A SOCIAL HISTORY OF
ENGLISH RUGBY UNION

From the myth of William Webb Ellis to the glory of the 2003 World Cup win, this book explores the social history of rugby union in England.

Ever since *Tom Brown's Schooldays* the sport has seen itself as the guardian of traditional English middle-class values. In this fascinating new history, leading rugby historian Tony Collins demonstrates how these values have shaped the English game, from the public schools to mass spectator sport, from strict amateurism to global professionalism.

Based on unprecedented access to the official archives of the Rugby Football Union, and drawing on an impressive array of sources from club minutes to personal memoirs and contemporary literature, the book explores in vivid detail the key events, personalities and players that have made English rugby.

From an era of rapid growth at the end of the nineteenth century, through the terrible losses suffered during the First World War and the subsequent 'rush to rugby' in the public and grammar schools, and into the periods of disorientation and commercialisation in the 1960s through to the present day, the story of English rugby union is also the story of the making of modern England.

Like all the very best writers on sport, Tony Collins uses sport as a prism through which to better understand both culture and society. A groundbreaking work of both social history and sport history, *A Social History of English Rugby Union* tells a fascinating story of sporting endeavour, masculine identity, imperial ideology, social consciousness and the nature of Englishness.

Tony Collins is Professor of the Social History of Sport at Leeds Metropolitan University, a founding editor of the journal *Sport in History* and a member of the executive committee of the British Society of Sports History. He is twice winner of the Lord Aberdare Literary Prize for Sports History (1999 and 2006).

A SOCIAL HISTORY OF ENGLISH RUGBY UNION

Tony Collins

Routledge
Taylor & Francis Group

LONDON AND NEW YORK

First published 2009
by Routledge
2 Park Square, Milton Park, Abingdon, Oxon, OX14 4RN

Simultaneously published in the USA and Canada
by Routledge
270 Madison Avenue, New York, NY 10016

Routledge is an imprint of the Taylor & Francis Group, an informa business

© 2009 Tony Collins

Typeset in Sabon by
Keystroke, 28 High Street, Tettenhall, Wolverhampton
Printed and bound in Great Britain by
TJ International Ltd, Padstow, Cornwall

British Library Cataloguing in Publication Data
A catalogue record for this book is available from the British Library

Library of Congress Cataloging in Publication Data
Collins, Tony, 1961–
A social history of English Rugby Union / Tony Collins.
p. cm.
Includes bibliographical references.
1. Rugby League football–Social aspects–England–History. 2. Rugby Union
football–Social aspects–England–History. 3. Working class–Recreation–
England–History. I. Title.
GV946.C65 2009
796.3330942–dc22   2008040541

ISBN10: 0–415–47660–7 (hbk)
ISBN10: 0–203–88544–9 (ebk)

ISBN13: 978–0–415–47660–7 (hbk)
ISBN13: 978–0–203–88544–4 (ebk)

CONTENTS

PROLOGUE

Of the little that is known about William Webb Ellis, we can be certain of one thing: he did not invent the game of rugby football.

An unremarkable schoolboy, he lived his life in dutiful obscurity as an Anglican clergyman until his death in 1872. Four years later, however, a second life began for him when Rugby School old boy and benefactor Matthew Bloxam suddenly named Ellis as the boy who in 1823 first picked up the ball and ran with it. Bloxam offered no evidence for his claim. Nor did he provide any in 1880 when he reiterated his view.

At the height of the war that split rugby apart in 1895, the Old Rugbeian Society set up a committee to investigate the true origins of the Rugby football. Despite considerable efforts, not one person came forward to support Bloxam. The committee found not a single eyewitness, not a solitary written word, not even a syllable of hearsay evidence to support the William Webb Ellis story.

Nevertheless, the committee decided 'in all probability' that Ellis was the 'innovator' of running with the ball. In 1900 a plaque was erected at the school that proclaimed unhesitatingly that Ellis 'with a fine disregard of the rules of football as played in his time, first took the ball in his arms and ran with it' in 1823.

Not for the first time in the history of rugby, evidence had been outweighed by expedience.

1

THE SCHOOLBOY'S GAME

It is a sunny, brisk afternoon in November, with a slender breeze blowing across the pitch. In a few moments School House will face School in a match that would change the face of British sport.

Thwack! The ball is kicked off, far into the distance but no more than fifteen feet in the air at its highest. It is caught and taken back bravely by a School House player into the oncoming School forwards. As the two packs meet, the ball temporarily disappears. As struggle for possession seems to get increasingly desperate, the ball suddenly appears on the House side of the scrum.

Their forwards hesitate momentarily and in a flash the ball is taken up by the onrushing School breakaways and kicked down field, threatening to breach the House defence. But a covering House three-quarter cleans the ball up, sidesteps a couple of oncoming forwards and drop-kicks the ball deep into School's half. House forwards flood into School territory and the two packs pile into each other, desperate to regain the ball. House pile on the pressure and seem to have School penned into their own quarter.

The ball squirts free again but as soon as it appears in open play, it is once again entombed by a mass of scrummaging forwards. Two take their life into their hands and fight their way to middle of the scrum, determined to drive the ball through their School pack and out the other side. But the experienced School forwards get the better of them and they lose track of the ball, forcing them to fight their way back out of the wrong side of the scrum before re-entering it back on their own side.

Then Brooke, the House captain, takes charge, crouching low and driving the ball forward through the legs of the opposing school forwards. His skill and strength get it so far but he too is driven back. Slowly School begins to get the upper hand and House are driven back inch by inch, each step contested as if the forwards had the backs towards a precipice. The ball suddenly appears on the wrong side of the House goal line but the danger is averted by a sharp kick into touch.

As the line-out is formed, both sides jostle for position but Brooke takes the ball and throws into the hands of his brother, who scorches through the School line to take it deep into School territory. He beats one tackler, then another, kicks the ball forward and, just as the defenders rush in to kill the threat, throws himself on the ball as it bounces over the goal line and between the posts. Try! Try to House and the Brooke brothers' combination.

But the try counts for nothing if it is not converted into a goal. Crab Jones, the coolest player on the field, steps forward and amidst a swarming mass of defenders hoping to charge down his kick, calmly steers the ball over the crossbar and between the posts. First blood to House.

The two sides change ends and, following a brief break for refreshments, School kick off high into the air, giving their forwards time to advance deep into House's half. Their tactics are to keep the ball near the House goal through sheer weight of numbers but the House forwards meet them blow for blow. Each time the ball emerges from the scrum, it is a House player who retrieves it and takes it back up the field. Those loose balls they miss are cleared up by Crab Jones and his fellow backs, who drop-kick the ball out to safety, momentarily relieving the onslaught.

But the pressure refuses to go away and as the end of the match approaches, School forwards get the ball at their feet and drive it forward again towards the House goal. Brooke throws himself into the centre of the rush but fails to get the ball. As it heads towards the posts, Crab Jones manages to get his hands on it but before he can set himself for the relieving kick the School forwards bring him down and the ball slips from his hands and rolls behind the House goal posts.

As the rest of the House team hold their breath and School is about to salute the try that could tie the game, a slight and inexperienced boy playing in his first match rushes headlong towards the ball, a fraction ahead of the incoming School forwards. As the rampaging pack push him over, he manages to fall on the ball a fraction before they collapse in a mass on top of him. As his teammates rush up to congratulate him, the match ends and House celebrate a glorious victory.

The schoolboy was Tom Brown. The game was Rugby football.

And this was the match that would take the game and its values out of the school, across Britain and around the world.

Tom Brown and Rugby School

Of course, the School versus School House match described in Thomas Hughes' *Tom Brown's Schooldays* was entirely fictional.[1] And Tom Brown never existed. But the future popularity of the Rugby School code of football arose in large part to the remarkable impact of this fictional pupil of the school.

In contrast, the fictional exploits of William Webb Ellis, a real pupil at the school, had no bearing on the development of the sport. His tale belonged to a later time, when the story brought comfort to those concerned at the direction rugby had taken in the 1880s and 1890s. Thomas Hughes himself, a pupil at the school in the 1830s, knew nothing of him. '"The Webb Ellis tradition" had not survived to my day,' he told the Old Rugbeian Society.[2] There can be no doubt that if the Webb Ellis story had contained a shred of truth, Hughes would have woven it into *Tom Brown's Schooldays*, a veritable compendium of folklore about Rugby School.

First published by Macmillan in April 1857, *Tom Brown's Schooldays* became an instant best seller, almost single-handedly establishing a new literary genre of the 'school story', and creating the first schoolboy hero.[3] In it, young Tom Brown, the son of a country squire, is sent to Rugby School, where, through a series of moral lessons, including the importance of playing football and cricket, he matures into a model Victorian gentleman. *Tom Brown* was an attempt to describe public school life for young boys (Hughes originally wrote it for his eight-year-old son Maurice, who died just two years after its publication) and to bring the teachings of Rugby's most famous headmaster, Thomas Arnold, to a wider audience. Sentimental and sanctimonious in equal doses, it proved popular with boys and men alike, selling 11,000 copies in its first year and being reprinted almost fifty times by the end of the century. It was, said *The Times*, a book that 'every English father might well wish to see in the hands of his son'.[4]

In its tone and outlook it epitomised all the self-confidence that the middle classes felt during the decades that followed the 1832 Reform Act, which finally brought them the franchise. The final collapse of the threat of Chartism after 1848 guaranteed an unprecedented period of relative social and industrial peace that lasted for almost thirty years. The Great Exhibition of 1851 symbolised Britain's triumphant global ascendancy, and the years that followed saw exceptional economic growth both at home and overseas. New markets continued to be opened up to British trade and manufactures, profits and rents carried on rising, and the size of the middle class itself grew rapidly, thanks to the expansion of clerical, administrative and managerial work. The number of people employed in 'white collar' occupations grew by 69 per cent in the three decades after 1851 to over 900,000. Clerks, bankers and accountants multiplied fourfold over the period, while those employed in education almost doubled. It was also a period in which the professions began to consolidate organisationally, raising their social status and prestige. For example, the British Medical Association was established in 1856, the 1860 Solicitors' Act allowed the Law Society to organise entrance examinations, and the Royal Institution of Chartered Surveyors was founded in 1868.[5]

For the more adventurous, the discovery of gold in Australia and California offered opportunities to amass considerable fortunes. Industrial capitalism was now accepted, if not necessarily universally embraced, by the middle classes as an engine of their prosperity now and in the future. This was a world in which all sections of the middle classes – businessmen, churchmen, military men and country gentry – could feel that they, above all other classes, had made the decisive contribution to the success of their nation. Britain's position at the apex of world power, they confidently believed, was a result of ordinary middle-class families like theirs and, for Thomas Hughes, that of Tom Brown:

> much has yet to be written and said before the British nation will be properly sensible of how much of its greatness it owes to the Browns. For centuries, in their quiet, dogged, homespun way, they have been subduing the earth in most English counties, and leaving their mark in American forests and Australian uplands. . . . noble families would be somewhat astounded – if the accounts ever came to be fairly taken – to find how small their work for England has been by the side of that of the Browns.[6]

This sense of Britishness also encompassed an increased awareness of military responsibilities overseas. This was partly because of the growing newspaper coverage of Britain's frequent wars, most notably in William Russell's despatches from the Crimean War in *The Times*, but also because Britain's increasing international influence necessarily meant increased vigilance as its reach extended across the world.[7] The frustrations of the inconclusive Crimean adventure were followed in 1857 by the outbreak of rebellion in India, which was not only shocking in its violence but also in the way that it questioned Britain's right to rule. But such challenges to British authority became occasions not for doubt but for the reassertion of national and racial superiority. It was an age of self-satisfaction and moral certitude.

And it was the age that shaped and moulded rugby football, indelibly marking it with features and attitudes that remain with it to this day.

The game's birthplace, Rugby School, self-consciously expressed and promoted the spirit of mid-Victorian England. It had been founded in 1567 by a London grocer, Laurence Sheriff, to 'teach grammar freely' to boys from the midlands town of Rugby and surrounding area. By 1818 the school had become the second largest public school in England, with almost 400 pupils. By this time there was very little that was either free or public about it, although Sheriff's legacy of land in London's Gray's Inn Fields had ensured its prosperity. While it had attracted some boys from aristocratic families in the late eighteenth century, and continued to do so throughout the nineteenth, the majority of its pupils came from the upper middle classes, especially the clergy and the rural gentry. This tendency intensified under the headship of Thomas Arnold, partly because he appears to have discouraged the recruitment of aristocratic boys, but mainly because he himself was the archetype of the social layer from which the school drew most of its boys.[8]

He had been appointed headmaster of the school in 1828 and set about reforming it according to his belief that Christian principles were an inseparable part of everyday living. He changed the school's prefect system so that much of the responsibility for the social and moral welfare of pupils rested on the shoulders of sixth form prefects, or praeposters as they were know in the school. He also raised the importance of mathematics, science and modern languages in the curriculum, deepening a process that had started before his arrival, moving the school slightly away from the public schools' traditional exclusive concentration on Greek and Latin. In 1844 a poem entitled *The Masters of Science* won the school poetry prize, marking the small but significant shift in the curriculum.[9]

But Arnold's overriding concern was to create boys who had 'character', whose education would enable them to provide leadership to British society and the Empire. 'What we must look for here is, first, religious and moral principle; secondly, gentlemanly conduct; thirdly, intellectual ability' he explained.[10] Although not a term used by Arnold, this philosophy became known as Muscular Christianity. Under him, Rugby became distinguished by a sense of moral certainty hitherto unknown in public schools. He saw life as a continuous battle between righteousness and evil and the school's role was to produce young men who would pursue this struggle in every aspect of their lives.[11] He argued that the cause of evil was the 'natural but most deadly error of human indolence and corruption, [and the belief] that our business is to preserve and not to improve. It is the ruin of us all alike, individuals, schools, and nations'.[12] Shaped by his response to the French Revolution, Arnold's philosophy was a mixture of anti-aristocratic sentiment, Protestant self-help, political reformism and monarchism. In this, they almost perfectly expressed the piecemeal ideology of British capitalist society, combining as it did belief in free trade and opposition to aristocratic excess with a sentimental loyalty to the monarchy and other trappings of traditional authority. Rugby's view of itself and its place in the world was spelt out by an anonymous contributor to the school magazine in 1846, who described the school as

> the image of that most powerful element in modern English society, the Middle Class . . . [it] may even claim kindred and fellowship of spirit with Railway Kings and Cotton Lords, being equally with them the creation of modern, burning, life-like energy. Her golden age alluded to above, synchronises with the strong convulsions which attended the Reform Bill. . . . Save in the one article of birth a manufacturer may make himself an equal to a duke. In a late stage of civilisation, like the present, the idea of trade comes prominently and almost exclusively into notice, being able at length to connect itself with that from which it has long been kept apart, education and enlightenment. Even so, we feel that our power has of late begun to be acknowledged; and that feeling shall animate us to proceed, holding fast the birthright of moral thoughtfulness which our great teacher [Arnold] bequeathed to us.[13]

This also explains the importance that began to be placed on competitive sports in the mid-nineteenth century. The economic dominance of British capitalism was based on competition, both in the struggle for new markets and colonies and, more fundamentally, in the very nature of how society functioned. The success of the industrial factory system had been accompanied by the imposition of a new culture of time-work discipline that attempted to inculcate the virtues of hard work and thrift into the working classes. In a similar fashion, the leaders, managers and administrators of the economy and society also had to be educated in the competitive spirit that drove forward the engine of economic expansion.

Another aspect of that competitive outlook was the expression of English nationalism, of which Arnold was also a passionate advocate. He believed in the innate moral superiority of men of his own race and class: 'a thorough English gentleman – Christian, manly, and enlightened – is . . . a finer specimen of human nature than any other country, I believe, could furnish'.

The same sentiments were expressed about the Rugby code of football by the school's pupils. 'At football you must possess either muscular strength, or fleetness of foot, or true British pluck (the three points on which a Rugbeian prides himself most) to become even a tolerable player,' wrote one enthusiast in the school's *New Rugbeian* magazine in 1860. Thomas Hughes fully shared the nationalism of his mentor, declaring later in his life that he did not 'like any foreign nation much from the little I know about them and I am certainly a most thoroughly prejudiced John Bull'.[14]

Ultimately, however, the core of Arnold's beliefs, and of his disciples such as Hughes, consisted of a fervent conviction of the moral correctness of his view of the world. 'Perhaps ours is the only little corner of the British Empire which is thoroughly, wisely and strongly ruled just now,' suggests a master with oblivious self-importance to Tom Brown towards the end of Hughes' book.[15] Many critics have accused Hughes of distorting or even betraying Arnold's ideals in favour of a cult of athleticism, but Muscular Christianity was literally the embodiment of Arnold's struggle for righteousness against sin. If one was to 'fight the good fight with all thy might', as J. S. B. Monsell's 1863 hymn had it, it was not enough that it be fought in lectures and sermons. It had to be fought in the industrial cities and throughout the colonies of the empire. Although Arnold had no interest in sport, he shared Hughes' belief that Christianity was about action, not contemplation. Muscular Christianity gave British middle-class men of action at home and abroad a moral framework in which to justify their work.[16] Such was the intensity of the school's training and the effect it had on its boys that many former pupils came to see themselves, in the words of *The Times*, 'as members of a semi-political, semi-sacerdotal society; [with] an inclination to extend the monitorial system to the world'.[17]

Tom Brown's Schooldays was part of that crusade. The book portrays the social mores and values of Rugby School in ways that would be easily understood by its youthful audience. This leads to a highly idealised view of school life. Contemporary accounts make it clear that Hughes underplayed the daily brutality of the school even under Arnold. In addition to the violence of the football field, the school was a '"rough and tumble" sort of place in the [eighteen] thirties and forties' where 'pugilistic encounters' were not uncommon, according to old boy Reverend Bulkeley Jones.[18] Bullying was far more common than is portrayed in the book, in which it is almost exclusively the preserve of the cartoonish Harry Flashman character. Those who failed to meet such physical challenges, whether at football or in school life generally, were guilty of the grievous sin of 'funking'. The clunking didacticism of the book ascribes this defect to the suspect older boys, such as Flashman – who 'played well at games where pluck wasn't much wanted' – and the unpopular Snooks and Green, 'who had never faced a good scrummage at football'.[19]

But, as was the case with the sport of rugby football itself, Hughes had an ambiguous view of violence; it was not always condemned. At one point in the book he even describes how Arnold strikes a boy for mis-translating a piece of Latin. Moreover, he himself had a strong and regularly expressed belief that 'fighting with fists is the natural and English way for English boys to settle their quarrels. What substitute for it is there, or ever was there, amongst any nation under the sun? What would you like to see take its place?' He was also a keen pugilist throughout his life, being arrested for brawling with a Chartist speaker in London in 1848 and personally boxing with every recruit to the London Working Men's College he helped found in 1850.[20]

As *Tom Brown* makes clear, the school was a microcosm of a rigidly hierarchical world, in which all boys were educated to expect deference and servility from those considered to be of lower status. An escalator of rank operated, on which even the lowest boy could expect to acquire increasing status as he progressed up the school. But for the lower classes, Arnold's worldview was one in which they knew their place and kept to it. Trade unions, he wrote in 1834, were a 'fearful engine of mischief, ready to riot or assassinate'.[21] While his ideas of moral rectitude, hard work and leadership by example were the embodiment of British capitalism's self-image in the nineteenth century, the place of the working class in his worldview belonged to a mythical Merrie England in which masters and men (women never being thought of as worthy of consideration) coexisted in mutual respect, each happy to acknowledge the other's place in the social hierarchy. This idea is strongly expressed in the early passages of *Tom Brown's Schooldays*. Hughes idealises his own boyhood in the Berkshire Downs and fictionalises his own father in the character of Squire Brown, who tells the young Tom that 'it didn't matter a straw whether his son associated with lords' sons or ploughmen's sons provided they were brave and honest'. But this apparent equality was dependent on the lower orders' accepting that they were, in the words of Hughes' father, 'bound not only by diligence but to strict obedience and deference to the wishes of master and mistress'.[22]

Class distinction was central to the school and to *Tom Brown*. As he travels to the school for the first time, young Tom is told by the coachman how boys from Rugby use pea-shooters to fire from the coach at passers-by, including at Irish road builders with whom they subsequently got into a fight. On arrival he is informed by East, his initial guide to the school and his subsequent best friend, that local youths are known as 'louts'.[23] Tom is ludicrously ignorant about the lives of boys outside of his class. 'All boys are sent to a public school in England' he tells the sensitive George Arthur late in the book. The reality was that less than a quarter of one per cent did so at that time.[24] In 1864 the cost of a Rugby School education, including boarding, was 90 pounds, 18 shillings and 10 pence per year, almost exactly the same as a skilled manual worker's annual wage. Not all those who attended the school survived its stifling social snobbery either. The Clarendon Commission noted that foundationers, local boys who paid minimal fees to be educated at the school according to the terms of Laurence Sheriff's original endowment, usually left after their first two or three years. This was because they were 'the sons of persons of the town who happen to belong to a class in society decidedly inferior to that of the mass of boys in the school, [and who had] to encounter always . . . the knowledge that they were born and bred in an inferior position'.[25]

This was also a world in which conformity was encouraged and intellectual curiosity frowned upon. As Walter Bagehot pointed out, intellectual dullness among the middle classes, and deference, especially on the part of the lower classes, were two of the defining qualities of the period and essential guarantors of political stability.[26] 'I don't care a straw for Greek particles, or the digamma; no more does his mother,' confesses Tom's father as the boy leaves to go to Rugby. 'What is he sent to school for? . . . If he'll only turn out a brave, helpful, truth-telling Englishman, and a gentleman, and a Christian, that's all I want.'[27] On arrival at the school one of the first lessons that the new boy Tom is taught by East is that it is the boy who has 'nothing odd about him' who most easily fits in with school life.

The book's most famous, or infamous, declaration of conformist philistinism is that of the praeposter Brooke who, during a speech after he has led his side to victory in a football match, asserts 'I'd rather win two Schoolhouse matches running than get the Balliol scholarship any day', about which Isabel Quigley memorably remarked 'qualifies him as either a liar or an idiot'. This sentiment is echoed when Tom is asked what his ambitions are at the school: 'I want to be A1 at cricket and football, and all the other games, and to make my hands keep my head against any fellow, lout or gentleman. I want to get into the sixth before I leave, and to please the Doctor; and I want to carry away just as much Latin and Greek as will take me through Oxford respectably'.[28] Even after he leaves the school the same attitude is highlighted, approvingly by Hughes, in a conversation with his holiday companions: 'What a bother they are making about these wretched Corn-laws! Here's three or four columns full of nothing but sliding-scales and fixed duties. . . . Ah, here's something better – a splendid match between Kent and England, Brown! Kent winning by three wickets. Felix fifty-six runs without a chance, and not out!' This dialogue was memorably echoed eighty years later by the characters Caldicott and Charters in Alfred Hitchcock's 1938 *The Lady Vanishes* as they attempt to ignore the onward rush of the Second World War around them by burbling about cricket scores throughout the film.[29]

The promotion of sport over intellectual pursuits did not go unnoticed by contemporaries. 'Scholarship throughout this little volume is kept quite in the background,' noted a reviewer in *The Times* drily, who in an otherwise very positive review also took the opportunity to 'protest' at the growing tendency of public schools to make games compulsory.[30] This was a debate that was to rage over the next fifty years among public school educators. The phrase that was most commonly used to encapsulate the philosophy of Muscular Christianity was Juvenal's 'Mens sana in corpore sano': 'a healthy mind in healthy body'. This has been subsequently interpreted by many historians to suggest that Muscular Christians believed in a balance between an athletic body and a studious mind. But for Hughes and similar thinkers, a healthy mind did not mean one that was scholarly but one that was morally pure. 'Healthy' meant that one was observant of Christian obligation and free of sexual corruption, which for schoolboys meant the avoidance of masturbation and homosexuality.[31] Other Muscular Christians were more outspoken in their advocacy of brawn over brain. Loretto headmaster and rugby football evangelist H.H. Almond argued that 'from fourteen to seventeen, long hours of brain work are unnatural and injurious,' that there was 'an overdone system of examinations' and that boys should spend 'two to three hours daily' engaged in physical training.[32] Whilst there were undoubtedly examples of scholar-athletes who excelled in both worlds, they were few and far between.

The tendency for athletics to take precedence over academic work was also an issue that troubled the Clarendon Commission. Established in 1861 to examine the state of public school education in England, its main concern was to investigate the extent to which the public schools' stodgy curriculum of Greek and Latin met the needs of an increasingly scientific age. As part of its review, it also spent considerable time investigating the precise details of student activities and the place of games in school life. Perhaps in recognition of the passions that the debate stirred, the commission trod carefully, finding no direct evidence to support the view that games overshadowed study but, with a subtlety that suggested that its sympathies were not wholly in favour of sport's growing prevalence, noted that it was possible that there might be some danger of sport being taken too seriously. Football was compulsory at Harrow, Shrewsbury, Winchester, where younger boys were required to fag for seniors, and Rugby, at which failure to play meant 300 lines followed by a beating for a repeat offence, but not at Eton. The commission also enquired whether boys regarded sporting success as a substitute for scholarly excellence. It found that at Harrow, 'the importance assigned to games in the estimation of the boys is somewhat greater than it should be', but at Rugby the philosophy of the school meant that sport 'distinguishes the strong, strengthens the studious and spares the weak'.[33] If the commission was circumspect in its assessment of the other public schools, it was effusive in its praise for Rugby and its philosophy. The school, it declared, had 'become in fact a national institution, as being a place of education and a source of influence for the whole Kingdom. . . . It instructs everywhere, is known everywhere, and exercises an influence everywhere.'[34]

Rugby football and its rivals

The Clarendon Commission's unqualified endorsement of the school and its principles was crucial to the success of the Rugby code of football. It effectively gave an official seal of approval to *Tom Brown's Schooldays*. The huge sales of the book had brought Arnold's principles to a new and wider audience. Not only did its description of football make the game exciting and attractive but, crucially, and for almost the first time, the book also gave the sport a 'meaning', above and beyond the intrinsic enjoyment of chasing a ball around a field. Today it is a commonplace to talk about the 'meaning' of sport and its broader cultural importance. But, aside from the occasional references to boxing being part of the British character by early nineteenth century writers such as Pierce Egan, no one before Hughes had ascribed a set of moral values to a sport. Even cricket, which had been seen since the late eighteenth century as the signifier of pastoral England and its romanticised rural past, did not yet carry the same assumptions of individual moral purpose.[35] 'This is worth living for; the whole sum of school-boy existence gathered up into one straining, struggling half-hour, a half-hour worth a year of common life,' says Hughes during one of his descriptions of a game.[36] Rugby football now had an explicit social purpose. It was a way of implementing Arnold's teachings. To play it was to build on his moral tradition.

The values of *Tom Brown's Schooldays* became the moral foundation for what would become rugby union football wherever the game was played. Put broadly, these values – which will be discussed as they recur throughout this book – were a commitment to a masculine and anti-effeminate worldview; a defence of social hierarchy and order; a belief in British national superiority, with England as 'first amongst British equals'; and an absolute certainty in one's own moral purpose. The success of Hughes' book and the evangelical fervour of the school's former pupils with 'their nervous anxiety to look after other people's moral welfare', combined with the ringing endorsement of the Clarendon Commission, meant that Rugby School, its methods and its football code achieved a prominence far beyond its origins in a small English country town.[37] As much as it was a recreation, Rugby football had also become an idea, an ideology even.

Following the publication of the Clarendon Commission report, Arnold's Rugby became the model for the mid-Victorian public school. Older schools such as Harrow reformed the curriculum along Arnoldian lines and new schools such as Haileybury and Clifton, two of a burgeoning number of public schools founded during the mid-century, adopted Rugby's philosophy completely. Indeed, middle-class expectations of public school life came to be shaped in a large part by reading Hughes' book, causing many schools to adopt its principles in order to attract new pupils.[38] For a large number of schools, this meant that Tom Brown's game became their football code of choice. The authority which Rugby School commanded can be gauged by the fact that at Wellington College, which took up rugby football in 1860, the first rule of football was 'in case of any dispute arising during a match, the rules are the same as those used at Rugby'. Moreover, such was the fervour for the game that, upon leaving school, many of its adherents formed clubs in order to play the game as adults. The two oldest clubs in England – Liverpool, formed in 1857, and Blackheath, formed in 1858 – were both organised by boys who had learnt the game at Rugby School and Blackheath Proprietary School respectively.[39]

The book's influence also extended far beyond the narrow strata of the upper middle classes that could afford to send their sons to a public school. The expansion of the middle classes during the mid-Victorian years had led to a corresponding rise in the demand and opportunities for leisure. This was intertwined with a recognition that, for middle-class males at least, an urban and sedentary lifestyle often had a detrimental effect on their health. 'In an age like the present', wrote the anonymous 'Stonehenge' in 1857, 'when in the struggle for precedence in the senate, the bar, or the haunts of commerce, time is considered as of equal value with money, it can scarcely be wondered at that many of the competitors in the race lose health, both of body and mind. Nothing enfeebles and lowers the bodily and mental tone more than an entire giving up of all the energies in one single pursuit.'[40] The rapid urbanisation of society was also a major course for concern. 'The tendency of the population to congregate in large towns, the multiplication of artificial means of transit, the increased strain and competition of modern life, the calamitousness of change, by which business hours have begun and ended later, till crowds of sallow clerks are now released from offices after the expiry of daylight for many months in the years, are all causes antagonistic to this prime necessity of a nation which is to be long vigorous,' argued H.H. Almond.[41]

For many middle-class men the Rifle Volunteer movement, which had been created in 1859 in response to an increase in Anglo-French tensions, offered the opportunity for the necessary physical exercise through military training. Gymnasia also started to appear in major towns and cities, as did athletic clubs, most notably London's Amateur Athletic Club in 1866.[42] By the mid-1860s it was common for football clubs to be formed by members of the local middle classes who had not been to public school. For example, in Leeds a local cap manufacturer, J.G. Hudson, helped to found the city's first football club in 1864. One of its unfulfilled ambitions was to play a match against Rugby School. And common to all these initiatives was a firm belief in the Arnoldian philosophy of 'Mens sana in corpore sano'.

Of course, the Rugby School code of football was not the only set of rules played by these new football clubs. Most played a modified or hybrid version of a public school code of football, although clubs in the Sheffield area played their own independent form of dribbling-style football. Even those who looked to Rugby rarely followed the school's rules exactly. Many did not allow hacking for example. But as the number of clubs grew the desire to play matches against other sides – rather than between members of the same club, as tended to be the case initially – also increased. Although matches were organised where the teams would use the rules played by the home side, this was not seen as a satisfactory solution and ideas about developing a 'universal' set of rules started to emerge. Similar discussions had started to take place in the public schools, as the increasingly high public profile of football stimulated inter-school rivalry and opportunities for matches increased as a result of the growth of the railways.[43] It was the desire to find an answer to this problem that led a number of clubs in London to meet in October 1863 to discuss the formation of an association of football clubs with a common agreed set of rules.

Although hindsight has led some historians to make the formation of the Football Association (FA) the decisive act in the creation of the soccer and rugby codes of football, the reality was not so simple. The FA took six meetings and a not inconsiderable amount of political manoeuvring before it arrived at a final version of its rules. By the end of the fourth meeting on

24 November 1863 the nineteen delegates, representing just ten clubs, had voted to accept a set rules that included:

> 9. A player shall be entitled to run with the ball towards his adversaries' goal if he makes a fair catch, or catches the ball on the first bound; but in the case of a fair catch, he makes his mark, he shall not run.
> 10. If any player shall run with the ball towards his adversaries' goal, any player in the opposite side shall be at liberty to charge, hold, trip or hack him, or wrest the ball from him; but no player shall be held and hacked at the same time.[44]

To all intents and purposes, the FA's proposed rules were to be based on those of Rugby School. It is worth noting that hacking, or 'shinning' as it was known elsewhere, was not confined to Rugby School football at this time. 'Shinning', noted an Etonian in 1859, 'is carried out to such an extent at our public schools that it would be greatly increased' if inter-school football matches took place.[45] However, the secretary of the FA, Ebenezer Morley, was not a supporter of Rugby's rules and proposed a motion to endorse the football rules of Cambridge University, which forbade carrying the ball and hacking. This was not put to a formal vote, possibly because on a show of hands only eight delegates indicated their support, but a committee was set up to discuss with the Cambridge footballers. Confusingly, the delegates also decided that hacking was a non-negotiable principle in the discussions with Cambridge, but that running with the ball in hand was negotiable. The meeting was adjourned amid controversy over exactly what had been decided.

When the delegates reconvened the following week, procedural wrangling broke out when Morley failed to read correctly the previous meeting's minutes and left out the motion that was passed in favour of hacking. Despite there being four fewer delegates and two less clubs than at the previous meeting, C.W. Alcock successfully proposed a motion to strike out the previously agreed rules allowing hacking and running with the ball. From the discussion that followed, it is quite clear that Morley and Alcock were determined to adopt the Cambridge rules come what may.[46] Unsurprisingly, most of the clubs supporting the Rugby School game did not even bother to turn up at the following week's meeting that rubber-stamped the non-hacking and non-handling rules. Although the founding clubs of the FA numbered eighteen, it appears that at least six of them, such as Blackheath, subsequently left because of their adherence to Rugby rules.[47]

14

Even after the break with the adherents of the Rugby code, FA rules still allowed handling the ball. A ball could be caught with the hands before it bounced and the catcher allowed to take an unimpeded kick, similar to the 'mark' in rugby or Australian rules football. Even the Royal Engineers, who were to appear in four of the first seven FA Cup finals, still played their own code of football that allowed running with the ball. Such apparent anomalies demonstrate not only the fluid state of the various rules of football at this time but also how little difference the FA's formation made to the game. Most football clubs were not members and even those that were members did not rigorously follow its rules. In fact, the formation of the FA had little impact on immediate direction of football. The FA's minute book records that 'no business was conducted' at its meeting of 28 October and it did not assemble again until February 1866 when it met to revise its rules. Twelve months later it had just ten member clubs, nine in London and Sheffield FC, which played its own rules anyway.

By January 1871, such was the dominance of the Rugby code of football that *Bell's Life*, the premier sporting weekly of the time, pointed out that since the formation of the FA, 'every year has increased the superiority in point of numbers and popularity of the Rugby clubs over those who are subject to the rule of the Association'. This is confirmed by Adrian Harvey's painstaking research into football clubs of the time. In the period 1868–73 he estimates that twenty-five of the thirty-eight major British football clubs played a version of football based on Rugby rules. This is confirmed by the first issue of what became C.W. Alcock's *Football Annual*, published in 1868, which records eighty-eight football clubs in existence at the time, of which forty-five played according to the Rugby tradition with thirty Association clubs and thirteen Sheffield Association clubs. It was only once the FA Cup became popular in the mid-1870s that differentiation between the various sets of football rules began to harden – and the FA began to grow – as the increased rivalry and competitiveness of the cup forced clubs to choose a code in which to specialise and thus increase their chances of success in the competition.[48]

Yet, alone of all the public school codes of football, it was the Rugby School code that survived and flourished among adult clubs. Despite the considerable social prestige attached to Eton, Winchester and Harrow, their codes of football did not become adult sports. Apart from one or two isolated instances, for example at Oxford and Cambridge universities, clubs playing the Eton or Harrow football rules did not exist. To some extent this was because the FA incorporated some of the features of these schools' football codes. The FA rulebook was a conglomeration of football rules and preferences, with no direct link to any one public school. But the willingness of Etonians and Harrovians to sink their differences over football rules stands in marked contrast to the Rugbeians' belief in the superiority of their own code. This was despite the fact that, as could be seen in the discussions leading to the formation of the FA, a compromise was by no means impossible – indeed, former pupils of Rugby had participated in drawing up 1848 Cambridge rules.[49] But the adherents of Rugby rules had both the certainty of Arnoldian self-belief and the public profile generated by the success of *Tom Brown's Schooldays*. They had no reason to compromise with the FA or anyone else.

The close identification of Rugby School football and Muscular Christianity also gave the code a resonance beyond the British Isles. Whereas the FA's version of football never took hold in the English-speaking world beyond Britain, Rugby rules provided the basis for the development of football in the white settler colonies of the British Empire and the United States. In 1860, the Melbourne press noted that 'the advocates of Muscular Christianity have become the majority [in Australian society]. Such books as *Tom Brown's Schooldays* are among the most popular works of fiction.'[50] Although born in Australia, Tom Wills, the organiser of the first football club in Melbourne in 1858, had been educated at Rugby and based the club's form of football on the rules he had played at school. As with many football clubs in England, the new club adapted the rules, most notably by abandoning the off-side rule and restricting how the ball could be carried, but it retained the oval ball and eventually came to regard the 'mark' as one of the Australian game's most prized features. In a similar way to which the formation of the FA in 1863 has been retrospectively vested with an importance contemporaries would not have recognised, the rules of Melbourne's first football club have been elevated to the status of a proto-nationalist impulse to create 'a game of our own'. In fact, the founders of football in Melbourne saw themselves as being no less British than those living in Britain. They were merely engaging in the same discussions about how football should be played that were taking place among British footballers at the same time. They fully shared the belief that football of whatever rules was a mark of Britishness and of the superiority of the British race. In Sydney, Rugby rules were adopted unchanged, and the governing body of the sport named itself the 'Southern Rugby Union' to indicate its relation to the Empire, thus establishing a sporting divide in the country which persists with great passion to the present day.[51]

In South Africa, initially among English speakers, the Arnoldian model of public school life was adopted completely by white middle-class educators and sports enthusiasts. Although the Winchester School code of football had been originally played in Cape Town, seen as the cradle of rugby, this was abandoned in the 1870s and rugby quickly came to dominate white sporting culture. It was through elite schools such as Old Diocesans, Bishops and Hilton College that rugby acquired a social significance and the means to spread throughout white South African society. By the mid-1880s support for the Rugby game had spread to Afrikaaner settlements such as Stellenbosch and by 1891 the sport was sufficiently important to host a tour from a side representing Britain, a visit that was entirely underwritten by Cecil Rhodes, thus highlighting the imperial impulse that also now stimulated the growth of the sport.[52]

In North America, the Rugby code was taken to the United States by students from the elite McGill University in Montreal, who had begun playing the game in 1865 when it had been introduced by officers of the local British army garrison. In May 1874 the McGill captain challenged Harvard University footballers to two matches, one under Harvard's soccer-style rules and another under McGill's version of rugby. Despite a 0–0 draw, the Harvard players were sufficiently impressed with the visitors' game that they abandoned their own rules and took up the Canadians'. As with Victorian Rules football, the variations on the Rugby School game that had been introduced by the Canadians and embraced by the Americans – which at this point revolved around the organisation of the scrum as two single lines of forwards opposing each other – were not viewed by contemporaries as expressions of national identity but as natural adaptations within the general rules of Rugby. Even as late as 1888, the American magazine *Outing* could note that, the scrum notwithstanding, 'there is very little in which the American has varied from the English Rugby'.[53]

More importantly, the Rugby-style game flourished in an environment where sport was closely interwoven with the popularity of a specifically American form of Muscular Christianity, best exemplified by the Young Men's Christian Association. Amos Alonzo Stagg, after Walter Camp probably the most influential figure in the formative period of American football, embodied the tight interlocking of the Christian ideal and sport, being a graduate of divinity school and a seminal coach with the University of Chicago. Teddy Roosevelt, whose boundless physical energy embodied the spirit of America's imperialist appetites, thought that *Tom Brown's Schooldays* was one of two books that everyone should read. As historian Robin Lester has pointed out, the American handling code 'was greatly aided when football was linked with evangelical purposes by believer and secularist alike'.[54]

The sharpest example of the importance of ideology in rugby's spread beyond Britain can be found in France. Following the defeat in the Franco-Prussian war in 1870 a crisis of confidence wracked the French upper classes and many looked across the channel to learn from the British Empire. A number, most notably Pierre de Coubertin, believed that sports were a vital factor in the success of the British model and sought to introduce them into France to promote social coherence within the French upper and middle classes. De Coubertin visited Rugby School in 1886 and, standing in the school chapel, 'dreamed that I saw before me the cornerstone of the British Empire'.[55] Thus inspired, he returned to France to campaign for a modern Olympic Games and to play a key role in the founding of the Union des Sociétés Françaises des Sports Athlétiques, which oversaw the organisation of 'English' sports in France. Based firmly on Arnoldian principles and an absolute belief in amateurism, rugby became the most important of the sports promoted by the USFSA and rapidly gained the premier position in the elite lycées and universities. De Coubertin himself refereed the first French rugby championship final in 1892.[56] As with the English-speaking world, it was what rugby represented, as much as the intrinsic enjoyment of playing the sport, that enabled it to take root among the French governing classes.

Most of these overseas developments took place outside the control of or without the encouragement of the RFU. The initial international spread of Rugby rules and their variations took place before the formation of the RFU in 1871, emphasising the extent to which the spread of rugby football was based on shared cultural values, rather than organisational ambition. Most rugby-playing clubs had little use for a governing body, as their dis-dain for the FA demonstrated. The sport was played and organised according to a common set of values and assumptions among young men who had a shared social and moral outlook. They had learnt a code of behaviour at school that meant they could govern themselves without formal organisation. It was therefore only when confronted with external threats that the rugby clubs began to consider the creation of a governing body.

The issues that stimulated the formation of the RFU were two that were to be integral to its future development: the violence of the game and the sport's prominence in national sporting life. The debate on the violent nature of rugby, and particularly hacking, had continued to be an issue following the FA's rejection of it in 1863. In London, a number of clubs who played under Rugby School rules had abandoned 'unnecessary' hacking by 1866. Led by Richmond and supported by Blackheath, two of London's most prestigious clubs, the young men who played the game found that bloodied and bruised shins acquired on a Saturday afternoon were not ideal preparation for a day's work in the office the following Monday morning.[57] But the practice still continued in schools. Concerns over hacking came to a head in November 1870 when *The Times* published a letter from 'A Surgeon' complaining about the number of injuries he had dealt with that had occurred during games of football at Rugby School and ascribing the cause of them all to hacking.[58] The seriousness of his complaint could be gauged by the fact that the letter openly called into the question the competency of the school's administration for allowing hacking to continue.

Pupils and old boys leapt to Rugby football's defence, either by disputing the facts of the surgeon's claims or by defending hacking as 'entirely legitimate', in the words of an old boy now at Trinity College, Oxford.[59] This old boy went on to claim that hacking had been dying out but that 'a new evil has arisen, and to prevent this evil, known as that of "mauling" [whereby the ball was shielded from the defending side through the use of bodies and hands] a certain amount of hacking is absolutely necessary'. The controversy grew to such heights that the school's medical officer, Dr Robert Farquharson, felt it necessary to write to *The Times* in early December 1870 admitting that a boy had in fact been killed playing the game but that it was as a result of an abdominal injury caused by a collision rather than hacking, which he claimed was not responsible for any major injuries. Nevertheless, the disrepute that such publicity brought to the game was clearly beginning to undermine its legitimacy.

The second challenge to rugby football's position came from its rivals in the FA. For most of the 1860s the FA had remained a moribund body, but in March 1870 and then again in November it had organised matches between sides representing England and Scotland. Piqued by the fact that Association footballers were claiming to represent the English and Scottish nations, five Scottish rugby players issued a challenge to their English counterparts to meet them in a match under rugby rules, noting that 'the football power of the old country was not properly represented in the late so-called international football match. . . . almost all of the leading clubs [in Scotland] play the Rugby code'.[60] Such a match needed organisation, not least to ensure that the soccer matches – in which few of the Scotland side actually lived in Scotland – would be eclipsed as being truly representative of the nation.

As these two confluences drew together, a letter was issued in December 1870 under the names of Blackheath secretary Benjamin Burns and his Richmond counterpart Edwin Ash, which explained that an opinion has for some time prevailed among the supporters of Rugby Football that some fixed code of rules should be adopted by all clubs who profess to play the Rugby game, as at present the majority have altered in some slight way the rules as played at Rugby School by introducing fresh rules of their own. Each club plays according to its own rules on its own ground, and consequently the strangers in each match, finding themselves at once at a disadvantage through not knowing the rules of the ground, confusion and disputes are generally the result. We therefore hope that all clubs playing the rugby game will join with us in framing a code of rules to be generally adopted.

The letter called for all those in agreement to contact the authors to take part in a meeting to establish such a code.[61]

In contrast to the drawn-out manoeuvres that led to the creation of the FA, the meeting that established the Rugby Football Union on 26 January 1871 lasted a mere two hours and was conducted in an atmosphere of agreeable unanimity. Ash opened the meeting by declaring that its aim was to 'frame a code of football based upon the Rugby system of play' and the thirty-two delegates representing twenty-one clubs quickly agreed a constitution and appointed a sub-committee of three, all Rugbeians, to draw up the grandiosely titled 'Laws of the Game'.[62] When the new code was agreed the following June, law 57 outlawed hacking in all its forms. It was, however, generally understood that clubs playing each other could make their own arrangements about its enforcement during matches. Law 58, outlawing the use of 'projecting nails, iron plates or gutta percha' on boots, underlined the new body's opposition to the more extreme manifestations of manly 'pluck'.[63] The ban on hacking was not the only difference with the game played at Rugby School. The school's convoluted manner of converting tries into goals was abandoned and other minor variations to the offside and line-out rules were codified. Indeed, the school was not to join the body bearing its name for another two decades.

The men who formed the RFU came from a very narrow and close-knit stratum of the professional upper middle classes. Of the fourteen officers and committee members elected at the first meeting, all those for whom we have data had attended public school. Six had been to Rugby and the others to Wellington, Tonbridge, Lancing and Marlborough. Of the twelve whose occupations are known, seven were solicitors, two were brokers and the others were a doctor, accountant and military instructor. All lived in central or south London, except the Wellington College representative who lived at the school in Wokingham. And of the nine whose date of birth is known, the eldest was twenty-nine and the youngest twenty. This was, in every sense, a young gentleman's club, one of many examples of organised middle-class sociability that emerged in the mid-Victorian period.

The new body made rapid progress. Eight weeks later, at 3.30 pm on Monday 27 March, an English side met a Scots side under rugby rules at the Academy Ground at Raeburn Place, just a mile and half north-west of Edinburgh city centre. In front of an unexpectedly large crowd of 8,000 people, England, playing in white shirts with a red rose, played with thirteen forwards, three half-backs, three full-backs and just one three-quarter. The Scots, starting a tradition of forward play that would last for the next century, dispensed with the three-quarter and played with fourteen forwards. The extra man in the pack paid dividends when the Scots, after a scoreless first-half, scored and converted a pushover try. England responded when Reginald Birkett went over for a try in the corner but as full time approached, the Scots made sure of victory with a try to one of their three half-backs, William Cross. As a portent of what the fixture would produce in the future, controversy was created by a dispute over one of the Scottish tries and by the English claim that the Scots had violated a pre-match agreement forbidding hacking by resolutely kicking the shins of any English player who managed to run with the ball.[64]

Nevertheless, the match was a resounding success for the rugby fraternity, emphasising their pre-eminence over the soccer code and demonstrating the sport's geographical reach through the inclusion in the England side of seven northern players from the Manchester and Liverpool clubs. By 1875 the RFU's strength was such that it staged regular internationals against Scotland and Ireland, held an annual North versus South match and increased its membership fivefold to 113 clubs, twenty-one of them in the North of England.[65] As with the school from which its sport derived, the RFU was now exerting an influence throughout the 'whole Kingdom'.

Yet it was this very popularity that was about to bring forth problems that would eventually tear the game apart.

2

THE AMATEUR GAME

Since the 1880s the Welsh had dazzled their opponents through the brilliance of their backs and the innovation of their four three-quarters system. While England and the other nations still played with nine forwards and three three-quarters, Welsh clubs had moved a man out of the pack and into the three-quarter line, opening up play to create sweeping back line moves across the width of the pitch.

But now in January 1894, after years of debate and hesitation, England had decided to use the four three-quarters system. And the team they would use it against for the first time was none other than Wales.

This was no ordinary Welsh side. Captained by Arthur Gould, arguably the greatest Welsh centre of his or any other age, the side featured seven players from the Newport club, four of whom made up a mighty pack. Wales had carried off the Triple Crown in 1893 and were tipped to do the same this year. Even English reporters described them as 'a side whose combination was never more perfect'.[1]

The match was England's first and only international ever to be played on Merseyside, at the ground of Birkenhead Park. It had snowed on the Thursday before the match, necessitating straw being spread over the pitch to protect it from the elements. The temperature was approaching freezing when Bradford's Jack Toothill kicked off at half past two, but the weather was quickly forgotten.

Despite intense forward pressure from the Welsh, it was England who scored first. Fly-half Cyril Wells made a break from his own quarter, got the ball to Geordie scrum-half Billy Taylor who passed back inside to West Hartlepool centre Sammy Morfitt to score between the posts on his debut. Captain Dicky Lockwood converted and England had the initiative. Just before half-time Charles Hooper caught a Welsh clearing kick on the full and made a mark, allowing Taylor to successfully kick for goal and record a rare four point 'goal from a mark'. When the whistle blew for half-time England were surprisingly 9–0 ahead.

If the Welsh supporters, who had travelled up for the match in large numbers, expected their side to turn the tables, they were to be disappointed. After the break, Taylor and Wells combined again to put Halifax's Fred Firth in the clear. As he approached Wales full-back Billy Bancroft, he deftly chipped the ball over the Welshman, where it was regathered by Lockwood to score England's second try. Lockwood again converted to make 14–0.

A few minutes later, Bramley forward Harry Bradshaw picked a loose ball from a scrum and barrelled his way over the line for another Lockwood-converted try. Then from a scrum Wells slipped the ball to Lockwood who broke through tired defenders before being brought down on the Welsh twenty-five, where Billy Taylor picked up the ball and scored in the corner, converting his own try from the touchline. Complete embarrassment was partially avoided when Newport scrum-half Fred Parfitt scored a consolation try just before the final whistle but at 24–3 the match, in the words of the *Liverpool Mercury*, 'was not a beating, it was an annihilation'.[2] It was England's biggest win against the Welsh since their first meeting in 1881, when they had run in thirteen tries against a neophyte Welsh team.

More importantly, this was a very different sort of England team from that of 1881. Nine of the side came from clubs in the north of England. At least eight were manual workers. Only four players came from the traditional public-school based sides in the south. The captain, Dicky Lockwood, was an unskilled manual labourer from Heckmondwike. In this, the team was a vivid illustration of the way in which rugby had become a sport of the masses. No longer the preserve of the upper middle classes, it was vigorously played and keenly watched by all sections of society, from the doctor at Harlequins to the docker at Hull Kingston Rovers.

But it was not to last.

One and all enthusiasts at the game

The enormous change that rugby had undergone was a result of the way in which the influence of *Tom Brown's Schooldays* had spread far beyond the narrow strata of the upper middle classes who could afford to send their sons to public school. The novel had almost become a handbook for anyone who wanted to set up a football club. For example, in Leeds, J.G. Hudson helped to found the city's first football club in 1864, which immediately decided to write to Rugby's headmaster, Frederick Temple, seeking a match but the letter arrived in the school's holidays and Temple was able to decline the offer graciously. Similar enthusiasm for the game was repeated across England. By the end of the RFU's first decade of existence it had 117 clubs in membership plus as many as three times that number playing rugby but which were not members. Ten years later, it had 331 member clubs.[3]

Almost half of these clubs were based in the north of England. This enthusiasm of northerners for the game was to become a recurrent and increasingly ominous theme in the last quarter of the nineteenth century. The first adult games of rugby in the north had been organised by former Rugby School pupils who had returned home and wanted to continue to play their code. The inaugural rugby match played in the region appears to have been the grandiosely titled 'Rugby versus the World', organised by Rugbeians F.A. Mather and Richard Sykes in Liverpool just before Christmas 1857. A club seems to have been formed in the city following the match. In 1860 Sykes became the founding captain of the newly formed Manchester Football Club, where he was joined by old boys of rugby-playing Cheltenham College. Five years later the Hull club was formed by Old Rugbeians led by W.H.H. Hutchinson.

These clubs were formed to provide physical recreation and social opportunities for middle-class young men who spent their working lives indoors. The fact that these first clubs played the rugby version of football meant that anyone in the region wishing to play football usually chose rugby, soccer at this time being restricted to eastern Lancashire and south Yorkshire. Additionally, the high social status of the founders of local rugby clubs meant that a certain social prestige surrounded the game, adding to the incentives to play it. Rugby grew rapidly. The organisation of inter-county matches between clubs and especially the first rugby 'Roses Match' between Lancashire and Yorkshire in 1870 brought additional publicity to the game. The game was given a further boost in 1874 when, in recognition of the flourishing state of rugby in the north, the first North versus South match was played, which, until the advent of the county championship in 1888, became the most important representative match of the season after internationals.

But it was the industrial economy that shaped the life of the north of England that provided the impetus for the spread of the game. The intense competitive spirit of capitalism that fuelled the northern economy was also expressed through middle-class civic pride in their towns. From the 1850s towns across the north vied with each other to have the most elaborate town hall, the biggest and best laid-out park or the grandest concert hall and theatre. Football, of both codes, became part of that municipal rivalry. In the early 1870s rugby teams started to be formed by members of the lower middle classes who felt the need to express their local pride on the football field. Typical of this aspiration were those who founded the Halifax club: 'We saw reports in the papers of football matches being played at Leeds, Bradford and elsewhere, and we thought that Halifax ought to have a club' was how the founder of the Halifax club, Sam Duckitt, described his motivation for forming the club in 1873.[4]

In 1877 the leadership of Yorkshire rugby decided to bring a structure to local rivalry by organising a knock-out tournament, the Yorkshire Cup. Crowds flocked to the cup-ties. At Halifax, where four years previously there had been no club, 8,000 people flocked to see the team play Wakefield. The following season 12,000 people watched Wakefield Trinity win the cup. 'The operatives turn out in their thousands to witness the decision of an important club match or a County Challenge Cup match, partisanship running very high in the north,' noted *Bell's Life* in 1879.[5] From sixteen teams in its first year, the cup attracted sixty-four by 1881, a figure that would more than double over the next decade. Crowds grew in a similarly explosive way. By the early 1880s, cup-ties regularly attracted five-figure gates and the final itself consistently drew higher attendances than the FA Cup final.[6]

This pattern was repeated across England. A county cup competition began in Cheshire in 1877, in Durham and Northumberland in 1881 and in Cumberland in 1882. In Cornwall in 1877 Penryn were proclaimed as county champions after losing only one match all season, a Devon cup began in 1887 and a cup competition was organised by the Midland Counties Rugby Union in 1882. In 1888, some 14,000 watched the Midland Counties cup final between Coventry and Burton. Even in the south, cup tournaments began in 1889 in Hampshire and in 1891 in Kent. More often than not, the organisation of a cup competition coincided with the formation of county rugby unions. By 1885 there were over a dozen county unions affiliated to the RFU.[7] Almost uniquely in the north, the Lancashire rugby union turned its back on a county-wide cup competition, but a network of local cup competitions sprang up across the north-west, stimulating attendances and rousing others to play the game. Rugby, as *The Times* pointed out in 1880, was on the crest of a wave: 'the players of the rugby union game are probably twice as numerous as those of the Association. . . . In the North, the Leeds, Wakefield and Manchester clubs are prominent among a people who are one and all enthusiasts at the game'.[8]

As *Bell's Life* had intimated, the success of the cup competitions brought a new, mass public interest to the game. Clubs were formed by churches, pubs and employers to capitalise on this new enthusiasm. The overwhelming majority of the new players and spectators who came into the game were from the working classes who lived in the industrial towns and cities of the north of England. This was welcomed at first by the leaders of the RFU as being an opportunity for moral lessons of rugby to be passed on to these new adherents of the game, but it rapidly became apparent that the working class had a sporting culture and practices of its own and did not necessarily accept the leadership of the middle classes. First and foremost among these practices was an expectation of reward for results. The first rumours of payments to players in rugby emerged in the late 1870s. The leaders of Yorkshire rugby initially attempted to outlaw payments to players in 1879. This proved to be ineffectual, as leading players received, at the very least, payments in kind for playing or for time taken off work for training and playing. Generous travelling expenses, legs of mutton, suits, watches, bottles of port and offers of employment were the more common forms of remuneration. 'Poaching', or offering players inducements to change clubs, became commonplace.

The first paid player for whom records survive was C.E. 'Teddy' Bartram, a talented three-quarter, who in 1881 was appointed as assistant secretary of Wakefield Trinity for an annual salary of £52, although his duties were negligible – the provision of such sinecure being a common way for amateur county cricketers to be paid for playing while retaining their amateur status. His status was an open secret within the game, as Oxford full-back Harry Tristam remarked, 'his position was not entirely that of an amateur and the rugby union did not want to raise the question of professionalism'.[9] The middle-class leaders of Lancashire and Yorkshire clubs were similarly tolerant. Many even encouraged similar practices to attract and retain the best players to increase the local prestige that a successful rugby team brought. Those that attempted to resist working-class involvement and maintain middle-class exclusivity, such as the Leeds-based Yorkshire Wanderers and the original Hull, York and St Helens clubs, found themselves forced to disband or merge with less socially prestigious clubs.

The popularity of the sport was now viewed with some concern by officials. 'It is an open question whether this interest has not been attained at the expense of our noble sport,' pondered RFU secretary Rowland Hill in the *Football Annual* for 1882. By the mid-1880s, there was a widespread fear that working-class participation was driving out the middle classes: 'those who have worked hard to make the game an honourable pastime – one which gentlemen can indulge in and ladies patronise – will either have to stamp out the evil [of professionalism] with a strong hand or abandon the sport to its fate,' wrote the *Yorkshire Post* in early 1886.[10] Moreover, the growing number of clubs in the north gave rise to the fear that they would eventually outnumber those in the south and outvote the supporters of the RFU. Indeed, by 1895 clubs in Lancashire and Yorkshire made up almost 48 per cent of the RFU's adult membership. Unlike clubs with working-class followings in the midlands or south-west, the clubs in Yorkshire and Lancashire presented a serious numerical challenge to rugby's traditional leadership.

It was at this point that the RFU began to promote amateurism for the first time. In March 1886 it appointed a committee to draft its first anti-professional rules. In addition to the huge influx into the game of working-class players and spectators in the north of England, the leaders of the RFU had been chastened by the experience of the Football Association, whose legalisation of professionalism in 1885 had resulted in the rapid eclipse of the amateur teams of former public schoolboys that had hitherto dominated the FA Cup. 'Professionalism' became a shorthand method of expressing concern about the growing influence of working-class players. That this was seen as a class rather than a north–south issue is highlighted by the fact that five of the eight committeemen were from the north of England, including three from Yorkshire.

At its October 1886 general meeting, the RFU officially banned all forms of payment and inducements, monetary or otherwise. The aim was explicitly to curtail the influence of the working-class player. Arthur Budd, a future president of the RFU, argued that professionalism would inevitably mean the subordination of the middle-class amateur to the working-class professional. He argued that this had happened in soccer when the FA legalised pro-fessionalism two years earlier, and called for 'no mercy, but iron rigour' in order to 'throttle the hydra'. Harry Garnett of the Bradford club declared, 'if working men desired to play football, they should pay for it themselves'. Thus motivated, the RFU voted to become an amateur body with just four dissenting votes.

But the game in Lancashire and Yorkshire was now dominated by working-class players and supporters. It was also one of the most important forms of mass entertainment in the region, much to the concern of sup-porters of amateurism, such as the editor of boys' magazine *Chums*: 'it seems to me that the ball is often a superfluous element in a northern game of football, and the mob would enjoy the thing far more if the opposing fifteens simply took off their sweaters and enjoyed a free fight. And I do not doubt that a professional rugby match would in the end frequently amount to this.' N.L. Jackson's *Pastime*, the voice of unvarnished amateurism, contended that 'in Yorkshire football enthusiasm has reached such a pitch that it has increased the incomes of local clubs to such an extent that the difficulty is to satisfactorily expend the money so easily gained. Slowly but surely, professionalism . . . is creeping amongst us.'[11]

The implementation of the RFU's 1886 amateur rules ignited a civil war in rugby. Between October 1888 and January 1890 Brighouse Rangers, Cleckheaton, Heckmondwike, Leeds Parish Church, Leeds St John's (the future Leeds club) and Wakefield Trinity were all suspended for periods ranging up to fourteen weeks for violating the amateur code. Ten players were also put on trial by the Yorkshire committee for receiving money, testimonial gifts and, in one case, an unauthorised wedding present from his club. The financial and organisational chaos caused by these suspensions gave rise to significant opposition towards the amateur purity of the RFU. In 1889 the Halifax club proposed to the Yorkshire Rugby Union that working-class players who had to take time off work to play the game should be compensated with 'broken-time payments'. Unalloyed amateurism, it was argued, would 'deprive the pastime of its ablest and most numerous exponents, who are essentially the working men of the North, and of its most enthusiastic supporters, who are undoubtedly the wage-earning classes'.[12] At the same time, demands for the formation of a league system, which had successfully been introduced by the Football League in 1888, began to be voiced. Both proposals were rejected by the supporters of amateurism and relations between clubs in the north and the RFU leadership became increasingly adversarial.

The success of northern teams and players became an increasingly important factor fuelling the RFU's fear of working-class domination of the game. 'The majority of Yorkshire fifteens are composed of working men who have only adopted football in recent years, and have received no school education in the art,' wrote a London commentator in 1892. 'The majority of members of London clubs have played it all their lives, yet when the two meet there is only one in it – the Yorkshiremen'.[13] This was demonstrated with remorseless regularity by the success of the Yorkshire side in the County Championship which started in 1888. The white rose powerhouse won the title seven times in the first eight seasons of the championship. Of no consolation to the south was the fact that in the only year that Yorkshire did not prevail, the trophy went to Lancashire.

The debate over payments for play came to a head at the 1893 annual general meeting of the union. James Miller, president of the Yorkshire Rugby Union, proposed that 'players be allowed compensation for bona-fide loss of time'.[14] He argued that having made the game popular among the working class, 'the RFU at once did [the working-class player] an injustice. These men were constantly called upon to lose their wages in order to play for their

28

county or their club and at the same time they were debarred from recom-
pense for the loss of time involved. Why should not the working man be able
to play the game on level terms with the gentleman?'[15] The subsequent
debate did not affect the decision of the meeting, which voted against
broken-time payments by 282 to 136. Congratulating the RFU on the result,
Baily's Magazine of Sports and Pastimes identified the key issue at stake: 'in
some of the Northern clubs, which have so many mechanics and working
men in their teams, the passing of this compensation clause would have
meant increased strength'.[16] The RFU tightened its laws immediately after
the meeting, so that henceforth the first by-law of the Union allowed
membership only to those clubs 'entirely composed of amateurs'.

Two months later the RFU charged Huddersfield, one of the oldest and
most senior clubs in the north, with providing money and jobs to two players
from Cumberland. Found guilty, the club was banned from playing until
the end of 1893. The rest of the season became a 'phoney war' in which each
side waited for the other to make a decisive move. It came at the start of
the following season, when the Lancashire Rugby Union decided to strike
against 'veiled professionalism' among its leading clubs. After suspending
Leigh, the witch-hunt escalated and the union soon found itself investigating
all but three of the county's senior sides. It was now clear that the end was
nigh, as the RFU and the northern clubs sought to organise their forces for
a final showdown. In early August 1895 the RFU leadership announced, as
it had threatened the previous December, that it would introduce tighter
amateur regulations at the September general meeting, including a new
requirement that any club accused of professionalism would be suspended
until it proved itself innocent. Faced with this reversal of the principles of
natural justice, the leading clubs in the north decided that enough was
enough.

On 29 August at the George Hotel in Huddersfield, officials of Brighouse
Rangers, Halifax, Leeds, Bradford, Hull, Huddersfield, Hunslet, Wakefield
Trinity, Manningham, Liversedge, Dewsbury, Batley, Oldham, Broughton
Rangers, Rochdale Hornets, Leigh, Warrington, Tyldesley, Wigan, St Helens
and Widnes assembled. They proceeded to unanimously adopt the resolution
'That the clubs here represented decide to form a Northern Rugby Football
Union, and pledge themselves to push forward, without delay, its estab-
lishment on the principle of payment for bona-fide broken-time only.'
Broken-time payments were set at six shillings per day – the same amount
allowed to injured players under RFU insurance laws. The clubs announced
their intention to resign from the RFU en bloc, with the exception of
Dewsbury, who suddenly balked and made their peace with the RFU.

Stockport was also invited to join, which they did immediately, and Runcorn was drafted in for Dewsbury a few days later. The rebels were quickly joined by the clubs of the Hull and District Rugby Union, the first of more than two hundred other clubs and organisations in Yorkshire, Lancashire and Cumberland that would go over to the new body in the next decade.

Among the supporters of amateurism, inside and outside of rugby, the split produced an almost audible sigh of relief. *Punch* characteristically captured the mood in verse:

> Rowland Hill, and gentlemen all,
> Thanks to your efforts to 'keep up the ball'
> Out of Moneygrub's sordid slime!
> 'Professionalism' and 'Broken Time'
> . . .
> Keep it up gentlemen! Let not the shame
> of money-greed mar one more grand English game!

The invention of amateurism

As can be seen from the events leading to the split, amateurism was not an original, intrinsic part of the game but a reaction to what the RFU saw as an increasing threat to its authority from working-class players and spectators in the game. The FA's legalisation of professionalism and the almost immediate eclipse of the elite amateur clubs by professional teams was a prospect they wished to avert in rugby. A similar impulse animated both cricket and rowing in the 1860s, when both the MCC and Amateur Rowing Association formulated their amateur regulations in reaction to the power of the professional All England XI touring circuit in cricket and, in rowing, working-class rowers who were employed to work on the water. Furthermore, the RFU's amateurism was formulated during a period of renewed working-class self-confidence and organisation. The late 1880s saw the rise of 'new unionism' and militant strike action, which intensified in the early 1890s. In 1893 the Independent Labour Party was formed. Middle-class alarm about the potential political threat of the working class was deepening.

The amateur ideology in rugby evolved as a reaction to the influence of working-class players, both on and off the field, and articulated a worldview based very firmly on the ethos of the Arnoldian public school. Thomas Hughes himself had argued strongly against professionalism in cricket, contending that 'the romance of the game is fast disappearing . . . we cannot make sports into the serious business of men's lives without injuring them and spoiling the sports'.[17] Central to amateurism were three inter-linked components. A belief that sport should not be played for material reward; the idea that 'fair play' should govern the conduct of games; and the rather more nebulous notion that games should be played with a certain effortless 'style', which itself was connected to the ideal of the 'amateur body', tall, slim and graceful.[18]

Many of these ideas were non-contentious reiterations of common sense. The simple economics of sport meant that the vast majority of games were played as unremunerated recreation. Nor could any type of sport be played without a mutual recognition by its participants of the underlying and unwritten laws of on-field behaviour. But the repackaging of these ideas under the rubric of 'amateurism' meant that they could also be used as an ideology of control and exclusion, dressed up as a moral imperative for sport in general and rugby in particular.

Amateurism also became the norm for middle-class rugby players because it was largely an articulation of the way they *believed* they played the game. Most players had no desire for monetary reward, partly because there were very few matches that generated enough gate money to pay players but mainly because they had no need to be paid. They could afford to take time off work to play the game if necessary. Their idea of fair play was shaped by an environment in which young men played the game with those of similar social backgrounds and shared norms of etiquette and behaviour. And the aesthetic of 'style' was, and is still, deeply rooted in the social and intellectual values of the British upper and middle classes. To achieve success with the appearance of minimal effort was as important to the century-maker at Lords as it was to the student with a first from Balliol.

But the reality of how they played the game was often quite different to the ideal. Although direct monetary reward for playing the game was rare, it did occur. For example, when England cricket and rugby captain Andrew Stoddart took over the captaincy of Arthur Shrewsbury and Alfred Shaw's 1888 rugby tour of Australia and New Zealand, he received at least £200. The Welsh international and Cambridge rugby blue W.H. Thomas was paid £90 for the thirty-week tour.

Expenses, sarcastically dubbed the most 'beautiful word in modern English' by V.S. Pritchett, allowed many middle-class players to enjoy meals and accommodation while travelling to matches that was unattainable for most working-class players. Oxford blue and Tadcaster player William Bromet claimed expenses of £6/13 shillings to play for Yorkshire in 1895. In 1887 Bradford paid Blackheath players £57/15 shillings and those of

Richmond £42/10 shillings in match expenses. Even a confirmed supporter of the RFU and its policies such as E.H.D. Sewell was forced to admit that the payment of travel expenses was a well-known means of providing 'men of higher social standing [with] a free Easter or Christmas holiday'. This was not something unique to rugby football – the Corinthians, the self-proclaimed defenders of the amateur spirit, charged their soccer opponents £150 per match for expenses and W.G. Grace was famous for the amounts he earned in expenses as a supposedly amateur cricketer.[19]

The offering of inducements to switch clubs, often cited by supporters of the RFU as a primary evil in the north before the split and a focus for numerous investigations, was no less an issue among the socially elite clubs in London than it was for those lower down the social ladder. As early as 1890, complaints had surfaced about the recruitment activities of Blackheath, who had managed to recruit an array of talented players from their rivals in London. The issue had arisen again at the annual general meeting of the Middlesex RFU in 1898, when some of the smaller clubs had expressed concerns at the regularity with which their most talented players left to play for the leading London clubs.[20] Of course, in contrast to practices in the north, the difference was that money rarely, if ever, changed hands because a move to a more prestigious London club brought with it intangible social, employment and business benefits to the fortunate player.

Similar observations can be made about the commitment to 'fair play'. Even if we leave aside the question of violence on the rugby pitch, there is ample evidence to suggest that gamesmanship and cheating were rife in the game from its earliest years. Neutral referees were not obligatory in matches until 1885 and the captains of the teams were the arbiters of contested decisions. Far from encouraging disinterested gentlemanly discussion of the finer points of the rules, it led to constant disputes. Harry Beardsall of the Huddersfield club remarked that in his playing days in the 1870s, 'the captains were the referees and if any disputes occurred they squabbled until one or the other gave way'. In the 1880s a match between Richmond and Oxford University was abandoned after Richmond complained about an Oxford knock-on and Edinburgh Academicals had two matches abandoned because of disputes about the rules.[21] Time spent arguing over disputed points was added on to the end of the match, in a similar way that injury time was added.

Gamesmanship – using the letter of the law to undermine its spirit – was also common. During the 1878 Roses match, A.N. Hornby, who later captained England at cricket and was also an outstanding rugby and soccer player, told his team to kick the ball out of play as soon as it came out of the scrum to waste time and protect Lancashire's narrow lead. Most notorious were the events during the 1889 match between England and the touring New Zealand Native team at Blackheath. Andrew Stoddart's shorts were torn in a tackle and players from both teams formed a circle around him while he changed into a new pair. However, while this was happening, England's Frank Evershed picked up the ball and touched down for a try. The New Zealanders protested against this ungentlemanly act, but referee Rowland Hill, one of the leading spokesmen for amateurism, allowed the try to stand.[22]

Intimidation of opponents through violent play was also common, as will be explored in Chapter 4. Indeed, this was one of the sport's appealing features. Hacking retained its popularity for many, even after the RFU outlawed it in 1871. Leeds' J.G. Hudson looked back fondly at a Leeds versus Manchester match of 1865, which consisted largely of 'a good set-to at each other's shins in mid-field'. The Clifton versus Marlborough school match of 1868 was so violent that the fixture was not played again for another twenty-three years. The first Roses rugby match in 1870 was marked by the Lancashire players' keenness to indulge in hacking their opponents. Even the inaugural England versus Scotland match saw outbreaks of determined hacking.[23] When York played a game against the local teacher training college in the mid-1870s, they were surprised to see their opponents wearing shinguards and, thus provoked, hacked away at the shins of their adversaries throughout the match.[24] On their 1885 tour of Scotland, Bradford's game against Edinburgh Academicals witnessed 'some of the foulest play ever perpetrated' by the Scotsmen, which sent four Bradford players to hospital. Blackheath's C.B. Grundy described his side's tactics against a visiting Yorkshire team in 1881: 'Their idea evidently was, "There's a team of southern amateurs, let's frighten them by playing rough". And they did play rough! But they never made a greater mistake in their lives. At half-time Blackheath had thirteen men left and the others eleven. The rest had been take in cabs to the nearest hospital.'[25]

Examples such as these would also tend to suggest that the effortless style of the amateur was more of an aspiration than an achievement. Clearly it was harder for a rugby player than it was for a batsman in cricket to display such style, but the ability to play in this way was no more an attribute of the amateur than it was of the professional. Although amateurs disapproved of specialised training for sport, boys who went to public schools, or to grammar schools that based themselves on the public school model, spent considerable time playing sport. The Clarendon Commission found that boys at Harrow spent an average of fifteen hours a week playing or practising cricket during summer. And most leading public schools also employed former cricket professionals as coaches for the boys, giving them a level of training inaccessible to most other youths. The length of schooling for such boys could be four or five years longer than that of those from the working class. With the addition of time possibly spent later at university, sportsmen from a public school background served a far longer 'apprenticeship' playing sport than less privileged young men, for whom schooling rarely lasted beyond the age of thirteen.[26]

The quest for effortlessness was also a feature of public school education. To be a 'casual man', someone who appeared not to work while accruing accomplishment, was the ultimate indicator of status, whether academically or athletically. The epitome of this style was Oxford University and England centre three-quarter H.H. Vassall, who was described in a 1908 match report in *Isis* as 'strolling on to the field with his hands stuck deep in his pockets, and a supreme look of boredom on his face'.[27] Not working distinguished the gentleman from the labourer or tradesman, an aristocratic impulse derived from classical Greek culture and something that would be commonplace to boys whose lessons were dominated by the classics. The gentleman amateur was usually made, not born, no less than the working-class professional.[28]

Effortlessness of course implied a natural ability, and thus superiority over those who had to expend effort. The idea that there was a natural distinction between the tall, slender yet muscular amateur 'body' and that of the shorter, stockier professional was also widespread in the decades before the First World War. The 'amateur body' was an idealisation of the existing middle-class male physique, and by definition meant that the generally shorter working-class body could not be that of an amateur. The reality was that middle-class bodies were healthier than those of the working class. In the 1870s boys aged eleven and twelve at public schools were on average five inches taller than their counterparts at local industrial schools, as a results of diet, opportunities to exercise and different working conditions. Teenage public school boys were three inches taller than artisans' sons.[29] This association of body type with social class, and by implication with the notion that working-class players could not possess the natural gifts of the gentleman, was constantly reaffirmed in the years following 1895. Many of the narratives about pre-split rugby revolved around the idea that the northern sides' great contribution to the England team was the provision of hard-working and physically strong forwards, who would win the ball for the public school educated backs. In fact, of the forty-four northern working-class players to appear for England in the decade before the split, twenty-one were backs, including the incomparable Dicky Lockwood.[30]

The acceptance and longevity of the Webb Ellis myth was part of this creation of the amateur ideology. Matthew Bloxam's assertions would have remained an antiquarian's eccentric belief, on a par with the idea that Francis Bacon was the author of Shakespeare's plays, had it not been for the battle for rugby's soul that raged from the mid-1880s. By providing a narrative that claimed the sport exclusively for the public schools and separated it from the early plebian forms of football, and thus denying the legitimacy of the northern clubs' claim to leadership of the sport, the Webb Ellis story provided a comfort for those troubled by the development of rugby and a story with which to justify their beliefs.[31]

The components of the amateur ideology therefore offered a framework within which players could be categorised, judged and, if necessary, ostracised. Fundamentally, amateurism's underlying purpose was to provide a means of imposing social distinction. This can be seen most clearly in the definition of 'amateur' of the Amateur Athletic Club, forerunner of the Amateur Athletic Association, and the Amateur Rowing Association, both of which explicitly excluded artisans, labourers and mechanics from their ranks, with the ARA also barring tradesmen for good measure.[32] But such a move would have been impossible for the RFU, given the huge numbers of artisans, labourers and mechanics playing the game in the 1880s. And because of its belief that it had a moral mission, the leadership of the RFU was not opposed in principle to the working class playing the game. Its concern was to protect its own control of the sport and prevent it from becoming dominated by the lower orders. Thus its codification of amateurism was slow and piecemeal, driven by its reaction to the changing internal politics of rugby before the 1895 split and by what it saw as external threats following the split.

What is perhaps most striking about the RFU's amateurism is that it never actually defined what amateurism was. The term was defined only in the negative, as being the opposite of professionalism. The amateur regulations were known as the 'Rules as to Professionalism' and expended considerable energy identifying and categorising what constituted an act of professionalism. It was very clear what amateurism was *not*, but what it *was* proved to be somewhat more ambiguous. Such vagueness and imprecision in the definition of social distinction was characteristic of British upper- and middle-class society. For example, the Clarendon Commission had avoided defining the term 'public school education' but justified its use because it was 'a phrase which is popular and sufficiently intelligible' to its audience.[33] More famously, few people were prepared to offer a precise definition of 'gentleman' – as Philip Mason remarks in his history of the English gentleman, 'what was meant by this word is not at all easy to explain'.

Writing shortly after the end of the First World War the rugby journalist Philip Trevor linked amateurism to the 'public school spirit' but acknowledged that, 'of course, we cannot define the term "public school spirit" any more than we can define, by any amount of elaboration, the term "gentleman". But we all know exactly what we mean by both.'[34]

As Trevor implied, the crucial definition was not that of amateurism, but that of the 'we' who knew 'exactly what we mean' by amateurism. Thus, despite the labyrinthine maze of laws regulating professionalism, the RFU always abrogated to itself the ultimate decision of what constituted amateurism. 'The Union shall have the power to deal with all acts which it may consider as acts of professionalism and which are not specifically provided for [by the rules]' specified section eight of the regulations adopted at its 1895 annual general meeting. This ability to define its terms – above and beyond the formal, written regulations – allowed the RFU the power to decide who was and who was not an amateur, often in the face of plainly contrary evidence. In 1888, following the return of the unofficial side that had toured Australia and New Zealand under the auspices of the cricket entrepreneurs Alfred Shaw and Arthur Shrewsbury, the RFU took no action against Andrew Stoddart despite it being common knowledge that he had been paid handsomely for his efforts and the fact that Halifax's Jack Clowes had already been suspended for accepting £15 from the tour organisers.

This same flexibility helped to avert a split with Wales in 1897 over the Arthur Gould affair, when the RFU eventually decided to overlook a testimonial organised for him by the Welsh rugby union authorities, something the rules specifically defined as an act of professionalism in the rules. As well as the political exigencies of the situation, the compromise was made easier because it was felt, in the words of Surrey county union president George Berney, that Gould 'was in type, at heart and in fact, an amateur'. A similar dispensation was granted to Sidney Gedge, a Scottish international who as curate at Leeds Parish Church found himself administering the church's professional rugby league side, an offence that would normally warrant a lifetime ban. However, after discussing the situation with RFU secretary Rowland Hill, it was decided that the rules 'were not intended to apply to cases' such as his.[35] The refusal of the RFU to consistently apply the letter of its own laws was a source of outrage for its opponents in the Northern Union and of irritation to many of its own members. Ultimately the RFU adoption of amateurism demonstrated the truth of the assertion of one of the characters in Toni Morrison's *Beloved* that 'definitions belong to the definers, not the defined'.[36]

Exorcism and beyond

As soon as the northern clubs announced the formation of the Northern Union on 29 August 1895, the RFU immediately sought to create an impregnable barrier between itself and the rebels. At its September 1895 annual general meeting, held four weeks after the split, it defined professionalism as:

> asking, receiving, or replying to a promise, direct or implied, to receive any money consideration whatever, actual or prospective; any employment or advancement; any establishment in business; or any compensation whatever [for playing, training or 'rendering any service' to a club].[37]

The new professionalism rules carried on through twenty-seven clauses and a further twelve sub-clauses. As well as forbidding the acceptance or provision of any form of payment or inducement to play the game, the rules categorised as 'acts of professionalism' testimonial funds, playing in a benefit match of any type, officiating in a match taking place on the ground of an expelled club, and refusing to give evidence to the RFU committee. The provisions relating to clubs were just as stringent. As well as this mesh of regulation, the RFU also adopted a codicil that declared all members of NU clubs, whether paid or not, to be professionals, and barred rugby union teams and players from playing on NU grounds. Those unfortunates who were members of NU clubs but wished to retain their amateur status were given until 1 November 1895 to resign from their clubs.

Despite the RFU's desire for an airtight seal against the professional virus, the new regulations carried inherent problems. Although it forbade compensation for 'time lost to football or in travelling in connection with football', in the very next clause it explicitly allowed the payment of 'reasonable hotel or travelling expenses', offering the potential of practical ambiguity to those seeking a way around the regulations. More importantly, the rules seemed to violate logic by condemning as professionals even those members of NU clubs who were not paid to play the game. Like original sin, professionalism was now a stain that could mark those whose lives had been exemplary – indeed, the rugby union player who received travelling expenses was deemed to be more 'amateur' than the NU player who received no expenses.

The main concern of the rugby union authorities, both nationally and locally, came to focus not so much on whether a player had been paid to play rugby but the extent of his contact with the NU. After the split it was hoped by RFU loyalists in the north that players who had played as amateurs with NU clubs might be eligible to play for rugby union clubs, provided they had severed their connections with the NU. This quickly proved to be a vain hope and the RFU insisted that playing rugby for an NU club was itself an act of professionalism, regardless of whether money had changed hands. Players who merely signed a Northern Union registration form were banned for life from playing rugby union. The sinner had to be cast out. This draconian stance served to underline the fact that the RFU no longer defined amateurism in relation to payments for play; it was simply whatever the NU was not. The NU was now officially and unshakably the 'Other'.

The policy caused considerable heartache for the RFU's loyal supporters among the northern middle classes. From East Yorkshire A.R. Meek protested that the RFU's banishment of 'genuine amateurs' who had played amateur NU because there were no local RFU clubs 'is fast bringing the historic pastime into ridicule'. The Sugden brothers, scions of one of Brighouse's leading families and 'amateurs in the strictest sense of the word', resigned from Brighouse Rangers in protest against the NU's legalisation of full professionalism in 1898. Yet they too were banned from rugby union because they had 'professionalised' themselves. In Lancashire the Vale of Lune club committee protested to the RFU in 1902 about the refusal to allow two players who 'are landed proprietors, and may figure in Burke's [Peerage]' to play the union game because they had previously played for an amateur NU side, the only rugby club in their locality. But the RFU insisted on the letter of its law being obeyed.[38]

Despite the seeming illogicality of purging players who shared the sporting ideals and social status of its leaders, there was a logic to the mania. The RFU leadership was determined to carry out a scorched earth policy to prevent the possibility of professionalism arising anew in the north. In order to remove once and for all the threat of working-class dominance, compromise could not be countenanced. Moreover, many in the central leadership of the RFU blamed the rise of professionalism in the north on the inability or unwillingness of the local middle classes to provide firm leadership to working-class players. So, for example, at the 1895 general meeting, RFU secretary Rowland Hill hoped forlornly that 'those who have real social influence amongst the working classes of this country will use it to point out the evils which I am convinced are before them' and the Reverend Frank Marshall denounced 'men of superior intelligence' who 'pandered to the claims of their clubs and their working-men players'.[39] For many in the RFU, the loss of the sport's industrial working-class support came as a relief, as Frank Mitchell, dual cricket and rugby international, explained:

the working-man player has not taught us anything in the way of style or skill in playing the game. Physique and stamina above the average he undoubtedly has, but to say that he knows more about the game than one who has been brought up in the best traditions of the public schools and the universities is absurd. If in any way the game has improved his physical and mental capacity, we are more than repaid; but at the same time, if he cannot play the game for the game itself, he can have no true interest in it, and it were better that he left us.[40]

That the RFU's strategy was highly successful in changing the balance of forces in favour of the middle classes can be seen in the shifting class composition of the England team. Between 1890 and 1894 the percentage of England players whose occupations can be traced and who came from a manual labouring background had steadily risen to 36.1 per cent. But in the last five years of the Edwardian period, 1906–10, that percentage had fallen to 13.8 per cent.[41] By 1914, what working-class participation that remained in English rugby union was deferential, non-threatening and strictly controlled.

On the pitch, the effect of the purge was calamitous. Between 1890 and 1895 England won eleven of eighteen matches against Ireland, Scotland and Wales. With the exception of the 1895 matches, when pre-split manoeuvrings led the RFU to select only two players from future NU clubs, there were never less than four players in the England side from clubs that would break away in 1895. The 1892 team, which did the 'Grand Slam' to win the international championship for the first time since 1884, never had less than eight such players in the side. The team that defeated Scotland in the championship's final match of the championship had ten. Almost 43 per cent of the players who played for England between 1890 and 1894 came from clubs, or would join clubs, that went on to form the NU. But in the five seasons after the split, England won just four, and drew two, out of fifteen matches, as clubs in the north quit the RFU for the NU. Even worse, from 1901 to 1909 England won just six, and drew one, of twenty-seven matches with the three home nations.

The split had a similar effect on the RFU's membership. In 1895 the RFU had 416 adult clubs in membership, excluding schools, colleges and universities. Of these, 147 were in Yorkshire and 51 in Lancashire, almost 48 per cent of the total. But ten years later the number of adult clubs in England that belonged to the RFU had plummeted to just 155, of which a mere five were in Yorkshire and fourteen in Lancashire. By 1910 the total had inched up to 176, with the former stronghold of Yorkshire adding just one more club to its total.[42]

The decline would have been even greater were it not for the RFU's new-found flexibility of principle in the second half of the 1900s. In 1907 the RFU established a 'Commission on Veiled Professionalism' to investigate Moseley official and former England full-back J.F. Byrne's allegations of payments to players made by midlands clubs. Leicester, Coventry and Northampton had long been suspected of paying players and offering inducements of jobs to players they wished to recruit. Leicester had first been investigated for professionalism in 1896 and its local league structure was awash with allegations of players receiving gifts and remuneration.[43] When it reported back, the commission found extensive evidence of unaudited accounts, vague balance sheets, expenses being paid without receipts, 'unnecessary refreshments' for players and one case of a player being offered money to remain at a club. Yet, despite Leicester and Northampton players being told to refund payments that they had received from their clubs, the report concluded that there was no 'veiled professionalism' in the region. Byrne and his supporters were outraged and their motion condemning the commission was defeated by a mere nine votes. In response the RFU set up a committee to investigate the findings of the commission. Despite suspending four players for having played for Northern Union clubs, the committee cleared Leicester of all charges. Disgusted, Charles Crane became the first and only president of the RFU to resign the position. A motion to expel Leicester was voted down after a speech by Rowland Hill in which he argued that to expel Leicester 'would be to practically break up the union'.[44]

The RFU was prepared to ignore the evidence because implementing its own amateur rules would undermine its authority. As Hill warned, a literal reading of its regulations would have meant the expulsion of Leicester and the prospect of the Northern Union establishing a serious bridgehead in the midlands. This pragmatism was well illustrated by the events surrounding the Coventry club. Perhaps even more so than Leicester, rugby union in Coventry had a significant working-class following.[45] But the club lacked the size and the social cachet of its east midlands rival, and, possibly as a concession to its critics over the Leicester affair, in late September 1909 the RFU began an investigation into claims that the club had covertly made payments to its players. On 6 October Coventry was found guilty of professionalism and suspended until the beginning of 1910. The following week rumours emerged that club officials had met the Northern Union with a view to switching codes. The pro-NU faction in the club called a meeting for 29 November to establish Coventry NU club. Faced with the prospect of the NU club capturing public attention while the union side was still suspended, the RFU suddenly declared on 6 December that the sanctions against the union club had been lifted and that it was free to start playing again, once again demonstrating the flexibility of its principles.[46]

The most famous example of the RFU suspending its ethics when its interests were threatened by their implementation was the 1896 Arthur Gould affair. Gould had received a testimonial from the Welsh rugby union and the money was used to buy the deeds to his house in Newport. According to the RFU's rules, this constituted an act of professionalism. In February 1897 this was endorsed by the International Rugby Football Board (IB) and the Welsh withdrew in protest.[47] It seemed to be only a matter of time before a split took place. But at the start of the 1897–98 season the RFU changed its mind, citing 'exceptional circumstances'. Rowland Hill explained that the decision 'was a question of expediency' because it would put 'a serious strain on the loyalty of the West Country clubs of England if those fixtures [against Welsh clubs] were prohibited'.[48] To head-off the possibility that the Welsh would join the Northern Union and eventually take clubs in the south-west of England with them, the RFU had chosen to ignore its own principles.

Actions such as this fed accusations of hypocrisy against the RFU. More fundamentally, they offered no support for the belief that amateurism was morally superior to sports that allowed payments to players. Not only were amateur principles changeable to suit the particular needs of the RFU, but when they were implemented, they forced many players into a dishonesty which they would not countenance in other areas of their lives. A.W. Robinson, a former Keighley and Hull KR player who had moved to Stourbridge to take up a job as a teacher, played under a pseudonym for his local rugby union club until a zealous RFU supporter unmasked him. When confronted with evidence that they had played for Hull Marlborough NU club, some members of the Hull and East Riding rugby union side simply denied any knowledge of NU rugby at all. Manchester Free Wanderers were suspended for fielding an NU player by the Lancashire county rugby union despite being told to 'play him and say nothing' by a prominent member of the county committee.[49] And there was also the generous expenses paid to RFU officials. Members of the Yorkshire Rugby Union committee travelled to meetings by first-class rail, a privilege refused to those who merely played the game. A testimonial match for Lancashire and RFU president Roger Westray was organised to reward his long service to the game, something that was explicitly forbidden to players.[50] The RFU, claimed a critic in 1909, believed that 'what is professionalism in a working man is evidently something very different in a player of slightly superior social status'.[51]

It was not simply a matter of dishonesty and double standards. The pursuit of amateurism necessarily produced a culture of cynicism in which expediency triumphed over principle. This was not immediately apparent during times of social harmony within English rugby, such as the inter-war period and the two decades after the Second World War when the middle-class traditions of the game were relatively undisturbed. As England captain and RFU president J.E. Greenwood noted, before and after the First World War the RFU was 'very strict about expenses and not only was it a case of no sleepers but third-class and no taxis'. But at certain flashpoints in rugby history, such as the 1895 split, the Gould affair and the much later disputes over South Africa and the moves to professionalism in the 1980s and 1990s, the essential hollowness of amateurism came to predominate. It would take a century to do so, but ultimately the cynicism that amateurism fostered would be its downfall.

Soccer wins the code war

However, the winner of the battle for rugby's soul was neither the fifteen-a-side nor the thirteen-a-side code, but the eleven-a-side round ball game. As we have seen, until the early 1880s soccer trailed rugby for popularity. Ironically, given the future social division of the codes, it was believed by some in the early 1880s that 'it is quite possible that the lower classes prefer watching a Rugby Union game, but that the Association rules find more favour in the eyes of the middle and upper classes is made amply evident by the crowds of respectable people that assemble [for major soccer matches] even in apathetic London'.[52]

Although this was not an accurate assessment of the two codes nationally, to find itself in such a position was uncomfortable for the RFU. Its fear of mass, commercial spectator sport had led it to consistently oppose calls for a national rugby knock-out cup, along the lines of the FA Cup. In 1876 the Royal Military Academy at Woolwich had offered a cup to the RFU for such a competition but had been turned down. More famously in 1878 the RFU had been given 'a challenge cup to be annually competed for by all rugby union clubs' by the recently disbanded Calcutta rugby club. The RFU wrote back explaining the 'difficulties of all clubs playing together' and instead the trophy found fame as the Calcutta Cup for the England versus Scotland match. RFU secretary Rowland Hill argued against cup contests on the grounds that 'we again venture to enter our earnest protest against challenge cup competitions. Why are they continued? It is said that they aid materially in increasing an interest in the game. Football requires no such unhealthy stimulants.'[53] In fact, cup competitions were common in public school foot-ball. The 1871 *Football Annual* recorded six schools in which sides played for a trophy, including Rugby, Marlborough, Cheltenham and Haileybury. But the RFU and many of its adult clubs disliked the idea of not being able to choose one's opponents, as would be the case in a cup competition. This lack of a national focus for rugby clubs gave soccer an incalculable advant-age as the two codes battled for new supporters. Noting the growing popu-larity of the round ball code, a letter writer to *The Field* in 1884 argued with remarkable foresight that 'unless a Rugby Union Challenge Cup be speedily established, in a few years the Association clubs throughout the Kingdom will outnumber those of their rivals by at least ten to one'.[54]

The failure of the RFU to organise a national cup or league competition was felt most strongly in Lancashire. Here, with the exception of some of the East Lancashire mill towns, soccer had played second fiddle to rugby until the start of the 1880s. But the success of local soccer cups and leagues in providing an arena for civic rivalries had eroded rugby's hegemony. The refusal of the Lancashire rugby authorities to organise a county-wide cup tournament along the lines of the Yorkshire Cup meant that cities such as Liverpool and Manchester, strongholds of the rugby code, were gradually colonised by soccer. This process was given a huge fillip in the mid-1880s by the success of Lancashire clubs in the FA Cup, bringing a level of national prestige to towns such as Blackburn, whose Blackburn Olympic club became the first northern professional side to win the cup in 1883, which rugby could not match. The swing towards soccer from rugby can be gauged by the fact that Burnley and Preston North End, two of Lancashire's greatest soccer clubs, both switched from rugby in the early 1880s. The subsequent legalisation of professionalism by the FA in 1885 and the formation of the Football League in 1888 gave soccer a national prominence and competitive structure that further undermined rugby's appeal. In 1889 England inter-national winger John Sutcliffe switched to soccer and won five England caps as a goalkeeper in his new code.

Despite many warnings and determined efforts to force the Lancashire union to organise a Lancashire cup competition, most notably at the county's 1886 annual general meeting, there existed within the game a significant body of opinion that welcomed the rise of professional soccer. 'The loss of followers to the grand old game is regrettable,' wrote an RFU supporter in the 1889 *Football Annual*, 'yet looking at the present state of all professional sports we cannot but think that this possible loss is far preferable to legalising professionalism'.[55] The prospects for soccer were also helped by the civil war that broke out over the implementation of the RFU's 1886 amateur rules.

Sutcliffe himself had been banned by the RFU for accepting money to play rugby and the increasingly chaotic organisation of rugby contrasted sharply with the commercial efficiency of the Football League. Public perceptions of rugby as a fractured sport at war with itself did nothing to help it win new supporters or players.

Even after the 1895 split, the RFU recognised the threat from soccer yet consciously refused to make any move to increase rugby's popularity. In the north-east, where a decade previously rugby had been the dominant code, the sport became increasingly marginalised by the success of Newcastle United, Sunderland and the like. The Durham rugby union proposed in 1897 forming a league to offer an alternative to the immense popularity of the round ball game in the region. The RFU discussed the proposal the following year and refused to sanction it. A similar response was given to Cornwall, although they had actually already formed their own league.[56] In 1902 the Northumberland union proposed that the RFU should introduce a national rugby cup competition, to no avail.[57] Two years later at the RFU's annual general meeting Northumberland's Rockcliff – which had produced one of the architects of England's 1894 mauling of the Welsh scrum-half Billy Taylor – suggested awarding more points for tries than goals to make the game more exciting for spectators, but found no support.[58] For some clubs, the struggle with soccer was simply too unequal. In 1904 Tudhoe, a largely working-class club in County Durham, folded after a 'financially disastrous' season and its ground was taken over by Spennymoor United AFC. Two years later Blaydon Wanderers, one of the county's oldest clubs, collapsed. In 1906 Sunderland RFC, alarmed that 'gates at the rugby matches have been of the most meagre character and, outside the members of the club, very few people seem to have been taking any interest in the fixtures', discussed giving up and going over to soccer.[59] The relentless rise of soccer culminated in 1908 when West Hartlepool, arguably the most successful side in the north-east, gave up rugby completely and transformed itself into Hartlepool United AFC.[60]

In the south-west, where rugby union retained working-class support, the game found itself fighting for its life against the soccer tidal wave. In 1900, the Bristol and District union told the RFU that it 'was being killed' by round ball game and that if league competitions were not allowed, the 'younger portion of players would go over to the association code'. The RFU refused to give permission but, as in Cornwall and Devon, the district union decided that defiance was better than death and formed the Bristol Combination league.[61] Further to the south, Plymouth, a 'veritable hotbed' of rugby where soccer was 'practically unknown' according to the 1906 *Book of Football*, became a target for soccer expansionists and evangelical visits by Aston

Villa, Sheffield Wednesday and Arsenal led in 1903 to the formation of a professional soccer club in the city, Plymouth Argyle.[62] 'Soccer Mania' even started to encroach on rugby's middle-class heartlands. Frank Potter-Irwin of the Ilford Wanderers club and a future vice-president of the RFU, pleaded in 1904 for the RFU to 'do something to popularise the game', explaining that although the RFU numbered around 250 clubs nationally, 'in his own district there were 247 association clubs'.[63]

But the majority of rugby's leaders did not want to popularise the game. Many were horrified by mass spectator sport and wanted no part of it. For them rugby was a sport for the moral and physical recreation of its players. The commercialism and crowds of soccer and the Northern Union were an abomination. 'The football players of the future will be compelled to forget the honorable traditions of this great English game, and to pander to the howling mob that crowd the circular stands of some Yorkshire coliseum,' wrote Bertram Fletcher Robinson a few months after the split. Not to be outdone, the journalist Glyn Roberts explained that 'I visit a soccer match once a season to keep my disgust fresh', a sentiment that appears to have been widespread in the sport, if rarely expressed quite so sharply.[64] Little more than a decade after the 1895 split, the FA had over 7,500 affiliated clubs, roughly fifteen times the number of rugby clubs playing under either the RFU or Northern Union banner.[65]

Despite the devastation it had brought to rugby, RFU had got what it desired. The danger that the game might go the way of soccer and become dominated by working-class professionals had been vanquished. It was once more a sport in which middle-class gentleman could mix freely without fear. What working-class participation there now was in rugby was controlled and subordinate. Throughout the game, the RFU's principles were accepted by all and challenged by none. It therefore seemed appropriate that, as the purges and forced 'amateurisation' of the game came to an end in the late 1900s, the England team should once again emerge as the sport's premier force. Under Adrian Stoop, Harlequins' captain and old boy of Rugby School, England became a side noted for dashing backs and adventurous play. In 1910 the side left behind the previous two decades of turmoil and torment to lift the Five Nations title for the first time since 1892, when it still comprised the four home nations. In the same year Twickenham hosted its first international, an event rich in symbolic importance, as W.J. Morgan and Geoffrey Nicholson explained:

> After Twickenham had been built there was no need to worry about
> any similar threat from the provinces. London was in control of the

game in England, with all which that implies in the way of attitudes and influences. In the second place, Twickenham was an assertion that English Rugby had not been impoverished for all time by the loss of the Northern clubs. It was a well-timed gesture of self-confidence.[66]

Twickenham, as J.G. Ballard later described it, was to become the Maginot Line of the British class system. This self-confidence increased as the success on the field continued. The Five Nations title was regained in 1912 and then in 1913 the Grand Slam was finally achieved. The brightest star of the side was another Old Rugbeian, Ronald Poulton-Palmer, a three-quarter blessed with an almost supernatural turn of speed and body swerve. In 1914 he was appointed England captain, and led them to an unprecedented second successive Grand Slam. After almost three decades of discord and upheaval, the future of English rugby union had never looked brighter.

3

THE WAR GAME

It was a clear, crisp Edinburgh afternoon in early spring. Blustery wind had dried away the rain that had swept over the city earlier, leaving a sharp bite of anticipation in the air. It was Calcutta Cup day and England were in town. As the crowd made its way to Scotland's Inverleith ground in the northern suburbs of the city, the streets echoed to the talk of England's unbeaten run of two seasons, of the brilliance of its captain Ronald Poulton-Palmer, and of the chances of the underdog Scots that afternoon. It was March 1914.

The match was a classic. In the first half the Scots failed to take full advantage of the wind blowing behind them but, realising that a kicking game was impossible, the English backs relied on a passing game. For once it was not Poulton-Palmer who carved up the opposition with slashing runs but his centre partner 'Bungy' Watson. However, it was the Scots who took the lead midway through the first half when Scottish forward Fred Turner got a pass out to winger John Will who touched down with defenders still hanging on to him. But English pressure told and just before half-time Watson beat two defenders and threw an inside pass to his winger Cyril Lowe who tied the game up at three-all.

Scottish hopes of an upset rose even higher when their forwards over-ran the English pack a minute into the second half and Turner again laid on the final pass for debutant James Huggan to go over in the corner. This seemed to bring out the steel in the English: Watson and Poulton-Palmer took charge. Watson again opened the Scots' defence to send Lowe in for his second try, which Harrison converted to put England ahead for the first time. A passing movement involving four players put Lowe in for his hat-trick in the corner, which Harrison magnificently converted from the touch-line. Watson then stepped through a clutch of defenders to send Poulton-Palmer over by the posts, which Harrison inexplicably failed to convert.

Twenty minutes to go and England were ahead 16–6. The Calcutta Cup and a second successive Grand Slam were on their way back to Twickenham. But the Scots found their second wind. First an adventurous cross-kick from Huggan gave the fly-half Bowie the chance to score a drop-goal. 16–10. A few minutes later, Bowie gave a short pass to Will on the half-way line. He shrugged off Lowe and set off with Poulton-Palmer and full-back William Johnston in vain pursuit. Just as Lowe got back and tackled him, he touched down under the posts. Turner converted and it was 16–15 with minutes to play. As the clock ticked down, the action became more frantic. England forward Cherry Pillman suffered a broken leg as he was hacked down dribbling the ball towards the Scottish line. But the fourteen remaining England players hung on to win by a solitary point. The victory sealed England's second successive Grand Slam and their fourth championship in five years.

This was indeed a match to remember. No one at Inverleith that day could know that or anything of the fate which awaited them over the next four years. Bungy Watson would be dead within six months, drowned when his ship HMS *Hawke* was sunk by a German torpedo. Poulton-Palmer, the greatest player of his generation, was to be cut down by a sniper's bullet on the Western Front in 1915. Poulton-Palmer's winger, Arthur Dingle, was lost at Gallipolli, his body never recovered. Scrum-half Frank Oakeley went down with his submarine in December 1914. Front-rower Arthur Maynard was one of the tens of thousands who died on the Somme. And Harold Harrison and Cherry Pillman were both to lose their brothers, who were also England internationals. In all, twenty-seven England internationals died during the war

Of the Scottish side that came within a hair's breadth of defeating the champions, John Will, the double try-scorer, was killed in March 1917 while in the Royal Flying Corps. His opposite winger and fellow try-scorer James Huggan died less than a year after the match while serving in the Royal Army Medical Corps. Fred Turner, who converted Will's last try to bring Scotland within a point of England, met his end less than ten months later in Belgium. Full-back William Wallace died shortly after transferring to the Royal Flying Corps, while Eric Young, another debutant in the match, was killed in the summer of 1915. Scrum-half Eric Milroy was to become yet another victim of the carnage on the Somme. Twenty-five other Scottish internationals would also not return home from the war.

Yet it is doubtful whether a single one of them would have had a moment's hesitation in accepting their fate. In August 1914 they would rush to the colours with unbridled enthusiasm. They followed, and gave, orders that would lead to death without a moment's doubt. In this, they were only among the most prominent of a whole generation of young men who were willing to sacrifice themselves for the Imperial principles by which they had been raised and in whose spirit they played the game.

'We have come into our heritage'

The response of rugby union to the outbreak of the First World War was conditioned by its role in late Victorian and Edwardian society.[1] The RFU believed that rugby union had a higher moral purpose than mere recreation. Its goal was to train young men to be leaders of the Empire, to demonstrate the superiority of the Anglo-Saxon race in peace and in war. The link between rugby and military duty was woven into the narrative of *Tom Brown's Schooldays*, most notably to describe the face of the School House captain before a match as being 'full of pluck and hope, the sort of look I hope to see in my general when I go out to fight'.[2] In the late nineteenth century the game was seen as a form of military training. Without it, mused Bertram Fletcher Robinson in 1896, Britain would lose its place as Europe's leading nation to those countries that practised conscription. With his usual directness, H.H. Almond argued that rugby's purpose was to produce 'a race of robust men, with active habits, brisk circulations, manly sympathies and exuberant spirits' who were ready to lead and to follow in defence of the Empire.[3]

Rugby union saw itself as the very embodiment of the public school imperial ideal: vigorous, masculine, militaristic and patriotic. In boys' school stories of the later 1900s, there was an increasing tendency for the sporting hero to be a 'rugger' player and for the violence inherent in the game to be presented in a cathartic, character-forming way. Hugh Walpole's 1912 novel *Prelude to Adventure* is perhaps the most literarily accomplished example of this genre. His hero, Olva Dune, plays poorly in a game until almost knocked unconscious. The impact renews his enthusiasm:

> Now there was no hesitation or confusion. A vigour like wine filled his body. . . . he was amazing. He was everywhere. . . . For such a man as he there should only be air, love, motion, the begetting of children, the surprising splendour of a sudden death.

The link between violent death and rugby was expressed in an even more zealous fashion by the Dulwich College school song: 'fifteen fellows fighting full out for death or glory.'[4] As David Cannadine and others have noted, this

belief in the glory of death in battle was widespread in public school literature of the period.[5] Henry Newbolt's *Vitai Lampada*, with its rallying call
to 'Play up! Play up! and play the game' and Poet Laureate Alfred Austin's
cry of 'who would not die for England! . . . Duty and Death that evermore
were twin' set the tone for the era.[6] The importance of the warrior hero in
the Greek classics was transplanted to an England that felt threatened
abroad and was troubled by self-doubt at home. Military death for young
males was viewed as ennobling, something to be welcomed in the service of
one's country. H.A. Vachell's 1905 *The Hill* presented this in the starkest
possible way: 'To die young, clean, ardent; to die swiftly in perfect health;
to die saving others from death, or worse – disgrace – to die scaling heights
. . . is not that cause for joy rather than sorrow?'[7]

In the decade before the war, as it sought to re-establish the original
meaning of the game, the leadership of the RFU attempted to place itself
in the forefront of this militaristic, patriotic ideology. It embarked on a
campaign to increase the number of public schools playing its sport and
launched a determined effort to establish itself as a major sport with the
armed services. Initially, however, the Army did not share the RFU's belief
in the military importance of rugby. Soccer was the Services' game and such
was its popularity that in 1906 there were 578 soccer teams in the Army and
180 in the Royal Navy, against a mere handful of rugby union sides.[8] It was
only in that year that the RFU began to make headway in the armed forces,
with the organisation of an Army challenge cup tournament for regimental
teams and the first inter-service match between the Army and the Royal
Navy, although participation was restricted to officers. The growth of rugby
in the forces was also helped by the creation, again in 1906, of the Amateur
Football Association, which split the ranks of middle-class soccer clubs.
Although the Army FA stayed loyal to the FA, the rupture allowed the RFU
to stake a claim to be the one national football body truly committed to the
amateur ethos and it steadily grew in strength in the forces up to 1914.[9]

Paradoxically, the impact of international tours to Britain by New Zealand
in 1905 and South Africa in 1906 added weight to rugby's claims of imperial
importance, despite the heavy defeats usually experienced by the home
nations.[10] In the midst of much concern over the physical fitness of Britain
following the Boer War, the failures of the England team appeared to add
weight to the widespread belief that the nation was in physical decline.
In contrast, the skills, athleticism and success of the colonial tourists seemed
to demonstrate how rugby could help to develop a healthy, masculine nation.
In a comment typical of the time, P.A. Vaile, writing a year after the publication of the 1904 Report of the Interdepartmental Committee on Physical

Deterioration, went so far as to claim that rugby was the 'best trial of the relative vigour and virility of any two or more opposing countries'.[11]

Such sentiments were not mere observations; as fears of a European war grew in the years immediately before 1914, many rugby union clubs such as Harlequins, Blackheath and London Scottish developed close links with the Territorial Army. Indeed, one of the reasons many English rugby union players joined the Army so quickly in August 1914 was that they were already in the Territorial Army or had been trained in the Officer Training Corps at school or university. Both Adrian Stoop and Ronald Poulton-Palmer were keen Territorial officers. Poulton had joined the Officer Training Corps in his first year at Oxford in 1908 and declared himself to be 'frightfully keen on soldiering'.[12] In Ulster the link between the sport and the military was even more apparent; the 1913–14 season had been abandoned because the vast majority of players had joined Edward Carson's Ulster Volunteer Force. When the war finally came, it was regarded, in the words of a follower of rugby union writing in 1919, as 'the game for which they had been preparing for so many years'.[13]

It is therefore perhaps not accidental that the war poet who best captured the emotions of that generation of middle-class youth who rushed to the colours was Rupert Brooke. An old boy of Rugby School, where he had partnered Ronald Poulton-Palmer in the three-quarter line, he had remained a keen follower of the game. His poem *1914* was redolent with relief that war was finally upon England and anticipation of the personal challenge to come:

> Honour has come back, as a king, to earth,
> And paid his subjects a royal wage;
> And Nobleness walks in our ways again;
> And we have come into our heritage.[14]

War-time rugby

The declaration of war caught the RFU by surprise and it initially believed that the season should continue. But within hours, it found itself inundated with requests for guidance from members and on 13 August its secretary, C.J.B. Marriott, instructed clubs to carry on playing where possible:

> I have consulted my emergency committee, and they feel that they must leave it to those clubs that have sufficient players left to do as they think best with regard to carrying out their programme, but are

of the opinion that it will be advisable to do so where clubs can. The committee of the Prince of Wales Fund expressed a hope that a portion of the gates may be devoted to that fund, and the English Rugby Union hopes clubs will approve the suggestion.[15]

But hopes of a continuation of the season rapidly melted away as players flocked to the colours. Ronald Poulton-Palmer seemed to speak for most players when he wrote to his parents in August 1914 that 'Germany has to be smashed, i.e. I mean the military party, and everybody realises, and everybody is volunteering. And those who are best trained are most wanted, and so I should be a skunk to hold back.'[16] Clubs with strong military links found themselves unable to raise teams within the first week of the crisis. Old boys' clubs such as Haileyburians and Leysians announced they were cancelling all fixtures because 'practically every' player had enlisted.[17] Despite an initial belief that they could continue because 'their membership is scholastic rather than military', London Irish cancelled their season in mid-September.[18] Moseley voted to cancel all fixtures and offered their ground to the military authorities.[19] At Harlequins' annual general meeting most members turned up in khaki to demonstrate their commitment to the greater game and voted £500 to national war funds.[20] Of the 101 members of the Old Alleynians club, comprised of former pupils of Dulwich College, the school magazine reported that 'all are serving in H.M. Forces, with the exception of twenty-one, of whom eight are Government servants, three are under seventeen years of age, two have defective eyesight, three are not British subjects, and the remaining five are prevented from joining owing to special circumstances'.[21]

In the north, Birkenhead Park reported that they would not be able to fulfil any fixtures because 'our entire first XV, and practically all the remainder of our playing members, are in some service or another, and our ground is also being used'.[22] Liverpool declared that seventy members had joined up; New Brighton seventy-five, Sunderland eighty-nine and the Vale of Lune 'fifty or sixty'. The Cumberland county committee's belief that county representative games could continue was undermined within days by mass enlistment.[23] Walter Roberts of Harrogate Old Boys club commented that 'the feeling is very strong that football should be suspended for the season. Most of our boys have joined the "Terriers" [Territorial Army] or applied for commissions'.[24]

However, in Devon, where the game retained a significant following among the working class, especially in Plymouth and Torquay, a special conference of the county's rugby union had initially decided to follow the example of the

Football League and the Northern Union and continue playing after the declaration of war. Despite this willingness to continue, clubs in the region quickly found that the clamour to volunteer and the increase in working hours for dockyard workers meant that organising fixtures became virtually impossible and the season was abandoned.[25] By the beginning of September, club rugby union throughout England was at an end.

On 4 September, in recognition of this accomplished fact, the RFU Committee formally cancelled all club, county and international matches, and called upon all players aged between nineteen and thirty-five to enlist. It also proposed the formation of a rugby players' battalion. However, after discussions with the War Office, C.J.B. Marriott told the clubs that 'it is not feasible to form a separate battalion of Rugby men', but that 'various commanding officers . . . will gladly accept for their Regiments a company (about 120) of Rugby men who could be enlisted together'. He then asked volunteers to send their particulars directly to him.[26] In fact, the prospect of a national battalion had already been scuppered by the rush to join local regiments. Former RFU secretary Rowland Hill was one of many rugby administrators who reflected this trend when, a few days before Marriott's circular, he appealed to clubs in Kent to 'encourage their members to join the Second Battalion now being formed of the Twentieth London (Blackheath). Clubs and leagues coming forward in sufficient numbers will form a company, or section, which will allow friends to soldier with one another.'[27] The enlistment of players in local regiments was part of the same process that led to the formation of Pals' Battalions from late August onwards. Credited as being the brainchild of Lord Derby, the Pals' Battalions were initially formed by members of local middle classes as a way of serving together with their social equals.[28]

But for many in rugby union, enlisting was not enough. The imperial mission that the sport ascribed to itself led some in the game to appoint themselves as unofficial recruiters. The Yorkshire Rugby Union (YRU) called on its clubs to approach non-enlisted youths under nineteen and men over thirty-five 'with the object of forming a company in connection with your club, for the purposes of drilling and training in rifle practice', and warning that 'no excuse ought to be tolerated for his non-compliance'. This was too much even for some of the YRU's supporters, one of whom complained that the creation 'of various corps of "armed civilians" all over the place . . . are of more real danger to their country than they could ever be worth' and the plan was quietly forgotten.[29] Others devoted considerable energy to recruit volunteers, notably Leicester secretary Tom Crumbie who used his club's Welford Road ground as an enlistment centre to recruit 3,500 men in the East

Midlands to the forces.[30] Perhaps the most famous example was that of RFU committee member Edgar Mobbs. Mobbs had been a dashing three-quarter for Northampton and England and when war was declared he immediately volunteered but was unable to enlist as an officer because at thirty-two he was considered too old. Undeterred, he enlisted as a private and set about raising his own corps in Northamptonshire. In three days he recruited 250 men who became the Seventh (Service) Battalion of the Northamptonshire Regiment.[31]

Rugby union spokesmen were also at the forefront of those who clamoured for all sport to cease for the duration of the war. Rowland Hill claimed that by allowing soccer to continue, the FA Council 'had allowed one of the greatest sports in the world to be solely and entirely governed by commercial principles'.[32] In Yorkshire, James Miller – who had long ago made his peace with the RFU – felt that 'playing fields were being desecrated at the present time' and that 'it was necessary to compel those who idled around the streets – those shirkers and bullet-funkers – to join the ranks'.[33] The references to shirkers indicated the underlying class prejudice that lay beneath much of this criticism and Miller had little hesitation in pointing an accusing finger at 'members of other football bodies [who] had not responded in a like manner. It seems to me that a hot blush of crimson must come into the faces of those footballers who remained at play when others went abroad to fight their battles for them.'[34]

Nevertheless, despite its suspension at a club level, rugby union quickly reappeared in a military guise. Matches began to be organised almost as soon as the first volunteers arrived in training camps: a typical example being the Eighth Battalion of the East Surrey Regiment whose team met the Seventh Battalion of the West Kent Regiment while undergoing basic training at Purfleet. The Surreys won 37–3 thanks to a side that included five Welsh internationals and a Cambridge Blue. Inter-platoon tournaments played by battalions in training camp were commonplace. Games were also regularly arranged between battalions and nearby schools; for example, in late September 1914 Lancaster Royal Grammar School played host to a team from the Fifth (Reserve) Battalion of the Royal Lancasters.[35] On 31 October 1914 a match advertised as being between England and Wales was played between soldiers at Shoreham Camp in Sussex. In the north of England, a match was arranged at Doncaster between two regimental teams in the presence of the town's mayor; the sides included two internationals and seven county players. In early November, Leicester saw a Northern Command team defeated 38–3 by a team selected by Tom Crumbie.[36]

Despite its leaders condemning professional football, military rugby union itself became a significant wartime spectator sport. In early December, in what was to establish a pattern of regular matches in London, the Public Schools and Universities Battalion narrowly defeated a Canadian military side in front of 3,000 spectators at the Richmond Athletic ground. The sizes of the crowds that were being attracted to such games were potentially embarrassing to rugby union. The national campaign against 'shirkers' who preferred to watch football rather than enlist was at a hysterical pitch and there was a certain coyness in newspaper reports about the success of such games. *The Times*' reporter did not mention the size of the crowd but focused on 'the ring seats along the touchline presented the appearance of being almost solidly military – rows and rows of khaki caps and khaki figures leaning forward with hands on knees, rows of canes waving in time to the tunes or war cries that rose and fell'.[37] The contrast with the supposed crowds of 'loafers' attending soccer matches could not be made clearer – even a year later, when much of the hysteria had died down, rugby union correspondents were still seeking to emphasise the difference: 'the "shirker" does not patronise rugby union matches. He is not wanted at them', declared W.L.S. in *Athletic News*.[38]

Even so, major matches continued to attract significant attendances. On New Year's Day 1915, 20,000 saw the Canadians play at Leicester, one of four games played there over the Christmas and New Year's holidays. An August 1915 tournament at Northampton between English and Scots military sides attracted over 8,000 spectators. As well as sizeable attendances, the first few weeks of 1915 also saw something like a structured season develop. *Athletic News* noted that there were at least ten military sides in London looking for regular fixtures, together with a number of public schools keen to arrange matches. One such team was 'the Third Battalion of the Honourable Artillery Company, who are pleasantly quartered at Mount Felix, Walton on Thames, [and who] would be glad to arrange Rugby matches with regimental teams on Saturdays at home or away'.[39]

However, the war effort's ceaseless appetite for men meant that by September 1915 the new domestic season had fewer teams and less players, although the game was now being played by the services overseas. The first reported overseas game seems to have been that played by teams from an interned Naval Brigade at Groningen in Holland, which included the Oxford half-back A.C. Williamson. Rochdale's international Northern Union winger Jack Robinson, who was badly wounded at Neuve Chappelle in March 1915, reported playing rugby during the battle, saying that 'our boys out yonder will have their game of football under all sorts of conditions. It comes as a tonic and a relaxation from trench duty and I cannot understand anybody in England ever questioning the advisability of the game'. Before the Battle of Loos in September 1915, the Gordons played the Queen's Own Cameron Highlanders, while in the following year the commanding officer of the Thirteenth Battalion of the Rifle Brigade broke his collar bone in an Officers versus Other Ranks rugby match the day before the Battle of the Somme. Ronald Poulton-Palmer's last rugby match was played in Belgium in 1915 when he captained the South Midland Division (Forty-Eighth) versus the Fourth Division. The poet Robert Graves also turned out as a full-back for the First Battalion of the Royal Welch Fusiliers in a match in France.[40] However, these games were organised on an ad-hoc basis. There were no formal inter-regimental or battalion rugby competitions in the field, as was the case for soccer later in the war.

Rugby occupied a distant second place compared to the popularity of soccer with troops on active service. As a correspondent of *The Times* later lamented, 'it is strange that the game was so little played in France during the war. There was never any difficulty raising sides to play Association, and there was scarcely a squadron, cavalry, engineers or signallers, or a platoon that did not possess its own team and its own wonderfully coloured jersey. Yet Rugby games were few and far between.'[41] The war diary of Huddersfield and England Northern Union rugby forward Douglas Clark for 1917 describes a number of soccer matches of varying degrees of formality in which he played while in France but only one game of rugby.[42] The danger of injury and the difficulty of playing rugby on an improvised pitch naturally gave the round ball game an inbuilt advantage.

But soccer's popularity was based on more than its playing. As J.G. Fuller has noted, army soccer was a 'practical exercise in class collaboration', a sport which men of all ranks could play and which helped to cement *esprit de corps* among the troops.[43] Outside of those from rugby-playing regions in northern England, south Wales or to a lesser extent the Scottish borders, rugby was generally viewed by officers and men alike as a game almost exclusively for officers. Soccer was the sport of the ranks. Paul Jones, the former captain of the Dulwich College first XV, wrote home from France in October 1915 that 'the Tommies – the English ones, at least – think soccer the only game, so one must cut one's cloth to one's opportunities'.[44] Indeed, such was soccer's overwhelming popularity among soldiers that in winter 1917 every platoon was issued with a ball.[45] It is noticeable that in R.C. Sheriff's 1927 play *Journey's End* the protagonists play soccer at the front, despite being rugby players at home. Nor was it an accident that it was soccer balls which were kicked by rugby-playing officers into no-man's land for troops to follow when going 'over the top'. Although it was later claimed that both Edgar Mobbs' brigade and the 16th Battalion of the Northumberland Fusiliers had kicked a rugby ball out of the trenches, there is no contemporary evidence to show that either of these events occurred.[46]

The beginning of 1916 saw rugby union enter what, were it not for the circumstances of its playing, could be termed a golden age of domestic competition. The introduction of backdoor conscription by the 'Derby Scheme' in 1916 – which brought in many professional Northern Union rugby players who had not already volunteered – and the huge influx of troops from Australia, New Zealand and South Africa greatly expanded the pool of players available to military rugby union sides. The number of games played rose dramatically. For example, between March and April 1916, *The Times* carried results from twenty-two matches, mainly played between teams from the Dominions and the south of England, including services teams such as the Royal Military Academy, the Royal Flying Corps, the Welsh Guards and the Artists' Rifles. Many of the London hospital teams continued to play regularly too. Crowds of seven or eight thousand people were not exceptional for matches involving the Dominions teams. The enthusiasm for quasi-international matches was so great that in February 1917 it was announced that a crack team of New Zealanders serving on the Western Front was to tour southern England as the New Zealand Trench Team. *The Times* reported that ticket applications for their matches were already being taken, but within days of its announcement the tour was cancelled, no doubt because of disquiet about soldiers being withdrawn from the front merely to play rugby.[47] The spirit in which these games were played was never less than competitive, so much so that in 1918 the London Society of Referees refused to officiate in any further matches involving the Welsh Guards because of their 'foul play' – such was the scandal that the regiment immediately disbanded the team. Nor was it free of monetary consideration. Later that same season an Australian army side demanded £60 to play the Yorkshire county side.[48]

The year 1916 also saw a revival of rugby union in the north of England, spurred by the recruitment of top professional Northern Union rugby players into the Army. The first major match in the north since 1914 took place between a 'North of England Military Team' and an Australasian representative side in Leeds in April 1916, with the sides boasting four leading professional NU players each. Although this was not the first time NU players had played rugby union during the war – Wigan's Gwyn Thomas had turned out for the Barbarians against South Africa in November 1915 – the prominence of the players involved called into question the RFU's policy of forbidding NU players from playing rugby union. The ban was further undermined in 1916 when Major R.V. Stanley, the Oxford University representative on the RFU committee, unveiled his Army Service Corps (Motor Transport) team at Grove Park in south London.[49] It included Huddersfield's international NU players Harold Wagstaff, Douglas Clark, Ben Gronow and Albert Rosenfeld, together with three other star NU players, and was defeated once in twenty-six games that season.[50] The Devonport Royal Navy depot assembled a similar side, which eventually included nine NU players, of whom four were internationals. The fact that so many rugby union officials had included NU men in their sides meant that the RFU had to act simply to maintain control of the situation. On 4 October 1916 it issued a statement to clarify its position:

> Northern Union players can only play with Rugby Union players in bona-fide naval and military teams. Rugby Union teams can play against naval and military teams in which there are Northern Union players. Munitions workers cannot be regarded as naval and military players. These rulings only obtain during the war.[51]

This was not so much a concession as a recognition of reality. The exclusion of munitions workers from the edict was not surprising. E.H.D. Sewell undoubtedly spoke for many in the sport when in 1915 he hoped that soccer would 'remain the exercise of the munitions workers who suffer so much from varicose veins, weak knees, cod-eyed toes, fowl's livers and a general dislike for a man's duty'.[52]

Indeed, the central leadership of the RFU pulled up the gangway between the two codes of rugby as soon as the opportunity arose. On 14 January 1919, at its first committee meeting since September 1914, the RFU declared that NU players could only play rugby union in the services if they did not also play NU rugby.[53] There was some opposition to the re-implementation of the RFU's draconian policies. Welsh rugby union president Horace Lyne had written to the RFU suggesting that 'Northern Union players who had been on active service' should be eligible for reinstatement as amateurs but his proposal found no support at the meeting.[54] The RFU tightened its restrictions again in April 1919 when it announced that 'civilian clubs are not permitted to play against Service teams containing NU players'.[55] The May 1919 Committee meeting saw a series of appeals for reinstatement from players in Devon who had been banned for professionalism in 1913, all of which were met with the laconic response: 'Declined'.[56] The prestige that it had gained during the war and its close identification with the war effort easily allowed the RFU to brush aside the reformers in its ranks.

The blood sacrifice

The RFU's authority had been secured with blood. The England side contributed the lives of twenty-seven internationals. Bristol, with a broader social base than most teams, lost 300 members. Forty-five of the sixty players in London Scottish's four pre-war XVs were killed. Richmond lost seventy-three members, Rosslyn Park seventy-two, Liverpool fifty-seven and Hartlepool thirty-three. Of the Old Merchant Taylors' 1914 first team thirteen were killed and two permanently disabled; these are just some of the more prominent examples. Surveying the carnage that had been visited upon English rugby a few weeks after the armistice, a correspondent in *The Times* wrote without a hint of irony that 'of the English fifteen which played before the King at Twickenham early in 1914, scarcely one is left; they might indeed on that occasion have hailed their distinguished spectator, only too appropriately, with the ancient gladiators' cry, "Morituri te salutant"'.[57]

This harrowing toll of lost lives flowed directly from the conception that rugby was a preparation for war. The violent, physical nature of the game meant that it was the sport that lent itself most naturally to the vocabulary of war. Lord Jellicoe, Admiral and First Sea Lord during the war, wrote that 'Rugby football, to my mind, above all games is one which develops the qualities which go to make good fighting men. It teaches unselfishness, esprit de corps, quickness of decision, and keeps fit those engaged in it.'[58] In January 1915 the *Spectator* used rugby to explain the subtleties of trench warfare:

> The situation is not unlike that in the 'scrum' in Rugby football. Looked at superficially, almost total immobility seems to have been secured by the contending forces. If, however, one looks closer, there is seen to be a trend in one direction, and if this trend is not checked one knows that the unstable equilibrium will break up, with advantage to the side which is pushing just a little harder than the other.[59]

Nor did the use of rugby as a metaphor disappear when the full horror of the war became apparent. The return to England of two of the soccer balls kicked into no-man's land by the Eighth Battalion of the East Surrey Regiment was greeted by the depot's commanding officer, Colonel Treeby, in the language of rugby: 'our men have played and are playing the game. We are still in the scrum, it is true, but the ball is being carried forward, and we doubt not that in God's good providence the goal for which we are fighting – the goal of freedom, justice and lasting peace – will soon be won.'[60]

The most overwrought use of rugby as military metaphor was to be found
in a speech of Major-General Sir C.H. Harrington given in April 1919 after
a New Zealand services side had defeated a French XV at Twickenham, in
which he ascribed the Allies' victory to:

> the captaincy of that great soldier Marshall Foch, who developed
> his attacks so splendidly by means of those loyal and unselfish three-
> quarter backs, Sir Douglas Haig, General Pershing and the King of
> the Belgians, and those grand attacking forwards, our respective
> army commanders. Nor must we forget those wing three-quarters
> in distant theatres – namely our commanders in Egypt, Macedonia,
> Mesopotamia, Italy and Russia, where our forces all helped so much
> to increase the score. Behind all we had that sound full-back, repre-
> sented by the men and women of the allied nations.[61]

The response of those in the front line was more ambiguous. Some soldiers
quickly realised that the war was not at all a 'great game'. In December 1914
Leicester forward W. Dalby wrote home describing an attack on his trench:
'On one occasion all but one German [attacking the trench] turned and fled,
and he came on shouting, "Me no done for," but he was a second later. It is
nice to read of these things, but not so nice to be in it. We had this sort of
thing for four nights and lost half the men in that time.'[62] Ted Butcher,
a Devon county representative player and long-serving RFU committee
member who was one of a handful of surviving officers in Edgar Mobbs'
Brigade of the Northamptonshire Regiment, suffered from nightmares for
the rest of his life.[63] There is also evidence that some soldiers actively disliked
the use of sporting metaphors: 'we didn't dribble footballs, neither did we
say "This way to Berlin, boys" nor any of the phrases employed weekly in
the News of the World', wrote Roland Mountfort, a survivor of the first day
of the Somme. The same dismissals can be found in the magazines produced
at the front such as the *Wipers Times.* [64]

Even so, many other soldiers *did* believe in the rhetoric of their generals
and the propagandists on the Home Front. The letters of Billie Nevill, a keen
rugby player at Dover College who helped organise and lead the East Surrey
Regiment's football-led attack on German lines at the Somme, are full of the
gung-ho spirit to be found in the boy's stories of the Edwardian age: 'war is
the greatest fun imaginable', he wrote home at one point.[65] England international Jack King wrote in his last letter home before being killed in August
1916 that 'so long as I don't disgrace the old Rugby game, I don't think
I mind'.[66] Eleven months before he was killed in action, rugger-loving Paul

Jones of Dulwich wrote that 'in my heart and soul I have always longed for the rough and tumble of war as for a football match'.[67]

Indeed, this was where the true value of rugby union lay. Its real claim to occupy a special position in British sporting culture was not attributable to the military brilliance or the tactical astuteness of rugby-playing officers – it lay in their spirit of sacrifice, their willingness to die for their country. Within days of war being declared, Blackheath announced that they were 'immensely proud of the fact that in the list of wounded in the first engagement of the war in which the British Army was concerned' was one of their players, Lieutenant A.A.M. Durand of the Royal Field Artillery.[68] As the war drew on, the continuous recital of rugby union players who had been killed in combat became a source of pride and it became an accepted truth within the game that it had lost a higher proportion of its players than any other sport.[69]

When the available records are analysed, however, the validity of this claim is not so clear. Of the 160 England internationals who are known to have served in the forces in the First World War, twenty-seven were killed and another died shortly after partly as a results of wounds received during the war (16.9 per cent of the total) and twenty-eight (17.5 per cent) were awarded the Military Cross. Based on the not unreasonable assumption that the overwhelming majority of those England players serving were officers, we can compare these figures with those for officers in all services as a whole, of whom 13.6 per cent were killed and 16 per cent were awarded the Military Cross. Given such a small sample, it could be argued that the difference of less than three percentage points is statistically insignificant. These mortality figures are also lower than those of Oxford and Cambridge graduates, who recorded death rates of 19.2 per cent and 18 per cent respectively.[70]

How do rugby union's figures compare with the other football codes? Here the data are even less reliable, making any meaningful comparison impossible. Neither the Football League nor the Northern Union kept or produced comprehensive lists of players' war records or decorations. The only information available is that relating to fifteen of the twenty-five professional NU clubs published by *Athletic News* in 1919. Of 760 players who served in the armed forces, 103 lost their lives, 13.5 per cent of the total.[71] The limited statistical evidence available means that it is difficult to draw any firm conclusions. It is possible that rugby union players as a whole did suffer a higher casualty rate than other footballers but, given the overwhelmingly middle-class composition of the sport, this was as a result of social and demographic factors rather than the intrinsic nature of the game. Enlistment rates for the middle classes were higher than those for working-class males, many of whom failed military fitness tests or were engaged in munitions work. Casualty rates for officers were significantly higher than for the lower ranks, which, because entry to the officer class was restricted to those with a public school or university background until the latter stages of the war, meant a higher proportion of middle-class soldiers were killed. And the fact that many rugby union players were junior officers also meant that they were more likely to play a front-line role leading men into battle – in the first year of the war one in seven junior army officers were killed in contrast to one in seventeen of the ranks.[72] Given such factors, it does not seem unreasonable to claim, as did one the sport's supporters in 1918, that 'those who loved the game were just the type of men to be the first to volunteer, the earliest to be trained, and, from their very keenness and fitness, the quickest "over the top" – the most likely to be killed'.[73]

The huge toll of young lives lost does not appear to have caused anyone in the sport to question the war, with the sole exception of former Scotland captain John MacCallum, a doctor who in 1916 refused to serve and attempted to register as a conscientious objector.[74] Indeed, the opposite is true. Its blood sacrifice strengthened rugby's belief in its mission. RFU president Arthur Hartley led the way with his declaration that 'we are proud of the race that give us Rugby football at its best, and we would hold to the fine traditions now handed down to us by the fallen . . . Their supreme sacrifice will not have been in vain if we live nobly and carry into the game their spirit.'[75] It is possible to argue that such statements are merely enthusiastic expressions of imperial loyalty. However, the end of the war also saw RFU spokesmen freely using the rhetoric of the pre-war glorification of the warrior's death and enthusiastically helping to create what George Mosse has described as a 'cult of the fallen soldier'.[76] Writing in *The Rugby Football Internationals' Roll of Honour*, E.H.D. Sewell declared of the dead: 'there is not one among us who does not envy them for their glorious deaths for King, for Empire and for the Right.' Army chaplain and vice-president of Yorkshire Rugby Union Richard Huggard, who had lost two sons in the war, stated that 'we fathers miss our sons, but we thrill with pride, aye, and joy, when we remember the cause for which our boys died'. Future RFU president Bob Oakes, who organised many of the wartime matches in the north of England, shared similar sentiments: 'We now know how splendidly the Rugby footballer, in common with every British soldier, fought – aye, and how magnificently he died!'

Nor can it be argued that those making such statements were ignorant of the realities of war, as can be seen in the most chilling of eulogies to rugby union players, delivered by James Miller, now president of the Headingley club, in 1919:

And then, in the rotation of trenches and bullets, came the moment when they had to take their chance 'over the top'. With pulses quickened they waited through the night, their minds filled with the hidden fear, but no regret. For the same spirit possessed them, uplifted them, until, as the dawn rose and the signal was given, it carried them over and on through the blinding showers of lead, until one, then another, and another, and more and yet more then, called to the sacrifice, passed over into the shadows of the 'Beyond'.[77]

Jay Winter has suggested that such rhetoric was largely produced by those too old to fight, yet these sentiments were prevalent throughout rugby union.[78] Far from being 'devastatingly destroyed by the first experience of bombardment in the trenches' as has been claimed by David Cannadine, the comments of officials such as Miller and players such as Paul Jones demonstrate how deep and resilient was the belief that war was a variant of sport. In the *Boy's Own Paper* in 1919, Welsh international three-quarter George Hirst wrote of those rugby players killed in the conflict, 'they paid the greatest sacrifice of all; they scored for England, for the world, in the greatest contest the earth has ever known'.[79] Far from viewing the conflict as 'the war to end all wars', the leaders of the RFU emphasised their sport's war record as a demonstration of its willingness to go to war again. Sewell declared in the *Roll of Honour* that 'whenever [England] calls again, Rugby Football will be the first to line out; bending forward eager for the moment the fight begins, and ready to "stick it", come what may'. Former RFU secretary Rowland Hill was similarly keen when unveiling Blackheath's war memorial in 1921: 'Generations yet unborn will enter with spirit into the great games of England and will regard their country with such reverence and keen affection that should she ever again need the services of her young men they will be prepared to follow in the footsteps of the illustrious dead.'[80]

This view of the war adds much weight to the observation by Jeffrey Richards and many others that middle-class disillusionment immediately after the war, exemplified by writers such as Wilfred Owen and Robert Graves, was atypical and confined to small circles of the intelligensia.[81] The importance of sport to political or social discourse is that it provides an emotional framework based on the simple categories of victory and defeat. Rugby union provided a cultural vehicle through which to express conservative (both in political terms and through its re-assertion of traditional values) patriotic middle-class opinion. It articulated the feelings of those sections of the middle classes for whom victory in the war meant confirmation of the continuing validity of the values of the Edwardian era. The fact that it was a sporting body allowed it to express such thoughts in ostensibly non-political, cultural language.

Its writers tapped into the emotional resonance of the game by mining the same sources as mainstream middle-class opinion, especially through the use of poetry in the traditional styles that had been established by writers such as Newbolt. Rather than being the birth of 'modern memory', as Fussell has argued for high art, the memory of war fashioned by popular middle-class culture was solidly rooted in the past. August 1914 witnessed an explosion of patriotic doggerel and for rugby union the use of this 'heroic' style of poetry became almost de rigueur when writing about its experience of war. Both Sewell's *Roll of Honour* and the similar *Yorkshire Rugby Union Commemoration Book* were replete with patriotic poetry ranging in quality from schoolboy musings to Rupert Brooke. Sewell's book began with a call to arms:

Sound, sound the clarion, fill the fife
To all the sensual world proclaim
One crowded hour of glorious life
Is worth an age without a name!

The Yorkshire book was more extensive in its use of poetry. Bob Oakes, Yorkshire Rugby Union secretary, quoted Canadian poet R.W. Service, 'For all our beauty, and hope, and joy/We will owe to our lads like you.' Rowland Hill began his article with the words 'And us they trusted; we the task inherit,/The unfinished task for which their lives were spent.' Arthur Hartley ended his appreciation of the fallen with the words 'In grateful love I bow the knee/For nameless men who died for me.' Perhaps inevitably the portraits of the dead Yorkshire players was prefaced with extracts from Brooke's *1914*, starting with the famous words 'If I should die, think only this of me:/That's there's some corner of a foreign field/That is for ever England.' The phrase 'happy warrior', taken from Wordsworth's 1806 poem, was one of the most over-used phrases in writings about players killed in action, especially when referring to Ronald Poulton-Palmer. 'Amid his peers, a happy warrior sleeps' ended Alfred Ollivant's poem *R.W.P.P., Killed in the Trenches*.[82] Clifton, a club that lost forty-five members, commemorated its lost players with faux Rupert Brooke poetry:

Go search ye o'er the battlefields,
These names will be found again,
Each one inscribed on a cross

To show how they played the game.
They died; a handful of a mighty host
Who gave their lives that you and I
Might live. They died like men in foreign lands,
In the Club they will never die.[83]

Even as late as 1925 Brooke was being quoted by Leonard Tosswill in his article on the war for the revised edition of Frank Marshall's *Football: The Rugby Union Game*. Martin Pugh's observation that 'the Great War proved to be spiritually rewarding for British Conservatives' applies equally to rugby union and its supporters.[84]

Indeed, the most remarkable feature of rugby's use of poetry is not simply the way in which it used to convey a sense of debt and consequent duty, but also its linking of that debt to the greater glory of rugby union itself. It resembles, perhaps unsurprisingly, the way in which the histories of military regiments or biographies of saints are written. In much of the poetry and prose written, 'England' and 'rugby' are virtually interchangeable; the sport itself is the carrier of the imperial message. 'All's well with England; Poulton's on his game' was a key line in Ollivant's poem. No other sport abrogated to itself such a position. Soccer and rugby league certainly did not see themselves in this role and it is patently absurd to imagine a golf or tennis club with similar pretensions. Even cricket, the Imperial sport par excellence, was far more restrained and circumspect when discussing the war.[85]

The memorials, poetry, commemorations and the cult of its fallen were the means by which rugby union paid homage to itself as the embodiment of middle-class tradition and stability in a post-war world in which these certainties were being challenged. Fussell has pointed out how the literature of the immediate post-war period highlighted 'the persistence of the binary sense and the prevalence of the conception of "the enemy"' in British society during this period and this is very strongly reflected in rugby union writings of the time. One only has to look at the alacrity with which the ban on NU players was reinstated in January 1919 to see that the pre-war social divisions were not only preserved intact by the sport but were pursued with equal, if not greater, vigour.[86]

The 'rush to rugby' and beyond

It was this wartime record as a defender of Edwardian imperial ideals that laid the basis for rugby's ousting of soccer as the dominant sport in the public and grammar schools in the 1920s. In February 1919 an unnamed headmaster wrote to *The Times* to claim that:

it was a common experience before 1914 to read attacks upon the excessive athleticism of the country in general, and of the public schools in particular. Since then the war has come and gone, and the youth of the country has passed through the furnace of trial. In the test of that experience one game at any rate has been justified triumphantly, not only as a pastime, but as an instrument of true education, and that is Rugby football.

He went on to suggest that rugby

has proved itself to be unequalled by any other game as a school of true manhood and leadership. . . . It is all the greater pity that there should still be some great schools that follow the less inspiring and less severe discipline of Association, and a very few that play an esoteric game of their own. Now that all the world is devoting itself to reconstruction, and all institutions are making a new start, is it too much to hope that all schools will consider seriously the adoption of Rugby football as the winter game for all the youth of the nation.[87]

The following week another correspondent pointed to another source of its appeal: 'the way in which all Rugby clubs, aided very fully by the Rugby Union, almost ordered all players to the colours in August 1914, realising that the game for which they had been preparing for so many years had begun, made a deep impression on the country'.[88]

Before the war, soccer had been prominent in the public schools, although the efforts of the RFU, together with disquiet about the link between soccer and working-class professionalism, had helped to increase rugby's popularity. By the mid-1900s a number of previously non-rugger schools had begun to take up the game. Eton, for example, first started to play the game in 1908.[89] But rugby's prominence during and after the war provided the impetus for a major shift in the sporting geography of elite schools. Ampleforth, Rossall, City of London, Radley and Malvern schools, followed by many others, all took up the sport during or immediately after the war. In January 1919 a campaign began for Winchester to take up rugby led by old boy Brigadier-General Godfrey Meynell, a former commanding officer on the Western Front. Meynell took his lead from the fact that rugby was now played by Eton, 'our great rival and sister school with whom we have so much in common' but his main argument was simple. 'Rugby is the most character-forming sport in the world', he argued and suggested that many other public schools 'from the experience of the last war, will consider now the advisability of changing their game'.[90] In 1926 a sharp debate broke out in the pages of *The Times* over the move by Harrow headmaster Cyril Norwood to abandon soccer for rugby. Following overwhelming votes by the staff and the boys of the school to take up rugby, an advertisement appeared in the 'Personal' column on the front page of the newspaper urging Old Harrovians to protest. Norwood stood fast, not least because he claimed that the change had been in response to requests from parents.[91] A flavour of the anti-soccer sentiment that existed within some schools can be seen in a poem published in the school magazine of St John's School, Hurstpierpoint, during a debate to switch to rugby:

This Soccer has sapped the foundations,
Of honour, truth, justice and right;
Has made you traduced of the nations;
Has bedded and bushel'd your light.[92]

Countless other private and grammar schools opted for rugby in the 1920s. The haemorrhaging from soccer became so severe that in 1925 the Headmasters' Conference (HMC) was asked by concerned soccer supporters in the public schools for its co-operation to help 're-introduce Association football to those schools where it has been discontinued, and to bring about its introduction to those schools where hitherto it has not been played'.[93] The matter was discussed at its annual conference in December 1925 when representatives from Shrewsbury and Malvern proposed that the HMC should 'view with concern the present position of amateur Association football, and consider that a wholesale defection of Public Schools from Association to Rugby football would be a national disaster'. Shrewsbury's Canon Sawyer argued that

if the stampede from Association to Rugby football continued much longer, amateur Association would cease, a great game would be handed over to the professional, and there would be one game for the rich and another for the poor. The cleavage would be deepened between the larger public schools and the smaller grammar schools and secondary schools, which for the most part played Association.

Although a slightly watered down version of the motion was passed, no action was taken. The HMC issued a non-committal statement to the press which made no mention of the different codes, simply stating that it felt that 'it would be regrettable if there were anything of a social cleavage in the matter of football, [and] welcomed the opportunities which at present existed for boys of every social type to play games against one another, and hoped that it might be possible to extend them'. Three months later a concerned Football Association asked if the HMC could request that all boys be given the chance to play soccer. The headmaster of Repton and future Archbishop of Canterbury Geoffrey Fisher accused rugby supporters of 'rather insolent condemnation [of soccer] on grounds of prejudice and ignorance of those whose tastes are unlike one's own'.[94] It was to no avail. The 'rush to rugby' continued and, from twenty-seven in 1919, the number of public and grammar schools affiliated to the RFU had more than quadrupled to 133 by 1929.[95]

By the time that the Second World War broke out in 1939 rugby union was the dominant game both numerically and ideologically in the public schools. But the 1939–45 war did not follow the pattern of the 1914–18 conflict. Most strikingly from a sporting perspective, the witch-hunt against professional sport seen in 1914 did not occur in 1939. This was partly because professionalism itself now had a higher level of acceptance in society but also because the sporting authorities had learned their lesson from the last war. Sport had been proved to have a positive effect on morale, in both civilian and military life. Consequently, the leaders of the RFU did not engage in the previous baiting of their professional counterparts and were somewhat more circumspect about issuing orders to its clubs. In November 1939 the RFU also lifted its ban on rugby league players and allowed them to play rugby union while serving in the armed forces. As a Mass-Observation reporter noted 'rugby appeals to a section of the community which was the most likely to become war-minded, and to scrap everything to show some spirit of sacrifice', yet the impulse to shut down the sport was resisted, with the result that, in the south-east alone, around one hundred rugby matches were played each weekend. The only major victim of the outbreak of war was the touring Wallaby side, who arrived on 2 September and immediately made arrangements to return: 'we had one job in front of us now, viz., to return and get into Australian uniforms without delay' their tour manager told a farewell lunch at Twickenham ten days after their arrival.[96]

Clubs met with mixed fortunes. Some, such as London Scottish, closed for the duration as a result of both the loss of players to the services and the requisitioning of their grounds by the military. Others contrived to continue by joining forces with former rivals, the most notable example being the Blackheath–Richmond combination, a marriage caused partially by serious bomb damage at the former's Rectory Field ground. Harlequins kept their name alive by playing one match each season. But for a number the war brought considerable success. Coventry almost went through the war unbeaten, winning seventy-two consecutive matches before falling to St Mary's Hospital in January 1945. Rosslyn Park had a large number of guest players make appearances during the war and played a key role in maintaining public school rugby, which also flourished during the conflict. For some, the ease of movement between clubs and the shuffling together of players caused by service duties or other circumstances took the game back to its gentlemanly roots. 'War-time rugby has at last really become like club cricket, a game solely for the player. Present conditions are such that men are playing for any club they fancy', commented the *Evening Standard* in late 1939.[97]

Indeed, as *The Times*' O.L. Owen believed, 'the rugby game kept most wonderfully alive' throughout the war, especially at representative level.[98] In December 1939 an England/Wales side defeated Scotland/Ireland 17–3 at Richmond in aid of the Red Cross, signalling the start of a series of service-based encounters. In addition to Army and RAF matches, 1942 saw the beginning of regular service internationals being played between England, Scotland and Wales, including an April 1942 8–5 Scottish win over England at Wembley stadium. Eleven of England's sixty-seven wartime representatives were rugby league players. As in the previous war, army teams from Australia, New Zealand and South Africa added vibrant colour to the wartime scene. The Varsity match also continued in a different form, being played on a two-game home and away basis, although blues were not awarded. The fraternisation between league and union even went so far as cross-code encounters. In 1943 Northern Command organised a representative league versus union match at Leeds and the following year a Combined Services league XV met its union equivalent. Both matches were played under union rules and were won by the league players.

The playing of the matches against the league sides showed how much the tenor of the sport during the Second World War differed from that in the First World War. Even the memorials to players who were killed between 1939 and 1945 lacked the militaristic fervour of the earlier conflict. Fourteen England internationals lost their lives, including Alexander Obolensky, who died in a flying accident, and 1913 Grand Slam England captain Norman Wodehouse, who was a vice-admiral in the Royal Navy when his ship was torpedoed in July 1941. Six served in the RAF, five in the army and three in the Royal Navy. The cult of sacrifice and commemoration of the First World War was markedly absent, as it was in British society in general.

To some extent this change in attitude was as a result of the Second World War being a 'total war' in which civilians were often as much at risk as combatants and because of the strong memory of the horrors of the First World War. But the RFU also found itself slightly out of step with the times. The 1939–45 war was presented as a 'People's War', of make do and mend equality, of all classes being in the same boat together. The social democratic rhetoric of the war, in contrast to the militaristic patriotism of 1914–18, was at variance with rugby union's worldview. This war could not be taken as a vindication of the RFU's principles or as proof of the correctness of its support for amateur ideals. It was sports such as soccer and rugby league, unashamedly mass popular games, that had a 'good war' and seemed to represent the mood of the 1940s.[99]

Fifty years later in the late 1990s it was the rhetoric and imagery of the First World War that had once again come to the fore in rugby union. The interlinking of war and rugby became commonplace. Praising England's Lawrence Dallaglio, *The Times*' Alison Kervin commented that 'genuinely good leaders do emerge in the English game, men who not only understand the game, but who would be equally at home leading businesses or men into battle'. Such sentiments extended from sports reporters to military professionals. 'Rugby as a metaphor for war is quite uncanny. In rugby you respect your opponent at all times, you can win yet still have taken a huge physical beating', the former commandant of Sandhurst Major General Arthur DeNaro told a *Daily Telegraph* journalist. 'Things can go badly wrong, at some time you are definitely going to get beaten and it will hurt. Yet you learn to deal with disappointment and defeat. You learn to bounce back and get the job done.'[100] Following the example of Australian and New Zealand touring teams in France, two days before their first match in the 2007 Rugby World Cup, the England team were taken on a tour of the Somme battlefield.

To some extent this revival of the earlier tradition reflected modern times. The Falklands War in 1982 and the subsequent rise of Western military intervention around the world in the 1990s made militarism fashionable once more after the ignominy of Vietnam. As Sir Tasker Watkins VC, former Welsh Rugby Union president, said in 2001, 'patriotism, I am glad to see, is making a comeback these days. . . . Sportsmen – rugby players and others – understand patriotism better than any sector of society'.[101] But it also played an important role in reasserting rugby union's sense of ethical superiority. The abandonment of amateurism in 1995 seemed to leave the sport bereft any moral authority in the sporting or wider world. The revitalisation of its tradition of militaristic patriotism, blood sacrifice and nationalist duty gave the sport, at least in its own eyes, a renewed supremacy of broader purpose than the mere playing of a game. Rugby was war, war was rugby, and the horror of the events that inspired such thoughts was forgotten.

4

THE MAN'S GAME

Twickenham, January 1925. The unbeaten All Blacks reach the climax of their tour with a match against England. Queues had begun forming at the gates of 'HQ' since the early hours of the morning and cars had quickly filled every inch of spare ground around the stadium. A record 60,000 spectators were joined at this carnival of Empire solidarity by the Prince of Wales, the future Edward VII and a keen rugger fan. Expectations ran high.

The All Blacks had laid waste to all that British rugby union could throw at them, recalling their historic first tour of 1905. In just twenty-seven matches they had wracked up 637 points and conceded just 87. In eleven matches, their opponents had failed to score a single point, Wales and Ireland being among them. But England, led by former RAF officer William Wavell Wakefield, were an altogether different proposition. Unbeaten for almost three years, they were back-to-back Grand Slam champions, boasting a fast, physical pack together with agile and intelligent backs. And they had a plan to beat the All Blacks.

Wakefield believed the All Blacks won many matches because they were physically 'assertive'. In other words, they set out to intimidate their opponents. He therefore 'made sure that before the English team went on to the field they had definitely made up their minds not to be so treated.' In fact, this determination not to be intimidated had become a hallmark of England under Wakefield's leadership. In 1921 they had kicked the Scots off their Inverleith pitch to win 18–0. When one of the Scottish forwards had complained to 'Wakers' that England were a little too keen to use the boot, he replied that Scotland had done the same to them in the past and now that the English were getting their own back 'they must not turn and grouse'. During the 1924 match with Wales, what Wakefield described as 'rough-housing' got so out of hand in the second half that at one point England had four forwards being treated for injuries. But the tactics were successful and England recorded a 17–9 victory, their first in Wales since the war.[1]

So as soon as Bristol's Len Corbett kicked-off, the England pack tore into the New Zealanders, asserting a dominance that was undermined only by the English backs' failure to turn their supremacy into points. Wakefield euphemistically recalled that the first ten minutes were 'very hectic', although *The Times* preferred to talk about 'more than one unpleasant proof that the forwards were taking things too seriously'. Corbett was more frank, calling the events of the early minutes 'plain rough housing'. In fact, from the first scrum the English forwards sought to dominate through the use of fists and boots. Reg Edwards, an Englishman who played his club rugby for Newport, allegedly struck the first blow and continued, in the words of England full-back Jim Brough, to be 'a bit free with his fists' until warned by the referee. The English journalist Denzil Batchelor saw an English boot land on a prostrate All Blacks. Things became so unpleasant that Albert Freethy, the Welsh referee, stopped the game three times to warn both sets of forwards about their behaviour. The next player to be cautioned would be sent off, he told them in the expectation that this would end the matter.[2]

It did not.

With barely eight minutes gone, Freethy once again stopped play and ordered Cyril Brownlie, the New Zealand 'side-forward' or equivalent of a modern flanker, to leave the field of play. The referee had seen him deliberately stamp on an England forward. Shocked, New Zealand captain Jock Richardson asked the referee to reconsider, who refused. Richardson then turned to Wakefield, who as the architect of the mayhem responded with even less sympathy. A momentary gasp seemed to echo around the stadium as the crowd realised what had just happened: Cyril Brownlie had become the first man ever to be sent off in an international.[3]

It looked as if Wakefield's tactics had worked. On seventeen minutes, the England pack wheeled a scrum. Tom Voyce dribbled the ball forward, guided it around full-back George Nepia and Ronald Cove-Smith followed up to score in the left corner. Brough failed to convert but England seemed to have consolidated their ascendancy against the depleted fourteen-man All Blacks. But in the last eight minutes of the half, slick New Zealand passing put Svenson and then Steel in for unconverted tries before a clumsy off-side by an English forward allowed Nicholls to kick a penalty. Another two tries in the second half extended the lead to 17–3 before England recovered their early form. Len Corbett dropped a goal from a penalty and then Harold Kittermaster ran from half-way to touch down under the posts on his England debut. At 17–11 to the tourists, it had been a memorable game, thrilling in its intensity but shocking to many for its violence. 'If that is international rugby I want nothing of it,' English forward Ronnie Hillard allegedly declared after the game.

It was to be his first and his last international match.[4]

Being a man

Hillard was an exception. For Wakefield and rugby union in general, the physicality of the sport was its essence. Wakefield was not only one of its most able exponents, he was also one of its most articulate, writing in 1927 that each player:

> must be ready to give and take hard knocks, but he will give and take them with a grin. . . . It would be a poor sort of game that had no sort of risk to be faced, and it is one of the glories of rugger that you can put your shoulder into a man with all your strength and bring him down with a crash, knowing that if you stave in a rib or two of his he will bear no grudge against you, while if he knocks your teeth out in handing you off it is merely your own fault for tackling him too high.[5]

This was true at all levels of the game, from internationals down to schools. There was little difference between a match such as the All Blacks game in 1925 and the schoolboy contest described by Alec Waugh in *The Loom of Youth*:

> 'Now lads,' shouted Stewart, 'fair or foul; shove the ball over the line!' Like a sledgehammer Gordon crashed into the scrum. Wilkinson was in his light, but Gordon was seeing red, his feet stamped on Wilkinson, and found the ball. His elbows swung viciously, as he cut his way through the scrum. Then someone caught him by the ankle. He went down hard. A boot caught him on the side of the head. He got up blind with wrath. 'Fight! Fight!' he yelled.[6]

The willingness to give and take violence, whether sanctioned by the laws of the game or otherwise, was for rugby the mark of a true man. More than any other quality, beyond even amateurism or patriotism, the game was built on the assertion of masculinity through physicality. 'I have never yet known a genuine Rugby forward who was not distinctively *a man*,' wrote

H.H. Almond in 1892. Almost eighty years later Geoffrey Nicholson and W.J. Morgan in their *Report on Rugby* endorsed this view: 'here is a world in which a man may be a man and demonstrate manly virtues without hindrances'. Even in the twenty-first century, this belief was eagerly promoted by the novelist Richard Beard. Rugby's appeal, he argued, is based on its 'universal masculine' values, adding that 'it's not just me' who wished to belong to this 'admirably like-minded band of men'.[7]

The use of violence to forge 'like-minded men' can be traced back to the very earliest days of the game at Rugby School. In *Tom Brown's Schooldays*, East introduces school football to Tom by proudly stressing its dangers: 'it's no joke playing-up in a match, I can tell you. . . . Why, there's been two collar-bones broken this half [of the term], and a dozen fellows lamed. And last year a fellow had his leg broken.'[8] Above all, it was hacking that was the measurement of manliness at the school. 'We all wear white trousers, to show 'em we don't care for hacks,' explains East to Tom before his first match. White was chosen because it would highlight the blood from a boys' hacked shins most vividly. Bloodied shins were a badge of honour, the crimson proof of adolescent toughness. Although the wearing of white trousers was not a tradition that survived in the sport, that of wearing caps did. Crimson caps were worn by boys of School House to distinguish themselves from their School opponents in the mass scrums that dominated the game. As old boy Sydney Selfe remembered, 'the *mot d'ordre* was "whenever you see a [bare] head, hit it".'[9] Trousers and caps were not the only sartorial equipment that were essential to the game. Older boys would have their boots specially fashioned for football, with thick soles added and the toes beveled so they could more easily cut into the shins of an opponent. Reminiscencing in 1860, an old boy described how 'fellows did not care a fig for the ball except inasmuch as it gave them a decent pretext for hacking. . . . Those were the days when fellows used to roll the ball out of touch, like sensible Christians as they then were, and bowl over the fellow who stood next to them with a stunning good place kick. My maxim is hack the ball on when you see it near you, and when you don't, why then, hack the fellow next to you.'[10] The sport's brutal nature was attested to by the Reverend Bulkeley Jones, a pupil at the school in the 1830s and 1840s: 'The games at football were positively ferocious. However they were an excellent training for the pugilistic encounters which were not uncommon.' Similar practices were commonplace at all public schools where the rugby code was played (and also at those where other codes prevailed). Remembering his schooldays at Clifton College in the early 1870s, Arthur Budd recalled that

it was an act of high treason to put down one's head in the scrummage, and if anybody did so, an opponent would probably remind
him of this breach of etiquette by raising his knee sharply against it.
Hacking was permissible and, as there were no umpires to appeal to
in the case of a breach of the rules, such as for example, off-side
play, the innocent party used to take the law into his own hands,
and with a shout of 'Off-side, sir' administer the orthodox punishment by violently kicking the shins of the offender.[11]

Opposition to the violence of rugby was generally dismissed by the sport's
supporters as either uninformed or evidence of the softening of British
manhood. And as the ethics of the game became systematised, the importance of physicality acquired a redemptive, restorative quality. This was
expressed most plainly when justifying the value of the game for adolescent
schoolboys. The player who holds back and suffers for his hesitancy but then
throws caution to the wind and becomes invigorated was a staple of the
schoolboy story. This supposed catharsis of violence was eloquently described in a short story, *The Wing Three-Quarter*, by Liam O'Flaherty:

This was the first time in his life he had gone down to a forward
rush. It was his first good bruising on a hard field, and it awoke
some element in him that nobody thought he possessed, of which he
himself was unaware. Standing now, leaning forward, waiting for
the ball, he felt that he wanted to fall upon the whole enemy team
and lay them low. His face was covered with earth. His right knee
was skinned. There was a big bruise on his left hip and his whole
body tingled with pain after the mauling he had received. But his
heart thumped with excitement and he felt fierce instead of feeling
afraid. Afraid! He knew he would never be afraid again.[12]

Regan, the story's revivified schoolboy, had previously been guilty of
'funking' – shrinking from a challenge – the schoolboy equivalent of
cowardice. For rugby's advocates, the boy who funked was more likely to
be injured than one who hurled himself selflessly at the feet of on-rushing
forwards. A young player must not make 'half-hearted grabs at the ball but
throw himself at it bodily,' explained the Reverend R.H. Cattell, one of
many Anglican clergymen who reveled in the muscularity of Muscular
Christianity. 'Funk is responsible for most of the accidents in football.' The
Manual of Rugby Football for Public Schools told its readers that 'it is
noticeable that it is always the 'funks' that get hurt at football, while the

plucky players seems to have a charmed life', although of course it offered no evidence for this assertion.[13]

There was a clear link between this belief in physical courage and concepts of military duty. War was a constant feature of the period in which Rugby School codified its rules of football and ideas about masculinity were shaped by British military history. In particular, British success in the Napoleonic wars was the reference point for manliness. 'What! Talk of *danger* to British boys! To the descendents of those men who were at Waterloo and Trafalgar?' wrote the *New Rugbeian* in 1861 in response to complaints about the violence of hacking. 'We are thankful to say we were never yet told by an *English* man to look out for our shins.' As Robert and Isabelle Tombs have demonstrated, the French were often portrayed at this time as effeminate decadents. If the critics of rugby were successful, its supporters claimed, they would reduce British football to the level of a 'pretty little skirmish in the Champs Elysees' rather than the 'gallant bayonet charge that won the field of Waterloo'.[14] Hostility to the French was a constant thread that ran through rugby's narratives of masculinity up until the 1880s. At the meeting of the Football Association that finally decided against hacking in December 1863, Blackheath's F.M. Campbell protested against the decision on the grounds that it would 'do away with all the courage and pluck of the game, and I will be bound to bring over a lot of Frenchmen, who would beat you with a week's practice'. The meeting which founded the Wakefield Trinity club in 1872 heard the Reverend W.M. Madden claim that, thanks to sport, 'one Englishman [was] equal to five Frenchmen'.[15]

Of course, rugby's defenders were quick to emphasise that there was a difference between the aggressive physicality that took place within the rules and foul play that took place outside of them. But in reality, the dividing line between legitimate and illegitimate violence was fluid and indistinct. Although formally outlawed, punching, kicking and the use of the foot within scrums and rucks were accepted as being part of the game, provided they took place in the right context. Violence could be legitimated by the heat of the game, as Wavell Wakefield intimated. It could be excused by humour, as could be seen in club journals or commemorative brochures. 'Hacking, hacking-over or tripping up are illegal – if you are seen,' explained a magazine produced by the Devon Barbarians club in 1931, before going on to mention that 'another writer has stressed the value of good kicking. Of course, he means the ball . . . the boot is the most important part of one's outfit. It certainly has its uses.'[16] Or violence could be acceptable as a form of summary justice: 'the only way to stop dirty work, which can seldom be seen by the referee, is to put the fellow guilty of it out of action,' admitted

E.B. Osborn in the mid-1930s. 'Such cases very seldom occur, but every experienced player must be able to recall the effective laying-out of a systematic offender by means that were certainly "not very conveniently civil", to repeat Davenant's polite phrase.' Despite his claim that this was a rare occurrence, he also suggested that a rugby referee, 'like the successful public school master . . . must take care not to see too much'.[17]

But for many, the violence of the sport was one of its most enjoyable and appealing aspects. The oral traditions of the game are steeped in stories of fights, illegal tackles and worse, as anyone who has ever heard a speaker at a rugby club dinner can verify. Like the tales of 'high jinks' on tours, little of this lore found its way into the public domain until the 1960s but it was a vital part of the culture of rugby, especially among forwards who prided themselves on being masters of the 'black arts' of the scrum, the ruck and the maul. Adrian Stoop recalled a Harlequins match at Bristol in the 1920s when some players complained about the home forwards kicking Wavell Wakefield as he laid on the ball. Wakefield dismissed the complaint by saying 'they didn't kick me hard enough and I should have been penalised'. Peter Howard, England captain in 1931, told his son that his half-time team talk went 'are we going to play like English gentleman or are we going to play to win?'[18]

Ultimately, the context for deciding on the legitimacy of violence was social. Its acceptability was determined by asking who was doing what to whom. Acts of violence between young men of similar educational and class background on the rugby pitch were largely acceptable because both parties shared a mutual respect and cultural code. What happened on the field had no wider social significance. As Nicholson and Morgan explained, one could 'recognise a gentleman by his ability to distinguish between various forms of roughness; and in the heat of the scrummage blows struck which seem to the casual observer to make it a wild brawl, will seem to those involved amiable and struck without malice'.[19] The subversion of this shared understanding had been one of the contributory factors to the 1895 split. Physical confrontation with, and a strong possibility of defeat by, those perceived to be working-class social inferiors was unacceptable to the leaders of the RFU because it appeared to undermine social hierarchy. The strict social segregation that marked rugby union in the decades following 1895 effectively removed cross-class violence as a problem for the domestic game.

But it was different at international level. In matches involving sides from outside the British Isles, it could not be assumed that they would share the same conceptions of violence and its relative acceptability. Even those nations that saw themselves as unequivocally British, such as New Zealand

and Australia, did not entirely share the attitudes of the RFU when it came to how to play the game. Thus the All Blacks' vigorous style of play was seen by many, especially the Scots, as tantamount to professionalism, while the Wallabies' first visit to Britain in 1908 was riven by controversy as they had three players sent off during the tour. The belief of the Australians and New Zealanders that they were equal members of the British family of nations was rarely shared by the British of the Mother Country, and certainly not by the English. Play that might be described as 'over-vigorous' if practised by a London side was an affront to English sensibilities in the hands of a deferential yet determined side from Down Under. 'We admire the touring teams who come from the Dominions to challenge us', wrote Howard Marshall in 1936, 'but they do not play rugby football as I understand it'.[20] In the late 1920s the play of the French was viewed as irredeemably violent, and served as one of the reasons for the expulsion from the Five Nations championship in 1931. Matches with the Welsh, whose national side had a much broader social mix than any of the other home nations, could also become flashpoints for controversy, as in 1924 and 1933. For their part, overseas opponents who expected the principles of gentlemanly fair play from the English were often shocked at the violence of the domestic game. Tours Down Under by British teams in 1899 and 1904 were continually dogged by Australian and New Zealand complaints about the tourists' aggressive style of play. Alan Valentine, an American Rhodes Scholar of the early 1920s, tried his hand at rugby while at Oxford and looked forward to the 'English tradition of clean sportsmanship'. After ten minutes of his first game he 'found himself on the receiving end of more deliberate foul play than he had met in four years of American varsity football'.[21]

The problem became even more acute by the 1960s, as English hegemony over international rugby began to dissolve and media coverage, especially through television, became more inquisitive and less deferential. The visit of South Africa in the 1960–61 season, which before the Second World War had been the most deferential of all the rugby-playing British Dominions, produced a match in which both sides punched and kicked their way through eighty minutes of 'rough housing and thuggery'. The context of the match – the tour had begun just days after South Africa had voted to become a republic and followed a series of disputes between the RFU and the South African Rugby Board – illustrated the way in which broader social factors impacted on the tenor of the sport. South African desire to show their superiority over their former colonial masters was demonstrated the following year when Northern Transvaal and Springbok centre 'Mannetjies' Roux broke the jaw of England and British Lions' fly-half Richard Sharp in a brutal head-high tackle. England's tour to New Zealand in 1963 and the reciprocal tour by the All Blacks in 1964 were accompanied by complaints about the New Zealanders' methods of play, especially at the set-pieces. The All Blacks' methods were summed up by Chris Laidlaw as being based on the principle that 'if an opponent begins to win too much possession at the line-out, for instance, he is thumped, sometimes by his marker, sometimes not . . . any member of the opposition who deliberately sets out to spoil All Blacks possession in ruck and maul by fair or foul means is summarily dealt with by knee, elbow or fist'. Again, the political context of these two tours provided at least a backdrop for the intense violence. Harold Macmillan's government had declared its intention to join the European Common Market without consulting either New Zealand or Australia, both of whom would suffer economically by the move. Although intimidation played a bigger role in the New Zealand and, especially, the South African approach to rugby, similar tactics were not unknown in England. Playing in an England trial match in 1960, Ray French found himself losing in the line-out to the six feet, five inches tall David Marques. During a break in play he asked British Lion number eight Alan Ashcroft if he had any advice. 'Bloody hit him', he replied.[22]

The prevalence and visibility of violence between national sides reached such a level that in March 1964 the International Board felt compelled to formally condemn, albeit in typical euphemistic language, 'rough and over-vigorous play' in international matches. Its words fell on deaf cauliflower ears, although the 1966 Wallaby tourists to the UK did see fit to send home second-string hooker Ross Cullen after he had bitten the ear of Ireland's Ollie Waldron in a match against Oxford University. The IB's concerns were reiterated in 1969 when, more explicitly, it denounced 'illegal and foul play, and spoiling tactics', which had become an almost permanent feature of the international game. Yet, if anything, the situation became worse in the 1970s. In 1974 the British Lions literally fought their way to their first series win in South Africa since 1896, helped by the famous – or infamous – rallying cry of '99' to signal an all-in brawl. 'The Lions went through South Africa like latter-day Genghis Khans', according to the normally unshock-able John Reason. 'Some of the teams, like Orange Free State, [that] they left behind looked as if they had been in a road accident.' On the eve of the third and deciding test, captain Willie John McBride told the Lions 'there is no escape. We will take no prisoners!' The following year England's tour of Australia became notorious for the 'Battle of Ballymore' in Brisbane, in which amidst generalised mayhem England prop Mike Burton was sent off shortly after the kick-off, becoming the first Englishman to be dismissed in an international.[23] The nadir came in 1980 when, in a match of thirty-four penalties, England slugged out a 9–8 victory over Wales in an ugly, brutal match which saw Wales' Paul Ringer became the first man since Cyril Brownlie to be sent-off in a Twickenham international.

By the 1970s English club rugby had also begun to exhibit similar signs of uncontrolled yet premeditated violence. Again, this was in part as a result of the changing social context of the sport domestically. From the mid-1950s the predominantly public school social composition of the English game became diluted by an influx of lower middle- and some working-class grammar school boys following the reforms of the 1944 Education Act. The codes of behaviour that had bound the game together began to dissolve, most notably in the way that overt competitiveness, hitherto regarded as a somewhat vulgar trait, became an accepted part of the sport. In 1966 and again in 1967 the RFU expressed its concern about the incidence of 'rough and dirty play', especially by forwards. In the 1970s the problem became a staple subject of RFU annual general meetings. A survey in the 1975–76 season recorded 1,039 players sent-off, ninety more than the previous season, 82 per cent of whom were dismissed for punching, kicking or tripping. The total continued to rise over the following two seasons reaching 1,394 players in the 1977–78 season, an increase approaching 50 per cent of the 1974–75 total.[24] Of course, the increase in dismissals could have been because referees became more vigilant of foul play and punished it accordingly, but the problem refused to go away. In July 1978 the RFU again warned that it 'would not tolerate anything but the highest standards of behaviour on the field of play' and in December it was decided that any player sent off would automatically be suspended for thirty days. The state to which matters had descended could be measured by the fact the Headmasters' Conference, historically one of the RFU's most loyal supporters, felt compelled to write to the RFU to express its concern about the prevalence of violence 'in the strongest possible terms'. In 1980 the London Society of Referees found that 75 per cent of sendings-off were for punching or kicking opponents.[25] In the late 1980s, the issue declined in importance for both RFU and the wider rugby union community, not least because the question of professionalism came to dominate politics of the game. However, there is little evidence to suggest that on-field violence decreased. The numbers of players sent off continued to rise, totalling 1,608 in the 1984–85 season, an increase of 70 per cent in ten years. Most notoriously, the Bristol versus Newport match at the start of the 1985–86 season saw referee George Crawford walk off the pitch in protest at the behaviour of the players. Describing the game as 'a street brawl', he explained, 'I am not a boxing referee. I was disgusted with what I have seen.'[26]

By the turn of the decade, overt violence had become less visible, partly because the prevalence of television coverage at elite levels meant that it was increasingly difficult to commit unseen fouls. And, as had already happened in rugby league, the game was becoming one of impact and collision in the tackle and the set-piece, in which strength and size were decisive, reducing the role of open violence in the physical subordination of opponents. Most importantly, the sport in the 1980s began to embrace the values of untrammelled competitiveness, the spirit of the Thatcherite age. As Anthony Sampson remarked about politics and business in the last two decades of the twentieth century, 'the ideal of the English gentleman had evaporated. No one talked about what's "not done": now anything goes, with enough aggression.'[27] For rugby union, violence or non-violence had become a means to an end: winning. The old values had been turned on their head, as Brian Moore, the epitome of the machismo battle-scarred front-rower, displayed in a Nike advertisement hoarding of the 1990s. According to the billboard, it was no longer a matter of 'it's not the winning but the taking part'. For Moore and rugby players everywhere it had become a case of 'it's not the winning but the taking *apart*'.

It was victory, victory that was crushing and merciless, that now made a man.

. . . and not being a woman

Rugby union was a game that sought to forge masculinity, and gender segregation was from its earliest days one of its most appealing aspects for the men who played and watched it. If conceptions of violence and its role in the sport shifted over time, one definition of what it meant to be a man remained unchanged from the sport's origins at Rugby School. Being a man meant not being a woman.

'We have no dealings with women here', the Reverend Frank Marshall told a meeting of the Yorkshire Rugby Union in 1889. In 1923 Dr Alcock of the Gloucestershire rugby union urged that every boy who left school should be given 'the opportunity of joining a rugby football club, in which he may at once become associated with real men, and himself be developed into a MAN!'[28] As John Tosh has noted, the latter third of the nineteenth century saw significant changes in the relations between the sexes, not least because of the advances made by middle-class women towards legal equality, such as the various Married Women's Property Acts, the growth of women's educational opportunities and, towards the end of the century, the idea of the 'new, emancipated women', together with campaigns against prostitution by women and moral reformers. The increasing wealth of the middle classes provided the basis for the increased importance of joint husband and wife collaboration in home-making and family activities. As John Stuart Mill told the House of Commons in 1867, 'in former days a man passed his life among men; all of his friendships, all of his real intimacies, were with men . . . the two sexes now pass their lives together; the women of a man's family are his habitual society; the wife is his chief associate, his most confidential friend, and often his most trusted adviser'.[29] The growth of sports clubs and mass spectator sport coincided exactly with these changes, providing a male respite from this new world. For Victorian and Edwardian men, rugby union, and later the rugby clubs that grew up rapidly in the first half of the twentieth century, offered a refuge from women, children and the responsibilities of domesticity.

This stress on male sociability was evident from the sport's earliest days. The initial impulse for the formation of adult rugby football clubs was for the sport to provide a means to continue the associations of schooldays and build up new social networks. As rugby's popularity grew, its social side was viewed as being almost as important as its playing. For much of the RFU's first decade, the minutes of its committee are heavily concerned with dinners and other social arrangements for international matches – and by the 1920s a special 'Dinner' sub-committee had been appointed to oversee all such activities. Away matches and especially tours were occasions for often lavish dining and jollity. This was consciously and explicitly an entirely masculine domain, an arena where men could socialise without the presence of women, a realm in which they could drink heavily, sing obscene songs and indulge in what were euphemistically known as 'high jinks' and 'horseplay'. Even the growth of women's rugby union from the 1980s did not dent the walls of the manly citadel; other than for those women who played the game, 'real' rugby was men's rugby, played by 'real men'.

Fear of effeminacy and a drive to remove any of its vestiges from adolescent boys was one of the defining features of nineteenth-century public school life. Muscular Christians such as Charles Kingsley were inclined to believe that their theological opponents, especially the Tractarians and those sympathetic to Rome, were by nature effeminate.[30] Indeed, effeminacy itself was seen as a sickness by many Arnoldian school masters. H.H. Almond declared that 'every school ought to regard it as part of its duty to and mission to rid itself almost entirely of delicate complexions, narrow chests and feeble limbs'.[31] Once again, *Tom Brown's Schooldays* both reflected the prevailing ethos of its times and shaped subsequent attitudes. One of the book's central messages was the danger of effeminacy. 'Don't you ever talk about home, or your mother and sisters', Tom says to a boy at one point. The book also remarks how a new boy would sometimes get 'called Molly, or Jenny, or some derogatory feminine name'.[32] More shockingly, especially in a book that is often held up as an anti-bullying tract, the effeminate (and by implication homosexual) boy is portrayed as a legitimate target for bullying. In the second part of the book Tom and East are approached by 'one of the miserable little pretty white-handed curly-headed boys, petted and pampered by some of the big fellows, who wrote their verses for them, taught them to drink and use bad language, and did all they could to spoil them for everything in this world and the next'. The anonymous boy asks them to help with his fagging for an older boy. Without provocation they trip him and kick him, two against one. As they leave him, Tom says 'Thank goodness, no big fellow ever took to petting me' to which East replies 'You'd never have been like that.'[33] The section had a clear purpose. In a footnote Hughes says that 'many boys will know why [this passage] is left in'. Bullying is portrayed as being acceptable when directed against a boy who is seen as effeminate and homosexual.

In this, the book echoed contemporary fears of adolescent sexuality. Indeed, the publication of *Tom Brown's Schooldays* in 1857 coincided exactly with the emergence of widespread concerns about masturbation among schoolboys. A year later, Frederick W. Farrar's schoolboy novel *Eric, or, Little By Little* was published with the explicit intention to promote 'inward purity and moral purpose' among its adolescent readership. Also in 1857 saw the publication of William Acton's *The Functions and Disorders of the Reproductive Organs*, which observed that it is 'the intellectual book-ish boys who develop sexual desire before the strong athletic boy'.[34] Acton recommended lots of physical exercise to discourage the practice – or failing that, tying-up the hands of a boy at night to stop it. In 1854 the *Lancet* had published a series of articles by John Laws Milton on 'spermatorrhea' (who recommended the use of strategically placed spiked rings to cure the problem of boys' sexual thoughts) and another series on the subject in 1856 and 1857. This campaign, which extended throughout the nineteenth century in varying degrees of intensity, was based on the same concerns that animated the drive to place sport at the heart of the school curriculum.[35]

Even to those educationalists with no intrinsic interest in sport, cricket, athletics and football of all types appealed because it was thought to take boys' minds off the topic of sex and to use up excess energies. As Bertrand Russell remarked some years later, public school masters encouraged 'boys to be constantly occupied so that they will have no time for sexual sin, and incidentally no time to think'.[36] The link between sport and opposition to so-called 'unnatural' sexual practices was bolstered by the involvement of leading sporting figures of the time. Edward Lyttleton, captain of the Cambridge University cricket team and a first-class batsman with Middlesex, published pamphlets and letters campaigning against what he called 'defilement by hand'. And of course it was the Marquess of Queensberry, one of the founders of the Amateur Athletic Association, racehorse owner and the man after whom the laws of modern boxing are named, who was fatefully sued by Oscar Wilde for calling him in 'Somdomite [sic]' in 1895.

Rugby from its earliest beginnings therefore defined itself against effeminacy and, albeit usually unspoken, homosexuality. Although later writers have occasionally suggested that the intense male sociability and physical contact of the sport indicates latent homosexual desire, rugby union's culture was based on an aggressive denial of effeminacy and, in certain cases, sexual activity outside of strictly defined norms.[37] Indeed, it was not unusual for homosexual schoolboys to define themselves in opposition to the rugby culture of their schools. The writer and jazz singer George Melly was slippered, no doubt bearing an air of insouciant defiance, for telling his sports master at Parkfield preparatory school that he would rather go to the ballet than watch a rugger match. 'Bunny' Roger, later a society couturier and, as gossip columnists of the time had it, a flamboyant 'lifelong bachelor', was asked by his father what gift he would like if selected for his school's first XV. 'A doll's house please, father', came back the gloriously camp reply.[38]

The somewhat tortured attitudes towards sex on the part of English middle-class males found their most distasteful expression in the tradition of the rugby song. Derived from public school and university drinking songs, rugby songs seem to have emerged in their own right in the interwar years. By the 1960s they had become so popular that a series of best-selling paperback books, each one featuring the words 'rugby songs' prominently in its title, were published. Each one set down in print lyrics that had hitherto been the preserve of oral tradition or badly reproduced typescripts. These songs dealt with a range of what were perceived to be 'dirty' or obscene topics, such as excretory functions, penis size, sexual encounters, and an entire universe of gender and racial stereotypes – 'Swing Low, Sweet Chariot,' now the unofficial anthem of England supporters, belongs to this tradition. Their predominant themes were sexually insatiable woman and male homosexuality. Both were relentlessly mocked and ridiculed, with the storylines usually ending in the humiliation or even death of their subjects. One can only speculate about the psychological satisfactions of such songs, which occupied a spectrum bounded by fear of personal inadequacy at one end and misogyny and homophobia at the other.[39]

The same themes were also to be found in the initiation ceremonies that many rugby clubs forced new members to undergo. Again because of their origins in school and university practices, these were – and remain today – elaborate rituals of degradation. Watcyn Thomas described new members' induction to the Barbarians in the 1930s as an

> ordeal by fire and water, with myself the chief priest clad in head-towel and bed-sheet, à la Ku Klux Klan. For fire worship, the carpets were rolled back and newspapers lighted, which novices and full members danced around the bonfire like dervishes, howling incantations and ending up on their knees facing Mecca. The initiates then underwent ordeal by water, being thoroughly soused by buckets of water thrown over them, but not before their shirts were ceremoniously burned.[40]

This, at least as described, was somewhat mild. Other ceremonies involved extravagant consumption of alcohol, enforced stripteases and the smearing of the body, especially the genitals, with vaseline, shoe polish or similar substances. In 2003, an 18-year-old student died following his initiation into the Staffordshire University rugby union club, choking on his own vomit after using his teeth to pick up deflated balloons from a tub of chilli, dog food and pig offal.[41] Even the somewhat milder compulsory pub crawl had its dangers, ranging from acute alcohol poisoning to road traffic accidents. In the vast majority of cases the victims were willing accomplices in their own humiliation. Not only did the ceremony permit them access to a closed world, but it also allowed them to demonstrate their imperviousness to embarrassment, pain or worse – in other words, their manhood. The prevalence of initiation rites in the sport paralleled their use in the military and medicine, both professions which promoted an aggressive masculine culture and both of which had close to ties to rugby union.

Once accepted into membership, heavy drinking was expected of the new recruit. Simply playing the game was not the done thing. In 1947 *Rugger* magazine discussed 'what makes a sound XV?' to which the answer insisted that

> it is not sufficient for an individual to appear at the ground, change, play, wash and depart to the connubial company of the female of the species. *Rather should a player join in the convivialities of the night in order that the full benefit may be derived from the ensuing bar counter inquest. . . .* an intelligent listener can learn a great deal

from the appraisal of others and a genuine spirit of camaraderie will pervade the ensuing cloud of alcoholic fumes and blue smoke.[42]

As can be surmised from the above, there was a strong element of social coercion to all this. Dave MacSweeney, a Cambridge Blue who played for Ireland in the 1950s commented that 'there is a compulsion if you play rugger, to at least try to be an extrovert. . . . because of the tradition [those who do not want to take part] can't decently do otherwise'.[43] Moreover, it was a culture of which the rugby fraternity was fiercely protective and proud. Behaviour off the field, as well as on it, built a player's reputation in the eyes of his team-mates.

Often this meant the more boorish the better. In 1929 Oxford University's *Isis* remarked that the future England captain Peter Howard 'seems to have conducted his life on the principle that what is worth doing is worth doing violently. . . . his sense of a joke is liable to lead him to drop his friends over the Magdalen Bridge, if he so inclined'. Even in the early 1900s J.E. Greenwood remembered being shocked to find players, especially on Barbarians' tours, smelling of gin at ten o'clock in the morning. He also suggested that the RFU stopped serving champagne at international after-match dinners in 1920 in an attempt to improve the behaviour of players.[44] Most club tours and trips back from away matches took place in a permanent haze of alcohol. Clubs tours during Easter and occasionally Christmas holidays had emerged in the 1870s as the number of rugby clubs expanded and the opportunities for social trips increased. Away matches were taken as an opportunity for socialising as much as for the playing of the game. Playing for Cambridge University in the 1900s, Greenwood recalled that:

> a saloon was always booked on the railway, the old Great Eastern, to Liverpool Street, and we usually had lunch at the railway hotel. For the return journey, the saloon was hitched on to the back of the train and in consequence it was a very uncomfortable ride as the first few miles from Liverpool Street was full of curves, which caused some of the side to keep their heads out of the window, having dined too well. It was always the custom of London sides to give us a good dinner, which was generally given in the Old Sports Club in St James's Square.[45]

For those who played for a well-heeled club or one supported by their employers, the benefits of touring could be significant. In the 1920s the Bank of England club played annual matches against the Bank of France, for which both banks picked up the bill. The fixture in Paris involved 'three nights in one of the best hotels in Paris, a magnificent banquet, a coach tour of parts of France (including the battlefields), seats for the France/England rugby international and an evening at one of the more exotic theatres'. A trip to the red light district in the Pigalle was often the final destination for teams on tour in Paris.[46]

A rugby club enjoying itself was generally something to be avoided by members of the public. In 1933 Saracens held a supper evening at the Adelphi Hotel in the Strand in London, which, according to a letter to the club from the hotel manager, resulted in:

> four bay trees (in outside porches) to be replaced. One screen smashed. The dining room had to be extra cleaned etc., owing to throwing of food about. Several mustard and pepper pots thrown down the area and broken, also three large glass water jugs broken. Towels torn and nails pulled down in gents' toilet. Weighing machine in hall broke and put out of order. Also a cask of beer was moved and disturbed and about six gallons of beer rendered unfit for sale.[47]

This was not atypical. In the same decade the Lancashire county side came back from matches with a free bar provided by the county committee: 'we had a system whereby the restaurant car attendant, on hearing three rings of the bell-push, would bring us bottles of beer', recalled Watcyn Thomas. 'The steward couldn't care less, since he was not paying, and a tip at the end satisfied him. I don't know what it cost the LRU on our long journey.' One of his team-mates liked to blow up a condom like a balloon, attach it to the air-conditioning fan and let it blow down the carriage, 'the downcast looks of the women who observed it gave him great cause for mirth'.[48]

The humiliation of women was a common theme of such behaviour. Indeed, deliberate acts of anti-social offensiveness such as drunkenness, vandalism and theft were an expected part of touring. In 1938 Albert Freethy complained to Bristol about its players' conduct on a visit to Neath, opining that 'this sort of thing is getting far too prevalent among a certain type of rugger player'. A quarter of a century later the Devon Rugby Union made the same complaint to the RFU, which responded by sending a 'confidential letter to the chairmen of all clubs and unions'. During his term as RFU president in the 1960s, Cyril Gadney felt compelled to regret the 'instances of ridiculous and disgraceful conduct when teams are on tour' that were prevalent.[49] But this behaviour was very much part of the culture of the game. Indeed, it was expected and excused by both contemporaries and subsequent club historians. It was not 'yobbo hooliganism' but 'high-spirited jollity' argued a historian of Harlequins because 'the club went out and played hard and entertaining Rugby football, and gave enjoyment to many thousands of spectators. The hotels knew very well what might be in prospect when they booked in an entire Rugby football team and its administration, and adjusted their prices accordingly'.[50] Such behaviour, and excuses, had its roots in the private members' clubs for students of Oxford and Cambridge universities. Drunkenness, riotous behaviour and the destruction of property were an integral part of the purpose of such clubs. Perhaps the most notorious – and the most prestigious – is Oxford's Bullingdon club, which still today specialises in devastating restaurants that are unfortunate enough to host them. Moreover, the aggressively anti-effeminacy of the rugby club is also paralleled by the Bullingdon, as Tom Driberg recalled: 'Such profusion of glass I never saw until the height of the Blitz. On such nights, any undergraduate who was believed to have "artistic" talents was an automatic target.'[51]

International tours gave even more scope for similar acts of 'jollity'. The RFU archives at Twickenham contain a letter from Blackheath's H.H. Vassall apologising for his behaviour on the 1908 Anglo-Welsh tour to Australasia. Writing about his experiences on the 1924 British Lions tour of South Africa, captained by England's Ronnie Cove-Smith, Rowe Harding confessed that 'we were thoughtless and careless of what other people said or thought of us and that contributed to our unpopularity'. The 1950 Lions tourists each had to post a bond of £50 before departing as an indemnity against the costs of any bad behaviour. In the 1960s, according to Cambridge University captain Chris Laidlaw, Oxford and Cambridge behaved so badly on tours to South Africa that they would never be invited back. A Combined Oxbridge tour to Argentina in 1965 resulted in the RFU writing to both universities deploring their conduct. The 1968 Lions tourists to South Africa boasted a group of players known as the 'Loyal Order of Wreckers', who could allegedly dismantle a hotel room in just six seconds. As late as 1986 the RFU expressed its regret at the 'increasing number of reports of poor behaviour by touring parties particularly while travelling on public transport or when staying in hotels at home and abroad'. It urged that club committees 'ensure that only responsible persons are given charge of touring parties and that strict instructions as to proper behaviour are issued and maintained'.[52]

Examples of similar types of antics could occasionally be found in the behaviour of rugby union crowds, especially at major matches involving students, such as the Varsity match of the Hospitals' Cup Final. The fact that internationals at Twickenham – the only English venue where internationals were played after 1923 – were major social occasions meant that crowd misbehaviour was rare. The greatest scandal in the inter-war years occurred during the 1931 London representative match against the touring Springboks, when a spectator booed South Africa's Gerry Brand as he was about to take a conversion. The incident made the front page of the weekly *Rugger*, which warned of the 'untold harm' such conduct would cause. The ensuing debate also highlighted the ambiguity with which committed rugby supporters viewed the large crowds that turned up at Twickenham. 'The ignorance of the present day crowd there is appalling. Judging by the astounding remarks one hears, it is doubtful whether fifty per cent of the spectators would know when to boo even if they felt so inclined', complained one correspondent. Howard Marshall found the stadium 'nauseating'. 'I would rather stand behind the ropes on the touch-line at the Old Deer park and watch a decent game between unnumbered players, than perch in a glorified hen-roost to see an efficiently organised international match, any day of the week', he proclaimed in 1932.[53] The atmosphere of the Twickenham crowd was memorably captured in A.G. Macdonell's 1933 satire *England, Their England* in which the crowd's appreciation of a Varsity match was not lessened by the fact that no one knew the final score or who had won or lost.

But by the 1960s regular complaints were being made to the RFU about the conduct of spectators at Twickenham. The 1960 Springbok tourists were booed and slow-handclapped during their match against England. In January 1964 it was decided to discuss disorderly behaviour at the ground with the police and the following year the bar staff complained about their treatment by spectators. At the end of the 1965 Varsity match the crossbar from one set of goalposts was stolen, eventually being returned by members of the Shirley Wanderers club in Surrey. In 1968 it was decided to stop people drinking on the terraces to try to deter loutish activity. Local residents complained to the RFU in 1975 about 'poor behaviour' after the Varsity match and the Middlesex Sevens. A 1977 leaflet for distribution to spectators warned that 'shouts from the touchline encouraging any form of violence, or practice against the law are NOT to be heard: e.g. "put the boot in", "kill him", etc'.[54] Anecdotal evidence from writers such as Frank Keating would seem to suggest that the standards of behaviour of Twickenham crowds actually declined from the 1970s onwards. The 1987 Bath versus Wasps John Player Cup final was ended two minutes early by referee Fred Howard after two pitch invasions by prematurely celebrating Bath supporters made play impossible. Moreover, the increasingly overt nationalism that had begun to manifest itself in the 1960s gave rise to a far more adversarial atmosphere at major matches. In 1991 spectators complained about the aggressive behaviour of some England supporters and similar disquiet had been expressed about their behaviour at away matches.[55]

The reluctance of the RFU or the clubs to publish attendance figures for matches means that it is impossible to analyse crowds or to draw any meaningful comparisons or conclusions about spectator behaviour. Outside London we do know that in 1904 Coventry were banned from playing at home for four matches by the RFU following a fight between spectators and players. The following year the Yorkshire Cup final ended in disarray after the crowd invaded the pitch. In 1906 the secretary of the RFU, Percy Coles, was attacked by a spectator as he refereed a match between Leicester and Devonport Albion. In 1924 the referee stopped the Leicester versus Army match until the Welford Road crowd stopped incessant barracking. Following bad behaviour on and off the field, matches between Bath and Bristol were not held for a number of years at the beginning of the twentieth century, a fate which also befell matches between Devonport Services and Devonport Albion.[56] But these were areas in which the appeal of rugby union encompassed not only the middle classes but also the working class, where crowds resembled those at soccer and rugby league games. Spectator misbehaviour in the Midlands and south-west was usually linked to an excess of local pride or overly fierce partisanship, rather than simply a recrudescent adolescent yobbishness.

Being a woman

Misogyny and male exclusivity did not mean that women were not involved in the game. But for most of rugby's history women had no part in its playing. 'It was perhaps the only game that was absolutely masculine in the country', the president of the Salford club declared in 1891. 'Women took part in cricket and other pastimes but he had never yet heard of them playing football.'[57] As far as we can tell, there were no examples of women playing rugby union in England for at least the first seventy-five years of its existence.[58] This should not be surprising. The same attitude was expressed in strikingly similar words forty years later when former RFU president Percy Royds told the diamond jubilee dinner of Ealing RFC that 'ours is a game not founded for women. It seems to me to be the only game today in which women cannot compete – thank goodness.'[59] An occasional dissenting voice could be heard. In 1923 the journalist Philip Trevor argued that, contrary to received wisdom, the sport 'was a game suitable for women' but he was very much a lone voice.[60]

Indeed, women had problems simply being admitted into membership of some rugby clubs, let alone playing the game. For example, in 1930 London Scottish discussed and promptly dismissed the idea of allowing 'ladies' to become associate members. It was to be another thirty-nine years before the decision was reversed. Even those that did admit women members often excluded them from voting rights or, as at Huddersfield RUFC, refused to allow them to attend annual general meetings.[61] Of course, much of the activity of the rugby club could not be carried out if it were not for the voluntary labour of women. Many clubs, especially those without bars, relied on women to provide refreshments at matches – Huddersfield opened their 'Ladies Pavilion and Refreshment Room' in 1935 – usually in the guise of the ladies' committee. And, of course, mothers, wives and girlfriends provided hours of unpaid labour in the washing and repairing of playing kits. The best they could hope for was a word of thanks from a senior (male) official, such as outgoing RFU president 'Ginger' Osborne, who mentioned the 'ladies' in his valedictory address in 1957: 'wherever I have been I have met ladies committees which are organising and running dances, whist drives and the social side of the clubs, and I do give thanks through you to them for their hard work and good spirit'.[62] Needless to say, no women were present to hear his gratitude.

Despite this complete lack of a voice within the sport, some women were enthusiastic supporters of the game. At the first England versus Scotland match in 1871 at Edinburgh 'a convenient slope of turf some 50 yards from the side of the ground was specially enclosed for the accommodation of ladies, of who several hundred were present, and added materially to the brilliancy of the scene'.[63] In London before the First World War, their numbers were such that the weekly *Rugby Football & Cricket* reported that 'at Wandsworth on Saturday they were nearly in the majority', while at Blackheath 'the middle portion of the stand is usually exclusively occupied by the fair sex'. Women were also conspicuous by their presence at Richmond and at Twickenham.[64] There is little evidence to make meaningful comparisons with areas outside of London, but we do know that, prior to the 1895 split, women spectators had been a noted feature of crowds in the north of England. But the elite and fashionable aspects of rugger in London may well have made the game attract a wider base of support than in other areas of England.[65]

Female interest appears to have grown in the years immediately following the First World War. Philip Trevor thought that more women could be seen at matches in 1923 than in the years before 1914. A writer in *Rugby Football* in the same year expressed satisfaction at 'the numbers of women and girls who flock to rugby matches nowadays'. Surprised at their knowledge of the rules, he believed that most of them were relatives or friends of players and dismissed their 'partiality' on the grounds that it was 'the privilege of their sex to take more interest in the players than in the play'.[66] The idea that women attended matches because of their interest in men remains common to almost all discourse about women and rugby. When the short-lived weekly *Rugger* started a column for women in 1931, it dealt with such issues as 'how to be beautiful though cold'.[67] In 1936, 'Sister Anne' – described as 'the wife of a very well known and enthusiastic London club player' – identified the three types of women she believe attended rugby matches: those who loved the game; those who loved someone playing the game; and those who loved someone watching the game. The first group was 'largely made up of people who at one time or another have belonged to either' of the latter two groups.[68] Writing in *The Tatler* two decades later, J.E. Morpurgo demonstrated that nothing had changed in the intervening years: 'thousands of wives and wives-to-be wrap themselves in figure destroying clothes and brave the complexion-wrecking winds in order to accompany their husbands and might-be-trapped-into-being husbands on a journey back to boyhood'.[69]

Although less frequently expressed openly, the idea that the women were involved in the sport in an adult role and men as children was also common. Morpurgo humorously, but perceptively, went on to explain to women readers that when at a match 'your companion is back in his boyhood'. The role of women in rugby was to provide for men: food, drink, washing and emotional support. In other words, to act as a mother. In the rugger environment, wives, girlfriends and female relatives were not sexual beings. The men's relationship to sex was through their songs and other antics (although on tour this would sometimes change on account of the availability of women interested in sex with players for profit or pleasure). In the 1960s and 1970s, when equal rights legislation and women's campaigns for greater equality made it increasingly difficult to openly exclude women, the culture of the rugby club seemed to be under threat. 'Girlfriends were just regarded as being in the way', explained London Irish's Brendan Quirke. The Bank of England's club found that the after-match singing of rugby songs 'became something of a challenge for the chorus masters – even a provocation – when ladies were allowed into the men's pavilion on Dance Nights [in the 1960s] . . . But it was still a men's pavilion and it wasn't too long before the girls learnt to sit back and enjoy it – discreetly of course.'[70] The admittance of women into the bar or clubhouse appears to have changed male behaviour very little. Informal but rigid gender segregation took the place of outright exclusion. If anything, the change made more explicit the mother–boy relationship. In the late 1990s, the writer Laura Thompson echoed the observations of Morpurgo when she argued that women playing 'mummy' was the 'role that has always seemed to underpin rugby players' relationships. The player is treated by his woman rather as a favoured child . . . he enjoys the thrill of being naughty under her watchful but indulgent eye.'[71]

As well as the entry of women into many clubhouses, the early 1960s also saw the first reports of women playing rugby in England when a handful of matches between men and women were organised by clubs as charity events. In 1963 women students played against male students in London and in 1966 Worthing RFC staged a similar event. It was not until the late 1970s, when the impact of the women's liberation movement had at last begun to affect even the masculine bastions of university sport, that women began to play rugby seriously. Teams were formed at St Mary's Hospital, Keele University, University College London, Loughborough University and Plymouth's College of St Mark and St John. The game progressed rapidly and in 1983 ten student sides formed the Women's Rugby Football Union. In 1987 the first England versus Wales international was staged, with England coached by Loughborough lecturer and former Scottish and British Lion Jim Greenwood. In fact, the British nations lagged somewhat behind the rest of the rugby union world in organising the women's game. The Association Française de Rugby Féminin had been founded in 1970 and the game had begun in North America in 1972, followed by the Netherlands, Italy and Spain. The first women's world cup took place in Wales in 1991.[72] As with the growth of gay men's rugby, it is noticeable that much of the initial impetus and support for the game came from outside the traditional rugby union-playing nations, where the link between the game and the dominant forms of sporting masculinity was weak.

Despite the advances made by women in securing the right to play the sports of their choice, the RFU viewed the development of the women's game with a jaundiced eye. In December 1977 Keele University women's team applied for affiliation to the RFU, a request that was immediately referred to the RFU's solicitors. They reported back that to be eligible for affiliation a club had to have been in existence for at least two years and proposed and seconded by two existing member clubs. Presumably confident that no two clubs would support the women's side the matter was dropped and nothing more heard. Six years later, in February 1984, the RFU Executive was approached by the initiators of the Women's Rugby Football Union (WRFU). Up to that point the RFU had ignored women's rugby but the establishment of a women's side by a university rugby union club had raised the issue of whether female players were covered by the RFU's insurance scheme. Aware that they could be in breach of equal opportunity legislation if they refused to work with women's rugby, discussions continued about the constitution of the new women's union until the two parties came to an agreement and the WRFU was recognised by the RFU. Although there were inevitably misgivings among traditionalists, clubs soon realised that a women's team not only brought in new members but also helped to assuage the fears of local and national politicians that the RFU was composed entirely of chauvinist backwoodsmen, a fact which came in very useful from a public relations perspective when applying for government grants and other financial support. Once more, women were playing an auxiliary role to the men's game.[73]

The women's game grew rapidly in the universities, spurred on by the fact that it was one of the few sports in which women were encouraged to use physical strength and engage in contact with other players. Unlike netball, soccer or hockey, rugby offered the opportunity for women to behave in ways considered to be 'unladylike' by the dominant culture. As one anonymous player explained in the 1980s, 'I don't care how tough it gets or how filthy I get . . . I love to pit my strength against women and outwit my opponents.'[74] It also provided an environment in which women could replicate the singing and drinking culture of the male game. In fact, despite the potential subversion of what would become known in academic jargon as a 'hyper-masculine sport' by the presence of women, a significant number of whom were also lesbians, women's rugby offered no challenge to the fundamental masculine nature of the game. Once the principle that women should be allowed to play had been conceded, the sport continued as it always had done. And, as Alison Carle and John Nauright discovered, even in 'enlightened' rugby clubs with women's teams, underlying male chauvinist attitudes remained as strong as ever.[75]

'Manliness' was perhaps the most unchanging feature of the culture of rugby. By 2007, rugby union had abandoned amateurism, moved away from its moral purpose and fundamentally altered the way it was played, yet it remained, as much as it had been at any point in its history, the mark of masculinity. As numerous journalists during that year's world cup pointed out, to be a rugby union player was to be a 'real man'. It was an ideal of manliness that Thomas Hughes and the founders of Rugby football would have recognised and endorsed. The more rugby union seemed to have changed, the more it had stayed the same.[76]

5

THE CLASS GAME

It was the middle of January 1947 and Britain was about to be plunged into its coldest winter of the twentieth century. But the 40,000 people who poured towards Cardiff Arms Park on a Saturday afternoon did so in anticipation of being warmed by the heat of renewed battle between Wales and England.

It was almost eight years to the day since the two sides had last met in the Five Nations tournament. Wrestling in a rain-sodden mudbath of a Twickenham pitch, England had ground down the Welsh pack and emerged as victors by a single unconverted try to nil. Prop Derek Teden had scored the decisive touchdown by diving on the ball after dribbling it across the Welsh tryline. It was to be the pinnacle of his career. Less than two years later he would be dead, missing in action after his plane was lost over the Friesian Islands. Three of his England team-mates would also lose their lives during the Second World War.

But time had eroded the teams of 1939 more effectively than even the war had. Only two players remained from the sides that had faced each other at Twickenham almost a decade ago. For Wales, Haydn Tanner alone continued at his post, while winger Dickie Guest maintained the link with the victorious England side. Nor had the Arms Park survived the conflict unscathed. Its North Stand and parts of the terracing had been damaged during a Luftwaffe bombing raid in 1941, reducing the maximum attendance by a third.

But for those fortunate enough to be admitted, these details merely added to their sense of expectation. At last, Five Nations rugby union was back and the English had returned to the stadium where they had suffered so many torments so many times before.

Yet it was England who took command after just seven minutes. Scrum-half Bill Moore broke through the Welsh defence on the right and cross-kicked into midfield where flanker Don White, in an act of 'most intelligent anticipation' according to his old school magazine, streaked away from the turning defenders, picked up the ball on the bounce and scored at the side of the posts.[1] Otley's Arthur Gray converted and England had the game at their command.

But at fifteen minutes the balance shifted when centre Edward Scott injured a knee and was forced to leave the pitch, reducing England to fourteen men. This was the era before replacements were allowed, so back-rower Mickey Steele-Bodger took over as a makeshift three-quarter. The pack shifted to a three–four formation – three in the front-row and four in the second – and proceeded to push against the eight-man Welsh pack as if they had decided to teach Sisyphus himself how to shove. Despite their numerical disadvantage, the English back-row closed down the Welsh backs, so much so that the experienced Tanner and the young pretender Bleddyn Williams were both reduced to impotency. Ironically, both of Wales' tries were scored by back-rowers. Rees Stephens went over from a long line-out after twenty-eight minutes and then Gwyn Evan dummied his way over the England line and momentarily put Wales 6–5 ahead just after half-time.[2]

It now looked like the numerical advantage would begin to tell for Wales. But missed penalties and a failed Tanner drop-goal allowed the under-manned English pack to get back on top. With fifteen minutes gone in the second half they created a whisker of space for fly-half 'Nim' Hall to snap a brilliant drop-goal. For the next twenty-five minutes the Welsh dominated possession but were unable to make any impression on the English line, thanks to the tenacity of the English forwards and the supposedly superior Welsh backs' failure of imagination. When the final whistle eventually went, the Welsh seemed stunned and frustrated by their inability to overcome their weakened opponents, while the English had yet another heroic, backs-to-the-wall performance to add to their long list of underdog victories.

This marked the return of the *status quo ante bellum*. England had once again fashioned a win from inauspicious circumstances against the pre-match favourites, a constant narrative of the inter-war period. The players had outperformed opponents supposedly more talented and skilful. And, just as important, despite the social-democratic rhetoric of the 'people's war' and Clement Atlee's Labour government, the England team had retained the social character that the RFU had so assiduously sought to maintain for the past fifty years. Nine of the side had been privately educated and four others had gone to grammar schools. Edward Scott, Norman Bennett and Nim Hall had all attended St Mary's Hospital medical school, three others had been to Cambridge, two to Oxford and one, the longevitous Dickie Guest, to

Liverpool University. With the exception of full-back Arthur Gray, a fruit salesman, and prop Harry Walker, a tool fitter from Coventry, all went on to successful middle-class professional careers. Three would become doctors, two company directors, another two sales managers, with the others becoming a vet, a university lecturer, an insurance broker, a manager with ICI and the headmaster of an Australian public school. In a post-war world of conflict, turmoil and unrest, rugby union remained proudly unchanged.[3]

The old school tie and beyond

It is a generally accepted truth that English rugby union is a largely a 'middle-class game'. Despite occasional half-hearted attempts to prove otherwise – 'surely it is time this particular ghost was laid and all this rubbish about Rugby football being a game for the classes finally swept away', bemoaned the secretary of Sheffield's rugby club unconvincingly in 1932 – this simple social observation is buttressed by sheer weight of numbers.[4]

Who exactly played rugby union? We can discover the educational, occupational and social backgrounds of the game's players by examining the life-histories of those who were selected to play for England. The elite level of rugby union gives a relatively clear portrait of those who played the sport. While questions of status played an important role in players' choice of clubs, the importance of international competition meant that the England side was usually picked on merit. Even at the height of the war with the northern clubs in the 1890s, the necessity of winning meant that working-class players would generally be selected regardless of rugby politics. For example, despite being widely suspected of professionalism, Yorkshire labourer-turned-publican Dickie Lockwood was chosen as England captain in 1894 because of his ability to win matches.

Between the first international in 1871 and the advent of professionalism in 1995, 1,143 players were selected to play for England. As Appendix 1 shows, we know the schools attended by 876 of them. The number of internationals who attended elementary, board, secondary modern or comprehensive state schools was just sixty-six, not a significantly larger number than the forty-seven who were educated at Rugby School itself. This leaves 810 who were educated at grammar or fee-paying schools. Of these, 155 went to schools identifying themselves as grammar schools, although this self-definition includes both independent fee-paying schools and state-funded secondary schools, leaving 655 who were unambiguously privately educated.[5] In other words, 92.4 per cent of all England internationals for whom we have school details went to fee-paying or grammar schools.

What is more, just nineteen fee-paying schools provided over a third of all England internationals whose schools we know. These 310 players came from Rugby, Marlborough, Wellington, Clifton, Uppingham, Cheltenham, Tonbridge, Durham, Haileybury, Bedford Grammar, Dulwich, Sherborne, Sedbergh, Mill Hill, Blackheath Proprietary, Bromsgrove, Cranleigh, Epsom and Giggleswick. With the obvious exception of Rugby, none of these schools are from the elite group of nine 'Clarendon' public schools such as Eton, Harrow and Winchester. These schools are from the tier below the elite and were founded on the basis of replicating Rugby's Arnoldian tradition. Leaving aside Rugby, the other Clarendon public schools produced just sixteen England internationals, of whom ten played before 1900.

Of course, there were also players who had originally attended non-fee-paying schools but won academic or athletic scholarships to private or grammar schools. Working-class scholarship boys such as Ray French and Fran Cotton featured especially in England sides of the late 1950s to the mid-1970s. But unfortunately there are no data available that would help us quantify their number. It is also the case that the social mobility of this period that was opened up in large part by educational opportunity proved short-lived and was certainly in decline by the mid-1990s. We could therefore assume that this group would not significantly alter the overall picture. Moreover, the phenomenon of the rugby-playing 'working-class scholarship boy' highlights the fact that rugby union was part of the acculturisation process through which talented young students were assimilated into the middle class, rather than rugby union becoming 'classless' and moving down the social ladder in its appeal, as was the case with soccer.

What about the players whose schools we do not know? Of these 267 players, twenty-five attended university, medical school, naval academy or the Royal Indian Engineering College. We know that sixty-eight of those for whom we have no educational data had what can be termed 'middle-class' jobs, ranging from sales managers and accountants to company directors and, in the case of John Matters who played for England in 1899, a rear admiral in the Royal Navy. And of those for whom we have neither educational nor occupational data, fifteen played for socially prestigious elite clubs such as Blackheath, Manchester or Richmond. This would indicate another 108 players that could be categorised as being clearly from the middle classes.

What of the remaining 159 players? There are fifty-five for whom we know only the name of the club for which they played. They played for clubs in the Midlands, south-west or pre-1895 north that traditionally had a socially mixed, cross-class playing personnel, making it impossible to draw any inference about their social background from their club. This leaves us with 104 players whose schools we do not know but who are recorded as having manual occupations, beginning in 1882 when storeman Harry Wigglesworth of the Yorkshire club Thornes made his debut. The most common employment was that of publican, which provided gainful employment for twenty-two England internationals. Becoming a pub landlord was invariably an inducement to a player to stay with a club or to join a new one, offering an attractive way out of direct manual labour. Thirteen of these publicans became rugby league players. Indeed, thirty-eight of the 104 manual workers went on to play league. The only other significant manual occupational groups were thirteen police constables and eight ship and dockyard workers who played for clubs on the south-west coast and were employed mainly in naval dockyards.

We can therefore say that of the 1,088 England players for whom we have verifiable educational or occupational information, only 170 (or 15.6 per cent) were unambiguously not part of the middle classes, either because they attended non-private or grammar schools or were employed in manual labour.

Which sections of the middle classes did rugby union draw its strength from? Much of it came from the universities. There were 415 England internationals who went to universities or medical schools, eight attended polytechnics, eight went to Imperial Service or Imperial Engineering colleges and seven were educated at physical education colleges such as Carnegie in Leeds or St Mary's in London. Another forty-seven attended military or naval academies such as Sandhurst or Dartmouth. Thus 485 internationals – 44 per cent of the total – had some form of higher education.

But, as with schools, these bare facts do not tell the full story. Of those that attended university, 169 went to Cambridge and 151 went to Oxford, 77 per cent of the total. The next three universities with the most internationals were Loughborough with twenty-five, the London medical schools with twenty-two and Durham with ten. Sixteen other universities accounted for the remaining thrity-eight internationals.[6] The sport's strength was thus historically concentrated on the elite universities, medical schools and the armed services' academies.

What jobs did they do? As can be seen from Appendix 2, we have the employment details of 952 players (82.6 per cent of the total). The occupation most likely to be undertaken by an England international was that of schoolmaster, the career chosen by 145 players. This includes those who became PE teachers in state schools, as well as those such as Basil Travers, who became headmaster of the prestigious Sydney Church of England Grammar School.

The next most popular category, with ninety-two internationals, was that of a commissioned officer in the armed forces: forty-eight were army officers, thirty-two naval officers and twelve RAF officers. Six of the naval officers attained the rank of rear-admiral, including Blackheath's Percy Royds, and Bob Weighell and Alfred Morris became air-commodores. In addition, seven other players were regular soldiers, sailors or aircraftmen outside of wartime. This should not surprise us, given the close links between the public schools and the officer class of the services. Indeed, Wellington, Cheltenham and Clifton schools, which between them produced seventy-one internationals, were renowned for their production of army officers.

The services were followed by the law, the choice of seventy-nine internationals who became solicitors, and then by medicine, made up of sixty-eight doctors, three dentists and one vet. The banking and financial sector accounted for sixty-nine players, of which thirty were stockbrokers and nineteen insurance brokers. A further forty were employed in sales, marketing or advertising jobs. Additionally, the professions of civil servant (twenty-eight), clergyman (nineteen), accountant (eleven) and civil engineer (ten) also recorded numbers in double figures. Thus 565 England internationals (59 per cent of the total occupations known) came from just ten professions.

There are five other occupations that reach double figures. The first is that of 'farmer', which numbers thirty-five players. This description of course can cover both wealthy landowners and farm labourers, especially for those who want to downplay or exaggerate their status. Certainly, it would not be unrealistic to assume that a reasonable proportion of the twenty-two self-described farmers who were privately educated were also landowners, although only one player, the future RFU secretary C.J.B. Marriott, described himself as a landowner rather than a farmer. 'Manager' accounts for twenty-eight players. This is a category with even more plasticity, covering factory and colliery managers, of which there were thirteen, and those who designated themselves simply as managers. There are also twenty-two publicans and fifteen policemen. As noted above, the publicans were the vestigial tail of covert professionalism, with only one, Coventry's Stan Adkins, being in the trade after 1908. Of the policemen, ten became internationals after 1967.

The final major category is that of company director or partner in a firm, a description that accounts for eighty-one players. Unfortunately these details are undifferentiated, so we cannot say in what type of businesses these players were decision-makers. We do know that in addition to these eighty-one, there were also nine merchants of timber, wool and hops, seven designated as 'manufacturers' in the glass, paper and textile industries, six ship owners, five cotton brokers, five self-described 'businessmen', three ship brokers, two tea planters in India, one colliery owner and one coal exporter. This gives us a total of 120 involved in senior roles either running or owning businesses.

These findings highlight the predominance of 'service' professions in the game. As others such as Peter Cain and Ross McKibbin have noted, these are professions that are non- or even pre-industrial, distanced from manufacturing industry and based around the law, medicine, the clergy and the armed forces. With the partial exception of medicine (although one should not underestimate the role of morality in shaping medical practice), these are professions that also play an ideological role in society.

Yet, although the sport was dominated by the service professions, there were also a considerable number of elite players involved in business. The idea that the 'gentleman amateur' was entirely the domain of the southern, non-industrial upper-middle-class professions is thus not entirely accurate. The manufacturers, merchants, brokers and ship owners came in large part from the north of England, especially from Liverpool and Manchester. Moreover, they were prominent in the first two decades of the sport, at precisely the time that the amateur ethos of rugby was being developed and implemented. Indeed, the majority of those in the 'business' category, eighty-one, played before the Second World War, with all those describing themselves as manufacturers playing in the period before 1890.

One further point remains to be made. This was a group of young men that was overwhelmingly Anglican in their religious outlook. Leicester's Edward Massey appears to have been the first Roman Catholic to play for England when he was selected against Wales in 1925, the first of six old boys from Ampleforth – the 'Catholic Eton' – to represent the national side in the amateur era. There is little evidence of substantial non-conformist interest in the game. The only Jewish England international to be identified as such was John Raphael, who won nine caps in the Edwardian era and was killed on the Western Front in 1917. In 1906 Raphael twice played in the same side as Jimmy Peters, a fly-half from Plymouth, who became the only black player to be selected for England until Chris Oti took the field against Scotland eighty-two years later in 1988.

These statistics give us a longitudinal portrait of the remarkably uniform social composition of the England side for almost 125 years between England's first international and the legalisation of open professionalism. However, we can also use the data to discover the way in which the composition of the England side changed over that period too.

Perhaps the most striking change is the decline since 1945 of the number of players who had attended leading public schools. The last international to have attended Rugby School was John Williams in 1951. Marlborough's final England international played in 1937. Richmond's Peter Ryan became the last of six Harrow-educated England players in 1955. Uppingham's last England representative played in 1950, Clifton's last in 1965 and Cheltenham's in 1967. In fact this was part of a slow decline in the number of privately educated elite players from the 1940s. To some extent this may be attributed to the gradual withdrawal of the upper echelons of the middle class from elite adult team sports.

But, more importantly, it is indicative of both the growth of the middle classes in the twentieth century and the proportional decline of middle-class children attending these elite public schools. Between 1911 and 1971 the proportion of higher professionals, administrators and managers among employed males in British society grew from 5.4 per cent to 16 per cent. Moreover, from the 1960s fee-paying schools began to move away from an emphasis on sports towards a focus on academic achievement. The merito-cratic culture of the 1960s meant that qualifications and especially university degrees became more important to middle-class parents. Competition from grammar schools and the upper end of the state school system, amplified later by the publication of league tables, meant that it was no longer enough to have been to the right school, one needed the right qualifications too. The rise of co-educationalism in fee-paying schools also undermined the hyper-masculine culture in which rugby flourished – for example, Clifton became co-educational in 1987 and Rugby itself opened its doors to young women in 1975.

In the decades up to the Second World War the percentage of privately educated internationals was never less than 82 per cent, but in the twenty-five years after the war this declined to 63 per cent, with grammar schools accounting for 28 per cent. Between 1970 and 1995 this process accelerated, with privately educated players dropping to 44 per cent. Grammar schools increased their representation to 33 per cent and non-grammar state schools rose to 23 per cent – although to keep a sense of perspective, one must remember that 86 per cent of all secondary schools pupils in 1996 were educated by the state.[7] This change was also matched by an increasing diversity of schools attended by England internationals. Only Barnard Castle in the 1970 to 1995 era supplied three players, although Ellesmere College, Haileybury, Millfield, Rossall and Wellington each provided two. To some extent this diversity of educational background also reflected the attraction of local grammar schools and high-quality comprehensive schools to parents who, armed with a copy of the *Good School Guide* and the wherewithal to move between school catchment areas, may have in previous times sent their children to private schools.

This was also the result of a conscious policy by the RFU to spread the game into grammar and later comprehensive schools. Echoing the 'rush to rugby' after the First World War, the 1950s saw a number of schools switch their sporting allegiances. A 1958 Football Association survey showed that twenty-three grammar schools had abandoned soccer for rugby union and another fifty-five had introduced rugby alongside soccer. No schools had abandoned rugby for soccer and only seven rugby-playing schools had introduced soccer. In 1968 the Chester Report on the state of football noted with concern the ousting of soccer by rugby in many schools, and ascribed some of its growth to the numbers of rugby-playing teachers being produced by universities and colleges. Perhaps somewhat counter-intuitively, the introduction of comprehensive education in the 1960s and 1970s also led to more schools taking up the game as former secondary modern schools saw the game as a method of gaining social cachet.[8] The success of the RFU's policy can be seen in the huge increase in the number of state schools that took up the game between 1960 and 1990. In 1960 there were just thirty-one state schools in membership of the RFU. By 1970 this had grown to 256 and by 1990 – at which point the percentage of school children educated in grammar schools was around 5 per cent – 1,704 state schools were playing the game. In contrast, there were 331 private and grammar schools affiliated to the RFU in 1960, a total that rose to 626 in 1970 and then dropped to 552 and 525 at the end of each subsequent decade, some of which can also be explained by the change of some grammars into state-sector compre-hensives.[9]

Despite the tailing-off of the involvement of players educated at elite public schools, the game continued to be dominated by the professions. In particular, the popularity of teaching among England internationals grew in the post-Second World War period. Sixty-one schoolmasters represented England between 1871 and 1939 but eighty-four played between 1945 and 1995. Banking and financial sector careers underwent a renaissance in the period 1970–95, which coincided with the 'Big Bang' in the City of London. Twenty internationals were employed in this sector, more than in any other period of the game. Sales and marketing also grew in the post-1945 decades, with twenty-two out of the total forty playing for England between 1945 and 1970 and another twelve in the next twenty-five years.

However, other traditional career-paths went into decline. Only thirteen solicitors played for England after the Second World War, whereas fifty-seven played before 1914. Medicine also faded, with just twelve doctors and three dentists being selected after 1945, in comparison to twenty-eight in the twenty-five years before 1914 and eleven in the interwar years. The influence of religion on the national side came to a complete end in the 1950s, its last representative being Rosslyn Park's Brian Boobyer in 1952. Members of the officer class of the armed services also went into steep decline. Forty-six commissioned officers appeared for England before 1914. Another thirty-one appeared in the interwar years but only fifteen over the next fifty years, with just one army and one RAF officer appearing between 1970 and 1995. Civil servants failed to produce any England representatives after 1965.

These changes reflected patterns within middle-class life in general. In the first half of the twentieth century the composition of the middle class shifted away from the 'service' professions to become much more technical, scientific and commercial as the nature of the British economy changed. The collapse of the influence of the church, the reduction in the size of the armed forces over the twentieth century and the 'proletarianisation' of major parts of the civil service all led to a decline in the attractiveness of such careers to middle-class young men.[10] Rugby reflected these broader changes in society.

And, as the law, medicine and the armed forces became increasingly professionalised, so too did elite rugby union, which meant that it became increasingly difficult to combine a career in the professions with playing international rugby. This professionalisation was also reflected by a decline in the number of players playing at international level. In the twenty-five years leading to 1995, 174 players were selected for England, the least of any equivalent period and fifty-nine less than in the previous twenty-five years and 136 less than the same length of time before the First World War. For the elite player, rugby was becoming a career choice in itself by the late 1980s. It was no longer the hors-d'oeuvre before the serious business of life, but the main course itself.

The 'Freemasonry of Rugby'

Of course, for most of its history rugby union had offered considerable employment opportunities to many of its players, especially to those of exceptional talent. Certain clubs used their links with local businesses to attract players with the prospect of employment. The number of Leicester players employed by the city's insurance brokers was not unconnected with the club's links to the industry. Richmond and Blackheath players were over-represented in stockbroking thanks to the two clubs' organic links with the City of London. But even leaving aside examples of clubs seeking to attract players through attractive career options, being a rugby player helped smooth the path into higher education and the professions. In 1923 a correspondent to *Rugby Football* dispensed with the usual euphemisms and described how when applying for 'certain scholastic and business posts the honours won on the football field are enumerated'. 'Why not let us be honest', he appealed, 'and confess that there is a commercial value attached to the gaining of an international cap or Blue?' Almost fifty years later, *The Sunday Times* could comment that 'more than any other sport, it can help a boy win a place at Oxford or Cambridge . . . a rugby blue is the most negotiable of all Oxbridge blues . . . especially in medicine, school teaching and business'.[11]

Perhaps the most famous example of the career value of rugby can be found in Richard Gordon's best-selling *Doctor in the House*. His fictional-ised account of being interviewed for a place at St Swithin's medical college by its Dean would have been familiar to any number of real-life prospective medical students:

> 'Now', the Dean began. 'Have you been to a public school?'
> 'Yes.'
> 'Your people can afford the fees and that sort of thing?'
> 'I believe so.'
> 'You play rugby, I suppose?'
> 'Yes, sir.'
> The Dean began to look interested.
> 'What position?' he asked.
> 'Wing three-quarter.'
> He drew a pad of paper towards him and pencilled fifteen dots on it in rugby formation. . . .
> 'Well, you may shape well. Lucky you're a three. The hospital's full of forwards', he added in disgust.

A few seconds later Gordon's hero was offered a place to read medicine.[12]

It was not only imaginary colleges where rugby ability counted as much, if not more, than academic ability. As Christopher Brooke recounts in his history of Cambridge University, 'a newcomer to a Cambridge Combination Room in the 1920s was startled to find the eminent academics about him discussing their applicants almost entirely in terms of rugger'. In business too, the rugger player was much valued. The boys' magazine *Chums* told its readers in 1914 that rugby players made good stock brokers because 'during a "boom" on the exchange, if a fellow couldn't stand his ground with a lot of fellows pushing and elbowing through a crowd, he would be of no use. . . . The chap who could pile up a scrum at Rugger was just the man he wanted.' At ICI in the late 1920s an internal memo circulated that specified that the type of person to be recruited for senior management positions was 'a man who takes a First or Second Honours, who plays Rugby Football or Cricket . . . for his University, who is president of the JCR of his College. . .'. In the mid-1990s, the rugby player had once again become fashionable in business, as the manager of a City of London securities firm explained: 'every [equity] desk needs a "face", someone who gives your clients a reason to trade with you. You might have a pretty girl or a famous wit, but a big, beefy rugby player is the best.'[13]

To some extent the doors that could be opened through rugby reflected the high level of esteem in which the amateur sports champion was held in the middle-class culture. The exalted position of the crack three-quarter or the star batsman in the school hierarchy was also replicated to a great extent within adult society. But, more importantly, to be a rugby player implied that one was 'clubbable' and possessed the social skills and shared the attitudes and cultural values of conventional middle-class society. One was reliable, a 'good chap' and 'one of us' – and rugby was the passport that demonstrated one's bona fides for entry to and progress within the appropriate social networks. Rugby itself was also one of those networks, and thanks to its matches, tours, committees and dinners offered considerable opportunities for the creation and cultivation of social and business contacts. Indeed, it was common, and remains so today, to hear rugby union supporters speak of the game as a 'freemasonry'. Those freemasons who were also rugby players were also keen to compare the two: 'I experienced the same camaraderie in rugby as I do being a member of freemasonry', explained Don White, scorer of England's first try in the post-war period, first-ever coach of the national side in 1969 and Assistant Provincial Grand Master for Northants and Hunts.[14]

The most visible manifestation of rugby's freemasonry was the rugby club itself. Unlike soccer and rugby league, where the club evolved into either a commercial organisation to promote an elite professional team or a largely utilitarian grouping that did little more than organise matches, the rugby club remained a club in the truest sense: a social organisation of men who shared similar sporting and social interests. In this, it was no different from the myriad clubs, societies and associations that had structured and nourished the social life of the middle classes since the seventeenth century. As Peter Clark has pointed out, for many clubs 'their secondary functions, whether promoting social alignments, facilitating social integration and social networking, or defining gender boundaries, were no less a priority [than their specialist activity]'.[15] Clubs provided the means by which like-minded men could pursue their leisure or business interests in agreeable company. They presented an entry point into the social and commercial networks of the local community – as Margaret Stacey's detailed account of the complex web of social organisations in post-war Banbury makes clear, the rugby club became a vital nodal point in local middle-class networks. Moreover, through affiliation to the RFU, clubs offered their members participation in a wider, national group. These aims were all part of the catalyst for the formation of the RFU itself, which announced in the 1871 edition of C.W. Alcock's *Football Annual* that, as well promoting a uniform set of rules, the new organisation would also 'promote a greater amount of sociability and good fellowship'.[16]

There was thus little difference between the impulse that led to the formation of the first rugby clubs and that which inspired numerous other types of clubs. Unlike the clubs that were formed after the mid-1870s that had civic or local pride as their prime motivation, the early clubs of London and the south-east were social associations. This can be seen in the names of the clubs that formed the RFU. With the exception of Blackheath, Richmond, Belsize Park and Clapham Rovers, none were specifically related to a geographical area. Marlborough Nomads and Wimbledon Hornets were old boys' clubs. The Civil Service and Law clubs were occupationally based. Others represented schools or colleges, while Harlequins, Gipsies, Flamingoes and Mohicans were geographically anonymous. Although many of the twenty-one original clubs fell by the wayside, clubs based on the professions or educational background represented the fabric of London and south-eastern rugby.

The London teaching hospitals began playing the game in the 1860s. Despite claims that Guy's Hospital club was founded in 1843, there is no supporting evidence for such an early date, and it appears that the core of the London hospital clubs were founded in the mid-1860s: St Thomas' in 1864, St Mary's in 1865 and Guy's in 1866.[17] Guy's were, however, one of the founding clubs of the RFU. The United Hospitals RFC, an umbrella organisation for rugby clubs that predated the RFU, was founded in 1867. In 1874 it organised the United Hospitals' Challenge Cup for London teaching hospitals. The tournament rapidly became infamous for the intensity of the play and the antics of its spectators, especially at the final itself, where competing sets of supporters would engage in outrageous acts of disorder against their rivals. As well as providing opportunities to demonstrate both athletic prowess and riotous behaviour, the clubs and the cup were a vehicle for the expression of corporate pride and social solidarity.

The same was true of those London banks that embraced the game. The banks began to play seriously in the mid-1880s when the Hong Kong and

Shanghai Bank and the London & Westminster Bank formed clubs, closely followed by the Oriental Bank and the Chartered Bank of India. The enthusiasm for the game of their employees was spurred by the banks' provision of extensive recreational facilities such as pitches, club houses and financial support for club tours for their staff in the 1900s and the interwar period. By 1928 the United Banks RFU had fifty affiliated teams. The Bank of England club, formally founded in 1908 although it had played sporadically since the 1880s, boasted a pitch that, it was claimed, was second only to that at Twickenham. In the 1920s the bank paid all the fares of the team to make annual Easter trips to Paris to play the Bank of France. Given such largesse, it is perhaps not surprising that by 1938 the club had over 1,100 members. But the importance to the Bank of the rugby club was illustrated by its nickname. Among members and supporters it was universally known, not as one might expect as 'the Bank', but as 'House'. This was because, as the historians of the club explained, 'the word "House" conveys the idea of a family or a community with strong ties of blood or business. Something just a little stronger than *esprit de corps* and the camaraderie which are naturally engendered by all lovers of games.'[18]

Similar sentiments were expressed by those who founded old boys' clubs. The game owed its existence to former public schoolboys who had created adult clubs. For example, Marlborough Nomads, a founder member of the RFU, was entirely made up of Old Marlburians, and Wasps had been founded by old boys of Merchant Taylors'. However, it was not until the late 1880s that clubs based explicitly on former attendance at a particular school became popular. This followed the development of old boy societies in the previous two decades that aimed to offer financial support to their alma mater and provide an adult continuation of school social networks.[19] But the formation of old boy rugby sides was also driven by the desire to reclaim the sport by middle-class rugby supporters following the split with the northern clubs. 'The public schools have made English football, and it is only the public schools which can preserve that splendid game from the degeneration of professionalism', argued the *Globe* in 1901. 'A good deal more might be done by some schools to encourage the formation and maintenance of these old boy teams.'[20] By 1914 twenty such clubs were affiliated to the RFU. Ten years later, at the height of the 'rush to rugby', there were eighty-four and by 1934 there were 112 affiliated old boy clubs. In 1923 it was announced that a separate 'union of old boys' clubs' was to be formed because of the numbers of such clubs now playing the game, although this appears to have been short-lived. Such was the strength of the old boys' system during the interwar years that seven players from old boys' clubs were selected for England.

Despite the public prominence of old boy players, sociability continued to be just as important to their members as the playing of the game. After-match hospitality was subject to far more elaborate planning than anything that occurred on the pitch. The organisation of the annual dinner was a centrepiece of a club's activities, while the rest of the year would often be enlivened by a succession of dinners and smoking concerts. By the turn of the nineteenth century most clubs were organising annual dances, where the steadfastly masculine kingdom of the club would welcome wives and girlfriends of its members. At Old Alleynians' first annual club dinner in 1905, the club chairman toasted the club, stressing the two most important principles of the club: 'the fact that it gave the opportunity of continuing the friendships formed at school and the chance of getting recreation to compete with the archfiend of man: his liver'.[21] He was only half-joking.

A sense of the importance of the social side of the rugby club can be seen in the committee minutes of Old Alleynians, which suspended activities during the First World War but immediately revived in 1919:

> though it was six years since the last [dance], there seems to be a general feeling that another dance should be held. Mr J.T. Caesar who, it was known, was a keen dancing man was requested to attend the meeting. He had taken the opportunity of making various enquiries regarding suitable rooms, but had only been able to get the offer of two dates at Prince's Galleries . . . Mr Caesar was requested to act as hon. Dance secretary and consented to undertake the duties.[22]

Thanks to the efforts of the hon. Dance secretary, the event was a huge success with 231 people in attendance.

This little episode also hints at the formalised and bureaucratic structure of most rugby clubs. The constitution of Old Alleynians itself specified that 'the affairs of the club be managed by a president, vice-presidents, all captains of teams, a vice-captain of the first team, all honorary secre-taries, honorary treasurer, a committee of seven members (three of whom shall form a quorum), with captain and secretary of the school XV'. Blackheath had a committee of between twenty-three and twenty-six members.[23] As a matter of course, all clubs had sub-committees to deal with team selection, financial matters, ground maintenance, social activities and often much more. Annual general meetings, usually held within a few weeks of the season's end, were occasions for parading the full panoply of admin-istrative procedure, culminating in the elevation to club president of the vice-president, accompanied by outgoing and incoming speeches. As with the local rotary club or freemasons' lodge, the rugby club combined sociability with hierarchy and bureaucracy.

The basis of such bureaucracy was, however, an intense voluntarism. Without the unpaid labour of its members, no club could survive or grow. This was true throughout middle-class associational life. Old Whitgiftians established an 'informal entertainment sub-committee' that raised money for ground and pavilion improvements by organising match-day refreshments, suppers and dinners. Old Cranleighans raised £2,000 from its members in 1928 towards the purchase of their ground. Twenty-seven Old Alleynians volunteered to work on the club's ground 'cutting down seven trees, cutting them into logs, filling a hollow on the first XV ground, cutting down and removing a hedge, erecting goalposts, sweeping out, cleaning and white-washing a stable, levelling a 70 yard ditch, marking out two grounds, and erecting a cow fence with logs'. All clubs profited from the 'invisible support' of wives, mothers and girlfriends who washed kit, sold raffle tickets and served refreshments on match days.[24]

However, in the Midlands and the south-west significant numbers of clubs existed that had been founded not as extensions of middle-class social networks but to represent localities, whether town, district or even street, as was the case with most soccer and rugby league clubs. These were organisations whose playing personnel and supporters encompassed the middle classes and the working classes. In Bristol, Coventry, Gloucester, Leicester and the towns of Devon and Cornwall, the game resembled soccer or rugby league in being a vehicle for fierce community rivalry, as it was also in Wales. Clubs were led and organised by business and professional men, who were generally educated at local private and grammar schools and tended to be members of a regionally conscious middle class, rather than the 'national' middle class defined by attendance at public school and Oxbridge. They drew their support, and a good deal of their playing strength, from across the social strata of the locality. Manual labourers could indeed find them-selves playing alongside managing directors. In this, these cross-class rugby union clubs differed markedly from professional soccer or rugby league sides, which drew their players overwhelmingly from the working class, and especially from league clubs, which generally had very few, if any, links with local middle-class social networks. Whereas a successful playing career could often provide a ladder of social mobility to a working-class rugby union player, the same was rarely true of the successful rugby league player.

The playing of rugby union also differed where it had cross-class support. As in the north, cups and leagues were common, much to the irritation of the RFU. Devon and Cornwall both had league competitions by the early 1900s. In Bristol, the Bristol Combination league competition was established in 1901, against the wishes of the RFU, partly in response to the growing popularity of soccer in the town but also to provide a focus for the large number of clubs in the area. These ranged from Avonmouth, a side composed largely of dockers, to Old Colstonians, made up of ex-pupils of a Bristol private school. By 1923 the Combination had thirty sides in membership, which grew to fifty by the outbreak of the Second World War. In 1908 a district league was formed in the south-west comprising Gloucester, Lydney, Stroud, Bristol, Cheltenham, Clifton and Cinderford.[25]

Leicester also had a thriving league structure which boasted five divisions and almost 1,200 players by 1904. In the 1930s the city also had a league for teams based on evening institutes and, perhaps uniquely, an old boys' league of seven clubs. The *Midland Rugby Football Annual* for the 1938–39 season gives a useful snapshot of the wide social base of the rugby union in the region. Of the 198 clubs in a region stretching from Northamptonshire in the south to Derbyshire in the north, and including Birmingham in the west and Lincoln in the east, thirty-eight were old boys' clubs, twenty-four were works-based teams and the rest based on geographical location. Works-based teams ranged form local civil servants' sides to engineering factories, although it is difficult to say whether these factory teams were comprised of white-collar workers or manual labourers. In many factories soccer was the game for the waged and rugger for the salaried, a reflection of the general division in factory life that was highlighted by a manager in a midlands factory of the 1930s: 'you would have staff and works, and the staff would be middle class, the works were certainly working class . . . they wouldn't share the same interests and hobbies and the same sporting pursuits, and they wouldn't relax in the same way'.[26]

Rugby union in Coventry also extended across the classes and included a number of predominantly working-class, factory-based teams.[27] There were other examples of industrial working-class involvement in the game too. In 1924 the Northumberland pit village Seghill had six colliery sides and in 1926 Cinderford RFC in the Forest of Dean organised a cup competition for four sides from the local collieries, Eastern United, Foxes Bridge, Lightmoor and Crump Meadow.[28] Both of these appear to have been short-lived. The Seghill teams were established as part of the local colliery company's welfare scheme and seem to have been an attempt to promote industrial harmony in an era of intense class struggle.

In addition to cross-class support, the Leicester club itself also differed markedly from other leading clubs in that it closely resembled its soccer and rugby league cousins. It was run on broadly commercial lines and prioritised winning above all else. As early as 1893 the club had employed a professional trainer but it was Tom Crumbie, a local stationer who became club secretary in August 1895, who drove the club forward, instituting a policy of player recruitment through invitation and seeking fixtures with leading London and Welsh sides.[29] Crumbie was aided by the fact that the club was widely seen as, in his words, 'the first line of defence against the professionalism of the Northern Union'. The RFU therefore staged representative matches, including England internationals, at Welford Road and turned an expedient blind eye to the club's inducements to players. Crumbie dispensed with a second XV and focused solely on building a successful first team. He also embarked on a huge building programme to increase the Welford Road capacity to 40,000, partly to counter the popularity of Leicester Fosse (later City) soccer club. The building of what became known as the Crumbie Stand began in 1914 just before rugby union shut down in 1914, leaving the club to service a debt without being able to generate any income. By the early 1930s the ground had cost the club around £40,000, resulting in a severe financial crisis.[30]

Crumbie's recruitment policies capitalised on the fact that amateur players had no formal contract to play for their club and could thus be 'invited' to play for another side, especially if their work took them to a new area. The relative social openness of Leicester also made it appealing to leading southern players who did not feel entirely comfortable in the social atmosphere of London rugby. Jack Hodgson, a forward for the club in the 1930s, captured this when he explained why he lived in London but played for Leicester: 'I haven't got a bowler hat and an umbrella so I can't join 'Quins and I certainly have not a got a sports car to admit me to Blackheath so I'm happy to have a couple of hours on the train and play for Leicester.' Among its more illustrious invitees were England winger H.L.V. Day, W.W. Wakefield and Alexander Obolensky, causing Ralph Buckingham, who played for the club in the 1920s, to remark that 'it was different from any other club I had known. . . . It was rather like playing for the Barbarians when you were invited to play for Leicester.'.[31] Crumbie's desire to see the club triumph also brought him into dispute with Leicestershire's county rugby union. He opposed county matches being played on Saturday because they interfered with club fixtures and allegedly told the club's players to take it easy in county matches if Leicester had an important match soon.[32]

Leicester and similar clubs such as Bristol, Coventry and Gloucester therefore appear to represent something of an anomaly within English rugby. Commercially minded, locality-based and 'professional' in their approach to the playing of the game, it seems largely to be an accident of geography that prevented them from becoming part of the Northern Union. Coventry actually discussed the possibility in 1910. But a significant difference with the northern rebels was that these clubs were also entirely deferential towards the RFU. It is noteworthy that there was no meaningful club opposition to the RFU from the end of the Edwardian age until the early 1970s. Even when its policies directly impinged on clubs' commercial viability, such as the ban on clubs staging greyhound or speedway racing or its opposition to the use of floodlights, the clubs meekly toed the line. During the financial crisis that hit rugby and every other sport in the early 1930s, Leicester and other sides established supporters' clubs to raise money. As with similar organisations in soccer and rugby league, these acted as adjuncts to official fund-raising activities, often with no small success – Leicester's supporters raised £2,225 within a year of their club being established in 1934.[33]

Of course, there was irregular grumbling about the RFU by clubs, usually about the failure of one of their players to be selected for England – 'clubs such as the Harlequins, Blackheath and Guy's Hospital and other popular London clubs [are] rather inferior to such teams as Leicester, Northampton, Coventry, Bedford and Moseley (Midlands), Bath, Bristol, Headingley, Devonport Services and Plymouth Albion, and yet you will find practically no men from these teams playing for England', complained a Mr Smallwood to *Rugger* in 1931 – but similar sentiments could be found in all sports.[34] Another perennial issue was that of fixtures. Lacking league or cup structures, clubs arranged fixtures among themselves, usually on the basis of social prestige rather than playing strength. An informal hierarchy operated with Blackheath, Harlequins, Richmond and the Oxbridge clubs at the centre of a series of concentric circles of status. Next came other London clubs such as London Scottish, Rosslyn Park and Wasps, alongside whom leading provincial sides such as Leicester and Bristol might take their place. And so it went down the social strata. Without a league structure, lowly clubs had no way of ever working their way up to play the leading sides, and without a national cup competition there was never the hope that, for example, a team of miners from the Forest of Dean could find themselves facing Harlequins. Of course, these were among the reasons why the RFU refused to allow such tournaments. Complaints about the impossibility of meeting the prestigious London sides were often voiced by other metropolitan sides who felt themselves to be of equal strength. In 1947 six leading Midlands sides signed a letter to the RFU, proposing that it should insist on clubs adding two new fixtures each season so that clubs played opponents of equal strength rather than social status. 'Class distinctions' should be ended, it argued.[35]

This was akin to asking the Catholic Church to abolish the papacy. Class distinction not only marked rugby union's attitude to those outside the sport, but also to those who were part of it. In the late 1930s, Blackheath's adult annual subscription rates began at seventeen shillings and sixpence but 'workman's tickets', available to 'bona fide working men' and offering limited admission to the ground, were sold for five shillings, the same cost as chauffeur's tickets.[36] Clubs in counties that had cup competitions often simply withdrew if they did not approve of the type of opponents against whom they might play. In 1923 Headingley withdrew from the Yorkshire Cup in order to attract fixtures with more prestigious clubs. At the schoolboy level, the class distinction was even more severe. In 1904 the English Schools' Rugby Union had been formed on the initiative of schools in Leicester and included board and elementary (later to become state) schools in Coventry and Bristol and the south-west. The ESRU had no links with the sport in private schools – a separate Public Schools' union was formed in 1948 – and the RFU continually refused the ESRU permission to stage its annual international match against Welsh Schools at Twickenham. In 1952 W.D. Gibbs, the chairman of the RFU's schools committee, exasperatedly referred to 'the public schools who are and will always remain a law unto themselves and with whom we must not interfere'.[37]

Social distinctions ran through the game like veins through marble. Bert Solomon, the brilliant Cornish centre-three-quarter who played one game for England in 1910, reputedly refused to play again because of the way he felt uncomfortable around those England team-mates who saw themselves as socially superior to him.[38] Jim Steel, Kingston's representative on the Surrey Rugby Union in the mid-1930s, complained that he had 'got very fed up with the amount of snobbery and hypocrisy' in London rugby.[39] England and British Lions' tourist John Bentley, who played in the north in the 1980s when the game was becoming markedly more commercial, summed it up in characteristic fashion: 'rugby union has always reeked of the old boy network and I have had to put up with it all my life'. This was also true even at the lowest levels of the club game. 'Most of the players [at St Helens rugby union club] seemed to have an inferiority complex when in the company of more "socially acceptable" clubs such as Liverpool, Fylde, Wilmslow and Harrogate', noted England international Ray French about his time at the club in the early 1960s.[40]

Why did clubs in the Midlands and the south-west accept a situation which was detrimental to their success on and off the field? The most obvious answer is that English society itself was deeply deferential to social position and that the clubs simply reflected society. But two other points can be made. Unlike the clubs that formed the Northern Union, these were not clubs that were dominated by working-class players and spectators. They did not feel the same pressure to satisfy working-class demands for payment for play that ultimately led to the split of 1895. Moreover, the RFU was, unlike in 1895, prepared to compromise with clubs in order to avoid another rupture, as it had done with Leicester in 1909. The cross-class clubs never presented a numerical threat to the RFU in the way that the Yorkshire and Lancashire clubs did in the 1890s. From the Edwardian period until the mid-1950s, clubs in London and the south-east always formed an absolute majority of RFU members, with those in the Midlands and south-west together making up around a quarter of the total.

And there was also the question of money. From the early 1920s the RFU had supplied its clubs with tens of thousands of pounds in low interest, long-term loans. Funded by the income from internationals at Twickenham, which by 1935 brought in over £30,000 per season in gate receipts, the RFU provided loans for the buying of grounds, the building of club houses and other capital costs, often at interest rates lower than those available on the open market. From 1920 to the 1980s, the RFU loaned an average of £10,000 annually to clubs, never having less than £40,000 on loan at any one time. In 1926 it felt so confident about its financial position that it borrowed £20,000 from the Bank of Liverpool at an annual interest rate of 5 per cent and loaned the money back out to its clubs at a rate of 2.5 per cent. Loans at less than commercial rates were ended in 1932 when the impact of the depression meant that there was both a greater demand for loans and an increased risk of clubs defaulting. In 1933 Plymouth Albion asked for a moratorium on interest payments because of financial difficulties caused by falling attendances, which the RFU refused, instead restructuring the debt into two separate loans. The RFU finance committee played the role of banker with characteristic conservatism, neither allowing clubs to escape their obligations nor placing unreasonable demands for payments on them. Even at the height of the 1930s depression it repossessed just two club grounds out of the dozens for which it provided finance.[41] Thus rugby union clubs also had a material basis for their conservatism and support for the RFU. In short, amateurism paid.

The 'other' rugby

None of these class, commercial or regional tensions ever threatened the unity of the RFU. Only one club, Darnall in Sheffield in 1922, left the RFU to join rugby league following the First World War, the last ever. In 1927 clubs in the south-west called for the formation of a league, the so-called Paignton movement, but this was to be the last heard of leagues in the sport until the late 1960s.[42] The fact that there was never any attempt at rapprochement with rugby league, a seemingly logical move for those clubs in the Midlands and the south-west, can be explained by the ferocious campaign waged by the RFU against the other rugby code. 'I have not taken part in rugby league football, either as an amateur or a professional, nor have I signed any rugby league form, after reaching my eighteenth birthday' was the declaration that prospective new members had to make on the application form to join Huddersfield rugby union club. An affirmative answer would have automatically excluded the applicant from membership. The echo of McCarthyism was not accidental. In September 1895 the RFU established its policy towards the new rival, laying the basis for the sporting McCarthyism it pursued more or less intact for the next century.[43]

It insisted on a rigorous policy of separation from rugby league – described approvingly as 'the strictest form of apartheid' by South Africa's Danie Craven. As we saw in Chapter 2, anyone who played the thirteen-a-side game either as an amateur or a professional was barred for life from playing rugby union. Every player had to be on his guard against inadvertently dealing with the league devil: 'Ignorance of the rules is no defence' warned a poster distributed to all clubs.[44] Although the amateur regulations on paper outlawed all contact with professional sport, they were really only ever intended to deal with rugby league. Rugby union players who had played alongside professional soccer players, such as Ireland's Kevin O'Flanagan, a dual international in soccer and rugby who also played for Arsenal in the 1946–47 season, were not subject to sanction. The fact that league was the target was made explicit in a 1958 IB resolution:

> in keeping with principles underlying the Rules as to Professionalism, persons who are or have been associated in any capacity with a Rugby League club should be regarded as being ineligible to participate in the affairs of Rugby Union clubs or teams. The Board also agreed that, while this must in practice be a matter for each Union to determine in the light of its own local problems, *there is in general no objection to persons who are or have been ranked as professionals in games other than Rugby League football being permitted to play Rugby Union football or to participate in the affairs of rugby union clubs.* [emphasis added][45]

This also goes some way to explain why the RFU and the rest of the Home Unions consistently turned a blind eye to the open semi-professionalism of the game in Europe. Questioned about the sport's indulgence towards the clearly non-amateur Rumanian touring side in 1956, former Welsh captain and prominent judge Rowe Harding explained that if rugby union was to 'pull down the iron curtain' and expel them, 'I have no doubt that the Rumanians will turn to rugby league, which will be a tragedy.'[46]

Attempts to stop such 'tragedies' led to a fierce campaign against those who transgressed, often creating minor tragedies in the lives of those who loved the sport. A player from County Durham called Armstrong signed for a league club in 1928 but changed his mind on the way home and returned the contract and the cheque to the club. In order to make a clean breast of things he wrote to the RFU to tell them of his mistake. On receipt of his letter, the RFU banned him for life. A Manchester referee was banned in 1935 after it came to light that he had been a 17-year-old rugby league player a decade previously.[47] Perhaps the most notorious example was the 1933 banning of Bristol and England full-back Tom Brown. He travelled to Lancashire and met with league officials. Although he decided to stay with Bristol he was paid his travelling expenses. For reasons that are still unknown, the meeting came to the notice of the RFU which, after investigating the matter, banned him for life. Despite Bristol appealing the decision twice, the RFU refused to budge and Brown never played rugby again. He had never even seen a game of rugby league, much less played in one, and only saw the sport for the first time in 1954 when he bought a television set. He was posthumously reinstated as an amateur in 1987.[48]

Nor were schools exempt from such zealotry. A 19-year-old schoolboy called Drinkhall was banned in 1935 for choosing to play rugby league although he could have chosen to play union at school.[49] In 1936 RFU committee member (and former president) James Baxter wrote to the Board of Education claiming that teachers who played rugby union were being forced to teach rugby league in northern schools and asked if the Board could make a ruling about which sports were played in schools. 'We naturally don't want to ostracise these people', he explained. The Board replied that it could not understand the RFU's problem, as the RFU had no objection to its players teaching schoolboys to play soccer. Rebuffed, the RFU decided that if coaching rugby league only took place as part of a teacher's duties, the teacher would not be banned from playing union. This did not satisfy some 'ultras', who believed that any teacher who taught league should be excommunicated from union.[50]

The long arm of the RFU also reached far beyond the pitch. In 1923 former league players were barred from involvement in training or assisting union teams. Ex-league players were also prevented from becoming non-playing social members of rugby union clubs. 'Past or present rugby league players could not be admitted to membership of a rugby union club', it pronounced in 1962.[51] In the late 1960s Bev Risman, the England international who starred on the British Lions 1959 tour of New Zealand before switching to league, was asked to leave Broughton Park RUFC's fancy-dress party simply because he played the thirteen-a-side game.[52] Coventry's Old Players' Association's request that former rugby league players be allowed to join in 1970 was criticised by the RFU because 'membership might allow them into rugby union club premises and later into management positions of clubs'. In 1970 Martin Regan, who won a dozen caps for England in the mid-1950s before switching to league, had to apply for permission from the RFU to join Liverpool as a social member.[53]

As the Coventry discussion hinted, an insecure paranoia lay behind the RFU's zealotry. League and players who had played it was discussed at twenty-two of the RFU's first thirty committee meetings in the decade after the First World War. In the late 1940s, as well as discussing bans on players, the committee also discussed league in the Army, the Midlands, Surrey and even Canada. A flavour of this type of discussion can be seen in a 1968 agenda point for an Executive Committee meeting. Dramatically titled 'Rugby League Infiltration', this did not reveal a mole at the heart of Twickenham who had escaped behind the iron curtain of the Wigan municipal town boundary. Instead it referred to a small advertisement for trials with a rugby league club that had been published in a Durham newspaper. In 1980 the Executive Committee requested 'reports of [rugby league] development from each constituent body and county schools' union asking for information on any trends or similar developments in recent times'.[54]

These insecurities were heightened by the renaissance of the thirteen-a-side game from the mid-1970s. The formation of the British Amateur Rugby League Association in 1973 and the emergence of a new leadership in rugby league saw the RFU regularly wrong-footed by campaigners for the movement of players across the rugby codes. Twickenham's initial dismissal of its critics was unsuccessful and over the next two decades it engaged in a series of dog-fights with league campaigners, which revealed the shaky foundations of its amateur ethos. By the mid-1970s it found itself under increasing pressure from the government and the Sports Council to moderate its stance. In 1969 the RFU had set up a sub-committee to deal with requests by retired league players who wished to be 'reinstated' as amateurs, usually so that they could coach or join clubs as social members. The trickle of reinstated amateurs undermined the RFU by demonstrating the arbitrary hypocrisy of the amateur regulations – confirming that there was no objective measure of amateurism other than whatever Twickenham decided – and by 1980 calls for a 'free gangway' for players between union and amateur league could no longer be ignored. In 1986, faced with league's growing popularity and finding that the Sports Council was becoming reluctant to provide grants to clubs that clearly did not support its 'Sport for All' policy, the free gangway was finally introduced, allowing amateur players to play union and league without formal sanction. Nevertheless, the ban remained for anyone who played with a professional league side. Wasps' full-back Steve Pilgrim was banned from rugby union for a year as late as 1993 for playing a trial game as an amateur for Leeds rugby league club. Less than a year before union junked any pretence of amateurism, Ady Spencer was forced to withdraw from the Light Blues side in the 1994 Varsity match because he also played league.[55]

There is no parallel in the history of sport for rugby union's hostility to league. Other closely related sports never took comparable measures. Netball's leaders never considered banning basketball players from playing their sport. Even rival governing bodies of the same sport, such as the National Football League and the American Football League during gridiron's NFL–AFL war in the 1960s, never sought to ban players in their opponent's competition. Quite the reverse in fact – capturing players from the other league was a vital part of the contest. Moreover, the banning of players who played rugby league harmed rugby union more than it did league. Those union players who switched to league and did not succeed in their new game – a not insignificant number – were precluded from returning to union to resume their careers. The ban on contact with league was, in the words of historian Norman Davies, 'one of the clearest and ugliest manifestations of the English class system'.[56]

What animated such animus? In many ways it appears to be a continuation of Charles Masterman's description of the Edwardian middle classes' fear of the working class and 'an uprising of the uneducated, suddenly breaking into its houses; their clumsy feet on the mantelpiece, their clumsy hands seizing and destroying all beautiful and pleasant things'.[57] Certainly the RFU believed that the growth of rugby league was bad for rugby union. At a special RFU meeting called to discuss the growth of amateur rugby league in 1983, Denis Shuttleworth expressed his concern at the success of league and 'considered that this was to the detriment of the rugby union game'.[58] The rule 'dispensations' granted to the Australian and New Zealand rugby unions in the 1920s – barring direct kicking into touch outside of the twenty-five yard line, for example – were motivated by a desire to counter the more attractive and open features of league. In the early 1980s the RFU's coaching sub-committee itself admitted that 'there was no easy solution to combating the growth of amateur rugby league'. Former Yorkshire and England fly-half Alan Old identified the end of compulsory rugby union in grammar schools as one of the reasons for league's new found popularity.[59]

The animosity towards league also helped to fortify the natural conservatism of the game and its followers. Those who sought changes to the game could easily be deterred by the fear that this may lead down the road of the rival game. Most importantly, it served as a major deterrent to any player wishing to try an alternative form of rugby. Being banned from rugby union would mean exclusion from the club, its social activities and many of the friendship and business networks of which it was a part. As Philip Trevor pointed out in his 1922 *Rugby Union Football*, ostracism was 'the supreme penalty'.[60] It is also important to recognise that rugby union's unremitting opposition to league had a corrosive effect on its own morality. The demonisation of the rival game led to an internalised system of double-think. Payments to players by union clubs, especially in France, the provision of jobs to players, and the commercial activities of rugby union players had to be defended as being within the amateur regulations or simply denied regardless of the facts. Once again, the pursuit of amateurism and its defence had led to hypocrisy becoming institutionalised.

Fundamentally, the enmity to league was part of union's self-identity. The split of 1895 had not only created rugby league but it had also played a crucial role in defining the RFU's self-image. 'The Rugby Union has really been given a new reason for its existence by the success of professionalism', commented the *Guardian*'s rugby correspondent in 1900.[61] It was rugby league that embodied the 'other' against which union defined itself. Of course, league itself never sought to challenge the sporting or social order. Until the mid-1970s, it rarely contested the RFU's ban and in general it accepted its place in the pecking order of British sport. It was not rugby league's policies that provoked the RFU's hostility but its very existence. Rugby league called into question what the middle-class leaders of the RFU saw as the natural order of things. Here was a form of rugby that did not appear to need the leadership of the middle classes. The advantages of education, family, caste or rank appeared to confer no benefit in this alternative sporting world. For the RFU it was as if the stoats and the weasels of the Wild Woods had declared that they were the rightful owners of Toad Hall and that Mr Toad, Ratty and their chums would have to take their chances down at the employment exchange like everyone else. This alone explains the absurd and unprecedented paranoia that overcame the leading bodies of rugby union when dealing with the activities of its rival.

Character, club and class

One of the arguments advanced by rugby union supporters for the absolute ban on rugby league was the idea that the true aim of rugby union was to build character in young men, not professional sportsmen. But exactly what type of character did rugby union build? In their *Report on Rugby*, Morgan and Nicholson spoke for many by suggesting that, as well as manliness, the two crucial virtues taught by the game were courage and self-control.[62]

However, this raised more questions than it answered. Courage was a prerequisite of participation in any sport that involved physical confrontation or danger, whether it be boxing, horseracing or motor sports. It was not unique to rugby. And physical courage was not the same as moral or intellectual courage. As can be seen in discussions of amateurism and masculinity, the moral values that the game promoted, such as fair play and playing the game for its own sake, were fluid and dependent on the circumstances of the time.

Self-control was portrayed as the quintessential characteristic of the English gentleman. But this too is a vague and imprecise phrase. In the Victorian public schools from which the game emerged, it was used as a euphemism for sexual abstinence. In modern usage, it is often used to describe the spirit in which the game is played, the implication being that without self-control matches would become free-for-all fights. Again, this truism applies to all physical sports, from soccer to netball. It is also argued that the respect shown to referees and the acceptance of their decisions, especially in contrast to soccer, demonstrates the self-control of players. Yet referees were only introduced into the game in the mid-1880s to reduce arguments between captains during matches.

Self-control could also describe the measured emotional response to the excitement of victory or disappointment of defeat, as in Kipling's 'if you can meet with Triumph and Disaster/And treat those two impostors just the same'. But this is not necessarily a virtue, merely a characteristic of the nineteenth- and twentieth-century British middle classes. To identify it as a universally desirable quality is rather like suggesting that the film *Brief Encounter* should be used as an instructional guide for those experiencing marital difficulties. At bottom, the importance of self-control to the game was its focus on discipline and the ability to follow orders. As was emphasised in *Tom Brown's Schooldays* and thousands of subsequent schoolboy stories, life was about being part of the team and not standing out from the rest. The willingness to do as one was told, whether by the schoolmaster, the referee or the team captain, was central to the ethos of the game. Conformity was valued almost above all other qualities.

Of course, few people like to think of themselves as conformists. Implicit in the description of rugby union as a 'freemasonry' is the belief that rugby players are different from the rest of society. Richard Beard, in his 2003 book *Muddied Oafs*, claims that there is an 'affinity between rugby and non-conformism'.[63] But this is merely a conceit, the self-justification of those who think it is a breach of their human rights not to be allowed to do exactly as they wish. It was also used regularly in the 1980s by players who played in South Africa and claimed to be 'rebel tourists' defying political orthodoxy. Beard and others have also pointed to Che Guevara's involvement in the game as a youth as an example of its rebellious nature. Yet rugby-playing was a result of his privileged family background in Argentina and bore no relation to his later political activity – rugby is virtually non-existent in Cuba and the country is not even a member of the IRB.

Rugby's dissent from society's norms was expressed only when it prevented players or clubs doing as they pleased, such as when drinking after a match or engaging in 'high jinks' when on tour. This outlook is perhaps most famously reflected in the philosophy and name of the invitational club the Barbarians. Although its histories offer no clue as to how the side's name was chosen, it is safe to assume that the education of William Carpmael – who went to Jesus College, Cambridge and founded the club in 1890 – gave him at least a passing knowledge of Matthew Arnold's 1869 description of the British aristocracy as Barbarians:

> The Barbarians brought with them that staunch individualism, as the modem phrase is, and that passion for doing as one likes, for the assertion of personal liberty. . . . The care of the Barbarians for the body, and for all manly exercises; the vigour, good looks, and fine complexion which they acquired and perpetuated in their families . . . [as well as] courage, a high spirit, and self-confidence.[64]

Over the years the Baa-baas, as they are known within rugby, became associated with the maxim 'rugby football is a game for gentlemen of all classes but never for a bad sportsman of any class', apparently coined by Oxford Blue and future Bishop of Bloemfontein Walter Carey. Carpmael's personal history gave little support to this apparently liberal statement. In December 1894 he was one of the organisers of a campaign for proxy votes to support an RFU proposal that players or clubs accused of professionalism should be suspended until they could prove their innocence. He also proposed that anyone providing information about alleged professionalism in rugby should be paid a £20 reward. At the 1894 special RFU general meeting he declared that 'this is the amateurs' last chance' and pointed to the Bradford club Manningham's tour to Paris earlier that year as evidence of veiled professionalism, a point which struck many at the meeting as a trifle rich considering that the Barbarians' fixture list consisted of nothing but trips away to play rugby.[65] As with much of the discourse of amateurism, the phrase 'gentlemen of all classes' also concealed a sleight of hand, referring not to all social classes but to the gradations of gentlemen within the middle classes. Despite being formed in Bradford in 1890, northern working-class players were notably absent from Barbarian team sheets. A team that was selected by invitation and carefully chose its opponents was the perfect antidote to the rising tide of working-class participation in 1890s rugby.

Insofar as political attitudes were expressed in rugby union, they were those of a deep-going conservatism. 'Rugby presents a world within a world, a fellowship in which old beatitudes survive, in which life is simple and good, and from which the complications of an unclean world are absent', explained Morgan and Nicholson. As we saw in Chapter 1, from its birth the game was inextricably linked to a conservative worldview. A dismayed Chris Laidlaw, a Rhodes scholar who captained both Oxford University and the All Blacks, wrote in 1973 that rugby was 'normally played and administered by conservative elements in society. . . . Today's players are by and large tomorrow's Tories.' There was also a long tradition of involvement in the Conservative Party. Rowland Hill was a Conservative councillor, Wavell Wakefield became a lower-ranking Conservative minister and in 1956 Denis Thatcher was the English touch-judge for the France versus England match at the Stade Colombes. But, in general, conservatism was expressed in attitudes rather than politics.[66] Player biographies were a common platform from which to lament the decline of modern society. 'We lose a good deal, I think, with our modern conveniences, a criticism which applies to life in general as well as rugby football', wrote Howard Marshall in 1936. 'Existence becomes too easy for us; we are cosseted, sheltered from the buffets of an unkind world.' Wavell Wakefield shared the same view, mulling that 'it is because of the freedom of rugger and its consequent risks that it breeds hardiness, which in these days of cocktails and lounge-lizards is a quality to be encouraged'. Watcyn Thomas believed that rugby had the answers to society's ills: 'it moulds character and personality, and promotes and inculcates discipline, self-control, manners, deportment and co-operation. If more youths played rugby, we should have less violence and hooliganism, fewer hippies, Teds, Mods, Rockers, Hell's Angels and other selfish enemies of society.'[67] Such opinions came to the fore during the 1969 Springbok tour of the UK and during subsequent debates on rugby union's links with apartheid South Africa. David Duckham's autobiography cast him as something of a Tory backwoodsman while still in his early thirties, accusing anti-apartheid campaigners of holding an 'extremist viewpoint against racial discrimination' that could not be justified unless they had 'witnessed the scene themselves and experienced local feeling'. He had been to South Africa on tour and was struck by 'the atmosphere of calm acceptance on the part of those at the "raw" end' of apartheid.[68] There is no reason to suppose that he was any different from the overwhelming majority of players or supporters.

It is therefore not surprising that many rugby union players were enthusiastic strike-breakers during the 1926 General Strike. 'Every member' of the London Irish club enlisted in the Special Constabulary. About sixty internationals were estimated to have volunteered for strike-breaking duties. Teddy Wakelam organised some of his Harlequins team-mates to do building work for the Office of Works. A total of 193 members of the Old Alleynians' club volunteered for the Metropolitan Police's Special Reserve, forming their own 'flying squad' of cars and motorcycles to guard 'vulnerable points' in Dulwich. Needless to say, 'every one of them thoroughly enjoyed the experience'.[69] One or two found an outlet for their attitudes in fascism. Peter Howard, who won eight England caps and captained the national side in 1931, became the secretary of Oswald Mosley's New Party Youth Movement in the same year, an organisation popularly known as Mosley's 'Biff Boys'. Even before his outright declaration of fascism in 1932 Mosley's politics were based on physical force and the Oxford student magazine *Isis* reported that Howard had left the university 'taking a knuckle-duster, the Pro-Milone [Cicero's speech in defence of a friend accused of murdering a political enemy] and a nice new pair of trousers. All this to protect Sir Oswald and Lady Cynthia Mosley.' Although Howard later claimed to have broken with Mosley before his espousal of fascism, other evidence throws this into doubt and he had previously praised Mosley as 'Mussolini-like'.[70] In some areas in the mid-1930s, the Labour Party believed that British Union of Fascists (BUF) recruiters targeted 'younger members of the Tory Party, particularly those interested in sports, rugby and golf players (the boisterous kind of young bloods)'.[71] For their part, the Mosleyites were well-disposed to rugby union. 'It is a real Fascist game, for a man who plays Rugger must be determined to "get there" by co-operation with the rest of the team', proclaimed *Action*, the newspaper of the BUF.[72]

But Howard and those like him were exceptions. In general the great mass of rugby lovers were happy to be part of a social grouping that valued convention and hierarchy. The values of Tom Brown were replicated down the generations. In 1929 Richard Aldington, in his novel *Death of a Hero*, described the archetypal rugger-playing army officer Evans as having

> a strength of character which enabled him to carry out whatever he had been taught was his duty to do. He accepted and obeyed every English middle-class prejudice and taboo. What the English middle class thought and did was right, and anybody else thought and did was wrong. He was contemptuous of all foreigners . . . [he] possessed that British rhinoceros equipment of mingled ignorance, self-confidence and complacency which triple-armed against all shafts of the mind.[73]

Chris Laidlaw noted in the 1970s that in rugby union 'there existed a rigid code that demanded a sameness among all players that on first experience was extremely depressing. . . . No expression of feelings or emotions must ever be revealed, for that would infer soppiness, a quality reviled by every *compleat* rugby player.'[74]

Ultimately, the question of character always returned to that of class. The importance of character achieved a certain prominence in the 1960s when Oxford and Cambridge instituted more meritocratic selection methods, thus barring the way for well-born sporting hearties with little or no academic ability. J.E. Greenwood lamented the absence from Oxbridge of 'boys who were very good at games, who had character and definite powers of leadership and who were not judged solely by their ability to pass exams'.[75] And in the early years of the twenty-first century, as English rugby established itself as a professional sport and occupied the top table of the international game, its success was attributed to character. It was the characteristics of 'sportsmanship, discipline, camaraderie and valour' that helped England win the 2003 World Cup, wrote William Langley in the *Daily Telegraph*. 'Only a relative few are ever likely to aspire to them', but they could be found he suggested, unconsciously echoing Thomas Hughes' description of Tom Brown's family, 'around the hearths of solid, traditional families, and in those schools – mostly, but far from exclusively, in the independent sector – where rugby is cherished.' Contrasting England rugby union fans with soccer supporters in the same year, the *Spectator* columnist Michael Henderson praised the character of rugby union's followers:

> They attended good schools, and now hold down decent jobs, live in good houses and pay their taxes. . . . Naturally, given the mores of our times, they are derided while the yobs are often praised for the purity of their proletarian roots.

> After all these years we are still Two Nations, and determined to remain so. Aren't you glad you are middle class?[76]

This was a sentiment that had been expressed ever since rugby began to fracture along class lines in the 1880s. The importance of sport to social distinction was aptly captured in Warwick Deeping's 1925 best-seller *Sorrell and Son*. In this saga of a lower-middle-class father and son's struggle to maintain their social position in post-First World War Britain, the decisive moment in Sorrell's decision to send his son to a private school occurs during a game of football against a local council school. The boy is mocked and fouled by his working-class opponents, which is interpreted by his father as proof that 'these sons of working men hated the son of the ex-officer. They hated his face, his voice, his pride, his very good temper. They hated him for his differences, his innocent superiorities.'[77]

The growth of rugby union in the interwar years reflected something of this desire for separation of the classes. In particular, the 1920s were shaped by the impact of the Russian Revolution abroad and the events leading up to the 1926 General Strike at home. Fear and distrust of the working class was common, alongside a more generalised disquiet about the declining economic position of the middle classes in the early 1920s. The formation of the short-lived Middle Class Union in 1919 was one of the more overt signs of middle-class 'class consciousness' but it found a more long-lasting outlet in newspapers aimed at the middle classes such as the *Daily Mail*. Much of the *Mail*'s appeal was based in its articulation of a 'yearning for pre-war certainties', a social nostalgia it shared with rugby union, which expressed the same desire through its adherence to amateurism and class distinction.[78] One of the main manifestations of middle-class identity was found in the sphere of leisure. By the mid-1930s there were 2,874 tennis clubs and over 1,000 golf clubs in Britain. Between 1919 and 1950, some 3,000 new Masonic lodges opened. And the RFU tripled its membership in this period, growing from 307 clubs in 1919 to 965 in 1939.[79]

This growth was remarkably uniform, with the number of clubs based on schools, colleges, localities and the professions accounting for almost the same proportion of the total RFU membership in 1939 as they had in 1914. Only old boys' clubs recorded any qualitative increase, doubling from 6 per cent to 12 per cent of the total number of clubs. Moreover, as Appendix 4 outlines, the regional distribution of clubs remained constant. The proportion based in London and the south-east remained almost unchanged between 1914 and 1939, moving from 58 per cent of the total to 56 per cent, with only the Midlands recording any substantive increase, from 8 per cent to 15 per cent.

The south-west provided 9 per cent of the RFU's clubs in 1939, the north-east 4 per cent, and Cumbria, Lancashire and Yorkshire, rugby league's heartland, 16 per cent, almost the same percentages as in 1914.

To some extent rugby's growth reflected the increase in the size of the middle classes during this period, from around nine million people in 1921 to thirteen million in 1951 according to Ross McKibbin. But rugby union's expansion was proportionally much larger than this, suggesting that people joined or formed rugby clubs because they wanted to be part of its older traditions, which also explains the consistent occupational and geographic distribution of clubs. Both William Rubenstein and Richard Trainor have argued that older divisions in the middle class declined in the 1920s and 1930s, giving way to a more unitary, national middle-class identity. Rugby union was an integral part of this process, offering both recreational opportunities at a national level and a recognisable ideological framework for them.[80]

The sport continued to play this role in the second half of the twentieth century, although the size and composition of the middle class changed considerably. The growth in scientific, technical and administrative occupations contributed to changing attitudes of sections of the middle class, which impacted significantly on the game. Geographically, the game shifted slightly to the Midlands and the south-west. By 1970 the percentage of clubs in London and the south-east had declined to 40 percent of the RFU's membership, with the south-west and the Midlands increasing their proportion of clubs to 38 per cent, figures which remained consistent into the 1990s. The percentages of adult clubs from the services, universities, professions, works and localities remained remarkably stable between 1950 and 1990. However, as we can see from Appendix 3, the game experienced huge growth in the numbers of schools playing the sport. The 192 private or grammar schools fielding rugby union sides in 1950 had grown to 625 in 1990. Even more remarkable was the growth in state schools playing the game, which totalled 1,704 by 1990. Indeed, of the 4,316 clubs playing the game in 1990, schools accounted for 54 per cent of all rugby playing clubs or organisation. In 1968 the Chester Report had noted that a number of soccer-playing schools had taken up rugby union because of the hostility of some headmasters to the overt professionalism of soccer. However, it was the impact of the switch to comprehensive schooling in the state sector that led to many more schools taking up the game, both to demonstrate their social status to parents and to be part of the sporting network of former grammar schools that had become comprehensive.[81] This growth was assisted by the RFU's pro-active policies towards schools, which by the

1980s included the funding of development officers, coaching seminars and promotional materials. And, of course, the popularity of the England side from the mid-1980s once more made rugby union fashionable.

But to some extent these figures also revealed a certain stagnation in the adult game. In comparison to the interwar years, when the number of adult clubs increased by 293 per cent, from 280 in 1914 to 820 in 1939, the increase between 1950 and 1990 was 136 per cent, from 843 to 1,987. This too may reflect not only the changing nature of the middle class and the growth of non-traditional attitudes but also the decline of middle-class sociability and associationalism. The club may no longer play the important role in middle-class social networks that it once did. Moreover, this transformation of the rugby club was accelerated with the introduction of professionalism in 1995, as leading clubs became businesses and profitability replaced sociability as the guiding principle. As rugby metamorphosised from a freemasonry into an entertainment, the importance of class remained yet the club, its traditional conduit, was in decline.

6

THE PLAYER'S GAME

There are few more eagerly anticipated matches in the rugby union calendar than Wales' biannual trip to Twickenham in the Five Nations. For decades Welsh fans have poured down the roads and railway lines that connect south Wales to south-west London, hoping to teach the English a lesson in how to play the game. And the English supporters have hoped for victory to put the Welsh back in their place. Sporting and social rivalry combine to raise anticipation levels sky high.

The 1962 encounter was no different. Some 72,000 people assembled at Twickenham to see a battle – but from the kick-off it became one of attrition and safety-first kicking. Both sides were wary of each other's backline and risk-taking was reduced to a minimum. The English pack kept the play tight and foiled Welsh attempts to provide decent ball to their backs. Ken Jones, the fastest man on the field, spent most of his time walking between set-pieces.

Nor did the kickers offer any respite. Kel Coslett, the Welsh full-back who was to find fame in rugby league at St Helens, missed all five penalty goal attempts. His opposite number John Willcox also missed two and the normally deadly England fly-half Richard Sharp failed with four attempted drop-goals, one of which was blown off course by the blustery wind when it appeared to be going over. A late Budge Rogers fly-hack of loose ball over the Welsh line was thwarted by a dubiously late tackle by Coslett.

When the final whistle came, it was merciful release for all concerned. 'Well, at any rate, we didn't have to pay to watch it', commented one journalist as the players trudged from the field. 'Faultily faultless, icily regular, splendidly null', quipped the reporter from *The Times*, in a somewhat unique use of a Tennyson love poem.[1]

It would not be the last time such sentiments were heard. The following year England played out another 0–0 draw in Dublin, and Wales won a tryless match at Murrayfield in a game that featured 111 line-outs as the opposing scrum-halfs simply belted the ball into touch as soon as the ball reached their hands. This should have surprised no one. Welsh captain and scrum-half Clive Rowlands had earlier announced that all that really interested him was to win and he exploited the rules to the full to ensure his desired outcome.[2]

The same attitude had begun to emerge in England's approach to the game. 'I don't think we thought about the game as a spectacle', admitted Budge Rogers, who also played in the 0–0 draw at Landsdowne Road the following year before becoming England captain in 1966.[3] 'We turned up to play and people either turned up to watch it or they didn't. Lots of captains were prepared to subjugate the experience of enjoyment for the crowd to make sure they got the right result.' With nothing in the laws to prevent it, teams could simply reduce a game to a procession of set-pieces, turning the three-quarters into passive spectators.

But the early 1960s were a time when television was beginning to play an important role in public perception of sport. By 1961, 75 per cent of all households owned a television. It was an era in which all sports faced intense competition from an increasing range of leisure and consumer activities now available to people. If rugby union was to maintain its position in this new world of consumer leisure, change was imperative.

Shoving and science

The ease with which rugby could be turned into a game of attrition, of endless scrummaging, constant kicking and interminable forward battles was not an aberration but deeply rooted in its genetic code. Indeed, that is how it began.

To its participants, the attractions of the game played at Rugby School in the 1830s were exactly the features for which it would be criticised in later years. It was a game of continual scrummaging. The number of players on each side was unlimited but usually numbered around fifty or sixty, dependent only on the number of boys willing, or forced, to play. Furthermore, it would barely be accurate to describe it as a 'handling code' of football at all. The mode of play revolved around scrummaging and kicking to set up scrummages. Handling the ball was severely limited. If the ball was caught on the full from a kick – a 'fair catch' – the catcher was allowed to kick the ball unhindered by the opposing side. But players were not allowed to run with the ball in their hands if it had been picked up from the ground. Running with ball in hand was only permitted if the ball was bouncing when it was picked up – even a rolling ball could not be picked up by hand.

Scoring was measured only by goals kicked. 'Goal keepers', a position occupied by the younger boys in the school, were spread out along the goal-line to prevent the ball going over the line and being touched down by the opposing side. A touch down by the attacking side would allow them a 'try at goal' (hence the term 'try'). Once the ball had been touched down behind the goal-line, the player who made the touch down had to punt it back out to a waiting player who would catch the ball and make a mark in the ground with his heel. The moment the ball was kicked to the catcher the defending side was able to rush forward and attempt to stop him catching the ball. If it was caught successfully, the catcher was allowed time to place the ball on the ground for the try-scorer to attempt to kick the ball over the bar and between the posts of the goal. It is reasonable to suppose that the fact that the place-kicker could be rushed at by the opposing side resulted in goals being scored by the ball going over the bar, rather than under it as in other forms of football.

The 'quarters' acted as a defensive line in front of the goal, whose job it was to kick the ball back down field when it came to them. This would hopefully set up a scrummage for the 'players up', who would then seek to push the scrum or dribble the ball forward to the opposition goal-line. Those who drove the scrum forward were known as 'chargers'. In contrast to the subsequent development of the game, forwards in the scrum stood upright and pushed, kicking the ball or their opponents' shins. Putting one's head down in a scrum was seen as an act of cowardice because it implied that the player was concerned for his own safety. Sometimes the brave, the foolish or the naïve would attempt to drive the ball through the middle of the scrum, thus incurring the pain of a severe hacking as his opponents took the opportunity to ruthlessly kick at his shins. Other players up, known as 'dodgers', would loiter on the edge of the scrummage, waiting for the ball to squirt out so as to be able to kick it to make extra yards. 'Foiking', or hooking the ball out of the scrum, usually at the side, was not a common occurrence and was viewed as tantamount to cheating. This was because the scrum was the focus of the game. As in soccer, forwards were the attacking players and their role was to drive the opposing scrummagers as far back as possible and then capitalise on their disarray by dribbling the ball. Backs were the defensive players, charged with defending the goal or kicking the ball to set up another scrum. The idea that the forwards would deliberately heel the ball out of the scrum for the backs would be seen as at best perverse and at worst cowardly.

Running with the ball in hand was allowed but it was a hazardous and usually short-lived activity. We have no way of knowing whether William Webb Ellis ever ran with the ball but we do know that Jem Mackie, a boy who attended the school in the late 1830s, became famous for doing so. His reputation may have been more for his bravery than his innovation.[4] William Arnold, Thomas Arnold's son, described the typical fate of a ball carrier: 'the hapless and too adventurous hero who first grasped the ball, and he who first dared to stay his course by his rough embrace, both roll on the ground, locked in each other's arms, the foundation of a pyramid of human flesh, giving vent to screams, yells and groans unutterable'.[5] Such groans may have become more widespread the longer a match went on without a goal being scored because there was no time limit to matches, the contest being won by the first side to score two goals. That this was more difficult than it might appear to modern eyes can be seen in rule twenty of the first set of published rules printed in 1845, which stated that 'all matches are drawn after five days, but after three if no goal has been kicked'.[6]

How different was the Rugby code of football from those played at other public schools? Not very. Each school had its idiosyncrasies and unique features, but by and large the similarities were greater than the differences. Handling the ball in some form was common to all public school codes of football. Eton's Field Game football rules allowed use of the hands to stop the ball, as did the rules of Charterhouse, Westminster and Winchester. These latter three, plus Shrewsbury, also allowed a player to catch the ball directly from a kick. There was no commonly accepted shape for a football. The oval ball used at Rugby was no more or less distinctive than the cylindrically shaped ball of Harrow or the small round ball of Eton. Rugby's scrum, seen as a feature unique of the rugby codes today, had its equivalent in Eton's 'bully' and Winchester's 'hot', in which significant numbers of players would collectively push and pull for possession of the ball. Even hacking, used to demonstrate the uniquely violent nature of Rugby school football, was widespread in other schools, where it was referred to as 'shinning'. In fact, the Rugby game's almost permanent scrummaging, lack of ball movement and difficulty in scoring led some contemporary commentators to suggest that it was related to Eton's 'Wall Game', a variation of the school's football in which two sets of continually scrummaging forwards attempt to propel the ball along a wall in a usually vain attempt to score a goal. 'We think we can trace in this very popular public school game the dim beginnings of Rugby football', wrote an Old Etonian in 1895.[7] So, although it would have been a matter of pride for public schoolboys to believe that their school's form of football was unique, the reality was that, until the 1860s, the various codes of school football had a great more in common with each other than the subsequent evolution of the modern codes of football might suggest.[8]

As the game began to spread and be played beyond Rugby in the 1850s and 1860s, the school's rules were varied and altered according to the tastes and preferences of players and their new clubs. One of the most common deviations from Rugby rules was to ban hacking, not least because it could have far more serious consequences for young men engaged in a professional career than for schoolboys. Richmond campaigned against hacking and were held to be responsible for the RFU outlawing it but they were not the only ones. Hull Football Club, founded in 1865 by local Old Rugbeians, allowed tripping of the man running with the ball but not hacking. Rochdale Hornets and Preston Grasshoppers played Rugby rules without hacking. Schools who took up the Rugby game also varied the rules. Marlborough banned hacking but otherwise played according to the Rugby rule book. Sizes of teams differed too. Schools tended to play with large numbers – for example, at Clifton forty-a-side was common – but clubs played anything from twenty-a-side to twelve-a-side, as Hull did against Gainsborough in the early 1870s, although fifteen-a-side had become the norm for club matches by the mid-1870s. No one, as far as is known, used Rugby School's convoluted method of converting a try into a goal. The school's rule forbidding the picking up of the ball unless it was bouncing was ignored by Blackheath, Woolwich and Sandhurst. At Blackheath School forwards were allowed to run downfield in front of the ball carrier, obstructing opponents who attempted to tackle him. The similarity of this tactic to 'blocking' in American football also demonstrates the fluidity of the sport's rules at the time and supports the idea that the changes that led to different codes of football, such as American and Australian, were not so much specifically national versions of football but part of the generalised discussion about different methods of playing a style of football that allowed the use of the hands.[9]

But despite these differences, the clubs that played the Rugby game were united on the centrality of the scrum to the sport. RFU secretary Arthur Guillemard described the main feature of play in 1877, explaining that as soon as the ball-carrying player was brought to the ground with a tackle,

> the forwards of each side hurry up and a scrummage is instantly formed, each ten facing their opponents's goal, packed round the ball, shoulder to shoulder, leg to leg, as tight as they can stand, the twenty thus forming a round compact mass with the ball in the middle. Directly the holder of the ball has succeeded in forcing

it down to the ground, he shouts 'Down' and business may be commenced at once.[10]

In this description of the scrum one can see both the origins of American football's use of the term 'down' for a completed tackle and the antecedent of rugby league's play the ball rule.

The centrality of the set-piece scrum to the early game inevitably led to problems, as depicted in England and Richmond forward Charles Gurdon's description of a typical scrum of the early 1870s:

> It would last, if skilfully manoeuvred (as we then thought), ten minutes or more, sometimes swaying this way, sometimes that; and on special occasions, when one side was much heavier than the other, this rotund mass would gravitate safely and unbroken, some thirty or forty yards towards the goal-line of the weaker side, leaving a dark muddy track to mark its course.[11]

'Straight ahead propulsion' was the primary tactic used in the scrum. Sometimes the most central forward would grip the ball between his feet while his fellow-forwards concentrated on pushing him through the opposing pack of forwards, allowing him to dribble the ball forward once they had broken through their opponents. A related variation that appeared in the 1870s was for forwards to form up in pairs, 'two and two', behind each other to concentrate their pushing on the centre of their opponents' pack.[12] There were generally few opportunities for backs, not least because there were so few of them. In a team of fifteen or twenty, there would be two full-backs, two half-backs and one three-quarter, although two three-quarters gained popularity in the mid-1870s. The rest would be forwards.[13] Passing the ball was extremely rare.

By 1875 these tendencies had brought the game to an impasse. 'How much longer are we to see forwards chosen simply for weight and solidity, and not for knowledge of the game or skill in its practice?' asked *Bell's Life*. 'How much longer are we to be wearied by monotonous shoving matches instead of spirited scrummages, and disgusted at seeing a 14 stone Hercules straining every muscle to move an opposing mountain of flesh a yard or two further from his goal-line, whilst he is all the time blissfully oblivious of the fact that the ball is lying undisturbed at his feet.'[14] Part of the problem was the fact that grown men were playing a game that had been originally developed by and for adolescent schoolboys. A scrum made up of various-sized youths was a very different proposition to one comprising heavy, mature men. But, more importantly, adult clubs, free of the restrictions and exigencies of school life, were committed to winning, and that meant that tactics were developed to ensure victory, or avoid defeat at the very least. The amateur ideal that it was not whether one won or lost but how one played the game was never mentioned during this period when the game remained exclusively middle class.

To lift the game out of the mire in which it found itself, often quite literally, proposals were raised to lower the number of players in a team to fifteen. In 1875 the Oxford versus Cambridge varsity match was first played fifteen-a-side and the following season international matches became fifteen-a-side, although strangely the law was not formally changed until 1892. As well as endless scrums, the game also suffered from the fact that matches were decided solely on goals scored. This led to the problem that a team could dominate play, score numerous unconverted tries yet still lose to a side that managed to score a lucky goal. A call for matches to be decided by a points system rather than just goals had been rejected by the committee that drew up the RFU's first set of rules in 1871. A proposal that goals should count as ten points and tries as five was voted down at the 1875 annual general meeting of the RFU, but similar systems were already used in the north of England and in the London Hospitals' Cup, which began in the 1874–5 season. Typically these unofficial scoring systems awarded the most points for goals converted from tries, less to unconverted tries, and single points, known as 'minors' against a side which touched the ball down behind its own goal-line, known by some as 'rouges', and to a side that managed to kick the ball over the dead-ball line. Some also offered a point for a 'poster', when an attempt at a goal saw the ball miss but hit the post.[15] The rouge continues today in Canadian football and Australian Rules still awards a point to a ball that strikes the goal post, fossils of rugby pre-history.

Arthur Budd, a future president of the RFU, later remarked that the change to fifteen-a-side 'marked the dawn of modern scientific football'.[16] It also heralded the start of almost two decades of radical and far-reaching reforms of the game, which were intimately connected to rugby's growth as a mass spectator sport. The move to fifteen-a-side led to a number of key structural alterations to the way the game was played. It meant that scrums no longer lasted for minutes, because it was easier for the ball to come out of the scrum. Forwards now started to put their heads down in the scrum to see where the ball was. The frequency with which the ball now came out from the scrum meant that forwards began to look for opportunities to break away from the scrum and dribble the ball downfield independently. And the danger of a forward breaking away with the ball at his feet meant that a third three-quarter had to be added in order to defend against the quick breakaway. Moreover, and to the horror of traditionalists who tried unsuccessfully to persuade the RFU to outlaw the practice, teams began to deliberately heel the ball out of the scrum in order to start a charge of backs and loose forwards up the field.[17] Wheeling the scrum also emerged as a tactic, as teams with an extra player in the scrum, following the withdrawal of an opposing forward to the three-quarter line, realised that they could turn the weaker set of forwards around.[18]

Above all, the change opened the way for the development of the passing game. The speed with which the ball left the scrum and the ease with which forwards could peel away from the pack offered a quick-thinking half-back the chance to move the ball quickly out to his three-quarter or loose forward. The process was helped significantly in 1878 when the rules were changed so that a tackled player, who, as we have seen, would previously hold the ball until his forwards gathered around him, was forced to release the ball immediately the tackle was completed. This meant that forwards now had to keep up with the play, rather than take their time to scrum down, increasing their fitness and expanding the available space on the field. As with many other aspects of the history of the game, a great deal of mythology surrounds the origins of the passing game. Richmond's Alan Rotherham is usually credited with inventing the pass from the half-back to the three-quarter when playing for Oxford University in 1882, but it was clearly happening before this date. Dewsbury won the Yorkshire Cup in 1881 with half-back Charlie Marsden passing to his two three-quarters, Alf and Mark Newsome, the latter later becoming a president of the RFU, a tactic they had begun to use at least a year before. J.H. Payne, the Lancashire half-back, was also noted for his passing ability in the early 1880s. At Cheltenham College in the 1870s, a move was developed whereby a forward would peel away from the scrum, take a pass from the half-back and then throw a long pass to a three-quarter who could capitalise on the overlap that the forward had created.[19]

Tactical advances on the field and innovation in the rules of the game became the hallmark of the following decade. Many of these were spurred by the tremendous expansion of the game that occurred in the 1880s, increasing both the pressure to make the game a spectacle and the need for the rule book to keep pace with the changing nature of the game. This could be seen at an international level, where the Welsh led the way with the introduction of the four three-quarter system in the mid-1880s, and at local level, where the importance of county and club cup tournaments led to players developing new and original tactics. In the north, the huge popularity of the Yorkshire Cup, in which crowds for the final regularly overshadowed those of the FA Cup final, propelled the game forward to new levels of sophistication. When Thornes, a team from a mining village near Wakefield, won the Yorkshire Cup in 1882, they did so by employing a wing-forward to protect their scrum-half, using fast heeling from the scrum, and allocating specific positions in the scrum and line-out to their forwards, anticipating the 1905 All Blacks by a generation.[20]

The use of four three-quarters did not take quite as long to become widespread. It had first been developed in Wales in the mid-1880s but it was only around 1890 that it began to be taken seriously in England.[21] In February of that year the Welsh had beaten England by a try to nil using four three-quarters for the first time. Despite Welsh enthusiasm for it, the new configuration did not immediately find favour in England, not least because England won the next two matches with Wales and outscored them in tries in the 1893 loss. But by 1892 a number of clubs, including Blackheath, Oldham and Dewsbury had begun using it and both sides employed it in the annual North versus South match that year. The catalyst for its wholesale adoption, however, was England's 24–3 demolition of the Welsh in 1894, when the Dicky Lockwood-led Englishmen used it for the first time with such devastating effect. Although a few clubs persisted with the old system until the early 1900s, no team that aspired to be successful ever again took the field with less than seven backs.

The increasing importance, and spectator appeal, of try-scoring led in 1886 to the award of points for tries and goals. This finally meant that matches were to be decided by the team scoring the highest number of points, rather than the one scoring goals, regardless of the number of tries scored. Previously tries only had value if both teams scored the same number of goals. Now a goal from a try or a dropped goal was worth three points and a try one. Minor points were not counted in the official scoring system. Despite this change, the value of goals still substantially outweighed tries. In 1889 this situation was exacerbated by penalty goals being awarded two points, further undermining the value of a try. Prior to this, a goal could not be scored directly from a penalty.[22] But the scoring system lagged behind the desire for spectacle of the huge crowds now attending rugby matches. For most spectators, especially in the north, the passing game, combinations between players and the scoring of tries were now the most attractive features of the sport, as a Yorkshire rugby correspondent argued:

> a try in the vast majority of instances is the most deserving point in the game, and calls for the greatest exertion on the part of the team

as a whole. On the other hand, the responsibility of placing a goal is an individual responsibility and is attended by none of the combined action which forms one of the chief attractions of the game. Goal kicking is a science and should be encouraged, I agree, but its value in the past has been, and in some respects still is, exaggerated . . . We have to see the scoring put on such a basis as will properly indicate the respective strengths of the teams.[23]

In 1891 the RFU partially acceded to these demands and once again changed the points system, awarding two points for a try and five points for a goal converted from a try – something that it had declared would 'never be sanctioned' in 1886.[24] But, giving with one hand it took away with another, raising the value of the dropped goal to four points. Two years later in 1894, the value of a try was raised to three points, making it equal in value to all goals apart from those scored from a drop-kick.

It was not only internal pressure that was pushing rugby to become a more open and spectacular game. The growth of soccer, fuelled by the tremendous success of the FA Cup and the Football League, formed in 1888, now meant that rugby was being seriously threatened by the round ball code. Many in rugby felt that the game was being pushed aside in its previous strongholds of Liverpool, Manchester and the North-East because soccer was easier to follow and the ball could always be seen by spectators. One solution was to emulate soccer and, against the wishes of the RFU, introduce league competitions into the game, as happened in Yorkshire and Lancashire in the early 1890s. But, more fundamentally, rugby had to be able to compete aesthetically by promoting tries over goals and reducing the number of scrums and line-outs. The game had to become more attractive to players and spectators alike. In 1892, James Miller, the president of the Yorkshire Rugby Union, hailed the move to fifteen-a-side and the introduction of four three-quarters, and went on to argue that

the game had now reached a period when another radical change must be considered, and that was the reduction of players from fifteen to thirteen. By lessening the number of forwards taking part in a game, he was convinced it would be a reform which would have precedence in the immediate future and the adoption of which would bring the game nearer the perfected state. It was clear to him that the end of the 'pushing age' had been reached and instead of admiring the physique and pushing power of those giants which took part in the game in the early stages, at any rate in the future they would be able to admire the skilful and scientific play of the game. He thought the adoption of this rule would enable the game in many parts of England to maintain an equal fight with the Association game for popular favour.[25]

The next steps in the evolution of rugby appeared to be emerging.

But the changes of the 1880s, let alone proposals such as Miller's, had profoundly disturbed many of the leaders of the RFU. They had been educated, not least at school, to believe that the game was about the scoring of goals and the importance of the scrum. Aubrey Spurling complained that the fourth three-quarter signified that forwards had become 'the servants and not the masters of the backs'. Arthur Budd regretted the increasing importance placed on try-scoring: 'the very fact that try-getters are plentiful while goal-droppers are scarce shows that the latter art is very much more difficult of acquirement. Now this being so, why, I should like to ask, ought the more skilful piece of play to be depreciated, while a premium is placed on mere speed of foot?' In 1896 he even proposed turning the clock back and making heeling the ball out of the scrum illegal.[26] Budd and his fellow traditionalists had been pushed much further down the road of reform than they had ever desired.

Thus when the split came in 1895 over the issue of broken-time payments – another proposal emanating from those, such as Miller, who were pushing for the reform of the rules – the leadership of the RFU also drew a line in the sand on the question of the rules of play. The rapid evolution of the game – which in less than twenty years had brought tries to the fore, given rise to the passing game, and started to move the sport away from its reliance on scrimmaging – was stopped dead in its tracks. It was to be another fifty years before the scoring system was amended, when dropped goals were reduced from four to three points in 1948. And another twenty-three years would elapse before a try would earn more points than a goal. The evolutionary process that had been snuffed out in rugby union would be continued by the renegade clubs of rugby league.

From Wellington to Wakefield

Although the purge of the northern clubs from the RFU removed the main engine for reform, the desire to make the game more attractive and move the focus away from goal-kicking and scrummaging continued to be expressed by many of those who remained loyal. Cambridge rugger 'Blue' and Test cricketer Frank Mitchell, as zealous an opponent of professionalism as could be found, called for the value of penalty goals to be reduced to two points and dropped goals to three. Wavell Wakefield wanted to get rid of the line-out, while Adrian Stoop doubted the usefulness of direct kicking into touch. As a wide-ranging debate in *Rugby Football Weekly* demonstrated in late 1923, many lesser figures in the game wanted similar reforms, among them a reduction in the number of players in a team.[27]

Among those lesser figures, at least in the eyes of the RFU, were the leaders of the game in Australia and New Zealand. Both countries had historically favoured the running game and valued the scoring of tries over goals. And in both cases internal tensions over financial reward to players led to serious splits in 1907 that resulted in the creation of rugby league competitions. Pressure from league coupled with a natural affinity for open rugby resulted in an eagerness to reform the playing of the game. Representative of this feeling was Colonel G.F.C. Campbell, the vice-president of the New Zealand Rugby Union, who in 1920 called for a fourteen-a-side game: 'alterations in the laws of the game will not however have the effect of making the game more open unless the number of players, especially those in the pack, is reduced'. The arrival of league in New Zealand had given rise to extensive calls for rule changes and in Auckland, where league was strongest, the provincial union had introduced a series of reforms as early as 1916, including a ban on direct kicking into touch. Moreover, antipodeans on both sides of the Tasman Sea allowed the use of substitutes and teams to return to the dressing rooms at half-time, both anathema to the RFU. Indeed, such was the gulf that W.L. Sinclair confidently predicted in the *Athletic News* at the end of the First World War 'in very little while we may expect to see Union and League united' in the southern hemisphere.[28] Less than a year after the armistice, the NZRU, supported by the New South Wales Rugby Union (then the *de facto* governing body of the Australian game), had proposed to the RFU a series of rule changes designed to speed up the game and also to relax the amateur regulations. Additionally, they called for the establishment of an Imperial Rugby Board with representatives of the three southern hemisphere 'colonies' sitting alongside those of the four 'home' nations. The RFU refused to countenance such change.[29]

The Australian and New Zealand rugby unions, deferential down to their socks towards all things British, backed away from confrontation. In exchange, the RFU, through the International Board, allowed 'dispensations' that enabled both countries to forbid direct kicking into touch from inside the twenty-five yards line, although this was withdrawn in 1931.[30] But tensions continued to simmer and the All Blacks unbeaten tour of the UK in the 1924–25 season highlighted differing rule interpretations, especially around the scrum, and conceptions of how the game should be played. These came to a head on the 1930 British Isles tour (they were not yet known as the 'Lions') to Australasia. Although comprised of players from all four home nations, the tour was entirely organised by the RFU and managed by former president James Baxter. Baxter had a reputation for what could euphemistically be described as 'plain speaking' but would be simple rudeness to those on the receiving end. Certainly that is how his hosts viewed his manners. On the first match of the tour, the British were dumbfounded to see the Wanganui players head back to their dressing room at half-time, contravening RFU regulations. They were also disturbed to see prominent All Blacks appearing in advertisements for products, contrary to the RFU's rules on professionalism. But most of all they were shocked at the New Zealanders use of the free-standing wing-forward or 'rover', who fed the scrum and shielded his scrum-half to allow quicker passing of the ball from the base of the scrum. At an official dinner, Baxter implied that Cliff Porter, the All Blacks captain who played as a rover, was a cheat, the worst possible insult to a British gentleman, which the New Zealanders most definitely believed themselves to be.

The All Blacks forwards packed down in the scrum in a 2–3–2 formation, with two men in the front row, three in the second and two in the third, with the wing-forward where the scrum-half would traditionally stand at the side of the scrum. The system was believed to allow more focused pushing and also, because the scrum-half was protected, to facilitate quick ball from the scrum. This method of opening up play from the scrum was very similar to that of the Northern Union, which in its first season had banned the defending scrum-half from going beyond his own front row until his opposite number had taken the ball from the scrum, thus providing more time to get the ball to the backs. The New Zealand scrum formation had been used to great effect on the 1905 and 1924 tours to Britain, so it should have come as no surprise to the tourists. But many in England had always felt that the wing-forward was unsportsmanlike at best and downright illegal at worst. Prominent among them was Baxter, who in 1926 had described it as 'a menace to the game'.[31] The fact that the British lost the test series 3–1 may also have exacerbated Baxter's antipathy. On his return he had little difficulty in persuading the RFU to change the scrummage rules to outlaw the wing-forward and the 2–3–2 formation. In somewhat typical dissembling fashion, the rule change did not formally outlaw the two-forward front row; instead, it insisted that the 'centre player' (the term 'hooker' had not come into everyday use at that time) could initially strike for the ball only with the foot furthest from the scrum-half putting the ball in.[32] This meant that a two-man front row would be completely unbalanced and easily pushed off the ball, rendering a two-forward front row useless.

This caused considerable dissatisfaction in New Zealand. 'Why should we give up our scrum formation, seeing that it is the best that has been devised, to please the English Rugby Union?' asked an outraged 'Old Timer'. 'It will make the game much slower than at present, and this will be serious, more particularly in Auckland, where league is so strong.' In Australia, A.G. Moyes wrote in the Sydney *Daily Telegraph* that 'the sooner these rules which make lazy thinkers and lazy footballers are thrown overboard the better. We want to see in action men properly attuned to the fray, playing the game of football, not slowing it down to such an extent that it is a paradise for half-baked forwards.' The fact that the IB had also withdrawn the dispensations on kicking directly into touch only increased Antipodean frustration.[33] But the deferential imperative always outweighed the reforming zeal of the Australian and New Zealand officials, blinding them to a truth that was obvious to their less reverential countrymen:

> Nothing has lost the English sportsman so many good games as his conservatism. And nothing has incensed him more with his rivals. This aspect of British sport has to be studied on the ground to be understood. So long as styles do not change – in boxing, in rowing, in football, in cricket – the Englishman can make himself good and can sooner or later get to the top of the tree and stay there. But when his opponents begin to introduce new strokes or to play new formations he is lost. But that is not the worst. He resents it. He feels that his opponent is hitting below the belt, and is not playing the game. He takes up a position of righteous indignation and refuses point blank to adapt himself to the change.[34]

The great irony was that many clubs in England had actually started to adopt the All Blacks system in the late 1900s and it had gained a certain vogue in the 1920s. Just months after the 1905 All Blacks had ended their tour, former Moseley and England forward J.H. Roger had speculated in *The Book of Football* that the seven-forward game represented the future of the sport, comparing its importance to the introduction of four three-quarters a generation previously. A number of teams, such as Old Leysians, actually put the theory into practice before the First World War. Although not an innovator in the scrum, Adrian Stoop's advocacy of running the ball rather than kicking it, which was based on the All Blacks system of playing two outside-halves and three three-quarters, had made Harlequins the most potent attacking force in England in the late 1900s. After the war, the seven-man scrum grew in popularity, most notably at Leicester where they began to play the formation in 1919. The club's adoption of the system was inspired by the fact that in Alf Bates and England international Tim Taylor they had two of the best outside-halves in England, and so simply decided to play with eight backs. In 1925 the Leicestershire county side, always dominated by Welford Road players, won the County Championship with the same configuration. The year before, Oxford had been on the verge of using the seven-man scrum for the Varsity match but felt they would be disadvantaged by the heavier Cambridge pack. Indeed, the fact that many teams now played with seven forwards was used by a correspondent to *Rugby Football* in 1924 to advocate a reduction in the number of players.[35]

A crucial factor in allowing the RFU to dismiss calls for reform during the 1920s was the success of the England side. Stoop's development of the passing game had come to full fruition for the English national team in the seasons immediately before the First World War, when the side had won two championships followed by back-to-back grand slams. Based on fast three-quarters and free-flowing passing movements, the side had vanquished all-comers just before the cataclysm of the war had engulfed Europe, taking with it much of the team. The success continued after the war, as England won grand slams in 1921, 1923 and 1924, losing only three matches – one against the All Blacks – in the first five seasons of the decade. Another grand slam followed in 1928, the sole interruption to Scotland's dominance of the Five Nations Championship in the late 1920s. The architect of this success was another Harlequins' player, William Wavell Wakefield. Educated at Sedbergh before going into the Royal Air Force, Wakefield brought an athleticism and a tactical planning to forward play that had not previously been seen in English rugby union. He almost single-handedly established a rugby tradition for the newest of the British services and then moved on to Pembroke College, Cambridge, where he set about moving the Light Blues away from a rather hale and hearty amateurism to an approach that was professional in spirit if not in remuneration. He aggressively scouted the colleges for players, re-ordered the fixture list to ensure that the team peaked at the right time and wrote a handbook of how Cambridge should play the game. He kept detailed records of all games and players, insisted on the necessity of training for every player, and focused training on movements and tactics, insisting that personal fitness was the responsibility of the individual player. In a move widely seen as tantamount to professionalism, he even introduced numbers on to players' jerseys for the first time at a Varsity match, as much for his own analysis of his team as for the benefit of spectators. The power of his teams, in many ways like that of the All Blacks, was based on having back-rowers (known as 'winging-forwards' to distinguish them from the New Zealand detached roving wing-forwards) who could cover every inch of ground defensively, then run, pass and back-up like three-quarters when on the offensive.[36]

As much as any tactical or organisational improvements, Wakefield's greatest innovation was himself. He defined what a modern back-row forward should be. Very quick – he was the RAF's 440 yards champion in 1920 – and extraordinarily aggressive, he was the rock from which every subsequent back-rower was carved. Scrum-halves and fly-halves were there to be devoured by him and his rampaging fellow back-rowers. As we have seen, he believed that the key to success was to establish 'moral authority' over the opposing team, and he was not above the use of fist or boot to do so. Moreover, he believed in what would now be termed the game plan, preparing his team in detail as to the strengths and weaknesses of his opponents. Each player had a role given to them; Wakefield even followed the Antipodeans in assigning each forward a particular role in the scrum and at the line-out. As he explained, he employed a 'deep theory underlying every move and counter-move on the field, and to learn and apply this theory successfully a man must have all his wits about him. . . . I would go so far as to say that it calls for quicker and deeper thought than any other game.' His views on building a winning side led him to reject New Zealand's scrum and wing-forward innovations. When playing for Leicester in the mid-1920s he was never comfortable with their seven-forward tactics and constantly fiddled with the formation, occasionally playing with four in the front row and three in the second row. In the final analysis, his vision of how rugby should be played was much more conventional than that of reformers Down Under, being based on a highly organised and modernised version of the traditional English virtues of hard scrummaging and forward domination.[37] In many ways, Wakefield, an engineering graduate and a qualified chemist, personified the emerging technocratic middle classes of the interwar years, whose scientific and technical skills allowed them to bring new expertise and techniques to industry and government administration, without funda-mentally altering the shape of social and economic structures. Wakefield's career in business and in parliament – he became a Conservative MP in 1935 – summed up this experience. On the boards of television and airline companies, he was also chairman of the Parliamentary Scientific Committee in the 1950s. Perhaps it is unnecessary to note that, following his retirement as a player, he became a bastion of conservatism as a member of the RFU Committee.

The spirit of the game

Despite the ultimately conventional nature of Wakefield's methods, they were still viewed with concern by many leaders of the RFU. Indeed, the early 1930s saw the RFU embark on a sustained campaign to roll back many of the changes that had occurred since the war. As well as reining-in the Dominions, the RFU sought to stop the advance of 'specialisation' in the game, by which they meant players being assigned specific positions in the scrum. This included not only the wing-forward but also what was becoming known as the hooker (for a time the position was known as the centre-forward), and was extended to encourage a return to the old scrummaging system of 'first-up, first-down'. Shortly before he became RFU president in 1926, James Baxter denounced specialisation in the scrum as being responsible for a deterioration in forward play since the war. Frank Mitchell warned against the trend in a review of Wakefield's book *Rugger* in 1928 and at the start of the 1932–33 season the RFU sent a circular to all clubs expressing its concern at this development and calling for a return to the old scrummaging methods. It also wrote to the Headmasters' Conference, the association of private schools, asking that games masters should follow its lead.[38]

Although etiquette forbade the critics from naming what they perceived to be the source of the problem, it was clear that the target was Wakefield's innovations. Although his tactics had originally overwhelmed opponents, as they began to be emulated by other teams matches became dominated by defensive back-row play. As Howard Marshall pointed out in relation to the Varsity match in the interwar years, the laboratory in which Wakefield's schemes were most intensely used, 'the midfield area was mined and enfiladed by quick-breaking specialist back row forwards and tries were scored by the calculated use of the crosskick or the punt ahead or the swift heel from the loose maul. Defence overcame orthodox attack, and the decay of real scrummaging set in.' The back-row forward had, he complained, 'got somewhat out of hand'.[39] The desire to receive or stop quick ball from the scrum led to interminable problems in putting the ball into the scrum, as front rows sought to stop their opponents getting the ball, and the keenness of the back-rowers to close down the half-backs led to constant penalties for off-side. The combination of back-row dominance and rule-changes designed to re-assert the centrality of the scrum meant that try-scoring dried up. In the first ten years after the war, England scored 107 tries. In the following decade that total almost halved to fifty-seven, reaching a nadir in 1939 when the team managed to share the Five Nations title despite scoring only a single try.

Reforms, whether from Wakefield or the southern hemisphere, were also viewed with suspicion because they seemed to smack of professionalism. Specialisation and the increasing speed of the game were seen as enemies of the amateur tradition. A schoolmaster writing in *Rugby Football* in the 1923–4 season spoke for many when he commented, 'the prevailing craze is to make the game faster. I should myself like to see it slowed down again. Why should people be compelled to keep in strict training for an afternoon's sport, as though they were paid gladiators?' This indeed was the crux of the matter. For most English rugby union players and spectators, the purpose of the game was neither elite performance nor the pursuit of excellence. It was a social activity that helped keep one healthy. 'The game is not intended for highly trained athletes, but for reasonably fit men who like their exercise on a Saturday afternoon. It changes subtly when the limelight is turned upon it', explained Howard Marshall in 1936. Moreover, the idea that the sport should be made more attractive to spectators was anathema. The RFU believed that 'nothing should interfere with the spirit of the game', vice-president Frank Potter-Irwin told an Old Alleynians dinner in 1926. 'They had no interest in making the game a spectacle and less of a real recreation, which was its original function. They did not consider the spectator as the real reason of the game.'[40]

The tactical sophistication of the game was also felt to be a threat to schools' rugby, where it was viewed as a vital character-building part of a good education. Throughout the 1920s there were accusations of foul play, biased refereeing and coaching from the sidelines. Much anxiety was expressed at the fact that private schools had become intensely competitive and that some, such as Felsted and Sedbergh, had adopted coaching methods similar to those used by Wakefield at Cambridge. These two schools had recruited first-class players such as H.L.V. Day and G.H. Todd as games masters, 'a title which makes the older generation shudder and which savours of professionalism' in the words of W.D. Gibbon.[41] Gibbon was writing in *First Steps to Rugby Football*, a training manual written for schoolboys in 1922. This was one of twenty-seven such handbooks published between 1919 and 1930 (compared with just ten for the immensely more popular soccer), each of which contained detailed and lengthy expositions on the skills, tactics and strategies of the game. While they all religiously stressed the importance of the amateur ideal, their focus on studying and improving the technicalities of the sport carried the unspoken implication that mere enjoyment was not all there was to the sport.

Such developments were seen by many as undermining the 'spirit of the game'. This was the essence by which the game should be played. But, as we have seen over the questions of amateurism and character, the 'spirit' was impossible to define. Even at the level of how the game should be played, differences arose over whether the scoring of tries or the kicking of goals was the object of the game, or whether the fast passing game or the traditional heavy scrummaging battle was the purest method of playing the sport. Of course, this also changed over time. Each generation assumed their method of playing the game represented its true nature. In the 1870s the idea that a forward should run with the ball was felt to be 'utterly and radically wrong'.[42] In the 1890s the conception that tries were more valuable than goals was commonly scorned. Indeed, the 1920s' idea that rugby was a passing game, with backs and forwards both handling and backing-up and kicking kept to a minimum, was originally the belief of the northern clubs that went on to form the Northern Union.

In fact, the spirit of the game was not an eternal and unchanging essence but the expression of the shared social assumptions of the English middle-class males who played and administered the sport. As with the question of the acceptability of violence in the game, the 'spirit' was not expressed in the written rules of the sport but in the acceptance of a common set of values and attitudes that they had been taught at home and at school. It was not therefore necessary for players to know or understand the rules in any great detail. Alec Waugh, a keen rugby fan despite the jaundiced view of the public school system he expressed in *The Loom of Youth*, captured this when he wrote that every player 'knows that the game is only worth the playing as long as he can trust his opponents to keep within the spirit of the law. That they should keep within the letter of the law would be a vain and unpro-fitable expectation, vain because only one player in ten has ever read the rules; unprofitable because it is unlikely that the referee will be conducting the game in accordance with the latest rulings of the Rugby Union.' The idea that the rules themselves were not important was a commonly expressed idea up until the 1950s. 'How many internationals', asked E.B. Osborn in 1936, 'who have been playing since they were small boys, could score 50 out of 100 marks in an examination on the rules?' Indeed, it was often a matter for self-congratulation that the game was not played strictly to the rules: 'the game is so complex and the laws relatively simple, the opportunities for petty evasion and obstruction are many, and of all games rugby football is pre-eminently the one which must be played to the spirit rather than the letter of the law', argued Howard Marshall.[43]

There was an element of smug philistinism in this attitude, a belief that even the dullest public school-educated male instinctively understood the game better than someone from a less exalted social background who had actually taken the trouble to learn the rules. This was indeed believed by many in the game to be the case. 'If from early childhood the working man's self-training makes him deal only with letter of the criminal law, why should you expect him to read into the laws of Rugby football more than what the letter of them would seem to contain?' asked Philip Trevor. For Trevor, the essence of the game was the 'public school spirit', which only those who had the privilege of a private education could understand or appreciate. Taking this attitude at its most absurd, J.M. Kilburn, the rugby union and cricket correspondent of the *Yorkshire Post*, suggested that ignorance of the written rules of the game actually made for better players: 'there is, indeed, something to be said for the theory that the player who does not know the rules in all their detail will not seek to circumvent them', a theory that did not extend to players who innocently transgressed the RFU's amateur regulations.[44]

In such a culture, referees were not expected to implement the rules literally. They 'interpret the rules more by "the spirit of the game" than by the bold letter of the law', the *Boy's Own Paper* told its young readers in 1920. Many of their decisions revolved around the question of intention. In many cases, the awarding of a scrum or free-kick was dependent on whether the referee thought the offending player had intentionally infringed the rules. And, of course, it was difficult to believe that a player of character would ever intentionally seek to break the rules. It was not until 1919 that a penalty goal was scored in the Varsity match, and even that, for off-side at a scrum, was the cause of much controversy.[45] The importance of intentionality to the game was also captured by Waugh:

> That word 'intentional' is the most important of the three or four odd thousand words that go into the construction of the rules. It is a key to the spirit of the game; it shows why the game can only be played only by those who are playing it for its own sake simply; shows why there can be no professionals; shows also perhaps why it is that eighty per cent of the men at an International are present or past public schoolboys; why the rugger world has come to a kind of family party.[46]

And this was the crux of the matter. By placing the informal appreciation of the rules above their formal application – favouring the spirit rather than the letter of the law – the sport was privileging the insider who understood the implicit unwritten conventions of the sport over the outsider whose understanding was based on the explicit written rules. Such unwritten codes of behaviour were central to middle-class culture, especially in the professions. In the City of London, 'Everybody tried to obey the code. If your client tried to cut corners and break the code, you stopped him and directed him back to the proper course of business ethics', explained a stockbroker who started work in the city in the 1940s. 'Now, of course, the code is not a code, it's a law. People are paid to find ways round the law, so that the difference is that instead of being paid to keep a straight course, many people are now being paid to avoid the penalties of keeping to the strict letter of the law.'[47]

This clash between the informal code and the formal rules could be seen in the disputes with the northern clubs in the 1880s, in which the northerners could not understand why the RFU refused to introduce penalties for rule infringements. It was not until 1882 that a penalty kick was awarded for infringing the off-side rule but a goal could not be scored directly from a penalty. A penalty goal for off-side was allowed in 1888 and in 1892 penalties were introduced for all infringements. Before 1882, there was no official sanction against those who broke the rules, but informally it was understood that the miscreant could be hacked below the knee.[48] Although there was discussion about introducing a penalty kick in the mid-1870s, it was only the growth of the game and the need for detailed rules that could be understood by everyone that forced the RFU to bring in formal written regulations. But formal rules, because they were separate and distinct from the people who led the game, could be used to undermine the RFU's authority, as had happened in the 1880s. Thus outsiders, such as the northern clubs or the Australians and New Zealanders, who did not share the same cultural code as those who led the game were a threat to what Waugh described as the family party. And so, inadvertently, were innovators such as Wakefield, who pushed the limits of the rules to breaking point in pursuit of victory, thus undermining the shared common culture that united the whole sport, from the fourth XV of the lowliest Old Boys' club to the grandest of England sides running out at Twickenham.

New times, old problems

The game continued to be oppressed by forward domination and kicking throughout the 1950s. It was a decade book-ended by Howard Marshall's 1951 observation that 'it may be that temporarily we have reached another period of stalemate, where defence is in the ascendant', and by Wilf Wooller's 1961 comment that 'the balance of power lies too strongly in the hands of eight forwards. Some redress is necessary to swing back the balance towards the seven backs'. No better illustration of the problem could be seen than in the performance of England. In 1957 they won the Grand Slam for the first time since 1928, scoring seven tries. They won the Five Nations somewhat luckily again the following year, scoring a mere five tries. But in 1959 they did not manage to score even a single try.[49]

There was no lack of ideas to improve things. New Zealand proposed in 1953 that penalty goals should be reduced to two points. The following year the Australians suggested that kicking the ball directly into touch should be punished by a scrum from where the ball was kicked. BBC radio commentator G.V. Wynne-Jones called for the number of forwards to be reduced to six. Wavell Wakefield thought that penalty goals should be made harder and also wanted to see an end to direct kicking into touch. The International Board made significant changes to the rules in 1954 to stop the deliberate collapsing of the scrum and to clean up the line-out. It returned to the rules again in 1958, once more to reform the scrum and to speed up play through a variety of minor measures.[50] But far from opening up the game, the IB reforms added to the problem, not least by significantly adding to the technicalities of the scrum. It was not coincidence that the French, frustrated with their failure to win the Five Nations despite the strength of their club competition, finally found success in 1959 by emulating English forward play, rather than by playing the open game that supposedly marked the essence of the Gallic game. Scrum work, argued the leading French rugby writer Denis Lalanne, was the basis for winning rugby: 'we know where rugby begins and where it must begin all over again. It certainly does not begin in the back row. It begins in the FRONT ROW.' [emphasis in original][51]

Despite the lack of improvement on the field, the 1950s and 1960s probably saw more discussion about the rules than at any other time since the 1880s. This opening of debate was caused both by the declining authority of the RFU in the International Board and by the increasing importance of international competition. The RFU could no longer insist on its view of the game being accepted by fiat. In 1948 Australia, New Zealand and South Africa had been given seats on the International Board and, as their countries' own relationship with the British government changed, so too did their own assertiveness. This was especially true of South Africa, hitherto the most deferential of the three towards the RFU. By the late 1950s, the South African Rugby Board had begun to challenge many of the traditions of the game, not least the purity of its amateurism. As well as allowing replacements during the 1958 tour of South Africa by France, contrary to the regulations, in 1963 SARB introduced a series of 'experimental' rules designed to open the game up. These included no direct-kicking into touch from inside the twenty-five yard line, backs to retire ten yards at set-pieces and reform of the line-out. To some extent these were a domestic response to the growing popularity of soccer and the emergence of rugby league in South Africa. They were withdrawn when it became clear such radical changes would cause serious conflict with the IB but they were indicative of the strength of feeling for reform.[52] In 1966 RFU president Gus Walker felt compelled to lament that 'the standard of play in top games in the two or three seasons has been in general – but certainly not exclusively – disappointing' caused by a reliance on kicking over passing, and the following year the IB issued a statement noting that standards of play were falling.[53]

By the late 1960s the pressure for change had become irresistible, not least because of the increasing importance of television to the game. In 1968 the International Board finally allowed replacements to be used, although Australia and New Zealand had used them domestically and, as a one-off, in their 1907 test series. In 1970 kicking the ball directly into touch from outside the kicker's twenty-five was punished by the ball being returned to the opposition at the point from which it was kicked. The following year the value of a try was raised to four points, making it worth more than a goal for the first time in the history of rugby union. In 1972 the RFU's laws committee even discussed abolishing the line-out.[54] The rule changes appear to have made some difference. England scored twenty-six tries in the last five seasons in which it was worth three points and thirty-eight in the first five seasons of the four point try. But the changes were overshadowed by the growing importance of the international game, which effectively meant that the desire for open rugby was often cancelled out by the imperative of winning. This could also be seen in the domestic game, as the introduction of the national club knock-out competition in the 1971–2 season demonstrated, most notably in the final when Gloucester kept the ball tight despite facing a Moseley side reduced to twelve players. Denis Shuttleworth's hope that the RFU's support for the introduction of the John Smith Merit Table in 1985, the first incarnation of the league system, would 'get rid of the ponderous, limited, unambitious, heavy infantry style prevalent over recent years' was not fulfilled.

This should not have been surprising. English rugby had always been based on a forward-dominated game that, at the international level, subordinated style to the necessity of victory. The idea that dashing three-quarters were the spirit of the England team had not been true since the 1914 side led by Ronald Poulton-Palmer. Indeed, one could trace the thread of English belief in the forward game all the way back to the opposition to four

FOOT BALL AT RUGBY.

SMYTH.

Plate 1 Football at Rugby School in 1845, possibly the earliest ever illustration of the game. Almost all the players are in the scrum and the scrummagers are standing upright.

Image © Lordprice Collection, www.lordprice.co.uk

J. E. Bentley. A. E. Gibson. F. Tobin. D. L. P. Turner. F. Stokes. J. H. Clayton. R. R. Osborne. J. H. Luscombe.
A. St. G. Hamersley. W. Maclaren. C. W. Sherrard. H. J. C. Turner. R. H. Birkett. J. F. Green. C. A. Crompton.
A. Davenport.   A. G. Guillemard.   J. M. Dugdale.   A. Lyon.   B. H. Burne.

ENGLISH TEAM *V*. SCOTLAND: EDINBURGH, MARCH, 1871.

(Scotland—1 Goal, 1 Try.   England—1 Try.)

Plate 2 The first England team. The side that played Scotland in Edinburgh in the very first international rugby match in 1871. Note the size of the shin-pads worn by the players at the front.

Image © Lordprice Collection, www.lordprice.co.uk

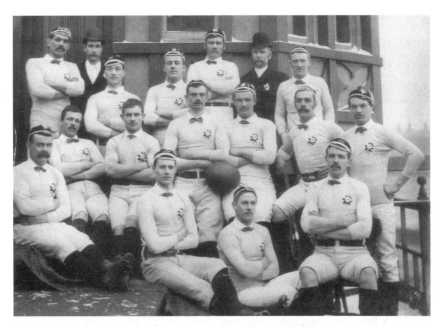

Plate 3 The all-conquering Yorkshire county side of 1889. Dicky Lockwood, the future England captain, is seated in the middle row, third from the left.

Image © Rugby Football League Archives, Leeds

The Milk in the Cocoanut.

COMPLAINTS HAVE BEEN MADE THAT OUR FOOTBALLERS PLAY UNFAIRLY.

LEO : "Look here, you don't play fair !"

KANGAROO : "What do you call fair ?"

LEO : "Well—er—you see, I didn't come out here to get licked."

Plate 4 A Brisbane newspaper complains about the 'fair play' of the 1899 British touring side to Australia, foreshadowing the 1932–33 'Bodyline' cricket crisis.

Image © Rugby Football League Archives, Leeds

Plate 5 The March 1905
edition of the
boys' magazine
The Captain,
which described
itself as 'a
magazine for boys
and "old boys"'.

Image © Lordprice Collection,
www.lordprice.co.uk

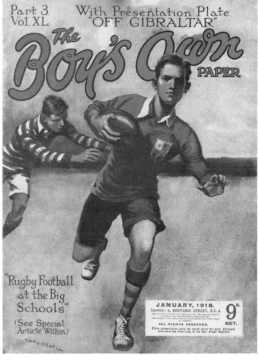

Plate 6 *The Boy's Own
Paper* for January
1918, the last year
of the First World
War, featuring a
special article on
'Rugby Football at
the Big Schools'.

Image © Lordprice Collection,
www.lordprice.co.uk

Plate 7 England's double Grand Slam side of 1924 after beating Wales at Swansea. Wavell Wakefield is third from the right in the scrum cap.

Image © Lordprice Collection, www.lordprice.co.uk

Plate 8 Twickenham 1925: All Black Cyril Brownlie is ordered from the field by referee Albert Freethy, a casualty of Wavell Wakefield's determination to beat New Zealand.

Image © Museum of Rugby, Twickenham

MEDICAL BROTHERS IN ARMS; OR, WAR TO THE SCALPEL AT RICHMOND.

To the general surprise, St. Bartholomew's beat Guy's in the Hospital Cup tie last week at Richmond and so qualified for the semi-final round. Our picture shows an amusing, rather than an orthodox, tackle in a game which was keen and violent, and in which Guy's, being the greater attacking side, found Bart's closing up the game, and not always on-side. After a pointless first half, Bart's snatched two tries and converted one of them, without letting their opponents score at all. Guy's, the holders, have won the cup twenty-four times to St. Bartholomew's four times.

Plate 9 Bart's versus Guy's in the Hospitals' Cup in 1931 in a scene similar to those immortalised in Richard Gordon's *Doctor in the House*.

Plate 10 The women's magazine *My Home* from 1932 featuring an illustrated half-time chat between a fashionably dressed woman and a player enjoying his orange.

Image © Lordprice Collection, www.lordprice.co.uk

Vigour of body, vigour of opinion ... "feet ... FEET ...
Oh, well kicked, sir ... Now ... go on man! ... he's
over ... He's not ... a-a-ah!! ... Going on Saturday?"

Plate 11 The unbreakable bond: rugger and beer, as captured in an advertisement for Worthington's Pale Ale

three-quarters and the passing game in the 1880s. The 1963 Five Nations title had been won by a side that scored just four tries. Players such as the elusive Coventry wing Peter Jackson, the inventive fly-half Richard Sharp and the mercurial David Duckham were rare exceptions rather than the rule, jewels in a base metal crown of forward efficiency. When the title was regained in 1980, a seventeen-year gap that included six wooden spoons, the side again was built around a ruthlessly physical pack led by Bill Beaumont, whose scorched earth policy cleared the ground for the backs. Similarly, when the Five Nations title was again lifted in 1991 by a Geoff Cooke-coached England, the side was built around the howitzer kicking of Rob Andrew and a fearsome pack, a formula revived by Clive Woodward that led to the World Cup triumph of 2003.

It was the introduction of the World Cup in 1987 that led to renewed soul-searching about the rules. The success of the competition, not least in the high levels of media interest and television viewing figures, brought into focus the fact that the game could not regularly provide the entertainment value of other sports. It also brought maximum pressure to bear on the belief, still held by many in the game, that the sport was played primarily for the benefit of the players, and only secondarily, if at all, for the enjoyment of spectators. In a world that was seeing the beginnings of satellite television and global communications, this was not an attitude that could be seriously maintained. Following the 1991 World Cup, the International Board announced in April 1992 the most wide-ranging revisions of the rule book for a century, designed to make the game faster and more attractive. Tries were increased to five points to encourage try-scoring and the ruck and maul rules were changed in an attempt to force teams in possession of the ball to open up play. The emphasis was on encouraging the spectacular and the exciting. Steve Bale of the *Independent* hit the nail on the head when he described the changes as 'the first official acknowledgement that rugby union is no longer exclusively a players' game'.[55] This was only the beginning. The advent of professionalism in 1995 was accompanied by almost continuous attempts to improve the game as a spectacle, from the legalisation of lifting in the line-out (or 'supporting' a player, as the rules now read in classic euphemistic style) to yet more tinkering with the ruck and the maul in order to ensure quicker ball and more continuous play. In 1995 there were even experimental games of thirteen-a-side played in Scotland.

That, of course, was the spectre hovering behind all discussions about rule changes. Ever since 1895 the RFU and its supporters had been able to dismiss calls for reform by pointing out that it would take the game down the road of rugby league. From making the defending scrum-half stay behind his own forwards to reducing the size of teams, all had been rejected because they were tarred with the brush of the renegade code. But rugby union's renewed evolutionary impulse, spurred by the impact of commercialism a century after it had originally shut the door on radical change, was taking it down exactly the same path that league had travelled. Despite the claims of some of the more jaundiced union commentators that league had abandoned rugby's traditional virtues, it had remained squarely within the tradition of the passing game. League had evolved on a trial and error basis by providing answers to the traditional problems of those football codes that had emerged from the rules of football at Rugby School. The problem of the breakdown, or what to do when the player with the ball had been tackled, had been solved by replacing the ruck or the maul with the orderly play-the-ball. Excessive touch kicking had been curbed by penalising direct kicking into touch. The domination of the forwards had been diminished by reducing the number of forwards and cutting the opportunities for scrummaging. Other branches of rugby football's evolutionary tree, such as Australian and American football, had also responded to those same problems but with different answers, such as abolishing the off-side rule or legalising obstruction and the forward pass. Moreover, experience had led league to gradually abandon the idea of the struggle for the ball. As professionalism and the importance of winning had become paramount, it had discovered, as union has begun to, that no matter how precisely the contest at the scrum or the breakdown was legislated, players and coaches would always find a way to circumvent or undermine the system. In its place, league had evolved into a struggle for territory and position. And no matter how hard union tried to resist, the contest for possession was steadily declining in importance. A 2005 study by the IRB comparing rugby union in 1983 and 2003 found that the side in possession now retained the ball thirteen out of fourteen times at the breakdown, nine times out of ten at the scrum and eight out of ten at the line-out.[56]

The growing 'treizification' of rugby union from the early 1990s was nowhere more noticeable than in the flood of rugby league coaches into union from the late 1990s. Of the eight 2003 World Cup quarter-finalists, only New Zealand did not have any former league personnel on their coaching staff. At club level in England ex-league coaches proliferated. They brought rigorous defensive systems and new attacking patterns to the game. But although union may be following down the same road as league, the two sports travel in different vehicles. Unification was no more likely in 2005 than it had been in 1905. Tradition weighs heavily on both games, in the ways that they play the game and the ways in which they see the world. The split that began to emerge a century and a quarter ago has resulted in two separate and distinct sports. One only has to discuss the essence of rugby with supporters of each game to realise that the struggle for the ball by the forwards is at the spiritual heart of the union game, whereas for league it is the open, passing game that is its soul. These two approaches to the way in which rugby should be played have remained exactly the same ever since they were first fought over at the end of the nineteenth century. The ghosts of Arthur Budd and James Miller will remain guests at the feast of rugby for as long as it is played.

7

THE IMPERIAL GAME

England had only ever managed a single draw against South Africa. The Springboks had never lost to the English. Yet there was something in the air on Saturday 20 December 1969 at Twickenham that suggested that an upset might be on the cards.

Just weeks before, the RFU had appointed its first ever national coach, Northampton's Don White, who had been a fixture in the England pack of the 1940s, in an attempt to reverse the decline of the side. Five new caps had been brought in and a new captain appointed. There was a new look and feel to the side as they looked to put English disappointments of the past few years behind them. What was more, a fortnight earlier Scotland had made history by recording their first-ever victory over the Springboks.

As soon as the whistle went, the two packs tore into each other and the game became a battle for forward domination. Springbok fly-half Piet Visagie broke the tension after six minutes with a penalty goal following an England line-out infringement. The arm-wrestle continued until the thirty-fourth minute when the match suddenly burst into life. First, a wild pass from debutant scrum-half Nigel Starmer-Smith was picked off by Don Walton who passed it on to Piet Greyling who ran across to score in the corner. Visagie converted to make it 8–0. But then almost immediately the England scrum-half atoned for his mistake when he ran directly from a scrum, swapped passes with his fly-half Ian Shackleton and hurtled past the Springboks' twenty-five yard line where he off-loaded to Tony Bucknall whose quick hands got the ball to Peter Larter who swapped passes with Keith Fairbrother and touched down ten yards in from the Springboks' right corner.

England pressure in the second half promised much but resulted in only a penalty goal twenty minutes into the half from Bob Hiller, captaining England for the first time. The game was in its last ten minutes when a South African line-out five yards from their line turned into a maul. The ball somehow squeezed out and Bristol's John Pullin threw himself over the line onto the ball to claim the three points. Hiller kicked the conversion from the sideline and the game was within England's grasp. But the Springboks refused to relinquish their unbeaten record. Visagie missed with a drop-goal attempt, Sid Nomis almost got over in the right-hand corner and then Andy van der Watt failed to score on the opposite flank. When the final whistle went, England had vanquished the Springboks for the first time ever.

But to large numbers of people, the events on the field were irrelevant. Since they had arrived in Britain two months earlier, the Springboks had been the focus for anti-apartheid demonstrations across the country. Like every other match of the tour, the game had been organised under the tightest police security to prevent it from being disrupted. Thousands of police confronted thousands of demonstrators around the ground. Just hours before kick-off, demonstrators had tried to disrupt the Springboks' preparation by locking some in their hotel rooms and then by driving off the team bus with half the team on board.

Rugby union was coming face to face with its imperial past. This was the 1960s and the old certainties of the British Empire were disintegrating. The international order that the sport had taken for granted for the previous century, of which it had been a symbol and which was a cornerstone of its very existence, was slipping away.

'The English, the English, the English are best . . .'

Twickenham itself was the arena that embodied the importance of international competition to English rugby union. As we have seen, the RFU owed its existence in part to the need to establish a national side and much of its energy in its first century of existence was spent establishing and maintaining its leadership of the international game. Following the inaugural match with Scotland in 1871, England's first played Ireland in 1875 and Wales in 1881. But its leadership in the 1880s was challenged by Scotland and the decade was marked by long-running disputes between the two nations.

The friction first emerged during the 1884 Calcutta Cup match at Blackheath's Rectory Field. A dour game in bitterly cold weather found itself heading into notoriety when, following an equalising England try to Richard Kindersley, the game was stopped for ten minutes by an argument over the legality of the try. The Scots claimed that one of their players had knocked the ball backwards with his hands and therefore a scrum should have been awarded to England. Eventually the try was allowed to stand and Wilf

Bolton duly converted to give England victory. The dispute highlighted the fact that each country played slightly different rules – knocking the ball back was not classified as a knock-on in England, as it was in Scotland. The dispute reverberated for the next year, causing the 1885 Calcutta Cup match to be cancelled amid a mountain of acrimonious correspondence between the two unions. The English claimed, with some justification, that if the try were disallowed, Scotland would benefit from its own illegality. The Scots insisted that the issue be judged by a neutral union, and supported by Wales and Ireland, proposed the setting up of an International Rugby Football Board (IB).[1] The model was taken from soccer, which had created an International Board of the four 'home' nations in December 1882 to agree on a common set of rules for the British Home International championship, which began formally the following season. But the RFU, sensing a challenge to its authority, kept its distance from the IB, arguing that it could not agree to equal representation on the board because it had three times as many member clubs as the other three unions combined.

In 1886 the RFU had introduced a points system for deciding matches, with three points for a goal and one for a try. This was not accepted by Ireland, Scotland or Wales, who preferred the old system of deciding matches by goals alone. More importantly, they insisted that the International Board, not the RFU, should adjudicate on the rules of the game. Stalemate ensued and England did not play any home internationals in 1888 or 1889. In late 1889, fearful of another anti-climactic international season, the two sides agreed to appoint arbitrators to reach a binding decision. They reported back in April 1890. On the face of it they sided with the three 'offshoots', as *The Times* witheringly called the other nations, who believed that the International Board should be solely responsible for drawing up the rules of the game. But they also acceded to England's demands for dominance of the IB. Of the twelve members, six would be from England, with two each from the other nations. Changes to the rules could only be made with a majority of 75 per cent, ensuring that England stayed in control.[2] The RFU had seen off the Scottish challenge to its authority and emerged even stronger.

The rivalry between the SRU (which was known as the Scottish Football Union until 1924) and the RFU was a struggle about who was the best representative of British sporting values. Many of the leaders of Scottish rugby, such as H.H. Almond, were strong Anglophiles who saw themselves as almost more English than the English, defending rugby in its purest form, on and off the playing field. Moreover, they had a history of playing rugby that rivalled England, Edinburgh Academicals having been founded in 1857. Even in the 1890s one could still find Scots who opposed the reduction in team size from twenty to fifteen, and the characteristic Scottish playing style of forwards dribbling the ball ahead of them – immortalised in the cry of 'Feet Scotland, Feet' – was felt to be nearer to the original spirit of the sport than the modern handling and passing game. The Scots were resolute in their opposition to speeding the game up or making it more appealing to spectators. In 1927 a number of heads of Scottish schools wrote to the Headmasters' Conference to express their anxiety at suggestions that the RFU might change the rules and move it away from 'what it always has been, a game suited for schoolboys'. The following year the SRU committee stated that it was 'satisfied from the public interest at present taken in our game that it is both sufficiently fast and interesting enough'.[3] The most famous, if perhaps apocryphal, expression of Scottish rugby's neolithic conservatism came from SRU secretary James Aikman Smith at Twickenham in 1922 when, in response to King George V's question about why the Scottish side did not wear numbers on their shirts like England, he replied 'my players are men, not cattle'.

Off the field, Scottish defence of amateurism was so ferocious that it made even the RFU's irreconcilables look like lily-livered backsliders. The SRU believed that the 1905 All Blacks were professionals because they received regular expenses' payments of three shillings a day.[4] They had asked to see the accounts of the tour, which they expected would fully confirm their suspicions, but these were not forthcoming. Their ardent pursuit of the professional devil led them to suspend one of their own players, Tom Wilson, in March 1908 merely for accepting a place on the 1908 Anglo-Welsh tour of New Zealand because he would receive regular expense payment and therefore professionalise himself. Scottish dissatisfaction reached its peak with the 1908–09 Wallaby tour, on which the Australian players also received three shillings per day expenses. Frustrated at what they saw as the RFU's compromise – 'there can be no halfway house in Rugby football', James Aikman Smith lectured the RFU – the Scots declared on 12 January 1909 that they would not play against England in that year's Five Nations tournament.[5]

Principle may have been on their side, but precedent was not. As many pointed out, the Scotsman David Bedell-Sivright had captained the 1904 British rugby union tour of Australasia, on which players were also paid three shillings per day expenses and no one in Britain had batted an eyelid. The RFU's secretary C.J.B. Marriott claimed that the Scots knew full well that the three shillings allowance was intended merely to pay for drinks taken with meals. Nevertheless, the RFU clearly felt uncomfortable having to justify payments to players and a fortnight later offered an olive branch to the SRU, under which the three shillings would still be allowed but could not be simply given to players but must cover actual expenses paid. Agreement was duly reached and in February the International Board declared that 'the making of any allowance to players in cash is contrary to the principles of amateur Rugby football, and in future no such allowance will be made to any player'. That year's England–Scotland match took place on schedule and the Scots scored what they believed to be a double victory by winning the Calcutta Cup.[6]

This was to be the last time that the authority of the RFU was challenged by another home nation. Among English-speaking countries its authority became unquestionable following the First World War. Until 1950 it was responsible for organising British Isles tours overseas (the side does not appear to have been known as the Lions until the 1950 tour of Australasia).[7] It was not until the 1970s that controversies between the home nations re-emerged. In 1974 the Welsh Rugby Union complained that *Land of My Fathers* was not played at Twickenham. The RFU agreed that it could be played only when the teams had come out on the field but that *God Save The Queen* must be played immediately before kick-off – if the British national anthem did not occupy this central place in the proceedings, it decreed that no other 'national tunes [sic] could be played'.[8] Scotland started to play *Flower of Scotland* as its anthem in 1990. These disputes over anthems were yet another manifestation of the decline of the RFU's authority from the 1970s, and reflected the emergence of nationalist political feeling in Wales and in Scotland that had begun to affect even the conservative ranks of rugby union, giving anti-English sentiment a degree of acceptability.

Even so, images of the four 'home' countries still remained locked into a reassuring and mutually reinforcing hierarchy of stereotypes, with England at its head. As Jason Tuck has described, the Scots were portrayed as fiery and dauntless yet erratic. The Irish combined native flair with primitive enthusiasm. The Welsh were violent, wild and magical, hallmarks of much-quoted Welsh *hwyl*.[9] Such descriptions were more indicative of national pre-conceptions and journalistic clichés than reality. The majority of Scots and Irish players had been educated at elite schools and universities and had more in common with their English counterparts than their supposedly more primitive countrymen. Even the Welsh, with a significant working-class component to their national team, were part of an Anglicised network of elite educational institutions or an industrial proletariat that had little to do with the rural Welsh past. At the top of the tree came the English, courageous, stout-hearted and orderly. Their leadership qualities were underlined by the fact that, unlike the three other nations, they were never referred to in terms that implied that they were emotional or in the grip of any primal or irrational force. For English rugby, as with English society in general, 'Britishness' was a subordinate sub-set of Englishness. England was not an equal member of the British family of nations, as those in Scotland, Wales, Northern Ireland and the rest of the Empire liked to believe. It was not even first among equals. As the attitude of the RFU to its international partners demonstrated, echoing the English nationalism of Arnold and Hughes, England led and expected everyone else to follow. Even as late as 1991, something of this spirit could be seen in the theme song for that year's first world cup, Kiri Te Kanawa singing 'World in Union'. The song was an adaptation of the patriotic hymn, 'I Vow To Thee My Country', which in its original form combined English nationalism and military fervour. Although the lyrics had been changed, Holst's stirring melody remained quintessentially English. Perhaps it would be only a slight exaggeration to compare the RFU's attitude to its neighbours to that parodied in Michael Flanders' and Donald Swann's 'Song of *Patriotic Prejudice*':

The rottenest bits of these islands of ours,
We've left in the hands of three unfriendly powers.
Examine the Irishman, Welsh or Scot,
You'll find he's a stinker as likely as not.
The English, the English, the English are the best,
I wouldn't give tuppence for all of the rest.[10]

Within England itself, a hierarchy of regions emerged within the game, with London and the south-east at its head, alongside the Oxbridge universities and the public schools. This was both a numerical fact, with more than half the RFU's clubs being in the south-east, and also an ideological dominance. Next came the Midlands, combining the rural middle class, the technological managerial class of the new industries and a leavening of working-class players. Behind this and jostling for attention were the north, where the game was now almost entirely shorn of its links with the industrial working class, and the south-west, where distance from the metropolis and the cross-class nature of the game meant that it constantly harboured resentments towards the capital. 'London [rugby] publications generally treat us very badly in the West, as our good performances are always belittled, and we are looked upon as being very much provincial', complained a West Country correspondent to *Rugby Football* in 1923.[11]

These regions of England were united by a sense of what might be called 'rugby pastoral', in which rugby was perceived to belong to an older, non-industrial England. The home counties, the south-west countryside and the county shires of the Midlands were seen as its natural home. Even the stereotype of the portly and jolly West Country working-class prop forward, personified perhaps best by Bath's Gareth Chilcott in the decade before open professionalism, was firmly rooted in a Merrie England 'Neverland' of Toby Jugs and John Bull. In the north, rugby union had largely abandoned, and been abandoned by, the industrial cities. Instead it was a sport of the market towns and commuter villages and suburbs. Otley, Ilkley and the Vale of Lune were all names that spoke of a rural, non-industrial north, the 'deep north' of H.V. Morton's *In Search of England*, which he believed had existed before the industrial revolution and would re-emerge after the industrial age had passed. This was a vision of England without industry and, crucially for the middle classes who feared the power of the trade unions and the labour movement, without the organised working class.[12] Indeed, this was a theme that was alluded to in J.M. Kilburn's 1938 book *In Search of Rugby Football*, in which the rugby correspondent of the *Yorkshire Post* said not one word about the league game in the cities and towns of West Yorkshire. The belief that rugby is not an urban game is one of the sport's enduring myths. John Reason and Carwyn James believed that it was not possible to play the game 'within the cobbled streets of towns and cities'. *New Statesman* editor Peter Wilby echoed this view when writing about rugby in Gloucester, reporting that the clubs' fans believed that the urban working class did not play the game because of the lack of nearby fields in cities.[13] Of course, this was nonsense, as the history of rugby league and pre-1895 rugby union demonstrated, but the idea that rugby union was part of the rural English past became a unifying and strong myth of the game. In this the sport reflected ideas about English identity that had also emerged in the late Victorian period that were based on a rejection or questioning of mass, urban society and gave rise, in Alun Howkins words, to 'a ruralist version of a specifically English culture'.[14]

Above all, rugby union carried with it a unifying sense of Englishness that could be traced back to Thomas Arnold and *Tom Brown's Schooldays*. Northern rugby was proud of its differences with the south but, as with cricket in Lancashire or Yorkshire, these were seen as strands that made up the threads that held the nation together, rather than a source of opposition or division. Similarly in the south-west, despite grumblings about metropolitan snobbery and attempts to link the game to the rise of political Cornish nationalism in the 1980s and 1990s, the game was always a unifying rather than a separatist force. Following its crushing 29–0 defeat at the hands of the 1924 All Blacks, Cornwall never played a major national touring side under its own name again, playing tourists either as Devon–Cornwall or the anonymous South-West Counties.[15] The county's famous extra-time County Championship victory over Yorkshire in 1991 in front of 54,000 at Twickenham undoubtedly harnessed much of the resentment of the Cornish people at rising levels of poverty and unemployment in the previous decade. Yet despite the huge display of Cornish flags and symbols, the imagery of 'Trelawny's Army', as the supporters dubbed themselves, fitted perfectly with the invented pastoral traditions of the game.[16] The late seventeenth-century royalist Baronet and Bishop of Bristol Jonathan Trelawny was jailed in 1687 by James II for opposing moves towards Catholic toleration. As a figure who embodied paternalism bolstered by popular support, he symbolised the Cornish variant of a mythical 'Merrie England' of pre-industrial social hierarchy and unity. Historically, the Cornish Rugby Football Union was strongly monarchist, appointing Edward VII, George VI and Prince Philip as its patrons.[17] As it was everywhere else, rugby union was not a vehicle for social or regional change but a force for English, and ultimately British, unity.

This sense of the unifying Britishness of rugby union could be seen in the ease with which players seemed to shift their national allegiances. In the 1990s concerns about players appearing for countries other than those of their birth or switching between national teams, dubbed 'Grannygate' scandals by the press, were pointed to as examples of globalisation. In fact, interchangeable national identities had been a feature of the international game almost since its inception. In 1883 the Australian Charles Wade had appeared on the wing for England against Scotland before returning to Sydney and playing for New South Wales against the visiting unofficial British side in 1888. Wade, like many subsequent non-native internationals, was a student at Oxford. Ernest Fookes, who won ten caps for England in the 1890s, was a New Zealander studying at Manchester's Owen's College. For a considerable number of Welsh internationals before the First World War, including Gwyn Nicholls, captain of the side that beat the 1905 All Blacks, the land of their fathers and themselves was not Wales but England. When Scotland defeated England at Richmond in 1903, their three-quarter line comprised a South African, a New Zealander and two Australians. 'Bruno' Brown had played for Queensland against the 1908 Anglo-Welsh touring side before studying at Oxford, going on to win eighteen England caps and become president of the RFU in 1948. In addition, disputes between the home nations over the selection of players were not unknown. In 1920 Newport centre-three-quarter Ernest Hammett was selected by both England and Wales for the same match, although he eventually opted for the English as they had been the first to ask him.

This was probably as good a basis as any other to choose a national team. As the rugby correspondent of the *Athletic News* pointed out just before the First World War, there were no formal guidelines for national selection: 'sentiment enters the process of qualification to a very great extent and if the stranger from afar has a reasonable sort of association with the land wherein he is domiciled he may, if he possesses no previous national distinction, be picked for that very land of temporary residence'.[18] The IB had been asked to make some ruling on the matter in 1921, partially because the aftermath of the war led to something approaching a state of flux in player movement – perhaps most uniquely in the case of New Zealand-born Henry Tancred, who had captained the 1921 New Zealand rugby league tour to Australia, emigrated to Sydney and then played three test matches for the Wallabies in 1923. Even so, the IB refused to 'take any steps towards defining international qualifications' but suggested cryptically that if a player took part in a trial match for a national side, that fact should be 'worthy of the sporting considerations of several unions', thus avoiding taking any position whatsoever. The immediate beneficiaries of the IB's fence-sitting were the Scots, who won a Grand Slam in 1925 with a three-quarter line that included Melbourne-born and New Zealand-educated Ian Smith, 1921 All Black captain George Aitken and A.C. 'Johnny' Wallace, who was to captain the New South Wales tour of the UK in 1927.[19]

Despite the Scots' spectacular success, it was the English who reaped the most benefit from overseas players, especially the university game. In the late 1900s the first Rhodes Scholars began to arrive at Oxford. The scheme had begun in 1902 through a bequest of arch-imperialist Sir Cecil Rhodes with the aim of bringing the future leaders of the English-speaking world to study at Oxford. One of Rhodes' original criteria for selection was a 'fondness of, and success in, manly outdoor sports' and a considerable proportion of the scholars, such as Bruno Brown, were talented and keen rugby players. Indeed, according to England captain and RFU president J.E. Greenwood, 'anyone who was a very good athlete and had sufficient scholastic ability was pretty certain of a Rhodes scholarship'. Between 1920 and 1970, twenty-seven of them played for Oxford in the Varsity match.[20] As early as 1911 the fact that Rhodes Scholars only played for Oxford had caused considerable controversy, not least because they were older and more experienced than most of their Oxbridge rugby peers.[21] It was also pointed out that Cambridge's four successive Varsity match victories from 1925 to 1928 occurred when the Oxford side contained its lowest number of overseas players. As well as Rhodes Scholars, the two universities attracted many other overseas players – between 1945 and 1959, thirty-seven turned out for Oxford and fifteen for

Cambridge. In 1949 a debate even broke out in *Country Life* over the number of overseas players, and South Africans in particular, who appeared in the Varsity match.[22]

The issue of overseas players' eligibility for England was a constant issue in the 1930s and 1940s. In the interwar years South African players were a common sight in an England jersey. Frank Mellish had played six times for England in the 1920s and returned home to win six caps for the Springboks. Brian Black won ten England caps in the early 1930s. Hubert Freakes won three caps in the late 1930s. Full-back Harold 'Tuppy' Owen-Smith, a South African medical student who scored a century for South Africa against England in 1929, won ten caps and captained England three times between 1934 and 1937. Following the end of the war, five South Africans and one Australian appeared for England. In 1946 *Rugger* devoted its first editorial to the matter after three overseas players had been selected in an England trial match: 'the truth of the matter is that international qualification hangs on the thinnest of threads. A second cousin, ten times removed, is the sort of thing that provides sufficient qualification.' Welsh rugby commentator G.V. Wynne-Jones was even more scathing, claiming that England believed they 'could select any Colonial player and call him English' and pointing out that the side for the 1949 match against France included the Argentinian Barry Holmes, the Rhodesian Robert Kennedy, the South African Clive van Ryneveld and the Australian Basil Travers.[23]

Indeed, apart from an 1898 ruling that no player could play for two home nations, it appears that the only serious discussion that the RFU had about player eligibility was in 1935 about Alexander Obolensky, a Russian prince educated in England whose parents had fled from the October 1917 Revolution, shortly before England's defeat of the All Blacks in which he scored two spectacular tries. At least four members of the RFU committee opposed his selection.[24] No action was taken to control the movement of players until the 1980s, despite the apparent anomalies in international representation. This was because the game saw itself as part of an imperial British network through which players, like businessmen and members of the professional classes, could move without restriction. It was the shared sense of Britishness of the 'home' nations and the white dominions of the empire that enabled players to move between national teams. There was a similar but less frequently used convention in cricket, which also based itself on a common British imperial identity – at least for the white nations of the empire. But as the British Empire started to unravel from the 1950s, so this sporting link also started to dissolve, as first South Africa and then Australia and New Zealand began to detach themselves from the 'Mother Country'.

The imperial bond

This free movement of players within an imperial network was an important component of the RFU's belief in the indivisibility of its game from the British imperial mission. Rugby became the dominant football code in the southern hemisphere because it offered both a common framework of British sporting morality and the opportunity for the white dominions of the empire to compete against the 'Mother Country'. In 1888 an unofficial British rugby tour organised by the sporting entrepreneurs Alfred Shaw and Arthur Shrewsbury had given added impetus to the popularity of the game. Rugby quickly became an important part of the imperial sporting network that included cricket, rowing and athletics. Welcoming the 1904 British rugby team to Australia, J.C. Davis, Sydney's leading sports journalist, encapsulated this when he wrote that sporting tours created 'an extended feeling of appreciation and racial sympathy. They have incidentally shown to the muscular Britisher at home that the Britisher abroad and his sinewy colonial descendents are not aliens because thousands of miles of sea intervene.'[25] The symbolism of tours to Australia, New Zealand and South Africa heightened the RFU's belief in its own imperial importance. RFU secretary Rowland Hill articulated this belief stating that international tours were 'of great Imperial importance in binding together the Mother Country with the Overseas Dominions'.[26]

The imperial landscape of the game was also shaped by the consequences of the 1895 schism in England. In Australia, rugby split along exactly the same fault line as in Britain, with rugby league being established in 1908. Rugby union owed its prestige as the national sport of New Zealand to a great extent thanks to the success of the 1905 All Blacks tour of Britain. The huge impact of the 1905 tour on New Zealand society would undoubtedly have been less if the All Blacks had met the same quality of opponents that faced A.H. Baskerville's pioneering 1907 New Zealand rugby league tourists to Britain. And in South Africa, the success of the 1906 Springbok tourists to the UK gave rugby a national importance that helped to consolidate its position as the country's dominant winter sport. For Afrikaners especially, for whom cricket was too closely identified with British provocations before the Anglo-Boer War such as the Jameson Raid, rugby offered the opportunity to beat the British at their own game.[27]

One of the sport's greatest strengths was therefore the weakness of the England national side. The loss of northern clubs and players in 1895 had destroyed England's potential to dominate the game. The national side's limitations gave smaller countries such as New Zealand, South Africa and

Wales the opportunity to compete on an equal footing with, and defeat, the imperial Mother Country. Without this ability to regularly overcome the English, the importance of rugby union to those countries where the game became the national sport would not have been so great.

Given the national pride at stake, rugby tours were rarely as straightforward as the imperial ideal suggested. The first official tour to Australia by a British representative side took place in 1899. Captained and managed by the Reverend Matthew Mullineux, the tour proved to be unexpectedly controversial. Mullineux was disappointed at how the Australians played the game and was horrified by widespread rumours that players received money for playing. [28] For their part, the Australians were shocked at the highly competitive manner in which the British played the game. Mullineux's side played to win, rather than according to the rules of 'fair play'. The contrast between the rhetoric and the reality of British tactics was highlighted in a newspaper cartoon published during the tour, in which a British lion confronted a kangaroo:

Lion: 'Look here, you don't play fair!'
Kangaroo: 'What do you call fair?'
Lion: 'Well-er-you see, I didn't come out here to get licked.'[29]

These problems worsened during the 1904 British tour Down Under. Captained by David Bedell-Sivright, the side departed Australia unbeaten before going on to face sterner opposition in New Zealand, but left a trail of controversy behind them. Foreshadowing Douglas Jardine, the captain of the 1932–33 English 'Bodyline' cricket tour, much ill-feeling was generated by the behaviour of Bedell-Sivright, about whom it was said 'his conception of football was one of trained violence'.[30] Two of the three test matches were punctuated by brawling between the British captain and his Australian adversaries and a match in Newcastle against Northern Districts was interrupted when he led his men off the field in protest against the dismissal of British forward Denys Dobson.[31] Eventually they were persuaded to return, but the incident became notorious as another example of the ease with which the British dispensed with their principles of fair play when it suited them. The New Zealand leg of the tour was also marred by complaints about British gamesmanship and sharp practice.

When the first All Blacks toured Britain in 1905, amazement at their speed, skills and organisation was tempered by distrust of their methods and suspicions about their amateur purity. Although the New Zealanders were to some extent seen as evidence of the physical virility of the 'colonial

Britisher', their tactics, and especially their use of the wing-forward, were seen as tantamount to cheating. The side was also criticised for its vigorous play, its supposed gamesmanship and for taking advantage of the referee.[32] These issues were exacerbated during the first Australian tour to Britain in 1908. Dogged by accusations of professionalism, unfair tactics and the shame of having the Australian rugby league team touring at the same time, the Wallabies' relationship with their hosts began awkwardly and rapidly deteriorated. The Scottish and Irish rugby unions simply refused to play them. On the pitch, the tourists were accused of being violent and playing to win at all costs. Three players were sent off during the tour, including Syd Middleton against Oxford University. For many in Britain, the tour demonstrated the moral deficiencies of the typical Australian. Scottish rugby writer Hamish Stuart claimed that 'custom and the national idea have so blunted their moral sense that they are sublimely unconscious of their delinquency and are sincerely surprised when accused of unfair practice'.[33] The Australians were less than enamoured by their treatment in Britain. James McMahon, the tour manager, complained that 'as visitors to the Mother Country, as representatives of part of the British nation, [the players] could not understand and were certainly not prepared for such hostility as was shown them by a section of the press'.[34] It was to be almost twenty years before either the Australians or the New Zealanders were invited to tour Britain again. Again, the lyrics of Donald Swann capture uncannily the attitude of the RFU:

> And all the world over each nations the same,
> They've simply no notion of playing the game.
> They argue with umpires, they cheer when they've won,
> And they practise beforehand which spoils all the fun.[35]

In contrast to the real and imagined delinquencies of Antipodean tourists, South African tours took place largely without controversy about playing methods or suspicions of professionalism. Until the 1950s, the South African Rugby Board was the RFU's most loyal ally. Unlike the New Zealanders and Australians, it rarely sought even to question English decisions and was viewed by the RFU as the overseas body nearest to its own values. 'The clean character of the South Africans' game has won for them a higher reputation all through the country than that which the New Zealanders secured', the *Guardian* congratulated the 1906 Springbok tourists. 'Men who have played against both sides confess that for the sheer pleasure of sport the South African matches have been unequalled. They have no system of tricks for execution when the referee was not close at hand, and the penalties against them for infringing the rules have been surprisingly few in number.'[36] For their part, the South Africans saw the 1906 tour as an opportunity to unite the English-speaking and Afrikaner population following the Anglo-Boer War, which had ended in 1902. The tourists' success, winning all but two games and drawing with England, cemented the game's place in South African society. At a reception to celebrate their arrival home, J.F. Hofmeyr claimed that they 'had made Dutch and English almost one, and had taken a great step in the direction of racial unity'. This of course referred only to those with a white skin.[37] The English affinity with the South Africans only increased following the RFU's experiences in Australia and New Zealand. George Harnett, manager of the 1908 Anglo-Welsh tour Down Under, returned home to announce that the RFU 'should keep in touch with the South African players, who besides being amateur to the core, are genuine sportsmen who play clean and honestly'.[38] It was therefore no surprise that the Springboks were the only side invited back to tour Britain again before the First World War. Shared attitudes about the playing of the game and the relative ease of travel, meant that of all the southern hemisphere countries, South Africa shared a unique bond with English rugby. This 'special relationship' would survive throughout the years of the boycott, isolation and ostracism of apartheid South Africa until the 1990s.

Yet despite undoubted antagonisms, the Australians and New Zealanders never directly challenged the RFU. Its authority among the rugby-playing countries of the Empire was based partially on its status as the founding body of the sport, but also and more importantly on the fact that it represented 'Britishness' and the centre of the Empire. It was this unique status of the RFU that led to the dominion rugby unions' default adoption of amateurism, rather than any intrinsic opposition to payments in sport. Distance from the imperial centre, less rigidity in social divisions among whites in the colonies, and the development of local sporting traditions all tended to create a slightly more liberal outlook towards monetary questions on the part of rugby administrators outside the 'Mother Country'. Payments for play do not appear to have been a major concern in southern hemisphere rugby before the establishment of rugby league in Australasia. Although there was opposition to outright professionalism, the dominions' experience of cricket and other sports suggested that there was no imperative to remove monetary reward from sport completely. Nor were the governing bodies of colonial rugby completely adverse to paying players themselves when expediency warranted it. In 1907 the New South Wales Rugby Union (NSWRU) paid star three-quarter Dally Messenger two pounds and ten shillings to compensate him for loss of earnings in order to play in the second test for Australia against New Zealand.[39]

Even the question of rugby league was viewed differently. That the 'colonial' unions did not always fully share the RFU's instinctive recoil when faced with league was shown in New Zealand. As Geoff Vincent has pointed out, the impact of A.H. Baskerville's 1907 rugby league tour on domestic rugby union was much greater than conventional histories have supposed.[40] The 1908 'Anglo-Welsh' tour to Australia and New Zealand turned into something approaching disaster: one member of the touring party was revealed by the press as former Swinton league player Frederick Jackson, and the British management alienated their hosts by their high-handed behaviour. In Auckland, where the struggle between league and union was at its most intense, rugby union regularly reinstated league players to its ranks.[41] 'Actaeon', the rugby correspondent of the *Auckland Star*, appears to have been speaking for many when in 1917 he blamed the hostility to league on 'the bitterness [that] is a legacy from that conservative body the English Rugby Union, which unfortunately has been made a fetish with a number of our New Zealand football legislators'.[42]

The most graphic example of the relative liberalism of the NZRU in comparison to the RFU can be seen in the career of Auckland's Karl Ifwerson. He played league for New Zealand against the British tourists in 1914, captained the Kiwis in all four tests against the Kangaroo tourists in 1919 and then again against the 1920 British tourists. In 1921 he switched to union and played for the All Blacks against South Africa that same year. Deference to British sensibilities meant that he was not considered for selection for the 1924 All Blacks tour to the UK.[43] In contrast, it is unlikely that a league international would even have been allowed into the bar of a British rugby union club, let alone play for a national side.

In March 1920 the New South Wales Rugby Union (effectively Australian rugby union's governing body at that time) voted to support a New Zealand proposal for changes to the laws of the game and to relax the code's strict amateurism. It also decided to press the RFU for representation on the game's International Board (IB), which was dominated by the RFU and comprised only England, Ireland, Scotland and Wales.[44] Consequently the Australian and New Zealand rugby unions submitted to the IB a joint document proposing thirteen rule changes, many of which were modelled on rugby league rules. On all substantive issues, the IB voted to reject the proposals but a 'dispensation' was granted to the Australasian unions to allow them to ban direct kicking into touch from outside the kicking team's twenty-five yard line.[45] Beyond this, the IB was not prepared to go.

More to the point, it was determined to roll back what it saw as a dangerous backsliding over the central tenets of the rugby game. For the RFU and its supporters, the war, and especially the huge toll of death among rugby union players, had been a powerful vindication of their belief in the moral and patriotic role of rugby. In the eyes of the RFU, the debate of the sport's rules and the apparent softness towards rugby league from the southern hemisphere placed this heritage in danger. The blood sacrifice that had been made during the war became the ultimate answer to those who questioned the sport's leadership. Thus the response of the RFU's supporters to calls for change was not primarily to argue the merits of any proposed changes but to use its moral authority to question the patriotism of its critics. This can be seen with stunning clarity in a letter to the Sydney *Referee* in early 1921 that signalled the end of meaningful discussion about change within the rugby union world:

> I believe that there are still some people in Australia and New Zealand who want to see rugby played. . . . I believe the Great Public Schools of Sydney will never desert the rugger game – a beautiful edifice, built up by years of patient labour, and over which is shed the lustre of a tradition that will live as long as red blood flows in Australian veins – this tradition (I quote from the 1919–20 *Rugby Football Annual*):
>
>> 'On the last Saturday of the 1913–14 season the London Scottish [club] placed four teams in the field, of these sixty players, forty-five have been killed. Altogether the club had seventy of three hundred members killed and fifty-two wounded. Some of the smaller clubs have lost almost all of the playing members.'
>
> Now, Billy Hill [the Australian official who had called for rule changes], old friend, that's the sort of game whose fortunes are entrusted to your (amongst other) hands. You know the record of the New South Wales and New Zealand rugby unions in the terrible but wonderful years of Armageddon.
> Before you and your friends, in this sudden, new found zeal of yours for 'improving the rules' destroy that edifice – think! And think again! In England it is imperishable and indestructible.[46]

For the colonial British patriots who led the game in Australia and New Zealand, this was an unanswerable challenge. It effectively destroyed any thoughts of substantive rule changes, amendments to the amateur regulations or reunification with rugby league. 'Dispensations', such as the limited ban on direct kicking into touch, were allowed by the RFU in the southern hemisphere only insofar as they would help constrain or defeat the league threat. Throughout the interwar years, the main focus for debate between the Australians and New Zealanders and rugby's British leadership centred on representation on the IB. In the mid-1900s the success of their touring sides to Britain had led to calls for Australia, New Zealand and South Africa to be represented on the IB. This was dismissed at the time by the RFU, but the joint sacrifices of the First World War and the continuing success of antipodean sides in the 1920s led to increasing pressure from the Dominions to have delegates of their own on the IB. In recognition of this, in 1923 the IB decided to agree to convene a conference 'with the Unions in the Colonies' for 1924.

To some extent this reflected the changing post-war political relationship between the British and Dominion governments. The idea of an imperial rugby conference was inspired by the series of Imperial Conferences that were held between the leaders of the major nations of the Empire in the interwar years. The discussions that led to the declaration of the 1926 Imperial Conference that the Dominions and Britain were self-governing nations of equal status could not fail to have found a sympathetic response from rugby administrators in the southern hemisphere. However, the IB's terms for the 1924 conference harked back to the Empire's pre-1907 Colonial Conferences that were only held when visiting statesmen happened to be in London for other events. The IB specified that any conference must be held in London and that it would not pay for delegates to travel to the conference. The gathering was eventually held in December 1924 during the New Zealand tour of the UK and served only to emphasise the complete resistance to reform on the part of the leaders of the British game. The IB proved to be less amenable to the idea of equality for the Dominions than British politicians, vetoing any discussion on relaxing the amateur regulations and voting against any Dominion representation on the IB. As a concession, it was agreed to hold an 'Imperial Conference' every five years at which the IB would meet with Dominion representatives. However, its decisions would not be binding, it would always be held in London and the IB would not pay travel costs. Needless to say, the resulting conference was a damp squib, with the Australian game being represented by two Australians already resident in the UK.[47]

The New Zealand delegates to the conference had suggested the formation of an Imperial Rugby Advisory Board, the word 'advisory' being carefully chosen so as not to alarm the IB. But at its meeting in March 1925 the IB still found this too strong and voted instead to organise an 'Imperial Rugby Conference' to be held every three years in London. The issue was debated again the following year and the RFU delegates this time proposed that a conference should be held to establish an Imperial Advisory Board, comprising two delegates each from the four home countries and the three rugby-playing Dominions. When the conference was held in November 1926, it yet again proved to be highly resistant to change. The NSWRU and the South African Rugby Union both submitted suggestions for amendments to the rules, with the NSWRU proposing that the Imperial Advisory Board should provide 'uniform international government' for rugby union. However, the IB ruled these proposals out of order and they were not formally discussed at the conference. In the report of the conference in the 1927 NSW *Rugby Annual*, the NSWRU sought to cover its embarrassment at the summary dismissal of its ideas by claiming that 'although not on the agenda for the conference . . . the Dominion unions' views [were] informally placed before the assembled delegates'.[48]

This was about as far as they would get in the interwar years – there was to be no rugby equivalent of the 1931 Statute of Westminster that granted a measure of representation for the Dominions in the Empire. The RFU manoeuvred effectively between the Dominions and the other Home countries, playing on the latter's fear that they would be reduced to third place in the rugby hierarchy below the RFU and the stronger overseas governing bodies. The Scots in particular had no time for colonial rugby, the SRU declaring in 1928 that 'it must always be second in importance to Home Football, which is their first consideration, and they cannot be party to any arrangement whereby any Dominion is to have a say in the government of the game at home'.[49]

The RFU continued to dangle the carrot of consultation in front of the Australians and New Zealanders if they would abandon the rule 'dispensations' granted to them. 'Now the game is played throughout the British Empire', wrote Sydney Coopper, the RFU secretary, in 1930, 'there should be no exceptions anywhere. We have found the particular dispensations once granted to you, of late a growing embarrassment to other Dominions and are desirous of checking a growing tendency to take advantage of a special arrangement made with you.'[50] In exchange for ending the dispensations, the RFU proposed the setting up of a 'Rugby Football Commission' representing Britain and the Dominions that would 'consider the laws of the game with the view of uniformity around the world'. But this would not be a decision-making body, being able only to submit suggestions to the IB, which would accept or decline them as it saw fit. Nevertheless, the NSWRU and the

NZRU agreed to end their use of the dispensations, despite the RFU proposal falling far short of their demand for direct representation on the IB.[51] Even in the face of humiliation, the antipodeans remained obsequiously sub-servient to the RFU, NZRU secretary A.E. Neilson telling the RFU that 'we desire to affirm our loyalty to the Parent Body [the RFU], recognising that the Dominions' ultimate object [of international representation] can, and will, only be obtained through your assistance'.[52] The Australians had been even more fawning:

> In all and to the furthermost ends of the British Empire the great Rugby game is played and all owe allegiance to the great controller of the game, the English Rugby Union. . . . At all times [Australian] rugby union stands behind its Alma Mater, not only because it believes and trusts in it, but also because it feels that by so doing the bonds of Empire are through the brotherhood of sport more closely knit.[53]

The imperial parent–child relationship, which domestic amateur zealots in the 1880s such as the Reverend Frank Marshall hoped would govern relations with working-class players, was a metaphor regularly used by RFU officials. Future RFU secretary Doug Prentice captained the 1930 British tour Down Under in the belief that 'each member of the side is an ambassador from the Mother Country, and if, by these, visits, the bond of friendship between parents and children is more firmly tightened, then that alone would be sufficient reason for sending out touring teams to the Dominions'.[54]

Winds of change

The RFU's paternalist control of international rugby was not to survive the new order established after the Second World War. In 1948 Australia, New Zealand and South Africa were finally given seats on the International Rugby Football Board (IB), which in the past were confined to the 'Home' nations. That same year the National Party came to power in South Africa, which at the time seemed to have little relevance to the sport but was to have profound implications for the game's future. And in 1947 France took its place in the Five Nations championship for the first time since being expelled in 1931.

The British had always had an uncomfortable relationship with French rugby, not least because in the 1850s and 1860s Gallic 'effeminacy' had regularly been contrasted to the manly British game of football. Despite the anglophilia of those such as Pierre de Coubertin who established the game in France, the Fédération Française de Rugby (FFR) never embraced amateurism with the enthusiasm of its Anglo-Saxon cousins. The English were always acutely aware of this. E.H.D. Sewell had warned in 1911 about the danger of 'veiled professionalism' in French rugby, something cheerfully acknowledged by a French correspondent who wrote to the Northern Union the following year describing how broken-time payments were commonplace across the Channel. To be sure, in the years following the end of the First World War French rugby resembled pre-split rugby in the north of England or Australia. Allegations of payments for players, inducements to switch clubs and protests about violence in what became known as 'le rugby de muerte' created intolerable tensions both within the French game and with the RFU. In 1923 *Rugby Football* reported that there were twenty cases of alleged professionalism under investigation across the Channel.[55] Appalled at the 'unsatisfactory condition of the game of Rugby football as managed and played in France', the IB stopped fixtures with all French teams in 1931 and expelled the French national side from the Five Nations championship. This was not universally supported, with *Rugger* magazine arguing that 'France must be brought back into the realm of international rugby championships as speedily as possible', a view shared by the Prince of Wales, the future Edward VII, who met with the FFR in October 1931 in an attempt to heal the split. Two years after the expulsion, French international forward Jean Galia compounded the FFR's problems by leading a rugby league breakaway to form the Ligue de Rugby à Treize, which soon began to rival the FFR.[56]

The emergence of rugby league across the Channel only confirmed the RFU's view of the French. Indeed, the RFU did not much care for anyone outside the imperial family of British peoples. A 1933 RFU meeting expressed the view that it 'should confine its activities to the English-speaking peoples', and in 1935 the RFU decided to stop accepting memberships from overseas rugby clubs, preferring instead to focus its attention on 'the British Commonwealth of nations'.[57] This was a commonplace view widespread among supporters of the game. Even in 1961 the journalist Hylton Cleaver could declare that 'the game of rugby began in this country and will remain here as part of our island rights; there is really nothing to be gained by dissipating these traditional principles in countries where the same attitude to the game is not respected, and in which we can really achieve no success on the field – and then get beaten'.[58] However, by 1939 the RFU had begun to rethink its attitude to the French, partly because of the growth of rugby league and partly because of France's Fédération Internationale de

Rugby Amateur (FIRA), a European version of the IB that included Germany, Italy and Rumania. In July 1939 the British unions accepted the FFR's renewed vows of amateurism at face value and allowed them back into the Five Nations, although the outbreak of the Second World War precluded their immediate participation.

When they did return, the relationship was no less fraught. Controversy erupted during the 1948 Five Nations tournament when it was revealed that French scrum-half Yves Bergougnan had previously been a professional with the Toulouse Olympique league club, one of ninety-nine French former league players who were now playing union. The issue flared up again in 1953 when former league international Jean Dauger was selected to play for France against Scotland.[59] In March 1951, the IB expressed its 'considerable misgivings' about the state of the French game and demanded immediate reforms, otherwise relations between France and the IB would be put in jeopardy. In response, the FFR executive voted to abolish its league competition, although a month later French clubs overwhelmingly vetoed the decision. The IB once again asked the FFR to affirm its amateurism in 1957 but by the end of the 1950s an unspoken *modus vivendi* had largely been reached where the French pretended to be amateurs and the IB pretended to believe them. The issue of France was discussed one final time in 1964 where 'it was agreed that it should be kept under review from time to time'. It was not until 1978 that the French were granted the honour of full membership of the International Board.[60]

Part of the IB's reluctance to act against the French in the post-war era was as a result of the changing balance of power within international rugby union and the decline of the RFU's authority. French rugby union had grown tremendously in the 1950s, when the successes of the national team gave it a centrality in French national and political culture. France's leadership of FIRA, which had seen the game expand into Eastern Europe, also meant that they could not easily be dismissed. But, more importantly, this shift was a direct reflection of Britain's decline and the end of its empire. Following the debacle of the Anglo-French attack on Egypt's Suez Canal in 1956 and the gradual granting of independence to many of its former colonies, British foreign policy began to focus on Europe and joining the Common Market (later to become the European Union). Rivalry between Britain and France intensified, especially after French president Charles de Gaulle blocked a British bid to join the Common Market in 1963. At the same time, Britain's moves towards closer economic ties with Europe and the introduction of new immigration laws severely alienated Australia and New Zealand, effectively ending their previously deferential attitude to all things British.

In 1962, the IB reflected this changing relationship by deleting the words 'Home Union' and 'Dominion' as categories of membership; now all countries were to be known as 'member unions'. If Harold Macmillan's 'winds of change' were blowing through a decrepit British empire, their breezes were also being felt in rugby union.

This was especially true in South Africa, although the prevailing winds there were travelling in the opposite direction. South Africa's relationship with international rugby had begun to change as a consequence of domestic and foreign politics. Rugby's national importance had been founded on an alliance between English speakers and Afrikaners. But this alliance had tilted heavily towards the Afrikaners following the National Party's 1948 election victory and the national euphoria surrounding the 4–0 humbling of the visiting All Blacks in 1949. This was heightened by the triumphant 1951 Springbok tour of Britain, the most successful yet. In 1957 the National Party abandoned *God Save the Queen* and the Union Flag as the country's national anthem and flag. As it grew in self-confidence, the South African Rugby Board (SARB) became increasingly critical of the RFU's leadership of the IB. From the mid-1950s it began to propose alterations to the rules and was criticised openly for the first time by the IB for allowing substitutes, then strictly against the rules, during the 1958 French tour of South Africa.[61] In 1963 SARB president Danie Craven called for expenses' payments to touring players to be increased and offered to make 'out of pocket' payments to players going to South Africa for its seventy-fifth anniversary celebrations. As early as 1937 there had been public grumblings among South African players touring Australia about low expenses payments, one going so far as to ask 'why can't rugby union players be amateurs and get an adequate allowance?'[62] Although all members of SARB loudly proclaimed their adherence to amateurism, it was apparent that many Afrikaners, like the French, did not entirely share the zeal of the Anglo-Saxons.

South Africa became increasingly isolated internationally following the Sharpeville massacre of township demonstrators in March 1960 and the subsequent imposition of a police-state 'state of emergency'. The IB's response to South Africa's expulsion from the Commonwealth in 1961 because of its apartheid policies was to express 'great pleasure to convey to South Africa the view shared by all the member countries that the change would not make any difference whatever in regard to South Africa's position in Rugby'.[63] Sporadic protests had taken place against links with apartheid since the late 1950s, most notably in 1960 when demonstrations erupted in New Zealand over the exclusion of Maori players from the All Blacks side to tour South Africa that year. South Africa was excluded from the 1964 and

1968 Olympics because of its racist policies and by the end of the 1960s the campaign against links with the apartheid system had become a key focus of political protest, especially in the former countries of the British Empire.[64]

In 1969 the RFU found itself at the very centre of this protest movement, buffeted by a maelstrom that was to have far-reaching and profound effects. The scene had been set by the events surrounding the selection of the England cricket team to tour South Africa in 1968. Basil d'Oliveira, the Cape Town all-rounder who had emigrated to England in 1960 in the hope of achieving international recognition for his prodigious talents, had seemed to be a certain pick for the tour, especially after scoring a century against the Australian tourists immediately before the touring party was selected. Under pressure from South Africa, the MCC left him out of the side on the ludicrous grounds that his bowling was not suited to South African conditions. Then, when Tom Cartwright was later ruled out of the tour, the MCC brought in d'Oliveira but the South African government refused to accept him and the tour was cancelled.[65] Anti-apartheid campaigners, partly in anticipation of a projected South African cricket tour to England in 1970, focused their attentions on the 1969 South African rugby tour of Britain. Led by Peter Hain, the campaigners undertook a determined and imaginative campaign against the tour.

The RFU also made preparations. A month before the tourists arrived, officials met with police to discuss tactics to deal with the anticipated protests. The police suggested that

> it would be best if the stewards employed by the RFU (aided by the police) did their utmost to keep all spectators off the playing area before the game, and . . . make the first attempts to persuade demonstrators who might try to interfere with the playing of the match by remaining on the pitch, to leave. It was confirmed by the police that the stewards were entitled to use the minimum amount of force necessary to achieve this end.

Thus advised, the RFU set about recruiting an extra one hundred stewards from local rugby clubs and looking for suitable security firms to provide dog patrols of the Twickenham stadium.[66]

When the Springboks finally arrived in Britain at the end of October, greeted at Heathrow by demonstrators chanting 'Don't Scrum with a Racist Bum', they made no attempt to conceal their racism. Tour manager Corrie Bornman told the waiting press that the tourists would mix freely with all races 'provided they are rugby players', which immediately led to calls for his prosecution under the Race Relations Act.[67] Five senior Oxford dons, including Sir Isaiah Berlin and Lord Franks, called for their first match against Oxford University to be cancelled. It was moved from the Iffley Road ground to Twickenham, where 500 demonstrators were joined by a similar number of police, the Scotland Yard Commando Squad and a sparse crowd to see a clearly unhappy South African side defeated 6–3. As the tour dragged on, the opposition grew stronger with matches being confronted by thousands of demonstrators and play interrupted by continual pitch invasions. On 15 November at the game against Swansea, the tour reached its nadir when stewards beat demonstrators mercilessly, sending twenty anti-apartheid campaigners to hospital, five of whom were knocked unconscious. Frank Keating described the violence against the protestors on the day as 'gruesome' and 'ferocious'. Home Secretary James Callaghan called for a report on the events and a week later banned stewards from being used against demonstrators.[68] The Springboks continued their sour trudge through Britain, outwitted by demonstrators and largely outplayed by their international opponents, drawing with Wales and Ireland and losing to England and Scotland. Over 50,000 people had joined the anti-apartheid demonstrations, two matches were forced to switch venues and one was abandoned, all at a cost of £50,000. Above all, the tour had, in the words of Chris Laidlaw, who captained the Oxford team that defeated the Spring-boks, ensured that 'rugby has gained international infamy as the key activity by which South Africa seeks to legitimise its doubtful sporting and cultural links with the rest of the European world'.[69]

The world of deference and order upon which the RFU was based was falling apart. RFU administrators were not used to having their authority questioned and their decisions challenged. Officials began to lash out at those they saw as their enemies. Robin Prescott denounced Callaghan's description of stewards as vigilantes with the words 'Mr Callaghan does not run our game and never will. For his information, the police have to be asked to come on to private property to defend it. We asked these volunteer stewards to assist the police.' In a House of Lords debate, Wavell Wakefield claimed that he had a list of the Communist affiliations of 'the people behind all this'. Donald Biggs, the chairman of Gravesend RFC, wrote to *The Sunday Times* to suggest that rugby clubs should 'receive government grants of say £1,000 to £2,000 a year. The total involved would be relatively small in comparison to the grants paid to long-haired louts of uncertain gender that invaded the pitch at Twickenham. Such nuisance-makers should be washed, shaved and cropped before appearing in court to receive appropriate remedial sentences.' Peter Hain wrote to each member of the England team before their victorious match against South Africa asking them to withdraw from the side in the name of 'decency and conscience'. According to debutant Nigel Starmer-Smith, he and his fellow team members 'made a big bonfire on a table in the lobby of the hotel and burnt the letters. There was a lot of pressure on us individually and as a team but, by and large, the rugby people were behind us.'[70]

There were some honourable exceptions. The University of Manchester Institute of Science and Technology rugby club demonstrated against the Springboks' match against the Northern Counties and Aberdeen University's club organised an alternative match that included black players on the day of the tourists' match against the North of Scotland. Llanelli coach Carwyn James famously left the Stradey ground after briefing his side before the kick-off of their match against the Springboks and London Welsh flanker John Taylor, who had seen the reality of apartheid on the 1968 Lions tour, courageously risked his career by refusing to play again against South Africa.[71]

But these were a small minority. Fundamentally the leadership and much of the membership of the RFU shared many of the conceptions of the South African rugby authorities, if not their politics. For example, RFU secretary Robin Prescott unashamedly blamed the MCC for not acquiescing to the demands of the South African government over the cricket tour, saying that the MCC 'made a complete mess of it. If they hadn't chosen d'Oliveira in the first place, the problem would not have arisen.'[72] Dudley Kemp, that season's RFU president, was interviewed by Rene Cutforth on BBC Radio 4 and implied that it was the demonstrators who were racist: 'I believe there is an act passed fairly recently which acts against racial discrimination of any sort [the 1968 Race Relations Act] and I would think that anybody who incites racial hatred of any kind is breaking the law and should be treated as such.' The RFU Executive sought advice about pursuing this course of action against demonstrators but abandoned it when legal counsel suggested that it 'would exacerbate rather than sooth the situation'. Intriguingly, Paul Dobson's biography of Danie Craven revealed that the Transvaal Rugby Union also considered raising money to take Peter Hain to court after the tour.[73]

These attitudes were not based on ignorance or misunderstanding but on firmly held beliefs that had not changed since the zenith of the British Empire. Larry Lamb, international referee and senior RFU official outside of his day job as an air commodore of the RAF, submitted a thesis to Royal College of Defence Studies in 1971 titled 'The future of South Africa as an apartheid state'. It concluded with the statement 'I see the Afrikaaner race and its English-speaking counterpart producing again from within their ranks men of vision like Hertzog and Smuts under whose wise guidance all races will develop separately but fruitfully "in a land blessed in the freedom and prosperity of all her peoples".' The last phrase was taken from a 1968 South African Department of Information document entitled 'Progress through separate development – South Africa in peaceful transition'.[74] John Reason, rugby correspondent of the *Daily Telegraph* for many years, took this attitude one step further when he wrote in defence of sporting links with apartheid South Africa that 'any study of the world shows that not only is nationalism (i.e. racialism) here to stay, but anyone who is NOT [sic] racialist is a pervert. I am not a pervert. . . . When it comes to Us versus Them, South Africa are Us.'[75]

The belief that South Africa was one of 'us', even among those who did not necessarily share the above views, was to become a decisive factor in rugby union's evolution over the following two decades. Despite the huge international campaign to isolate South Africa, the RFU and the British rugby unions were determined to sustain the special relationship with South Africa, with Lions tours taking place in 1974 and 1980, and England touring under its own name in 1972 and 1984. By the 1980s their instinctive sympathy for white South Africa had been supplemented by rugby 'realpolitik' in which both sides realised that complete separation from world rugby union would inevitably lead to the game becoming openly professional in South Africa. Thus an increasing number of unofficial yet extravagantly financed tours took place from the mid-1980s with the connivance of, or at least a blind eye being turned by, national rugby unions, adding sporting and moral sustenance to the South African regime.

When apartheid was finally dismantled in the early 1990s and the Springboks once again took their place in the legitimate ranks of international rugby union, it was a major cause for celebration for the RFU. Not because a system that condemned the vast majority of its population to second-class status and much worse had ended, but because it allowed the renewal of the networks and shared culture that had linked England and South Africa for a century. The strength of these links was underlined in 1992 when South Africa finally appeared again at Twickenham after twenty-three years. The RFU president that year was the South African born Danie Serfontein. To the dismay of many, the rehabilitated Springboks ran out against England and were greeted by the RFU as returning prodigal sons. 'Unctuously pious and overtly political', was how Frank Keating described their welcome by Peter Yarranton, while Mick Cleary described it as 'almost an apologia for the old South Africa'. The Springbok captain Naas Botha was thrilled: 'it was just like being at home', he declared.[76] In an age in which the authority of the RFU over the international game had shrivelled to almost nothing, in which its principles were being thrown aside by those who once gratefully deferred to it, the return of South African rugby seemed not so much the start of a new world, but the longed-for return of the old.

8

THE MONEY GAME

It had been twenty-eight years since England had last triumphed at Cardiff Arms Park. The Welsh citadel had stood impregnable since 1963, a time before some of the 1991 team had even been born, captain Will Carling included.

But these were different times. Coach Geoff Cooke had instilled a new professionalism into the England side, based on detailed game plans and driving intensity. The disappointment of 1990, when England had lost the Grand Slam dramatically to Scotland at Murrayfield in the last match of the Five Nations campaign, had been used to steel the side to pursue victory at all costs.

In this case, the cost of victory was open football, as the match became a penalty-kickers' duel. Nottingham's Simon Hodgkinson got the better of Paul Thorburn by booting a world record seven penalty goals in an international match. The normally deadly Thorburn missed four out of five attempts in the first half, before eventually handing over the kicking duties to debutant Neil Jenkins. The kicking contest was punctuated by forty-three line-outs and thirty-seven scrums.

England's game plan was built on the back row of Mike Teague, Dean Richards and Peter Winterbottom controlling the ball and relying on Rob Andrew's steamhammer boot to move the side downfield. The England wingers Rory Underwood and Nigel Heslop each received one decent pass. According to the *Observer*'s Clem Thomas 'there was hardly a three-quarter movement worth its salt throughout the afternoon' from either team.[1]

But fifteen minutes from time, Wales' defence was finally breached. England scrum-half Richard Hill chip kicked the ball into the Welsh left corner. The resulting scrum slanted slightly to England's left, Dean Richards waited with the ball at his feet and chose his moment perfectly to offload to

Mike Teague who drove through a ragged Welsh defence to go over for a try in the corner.

When the whistle finally went for no-side, England had won 25–6, their biggest ever win in Cardiff and their first away win in the opening match of a Five Nations campaign since 1967. It was a portent of things to come. They would not be defeated in the Five Nations until they returned to Cardiff in 1993, having racked up two consecutive Grand Slams in the meantime.

However, there was another cost of this victory. Journalists who went down to interview the victors after the match found themselves embroiled in an event that was unique in the history of international rugby.

Instead of finding players keen to talk about their victory and their prospects for the rest of the tournament, they were informed that the England side would not attend the traditional post-match press conference. Frustrated yet intrigued, the journalists made the short trip to the team's hotel, only to be met by players who simply refused to talk to them. 'The situation was farcical', reported *The Sunday Times*' Chris Dighton, 'normally communicative players walked around with fingers to hushed lips. One of them even used deaf-and-dumb sign language.' Caught in a lift by a Press Association reporter, Will Carling responded to his questions with 'I can't help you'.[2]

If the journalists were mystified, so too were the millions of viewers watching the match on the BBC. Instead of listening to a succession of bloodied players recounting tales of the triumph in post-match interviews, they were subjected to extended studio analysis.

In fact, it was a dispute with the BBC that had led the players to go on strike against the media. As part of the slackening of rugby union's amateur regulations, the RFU had appointed WHJ Promotions, a player agency run by former England cricket captain Bob Willis, to maximise the off-field earnings of England players. Its first significant act was to demand £5,000 from the BBC for post-match interviews. The BBC refused, on the grounds that they never paid anyone for post-match interviews, and the disgruntled team then decided that they would not speak to any journalists at all after the match.

Although the dispute was resolved within a couple of days by mutual claims of 'misunderstanding' all round, the affair left a bitterness that was to pervade English rugby throughout the decade. A new professional era was beckoning English rugby and it appeared that the game's best players were determined to get to there as quickly as possible. These really were different times.

Amateurism unravels

Such behaviour would have been utterly inconceivable to the English players who had triumphed in Cardiff in 1953 on their way to England's first post-war Five Nations title. Captained by Nim Hall and containing two future RFU presidents in Albert Agar and John Kendall-Carpenter, the team appeared to be part of a wider renaissance of England and its traditional values. The championship had been secured at Twickenham just weeks before the coronation of Elizabeth II, Everest was conquered by loyal members of the British Empire and the following year would see the Oxford medical student Roger Bannister break the four-minute mile barrier in an apparent triumph of the indomitable amateur spirit. After the privations of the war, the austerity of the 1940s and Labour's rhetoric of social-democratic equality, the time-honoured principles of middle-class England appeared to have recovered their rightful place in society. England's rugby triumph seemed to point the way to the future.

There were, however, other indicators to suggest things were not so rosy. The destruction of the England soccer team by Puskas and the Hungarian side in 1953 and 1954, the failure of the 1952 summer Olympic side to win more than a single gold medal and a general all-round dissatisfaction with sporting performances at the international level caused considerable discussion. Of course, this reflected a broader debate within British society about its loss of global power as the Empire was dismantled and decolonisation got underway. The ignominy of the Suez fiasco in 1956 brought home the reality of Britain's true status in the post-war world. Much of the unease about British sport and its standing was expressed in the Wolfenden Committee report into the state of sport. Appointed in 1957 to 'examine the factors affecting the development of games, sports and outdoor activities in the UK' the committee took three years to report, having undertaken the widest review of sport ever in Britain. Its main findings were that coaching and training facilities should be expanded throughout the country, but it also spent considerable time dealing with the question of amateurism. Many witnesses expressed their disquiet at the concept and its practice, with leading tennis player John Barrett stating openly that most top amateur tennis players received some form of payment. The final report noted the difficulties in defining amateur and professional, and went on to say that such 'anomalies produce embarrassment, uncertainty and, sometimes, bitterness. But even more important, in our view, than anomalies are the instances in which a sport's interpretation of its own rules about amateurism permit, or even invite, what looks to the outside world very much like hypocrisy or even plain dishonesty.'[3] Although it felt unable to propose the abolition of the amateur distinction, the report's findings still represented a significant shift in 'establishment' thinking on the issue. This move away from outright hostility to payments for competitors and a more open approach to commercialism was seen in sports such as cricket, tennis and athletics in the 1960s. Cricket was to abolish the amateur divide in 1962, leading to the end of the 'Gentlemen versus Players' match, the Lawn Tennis Association abandoned amateurism in 1967 and athletics, already engaged in commercial deals with outside companies, was also forced to grapple with the problem that international bodies, including the International Olympic Committee, had much looser definitions of amateurism. Even soccer found itself wrestling with issues of 'shamateurism'.[4]

For the most part, English rugby union felt itself to be insulated from such soul-searching. Apart from a very minor scandal in 1951 when Welsh rugby commentator G.V. Wynne-Jones accused clubs in the West of England of offering payments to Welsh players, it was secure in its amateurism.[5] There was, however, one barely perceptible change that indicated the game was not immune from outside trends. In 1951 the RFU decided to publish its own coaching manual and establish a coaching advisory team, which ran training courses for club and school coaches at Bisham Abbey in Berkshire. Although many such as Wavell Wakefield had argued for a more 'professional' approach to coaching in the interwar years, the majority of the RFU were opposed. In 1932 it condemned 'specialisation' by players, especially forwards. Even the 1951 initiative was severely restricted by the limits placed on training by the RFU and the IB. The first meeting of the newly expanded Board in 1948 had reiterated that 'the employment of a paid trainer or coach is contrary to the principles of amateur rugby football'. It also decreed 'that it is contrary to the spirit of amateur rugby football that teams should be assembled at a centre during a period prior to a match for the purpose of a change of air and training'. This was primarily directed against the French and the southern hemisphere nations and also the Welsh, who were suspected of preparing too seriously for internationals. This was relaxed slightly in 1957 when pre-match training camps of two days were allowed.[6] But the pressure for a more organised and systematic approach to team preparation continued to build, partly driven by the increasing importance of international competition and partly by the growth of physical education and teacher training colleges. Rugby union's strength in the teaching profession had been significantly boosted in the 1950s by the expansion of higher and further education, and this had slowly brought new attitudes into the game.

The first incremental shifts in the dynamics of post-war rugby could therefore be seen in the universities and colleges. Up until the mid-1950s the Oxford versus Cambridge Varsity match had effectively been a trial match for the Five Nations championship, which it preceded. But the boom in higher education from the mid-1950s saw institutions such as Leeds, Durham and Manchester universities and physical education colleges such as Loughborough and St Luke's in Exeter produce teams and players that could challenge the old order. More adventurous and willing to question traditional methods, not to mention possessing players such as Bev Risman and Ray French who had grown up with a rugby league background, these teams made full use of the fitness and coaching facilities available to them. St Luke's caused a major surprise in 1957 when they won the Middlesex Sevens tournament. They were followed in 1959 by Loughborough, the first of their five victories. By the mid-1960s Loughborough not only dominated the Universities' Athletic Union (UAU) competition but could also boast a first-class fixture list that included Leicester, Gloucester, Rosslyn Park and London Irish. Coached initially by the innovative John Robins, a former Wales and British Lions forward, the college included future stars such as Risman, Gerald Davies, John Dawes, John Taylor and John Mantle, and played what was known as 'Total Rugby', in which all players where expected to run with and handle the ball. This style of rugby saw its success continued as the Welsh students graduated, with many taking the same philosophy to London Welsh at club level and ultimately the Welsh and British Lions sides.

In contrast, the game at Oxford and Cambridge atrophied. Sport no longer held the central importance in the life of the two universities that it had before and immediately after the Second World War. Oxford University's *Isis* magazine ceased to have regular sports coverage in the late 1950s. The abolition of National Service in 1960 also meant that university players were disadvantageously younger and lighter than those in club sides, making it harder for most universities to compete with club sides. Of course, disdainful insularity meant that neither university took part in the UAU championships. Most importantly, possession of a good sporting record no longer offered an easy route to Oxbridge. Wilf Wooller protested in the 1967 Varsity match programme that an 'inflexibly high academic entrance level which ensures the greatest chunks of pimply swots enter Oxbridge' had excluded sporting types who would in previous years have been accepted, as he had been in the 1930s. In response, the young English don John Carey seemed to capture the spirit of the time in an article entitled 'Let's scrap Twickenham' in which he argued that 'allowing fifteen [students] to occasionally run around a large patch of grassland in the middle of a city [is not a] sensible or economic way of looking after the physical education of a college of three or four hundred busy students'.[7] The decline was starkly illustrated in financial terms. In 1949 Oxford University rugby club had a surplus of £5,390, which was used to subsidise less popular sports. By 1967 this had shrivelled to just £500. In 1973 Oxford captain Chris Laidlaw noted that over half of Oxford colleges no longer had a rugby team and by 1975 there was even talk about moving the Varsity match from Twickenham because of the dwindling crowds it was attracting.[8]

Teams from the PE colleges and the newer universities also differed from Oxbridge in attitude. These were sides that wanted to win and trained and prepared themselves to do so. They were not gentlemen amateurs, either by breeding or inclination. Their youth, social background and education meant that they were more open-minded and more likely to question traditional methods, a minor reflection of the questioning of traditional authority that was taking place throughout Britain and the rest of the world in the 1960s.

A similar process was taking place in the club game. 'The blood coming in now is not quite as blue as it used to be and lots of them are not going into the established rugby clubs', explained a delegate to the 1960 RFU annual general meeting. As with Oxbridge, Harlequins, Richmond and Blackheath, the big three of club rugby, found their traditional dominance challenged clubs of lesser social status. London saw the rise of the exile clubs such as London Welsh and London Scottish, as well as what were previously second tier clubs such as Wasps and Rosslyn Park. Moreover, London's traditional dominance of the club game was also threatened by Midlands clubs such as Bedford, Leicester, Coventry and Moseley, south-western clubs such as Bath, Bristol and Gloucester, and northern sides such as Gosforth, Orrell and Headingley. As with the colleges, the emergence of these clubs in the front ranks of the game was not unconnected to shifting attitudes in society, which gave them the self-confidence to challenge the RFU's authority and also allowed them to become more explicitly competitive. As we have already seen in the chapter on masculinity, from the mid-1960s there was considerable concern about rising levels of violence in the game brought about, so it was believed, by increasingly competitive play. Ken Chapman of Harlequins and a RFU president was not alone when he confessed that 'I have been considerably alarmed at what seems to me to be an increase in the desire to win at any cost, and in particular of the spread of rough over-violent play.'[9] It was hardly surprising therefore when clubs began to agitate for national cup and league competitions. The idea of national cup competition – last seriously discussed by the RFU committee in January 1878 when it decided not to use the Calcutta Cup for a national cup tournament as suggested by the Calcutta club that donated it – was raised by Bedford at the RFU's 1967 annual general meeting. Opposed by the RFU committee, the proposal was heavily defeated the following year but the idea refused to die. The following year a dozen northern clubs proposed the formation of a northern league comprising clubs in Cheshire, Lancashire, Northumberland and Yorkshire. This too was turned down by the RFU.[10]

But clearly something was changing. The leadership of English rugby was increasingly seen as being out of touch with the modern world, the sporting equivalent of the Conservative Party's 'backwoodsmen'. 'Hearty, smug, sensitive to criticism and self-perpetuating', was how a *Sunday Times* feature article described the RFU in 1969. 'Rugby is becoming distinctly unfashionable in Britain, a trend which is largely unnoticed within the rugby fraternity itself', noted Chris Laidlaw a couple of years later.[11] Most dramatically, the clashes during the 1969 Springbok tour had shown that the RFU could no longer take for granted its Colonel Blimpish belief in its own authority and the deference of others.

There was also another solvent that was beginning to dissolve the grip of tradition: money. The International Board had spent considerable time in the 1960s attempting to keep a lid on the burgeoning commercialism of the game in South Africa. In 1965 it had stopped players accepting awards 'presented by a commercial firm' and, after a series of regulations, in 1969 it had reiterated that 'commercial sponsorship is contrary to amateur principles. No gift or financial support should be accepted by any union or affiliated body from a commercial firm or any individual in his commercial capacity.'[12] The problem with this intransigence was that there were companies only too eager to put money into the game. The issue was highlighted by the BBC television programme *Rugby Special* in January 1969 when it revealed that it knew of eight companies willing to sponsor the game to amounts up to £500,000. The RFU denied the accuracy of the report and went on to state that, even if it were true, sponsorship 'could not be tolerated or even considered'.[13] Although in hindsight this may seem stupidly short-sighted, at that time the RFU was not so far from other British sports bodies in its suspicion of commercialism. Rugby league only allowed sponsorship of competitions in 1971 and the Football League refused to allow shirt sponsorship until 1978. What was actually remarkable about the RFU's stance was how quickly it changed. Barely two years after ruling that sponsorship was impossible, it changed its mind and decided that sponsorship was still bad but that 'patronage and commercial assistance are acceptable provided they benefit the game'. The following year it set up a 'Financial Assistance' committee to deal with sponsors, of whom it had eleven by the end of 1972.[14]

It was a similar story with the proposal for a national cup competition. Despite its previous 'unequivocal' opposition, the RFU backflipped in November 1970 and the first round of the new, uninspiringly titled 'RFU Club Competition' kicked off with thirty-two teams at the start of the 1971–72 season. Despite complaints about violence and the 'win at all costs' attitudes of some clubs, the tournament proved to be both a financial and a sporting success, complete with giant-killing exploits from Wilmslow who dispatched Harlequins in the quarter finals. The competition demonstrated the dominance in the game of the ambitious non-London clubs (of the old elite only Harlequins ever won the cup, in 1991), and was won by Gloucester, Bristol, Coventry, Bedford, Gosforth, Leicester and Bath in its first two decades. In 1975 Imperial Tobacco announced a three-year, £100,000 sponsorship of the tournament under its John Player brand, emulating a similar deal with rugby league. One of many tributaries of the Rubicon of professionalism had been bridged.[15]

The introduction of league systems proved to be a harder task. As was the case in the early 1890s, the RFU saw leagues both as opening the door to professionalism and, as would be the case in the late 1990s, a potential threat to its control of the sport. Moreover, Sir Anthony Wharton's traditionalist view that 'compulsory [league] fixtures between clubs have their dangers. Amateur clubs like to choose their own opponents', still had considerable support within the game. The *Daily Telegraph*'s unofficial 'Merit Table' gained substantial authority in the 1960s, so much so that some clubs, such as London Scottish, included their success in it as part of their official records. The *Telegraph*'s table allowed the RFU to deflect to some extent demands for league competition by pointing to its voluntary nature. But the popularity of the cup competition, and the successful introduction of a Scottish league structure by the previously antediluvian SRU in 1974, led to a clamour for something to be done. In 1975 thirteen English clubs and seven Welsh sides, led by Coventry secretary Alf Wyman, announced their intention to form an 'Anglo-Welsh Merit Competition' at the start of the 1976–77 season. As ever, this threat to its authority forced the RFU into action and in September 1976 it announced the creation of four regional merit tables comprised of over forty leading English clubs, an idea originally proposed in 1972 by the Surrey rugby union but dismissed at the time. The one caveat was that 'participation of clubs in any other form of merit table, league or combination without RFU approval is contrary to the bye-laws and cannot be condoned under any circumstances', which took much of the wind out of the sails of the Anglo-Welsh movement. But the desire for a competitive structure for the sport was not so easily sated. A survey of senior clubs in 1978 found that 92 per cent supported the national cup competition, 49 per cent supported merit tables and 37 per cent were for the introduction of an outright league system, with 19 per cent undecided.[16]

As well as the demands of clubs, the campaign for the formation of an English league structure was given added impetus by the abysmal performances of the national side. Between 1970 and 1975 England won just nine of thirty-one matches and finished bottom of the Five Nations table every season but one. *The Times*' Peter West argued for leagues on the grounds that 'there is a great yearning in England to see their international side consistently winning again. Young people – on whom the future prosperity of the game depends – react even more enthusiastically these days to success at the highest level. The case for a league rests on the contention that the cream – both corporate and individual – comes out on top – and on merit.'[17] He was not the first to argue for drastic action to raise national standards. The collapse in England's playing record after their 1963 Five Nations victory – they were not to win it outright again until the 1980 Grand Slam – occurred at precisely the same time as television was becoming the most important medium for sports coverage. Television sets not only became ubiquitous in homes but technological advances such as colour pictures and inter-continental satellite transmission of live events brought the political and national rivalry of international sport into the living rooms of millions of people. The 1968 Olympics and the 1966 and 1970 soccer world cups brought all these elements together and marked a turning point in sport's relationship with television – their destinies would now be forever entwined.

For its part, the RFU had long had a close relationship with the BBC. It had been the first sporting body approached by the corporation when it decided to broadcast live sport in 1927 and the inaugural BBC sports radio commentary was of England's 1927 11–9 win over Wales. Teddy Wakelam, who was to become the BBC's voice of rugby union in the interwar years, was invited to audition as commentator despite, as he freely admitted, 'up to that date, I had no journalistic experience'. He also commentated on the first live television broadcast of a rugby match, England's 1938 Calcutta Cup loss.[18] TV remained a novelty until the early 1950s, although a prescient Wavell Wakefield began his presidency of the RFU in 1950 by forecasting that the medium would have a 'major impact' on the game and would need to 'be closely watched'. In 1952 the BBC paid just £100 to broadcast the

England versus Wales match and offered fifty guineas for any subsequent internationals. However, things turned more serious in 1954 with the passing of the Television Act in July of that year. This paved the way for the launch of commercial television in the shape of ITV. Concerned to nip the potential threat in the bud, the BBC met with the four Home Unions a couple of days before the act became law to agree future broadcasts. Despite objections from the Scots, the RFU agreed to the live broadcasting of four internationals and the varsity match. Somewhat disingenuously the BBC claimed that there 'was no great demand for the televising of rugby union' in order to deflect questions about the value of broadcasting rights.[19]

This set the pattern for the next forty years. The Five Nations tournament was at the heart of the BBC's early year sports' schedule, focusing public attention on the showpiece fixtures of the game. Money was not an important issue for the RFU at this time. As late as 1970 the BBC was only paying £5,000 per international. The crucial aspect for the game's leadership was the portrayal of the sport. In 1958 a crisis meeting had been held with the BBC to complain about its emphasis on 'roughness' and 'toughness' in the game. The BBC's reporting of players who had switched to league was also criticised. Following hints that the Home Unions might approach ITV, the BBC's Peter Dimmock agreed to insert a clause into future contracts stating that 'the BBC would do its best to reflect rugby union football in the best interests of the game'. Complaints about the coverage of the game flared up sporadically, especially about coverage of demonstrations during the 1969 Springboks tour – when the RFU committee asked for 'appropriate action' to be 'taken to obviate the inclusion of such extraneous matter in television coverage' – and occasionally when rugby league was mentioned on BBC2's *Rugby Special*, but in general the game had a harmonious relationship with the broadcaster up until the 1990s.[20]

Indeed, the problem lay not on the screen but on the pitch. Live coverage of England's matches, with one or two honourable exceptions, simply highlighted the weakness of the national side. Throughout the 1970s, England won just eleven Five Nations games. The ease of air travel had also led in 1963 to the start of 'short tours' by individual national teams, in addition to British Lions tours. The inaugural overseas tour by England, in 1963 to New Zealand and Australia, had resulted in all three test matches being lost amidst some controversy in the England camp about, yet again, New Zealand tactics. Improbable touring victories against South Africa in 1972 and New Zealand in 1973 tended to raise expectations about the ability of the English team and to amplify further the importance of international rugby. One beneficiary of the increased emphasis on the fortunes of the national side was coaching.

Following the defeats in New Zealand, in January 1964 a new coaching committee was established by the RFU, which initiated manuals, posters, newsletters and conferences. Following defeat by the touring All Blacks in 1967, coached by the charismatic Fred Allen, the RFU appointed its first Director of Coaching, Don Rutherford, although in deference to older prejudices against professional coaches his official title was 'Technical Administrator'. The following year, in September 1969, as part of Rutherford's reforms, Northampton's Don White was appointed as the first coach of the England side. He began in style with England's first-ever triumph over South Africa at Twickenham, but this was as good as it got. In the ten years before a coach was appointed, England had a winning percentage of 43; in the following ten years after the appointment of a coach the percentage dropped to 33 per cent, leading some such as Dickie Jeeps to argue even in 1976 that coaching had undermined creative play in the game.[21] But coaching, like cup competitions, merit tables and worse, were here to stay.

'Sexy, greedy' rugby

Whether it recognised it or not, the RFU had begun to unconsciously and slowly dismantle its architecture of gentlemanly amateurism in order to respond to external pressures, whether they were from clubs, players, the media or the simple competitive imperative of having a winning England side. In this, it was a microcosm of broader trends in English society. In the 1960s 'amateur' had become one of the words that symbolised the problems of post-war British society. The use of the word as an insult was not confined to the left. On his accession to the leadership of the Conservative Party in 1966, the *Observer Magazine* noted that Edward Heath, along with rising stars Edward du Cann and Peter Walker deplored 'the amateurishness of British politics'.[22] It was not just politics. The culture of 'gentlemanly capitalism' was also being challenged, not least by North American entrepreneurs who engineered a series of spectacular takeovers, such as the Canadian media tycoon Roy Thomson. Between 1968 and 1986 the number of overseas banks and financial companies in the City of London increased from 125 to more than 400. Moreover, the values of the middle classes had begun to shift towards valuing success above character, as demonstrated by an eclipse of sporting prowess by academic excellence in the public schools and at Oxbridge. The middle class itself continued to expand – the category of 'higher professionals, administrators and managers' had grown from 9.6 per cent of the employed male population in 1951 to 16 per cent in 1971, the highest rise over any equivalent period thus far in the twentieth century

– further diluting the influence of those educated in or supportive of traditional gentlemanly norms.[23]

Although the RFU and many of its supporters had placed themselves in firm opposition to the changes taking place in Britain and the wider world – most infamously by the 1969 Springbok tour and its continuing support of South Africa – it was not immune to the forces that were reshaping society. Although a profoundly conservative sport, rugby union had a significant proportion of university-educated players and some of them were deeply affected by student protests against the Vietnam War and South Africa's apartheid regime. The late 1960s were a time when the fashionable model of a public school boy was no longer Tom Brown but Mick Travis, the rebellious hero of Lindsay Anderson's *If*. As we have already seen, in 1969 London Welsh, Wales and British Lions' flanker John Taylor refused to play against the South African tourists. This questioning of traditional authority seeped into other aspects of the sport too. Coming back from a match at Llanelli in 1975, Bedford and England winger Derek Wyatt queried his role in rugby: 'the crowd must have been 12,000 or more; the car park, which had a capacity of perhaps eight hundred cars, was full; the programmes were sold out; the bars were packed. Where, I pondered, was the money going?' He was not the only one.[24]

It was thinking like this that led to the 1970s witnessing a slow erosion of the fundamental amateur principle of no payment for playing the game. Initially the impulse for this came from South Africa and France. By 1976 the RFU and the other home nations were sufficiently concerned to register their alarm at the number of players 'being invited, in some cases with their wives and families, to South Africa to play and coach in what would normally be their close season'. Although this was no different from what cricketers had done for decades, it represented a not insignificant breach close to the core of the amateur ideal. In France, the situation was possibly more alarming. In a 1965 *Rugby World* article, Albert Lodge told readers that '*amateur* may be a French word, but in the rugby clubs of France and elsewhere on the continent attitudes are borrowed from professional sport that would make the turf at Twickers bristle'.[25] More than the turf bristled in the summer of 1973 when an advertisement in the classified section of *The Times* baldly announced:

> French Rugger Club, Grenoble – Seeks player to add Go to their game, in return would discuss either assistance in arranging university or other studies. Alternatively, would assist in job finding and settling in the area. Amenities winter sports, etc, adjacent.[26]

Needless to say, the offers of assistance in finding studentships or employment were contrary to the amateur regulations of the game. Although such help was also common in the English game, it was the openness of the offer that offended Anglo-Saxon sensibilities. Even so, a string of players made their way across the Channel to play for French clubs, most notably England lock Nigel Horton who joined Toulouse in 1977 and managed to find a job as a bar manager.[27] But the most shocking example of the distance the game had travelled from its roots came in April 1978 when Blackheath staged a charity match between a London XV and a Welsh XV. Minutes before they were due to take the field, the Welsh players refused to play unless they were paid to do so. Faced with the choice of abandoning the match or their amateur principles, Blackheath officials chose to discard the latter. A subsequent RFU investigation severely censured the club for breaches of rules relating to expenses and barred it from the John Player Cup for one season.[28]

The fact that Blackheath, a club that had historically been at the very core of the amateur tradition, could find itself in such a position spoke volumes for the state of the game. The pressures of commercialism had caused other bastions of the amateur tradition to buckle too. In 1975 Oxford and Cambridge universities agreed to the Varsity match being sponsored by city firm Bowring. A sense of the appetite for commercialism that had been awoken within the clubs, and many other parts of the RFU, can be seen in the comments of Leicester's Kevin Andrews, who told an RFU meeting in May 1979 that 'there is an enormous amount of money available and [who] asked whether we, in rugby football, were getting our fair share of it'.[29]

At the beginning of the 1970s Dudley Kemp had told the RFU that 'ours is an amateur game, organised and administered for pleasure and enjoyment . . . [We should not look] with envy at the top levels of other games which, being professional, are in fact organised for public entertainment'.[30] Yet by the start of the 1980s it had in practice abandoned virtually all its traditional objections to commercial involvement in the game. Perhaps the most egregious example of this was during the Adidas 'boot money' scandal of 1982, when the German boot manufacturer revealed to the Inland Revenue that it paid players to wear its boots. According to England prop Mike Burton, the going rate was £50 per international match.[31] The RFU carried out a desultory inquiry that, as usual, decided that not enough evidence could be found to take action. Nevertheless, untroubled by the fact that Adidas had been undermining the most cherished principle of the game for the previous decade, the RFU decided in September 1983 to approach them to supply free boots to the England side. The contract eventually went to Nike, who outbid Adidas and agreed to pay the RFU 'boot money' of £60,000 over three years.[32]

This was the spirit of the age. English society's slow move away from traditional middle-class values of character and status that began in the 1960s had assumed breakneck speed following the election of Margaret Thatcher's Conservative government in 1979. Her defeat of the trade union movement by the mid-1980s had vanquished many middle-class fears that were characteristic of the 1960s and 1970s. Her disdain for aristocratic privilege and identification with 'wealth makers' made the open pursuit of money not only acceptable but fashionable. This change was most spectacularly seen in one of rugby union's traditional bastions, the City of London, which in October 1986 experienced 'Big Bang', the introduction of major deregulation and 'free market' principles into the City. The old boy networks that had previously run the City were partially broken up and traditional methods of doing business through personal connections abandoned. As the Nolan Inquiry into Standards in Public Life later reported, the old codes of gentlemanly behaviour had dissolved and been replaced, in some cases, by 'a culture of moral vagueness'. The difference between the old and the new was summed up by a stockbroker who had begun work in 1946: 'it was very bad form to talk about money and still is among my generation. One would certainly never boast about what one earned or about one's successes.' Now the opposite was true. 'Sexy greedy' was how the new attitude was summed up in Caryl Churchill's satirical play of the time *Serious Money*.[33]

Those who played and administered rugby union were part of this changing world. Not only did it once more become commonplace for England and other international players to be seen working in the City – among them Rob Andrew, Peter Winterbottom, Tony Underwood, Brian Moore, Simon Halliday and David Pears – but the Varsity match and Five Nations games at Twickenham became part of the cycle of the new City's social and corporate entertainment life. The changed attitudes towards competitiveness and money were reflected in the RFU's embrace not only of open commercialism but also by the introduction in 1987 of a full league structure for the game. Sponsored by the brewers Courage, the new structure organised over 1,000 teams in 108 divisions, each with promotion and relegation between them. As with the John Player Cup competition, which had seen attendances and media interest increase each year of the 1980s, culminating in the first sold-out final at Twickenham in 1989 to see Bath defeat Leicester, the Courage leagues boosted crowds, club income and playing standards. In particular, it threw into sharp relief the dominance of a handful of clubs. The first league champions were Leicester, who had also won the John Player

Cup three times, followed by Bath and then Wasps. But it was Bath who proved to be qualitatively superior to the rest by carrying off the title another four times before the professional era, to go alongside their nine cup wins in twelve seasons. Of course, they were effectively a professional side – only two of their starting fifteen in their 1987 final win over Wasps were locally born – and their success only increased the pressures on other clubs to recruit and retain the best players. Stories of payments to players, signing-on fees and sudden moves from less fashionable to more glamorous clubs became legion.[34] In 1993, rumours that Rupert Murdoch's Sky TV – which had just paid £191m to televise soccer's new Premier League – was interested in broadcasting club matches even led to speculation about a possible breakaway by the leading clubs from the RFU.

The RFU attempted to keep some control over the disintegration of amateurism that was taking place beneath its feet by circulating in May 1993 *Inducements to Move, Incentives to Stay, and other Illegal Payments*, a memorandum to clubs outlining disciplinary measures they could face if they transgressed the rules. Danie Serfontein expressed his concern about

> the effect that intense competition through leagues is having. We all serve a club that, rightly, wants to do better, to win, to move up a league or to maintain a position in a top league. The pressures we as administrators have placed on the game are great and so the dangers of inducements to players which put the amateur game under threat are all too obvious.[35]

But the genie could not be put back in the bottle. No one took any notice of the memo. Moreover, the leagues were having a positive impact not just on the club game but also, as many in the RFU had hoped, on the national team. Even as early as 1990 that year's RFU president, Michael Pearey, was noting with satisfaction that 'the resurgence of England Rugby over the last two years has been due in large measure to the introduction of leagues'.[36] The added competitive toughness that the leagues brought to the England side was complemented by the methods of national coach Geoff Cooke. Appointed in 1987, after a disastrous Five Nations and a weak inaugural world cup campaign, he refashioned the team around a tight, aggressive pack, the kicking of Rob Andrew and a flowing three-quarter line including Jeremy Guscott and the Underwood brothers. He had no truck with RFU traditions, demanding total control of the side and eschewing the committees that had historically controlled the England side. As befitted an era in which success had triumphed over character and connection, he brought in his own technical backroom staff, committed to 'professionalising' the way that England played the game. To much surprise, in October 1988 he made 22-year-old Will Carling captain of the side. Carling was the very model of the modern rugger man, combining a public school and military background with an easy familiarity with the City and its new-found brashness. With back-to-back Grand Slams in 1991 and 1992 and a narrow world cup final loss to Australia in 1991, the England side had at last achieved the prominence the RFU had craved since the 1960s. Cooke, Carling, Guscott and company had made rugby union the sporting backdrop to the 'sexy greedy' era. England's 'Band of Brothers', as the press dubbed them, were one more reason why it had become fashionable to be proud to be middle class.

End game

If 1986 was the Big Bang in the City of London, 1987 had similar implications for rugby union. Not only did it see the introduction of leagues into the English game but it also witnessed the first rugby union world cup. In 1977 the Australian media mogul Kerry Packer, frustrated by what he saw as an old boy network running cricket, launched his own television-driven World Series Cricket competition. Despite the opposition of the cricket authorities, it was a tremendous success. This did not go unnoticed in rugby union circles. Indeed, plans for a Packer-style professional rugby union circuit based on New Zealand were unveiled in late 1977 and in 1979 SARB had also been approached by businessmen to discuss a joint venture to establish a professional tournament. In Australia and New Zealand, where pressure for rugby union to change was strongest and where the impact of Packer's WSC was deepest, discussion about the development of a rugby union world cup began in earnest.[37] The RFU had turned down as 'undesirable' an offer to discuss a possible world cup in 1968, and its attitude remained unchanged.[38] In 1983 the issue was formally raised at an IB meeting by Australia but rejected. However, in April of that year Australian journalist and sports promoter David Lord announced plans to sign up 200 of the world's leading players to form eight sides to play international tournaments around the world. Based entirely on Packer's cricket model, Lord promised payments of £90,000 each to players and seven international tournaments over the following three years. The cost of the venture would total £20 million. Lord claimed that eighty-eight British players had signed up in the first few weeks of the venture and that contracts had been agreed to play matches at Wembley stadium. Despite announcing that the first match would kick off on 14 January 1984 at Chelsea's Stamford Bridge stadium, by the end of the year the scheme was dead.

But for the supporters of the world cup concept, Lord had played a crucial role in strengthening their case. He demonstrated that if the IB did not organise a world cup, someone else would. 'If we were to save our game and not lose it to some entrepreneur, we would have to act promptly and organise a world cup', argued Nick Shehadie, the president of the Australian union.[39] In June 1984 New Zealand once again raised the issue and in March 1985 the IB voted 10–6 to stage a world cup in Australia and New Zealand in 1987. The voting followed a predictable pattern, with the three southern hemisphere delegations plus France voting in favour, and Scotland and Ireland opposed. The English and Welsh delegations split, each casting one vote for and one vote against the proposal. If they had not divided in this way, the motion would have been lost.[40]

Despite the seemingly inevitable direction that the world cup would take rugby union, the RFU still held out. Incoming president John Burgess told the 1987 annual general meeting that 'the RFU will continue to be a bulwark of amateurism as we believe that this is the wish of the majority of the game in England' and it increasingly dissented on the IB's relaxations of the amateur code. But its voice now carried little international authority. Amateurism had become little more than a hollow phrase. In France the pretence that the game was other than semi-professional had been dropped long ago. If the influx of overseas players from the mid-1970s did not raise suspicions, the signing of rugby league internationals Jean-Marc Bourret and Jean-Marc Gonzalez by French union clubs in 1981 should have alerted even the most comatose committeeman. Across the border, Italian clubs paid even less lip-service to the game's principles when recruiting considerable numbers of Australian and New Zealand players. Such were the rewards available that Wallaby wing David Campese could claim that he was 'rugby's first millionaire' as a results of his time spent playing Italy. For the more adventurous, the intertwining of sport and business in Japan meant that players could earn a handsome living through their rugby skills. 'Rugby is to a large extent financed by companies and on tours the players get leave with pay. In regards to poaching of players I don't think they are actually luring players with large contract money', Japanese rugby union president Shiggy Kono explained matter of factly in 1994. 'Many New Zealand and other overseas players seek to be hired by Japanese companies and play rugby. They are probably paid a good salary but nothing extremely out of [the] norm. The trouble is the current exchange rate. A salary of 8–9 million yen per annum is nothing extraordinary but when converted to NZ dollars it exceeds

NZ$150,000 which in New Zealand is big money.' By 1990 former All Blacks turned player agent Andy Haden could authoritatively claim that even English clubs were offering players up to £400 a week.[41]

Most importantly South Africa's desire for international competition had led to the extravagant financing of so-called 'rebel' tours. Thanks in large part to the astute political manoeuvring of SARB president Danie Craven, the threat of a professional breakaway competition led by South Africa had never materialised, despite the international sporting isolation of South Africa being almost complete by the mid-1980s. The last official tourists were the 1984 England side but the New Zealand High Court's ban on the All Blacks projected 1986 tour forced SARB to follow another route and, partly in connivance with other national unions, invite so-called rebel touring teams. In April 1986 the unofficial New Zealand 'Cavaliers' arrived in Johannesburg, boasting twenty-eight of the thirty players originally picked for the banned All Blacks tour, all of whom were paid. Three years later a World XV toured which, although sanctioned by the IB, was no less professional than the Cavaliers' tour. As a Welsh Rugby Union inquiry discovered, the ten Welsh players on the tour were paid around £30,000 each. 'SARB', the inquiry noted dryly, 'was prepared to tolerate the making of financial inducements to players to tour'.[42] There could be no doubt, admitted RFU president Denis Easby on his return from England's 1994 tour of South Africa, 'that South Africa paid its players and its referees contrary to the regulations'.[43]

Nor, despite formal protestations to the contrary, could there now be any doubt that the players themselves wanted to be paid. Like a fat man at a feast, the IB had been rapidly unbuckling the belt of restrictions on expenses and other payments to players from the mid-1980s, much to the irritation of the RFU. The payment of expenses to players on overseas tours had been a bone of contention since the advent of regular tours in the early 1960s. As early as 1959 a Cassandra-like O.L. Owen of *The Times* had predicted that 'if the Rugby authorities are unwise, and encourage too much play and too many tours overseas . . . the necessity [will] arise for substantial payments over and above those covered by the words "reasonable expenses".' The 1960s saw skirmishes with South Africa over the payment of 'out of pocket' expenses and gradually the amounts of 'expenses' that players could receive had risen.[44] The RFU viewed such developments as the thin end of the wedge of 'broken time' payments and in 1985 it had objected to the IB's liberalisation of the amount of daily allowance that could be paid to touring players and forbade England representatives in IB centenary matches from receiving their full allowances. The following year it openly declared that the

IB's proposal to allow increased payments for 'long tour allowances' would 'constitute broken-time payments'.[45]

But by the late 1980s, the target of the reformers had moved elsewhere. In 1990, in what was heralded as a decisive change, the IB allowed players to make money from 'non-rugby activities'. In order to placate the RFU and the remaining supporters of amateurism, it also contrarily ruled out commercial endorsements of rugby equipment and allowed local unions to stop players charging for speaking at rugby functions.[46] This did little to deter players who had a high public profile and the wherewithal to exploit it. Will Carling established his own self-promotional company to capitalise on his fame and Jeremy Guscott became a regular face in men's fashion magazines and on the catwalks. In an attempt to keep control of the England players' marketing activities, the RFU appointed WHJ Promotions to handle the commercial affairs of the side. This immediately blew up in their faces with the 1991 Cardiff post-match fiasco. For the next four years the players and the RFU maintained a barely concealed contempt for each other, exemplified by RFU secretary Dudley Wood's comment that 'we can easily find another fifteen players to play against Scotland in a month if it proves necessary' and Carling's famous remark just before the 1995 World Cup that the English game was run by 'fifty-seven old farts'.[47]

There was more than a hint of King Canute in the RFU's stance. Outgoing RFU president Ian Beer in July 1994 called for an international agreement to ensure that the 1995 World Cup remained amateur. Even in April 1995, when the seas of professionalism had already washed over the southern hemisphere and with the smell of the incoming tide in his nostrils, Dudley Wood was still asserting that, 'if you say to the England players "do you want to be a contracted, full-time professional rugby player?" I promise you the answer is no'.[48] The comment of a Foreign Office official in David Hare's play *Plenty* seemed to capture the outlook of Wood and his co-thinkers: 'as our empire collapses, there is little to believe in. Behaviour is all.'[49]

The success of Geoff Cooke's England side ratcheted up the pressure towards professionalism several notches. Not only did England reach the 1991 world cup final, ensuring massive media interest in the tournament, but the television viewing figures exceeded expectations, delivering to the broadcasters the prime market segment of young 'AB' (upper-middle- and middle-class) males with disposable income to burn. It also demonstrated that the desire for professionalism was not confined to the southern hemisphere, when the French side refused to play their quarter-final against Australia unless they were paid 7,000 francs each.[50] As the 1995 World Cup approached, to be held in the *laager* of barely concealed professionalism in South Africa, it was clear that something had to give.

Ironically, the final *coup de grace* to the amateur ideal was to come from a familiar source. Just as the formation of rugby league in 1895 had been decisive in subsequently shaping rugby union, so too did rugby league have a crucial impact on union in 1995. Since the late 1970s the growth of league had been a constant thorn in the side of national unions. The growth of amateur league in Britain in the 1980s had forced the RFU, under threat of legal action, to abandon key aspects of its ban on league players. Union players crossed to league with frequent regularity from the mid-1980s, especially from Wales. Even Springbok greats such as Ray Mordt and Rob Louw tried their hand at the forbidden game. But it was in Australasia where the effect was, in more ways than one, game-changing. The booming popularity of Australian rugby league had even begun to worry the NZRU by the 1990s, thanks to trans-Tasman television coverage and a steady haemorrhaging of All Blacks to league.[51] The southern hemisphere nations had attempted to mitigate the impact, partly by continually revising local interpretations of amateurism to keep players in union and also by reinstating to the 'amateur ranks' virtually any player who tried league but wanted to return to union. By the mid-1990s all elite rugby union players were receiving some form of payment, up to 30,000 Australian dollars in the case of Wallaby internationals, but it was clearly not enough to staunch the flow.[52]

In late 1994 rumours began to circulate that a 'super league' competition was being secretly planned by leading Australian league clubs. In February 1995, a proposal by Rupert Murdoch's News Corporation to create a Super League was vetoed by the Australian Rugby League (ARL) authorities and civil war broke out Down Under. Tens of millions of dollars were spent signing players to rival Super League and ARL competitions. Momentary *schadenfreude* in rugby union ranks rapidly dissipated when it became clear that union players would also be tempted by rugby league's new-found riches. 'We don't want our players sitting there like lambs to the slaughter. The advent of Super League could force us to move to professionalism much quicker than we were going', explained NZRU chairman Richie Guy. 'To protect ourselves from Super League, we must take the game global, we must become professional', echoed former Wallaby Ross Turnbull.[53] On 8 April ARU and NZRU representatives met and decided that the only realistic course of action was to embrace their potential nemesis and approached Murdoch for a deal. Four days later, the New South Wales Rugby Union officially announced that rugby union was no longer an amateur sport. By the time the world cup began in South Africa in May, the fate of rugby union had been settled. On 22 June the Australian, New Zealand and South African unions signed a £340 million ten-year deal with News Corporation. 'For some time rugby union has appeared to be threatened by other codes, almost like a wounded impala limping through the bushveld with lions nearby', declared SARFU president Louis Luyt. 'This agreement allows these unions to retain control of their destinies.'[54]

As ever, things were not quite so simple. The administrators' attitudes to payments may have changed but not towards their players. The hierarchy of the southern hemisphere unions had neglected to inform any of its players about their plans for professionalism. Flushed with their own self-importance, they had failed to notice that Ross Turnbull's World Rugby Corporation (WRC), backed verbally by Murdoch's arch rival Kerry Packer, had secretly signed up most of the cream of southern rugby union talent. To what extent Packer was genuinely interested in Turnbull's WRC rather than simply poking a sharp stick into the eye of News Corporation is a moot point. As players such as Welsh captain Ieuan Evans discovered, signing with WRC entitled them to nothing more than a promise of a down payment three months later and the responsibility to pay for their own match insurance. Certainly Turnbull's record as an administrator did not inspire confidence and his inability to back WRC contracts with ready money quickly allowed the ferocious Murdoch negotiators to outflank him. The project collapsed when Murdoch's general Sam Chisholm persuaded Springbok captain François Pienaar to switch sides and Turnbull was publicly humiliated on South African television by Luyt.[55]

For the leadership of the RFU these events were doubly humiliating. Not only had it lost the fight against professionalism but – like Anthony Eden during the Suez Crisis – it had also discovered that its international authority had simply evaporated. A man out of his time, Dudley Wood, who retired as RFU secretary in July 1995, imagined that the events of spring and summer 1995 were an 'opportunity for us to distance ourselves from the professional sport and remain a distinctive sport, based on whatever degree of amateurism we can preserve but certainly as a recreational sport'.[56] Faced with a *fait accompli* and with no stomach to split rugby in defence of what it had proclaimed as 'the first principle of the game', the supporters of amateurism simply gave up. On 27 August 1995 the IB legalised professionalism. It was just two days short of the centenary of the split with rugby league over the same issue.

The events of the summer of 1995 were the culmination of a process that began in the 1960s in which amateurism gradually collapsed in on itself. The growing status and financial worth of international sport had gradually yet fatally undermined the RFU's commitment to amateurism. From the late 1960s onwards, there was increasing frustration within rugby union with the acceptance of the mediocrity of the English national side – a legacy of the amateur idea that the game was about participation and not necessarily about winning. As the RFU slowly developed elite rugby, which would culminate in the 2003 World Cup triumph, the old mores of amateur play were cast aside. Faced with the determined thrust for professionalism by the southern hemisphere nations, the RFU and other supporters of amateurism had no ground upon which to fight.

Moreover, the claim that amateurism made rugby union morally superior to other sports could not be sustained. To take one example, in the 1993–94 season the RFU had circulated to its clubs a 'Declaration of Compliance' in respect of the amateur regulations of the game. Over 1,500 member clubs, including all those in the top six divisions of the Courage Leagues, signed and returned the declaration, confirming that they conformed completely to the regulations. Given the extent of covert payments, job offers and inducements to switch clubs that then pertained at the top levels of the game, only the very foolish or the completely naive could believe such affirmations. It was one more example of the cynicism that had for decades accompanied the pursuit of amateurism. Since the 1950s it had been rugby union's stock in trade to deny the reality of payments for play in European rugby. Then in the 1980s it had denied that players in South Africa were paid. Now the RFU had to pretend that its own players were not remunerated. The contradiction between maintaining the amateur ideal and the reality of modern rugby had led to a system of institutionalised cynicism, in which 'one does not have to believe everything is true, one only has to believe that it is necessary', as a priest in Kafka's *The Trial* tells Joseph K.[57] The culture of half-truth that now pervaded the game throughout Britain can be seen in the report of the inquiry into allegations of payments made to Welsh players who played in the 1989 centenary celebrations in South Africa. The inquiry found cynicism and lies to be rife in Wales: 'while individual lack of circumspection or even deceitful behaviour might be explicable, the vitally disturbing feature was that such behaviour seemed so widespread as to be almost endemic to the whole system and its operation'. As in England, the attitude of players to the Welsh union's committee 'bordered on the contemptuous', seeing it as 'being too large, too inexpert, unnecessary and out of place in the modern world'. The only criterion that the players used when deciding whether to accept illegal payments was the likelihood of being 'discovered or penalised'.[58] Amateurism had rotted from the inside.

One can get a sense of this collapse of ideology in the final discussions about amateurism. The IB had set up a 'working party' in 1994 to discuss the future of amateurism. When it reported back in February 1995, it could not even explain why the game was amateur: 'as to quite why it was considered that the question of compensation for bona fide loss of time was thought to be contrary to "the true interest of the game and its spirit", is not made clear in the surviving documentation of that time', it declared vacantly and, yet again, untruthfully. Moreover, if the game 'were to be first introduced as a sport in the latter part of the twentieth century, then [its amateur principles] would be considered socially unacceptable and divisive. It is not easily defensible as a social or moral ethic judged by the standards of today.' Although not acknowledged as such, this was a straightforward admission that the splitters of 1895 had been correct. In short, the leaders of the game had simply given up on what generations of rugby union players, supporters and officials believed to be 'the golden thread that binds us to our founders'.[59] Given the decayed state of the house of amateurism, there could be little wonder that it only took huffing and puffing from rugby league's Super League competition to blow the entire structure down.

From a broader perspective, the collapse of amateur rugby union was an example of the rise of the 'free-market' in the last two decades of the twentieth century. The collapse of the Soviet Union, the coming to power of leaders such as Thatcher and Reagan, and the worldwide defeats of organised labour had infused the middle classes with a new self-confidence. As Lawrence James noted, by the 1990s, 'the middle class has never been so secure. Old threats to its security, trade unionism and socialism, were neutered in the 1980s, a decade which ended with the universal triumph of free-market capitalism'.[60] Indeed, the financial deregulation of the City of London in the 1980s almost exactly paralleled the rise to international prominence of English rugby, not to say providing many of its players with jobs. Embracing the ideology of the market and shedding its traditional fear of organised labour – which had been the impetus for the introduction and consolidation of amateurism in rugby – the conservative sections of the middle classes that controlled rugby union no longer had use for the formal social segregation of amateurism. Indeed, in the battle against the rugby league 'other', amateurism had become an obstacle to the preservation of the game. As in the wider world, the old social hierarchies upon which rugby union was based had been dissolved by the exigencies of the 'marketplace' and the wealth now available to players and officials alike.

The gentlemen had become players.

9

THE WHOLE NEW BALL GAME?

It was a chilly, brisk evening in November, with a shimmering breeze blowing across the stadium. In a few moments England would face Australia in a match that would demonstrate just how much rugby had changed.

When the ball was kicked off, the two packs tore into each other. Six minutes into the match and England prop Trevor Woodman's enthusiasm overcame him. A couple of plays on from the resulting penalty and Australia's Lote Tuqiri caught a high bomb from Stephen Larkham and scored in the corner. But England's forward pressure took its toll and two Jonny Wilkinson penalties put them in the lead.

Then on 25 minutes England's defence forced an Australian handling error. Richard Hill hacked the ball on and just two metres from the Australian line Matt Dawson fed a simple pass to Ben Kay for a certain try. But in a world cup final nothing is certain. Kay, despite wearing gloves, let the ball slip from his hands.

Despite this, England continued to roll forward and Wilkinson landed another penalty. And as the match approached half-time England at last managed to break the grip of the Wallaby defence. From just inside the Australian half, England won a clean ball from a ruck. Dawson spread the ball to Lawrence Dallaglio standing wide on the left. He made an angled run to the twenty-two, put an inside ball through to Wilkinson who threw it wide to the left to Jason Robinson. With twenty metres to go, Robinson outstripped Wendell Sailor and Mat Rogers and went over in the corner.

Half-time and 14–5 to England. But as the second half progressed the tension grew. A series of English mistakes let Elton Flatley kick the Wallabies back into the match. In the last quarter, a desperate Wilkinson tackle stopped Stephen Larkham going over, while minutes later a try-saving tackle from Rogers prevented Will Greenwood from finishing off the game.

But with three points in it and just a minute and a half to go, South African referee André Watson ran out of patience with the English front row and penalised them for collapsing the scrum just inside their twenty-two. From wide out on his right, Flatley stepped up and kicked the ball sweetly between the posts to deny England victory.

Extra time. Two minutes after the restart, Wilkinson restored England's advantage with a penalty. For England fans, the tension was now unbearable, as first Catt and then Wilkinson failed with drop-goal attempts. Then Tuquiri broke through within sight of the England line but was foiled by Robinson and Ben Cohen.

With just three minutes left on the clock, Watson spotted Dallaglio using his hands in a ruck, just thirty metres to the left of the England posts. Flatley once more denied England their advantage and the match was again locked up at 17 all.

One minute to go and England drove the ball deep into the Australian half. Everyone watching the game knew that their aim was to create the space for a Jonny Wilkinson drop-goal. The Wallabies knew it as well, but there seemed to be little they could do to prevent the inevitable as first Dawson, then skipper Martin Johnson carted the ball closer to the Australian posts.

Eventually the ball was released and Dawson flung the ball back to Wilkinson standing slightly to the left just outside the twenty-two. With just twenty-nine seconds remaining of extra-time, he stroked the ball through the Australian uprights with his unfavoured right boot. As his team-mates rushed up to congratulate him, the match ended and England celebrated a glorious victory.

This was the game that Rugby football had become. And this was the match that showed how far the game and its values had travelled in 150 years.

In a state-of-the-art stadium highly paid athletes with no aim but victory produced a spectacle for a worldwide television audience. Each side had a team of coaches that had spent months preparing their sides for the tournament. The two tries of the match were both scored by former rugby league professionals. Even the rules of the game were subtly different from those of even a generation ago.

Yet beneath this shiny surface many things remained stubbornly unchanged. The very name of the world cup was the Webb Ellis Trophy, highlighting the continuity with the past. The eight teams that contested the tournament's quarter-finals were the same nations that had dominated the game for the previous century. And the players who took part in the match were still in the main, part of a privileged elite. Over half the Australian side had been to private schools. Of the twenty-two players in the England squad for the final, nine had been educated privately, five went to grammar schools and eight to comprehensives, one of which was Jason Robinson who had been educated at a rugby league-playing school in south Leeds.

And in Jonny Wilkinson, England had its own modern incarnation of Tom Brown: talented, brave, modest, he was embodiment of everything the English private school system hoped to produce. And as with Ronald Poulton-Palmer and other past heroes of the game he was even celebrated in verse, by no less than the poet laureate:

> O Jonny the power of your boot
> And the accurate heart-stopping route
> Of your goal as it ghosts
> Through Australian posts
> Is a triumph we gladly salute.

Everything had changed, yet everything had stayed the same.

The old as the new

This was not how things appeared to the various factions that fought over the soul of English rugby union after August 1995. The announcement that the sport was now professional found the RFU completely unprepared. The Canute-like approach of Dudley Wood's last years as RFU secretary meant that there were no plans for the arrival of the inevitable. Almost immediately the leading clubs came into conflict with the union. The clubs wanted the introduction of a system modelled on soccer's Premier League while the RFU sought to retain the same degree of control over the game that it enjoyed in the amateur era. Bolstered by backing from millionaires such as Nigel Wray at Saracens, Andrew Brownsword at Bath and Frank Warren at Bedford, the leading clubs saw professionalism as an opportunity for rugby union to make a transformative leap that would eventually see it compete with soccer. In the north-east, the owner of Newcastle United soccer club Sir John Hall, took over Newcastle Gosforth and transformed the side into a fully professional wing of his projected Newcastle Sporting Club.

But even the RFU's plans for lukewarm change proved to be too much for many at rugby's grassroots, who felt that the governing body focused on the elite clubs at the expense of the game's traditions. At a bizarre general meeting in January 1996 a motion to strike the word amateur out of the RFU constitution was defeated, the RFU's candidate for chairman was humiliated, and former president John Burgess effectively called for a split from the International Board to defend amateurism. The RFU was in the hands of those who, if not entirely wishing to return to the past, were none too keen on the future. Throughout the 1990s battles raged across the face of English rugby union as if it were re-enacting the Thirty Years' War. On almost every issue confronting the sport, the clubs and the RFU lunged into conflict. In April 1996 the clubs forbade their players from playing for England the following season, although a compromise was reached shortly after. The acrimony between club owners and RFU administrators grew so intense that RFU chairman Cliff Brittle and Newcastle's John Hall were allegedly involved in a physical confrontation. As with all long-term conflicts, the discord was occasionally punctuated by elaborate if ultimately fruitless peace treaties, such as the 'Leicester Accord', the 'Mayfair Agreement' and the slightly more successful 'Long Form Agreement' of 2001.[1]

It was not only with themselves that English officials were at war. In 2000 the England squad went on a short-lived strike and refused to play against Argentina in a dispute over contract payments. And the need to extract the highest possible funding from satellite broadcasters had led to the RFU negotiating an exclusive deal for England's Five Nations matches with Rupert Murdoch's BSkyB in 1996. The announcement of this, and its subsequent blowback, led to England being excluded, albeit temporarily, from the Five Nations' Championship in 1996 and 1999. In 1998 English clubs boycotted the Heineken Cup over a disagreement about the distribution of funding. Amateurism may have been abandoned but the RFU's high-handedness towards its non-English neighbours remained as strong as ever.

The labrythine and fratricidal divisions within the game were in many respects the continuation of the dispute between the RFU and the players that had marked the early 1990s. The battle between the proponents of the free market, such as the players and the club owners, and the traditionalists who believed that the RFU should control the sport was also in many ways a repeat of the broader debates that took place in British society over privatisation or patrician control. 'I cannot have amateurs running my business', complained John Hall shortly before he pulled the plug on his rugby adventure in 1999.[2] However hard they tried, the supporters of the RFU could not control the genie of professionalism, let alone put it back into the bottle. As the Northern Union had discovered a century earlier, professionalism was like being pregnant: one either was or was not. There was no halfway house. Once one club had started to play its players, every club that wanted to be competitive had to follow suit, all the way down the chain.

Yet those club owners who imagined they could simply replicate the culture of professional soccer had drastically misunderstood rugby union, which emotionally if not financially believed in a national pyramid for the sport, at the apex of which stood the England side. John Hall would have found few dissenters among his soccer club's Toon Army if he had banned Newcastle United players from the England football side but won the Premier League title. But it would be unthinkable for supporters of Newcastle Falcons, or even Leicester Tigers, for their players to eschew England caps for the sake of their club's fortunes. In soccer, the club versus country debate always resulted in victory for the club. But in rugby union, club would always eventually come second to country, no matter what the financial or legal resources available to club owners.

The clash of cultures and preconceptions was more often than not resolved to the detriment of the clubs. Richmond, which had been taken over by millionaire Ashley Levett, thrust itself to the forefront of the new professionalism with the signing of England forward Ben Clarke, reputedly rugby union's first £1 million transfer. Yet by 1999 Levett decided that he could no longer continue to underwrite the club and it was 'merged' with London Irish, leading to the original amateur club being reformed in 2000. The same fate befell London Scottish. Bedford too lost its millionaire backers but thanks to the depth of its links with the town was able to attract local businessmen to take over the club. Other former powerhouses of the game, such as Orrell, West Hartlepool, Moseley and Nottingham found themselves simply unable to compete in the market place or to survive the caprices of owners. Even Bath, the leading club of the pre-professional era, found it financially impossible to continue its on-field dominance of the game.

Eventually, a degree of equilibrium in the club game was reached by the mid-2000s, underpinned to a great extent by the success of the England side, which relieved the pressure on the RFU, and rising attendances in the Premiership, which relieved some of the financial stresses on the clubs. The bloodletting of the previous decade had resulted in a *de facto* franchise system operating at the elite level. With the exception of Harlequins, none of the elite London clubs played in their historic locality: London Irish played in Reading, Saracens in Watford and Wasps in High Wycombe. In 1999 Bristol even attempted to buy the ailing London Scottish side in order to take over their place in the Premiership.

Nevertheless, the jungle law of survival of the richest saw the average attendance of Premiership clubs rise to 10,880 in 2008, up from an average of 6,238 in 1998.[3] This was partly because of clubs adopting modern marketing methods and creating a colourful, noisy 'match day experience' –

ironically much of it taken from rugby league – to attract new fans, causing grumbling among older and more traditional supporters. But it was also because of rugby union becoming fashionable. England's success, in contrast to the consistently disappointing performances of the national soccer team, gave it a cachet that only cricket, at the height of its Ashes win over Australia in 2006, came close to matching. And the sport was also now more attractive for the casual spectator than it had ever been. In comparison with matches in the 1980s, the game was faster, the ball was in play longer and the scores were higher. IRB research showed that over the previous twenty years set-pieces had declined in importance, with the average number of line-outs and scrums in internationals declining from fifty-two to thirty-seven and thirty-one to nineteen respectively. The number of passes had risen but kicks had fallen. Penalty goals had decreased but try-scoring had increased. The rate of change of the game over the past twenty years had been greater than the entirety of the previous century.[4]

For some, these changes seemed to confirm everything they had feared about the professionalisation of rugby union. Rule changes, most notably the Experimental Law Variations introduced initially on a trial basis in 2007, appeared to be emasculating the very nature of the game. The coming of open commercialism had undermined the fabric of the game's freemasonry. 'I remember when, after a game at Leicester or Northampton, you might talk to their England internationals in the bar', lamented the chairman of Deepings RFC in 2004. 'That was only ten years ago. It would never happen now. Professional rugby players are a different species.' Indeed, the professional player now lived in a very rarified atmosphere. Identified by talent scouts at a young age, sent off to development camps and propelled through intensive training programmes, the young player was now someone for whom the playing of rugby was a full-time occupation, rather than a spare-time recreation. And the desire for increased revenue from the clubs and the RFU, together with satellite television's insatiable appetite for 'content', meant that players were now playing more matches at a greater intensity than ever before. Not only did this mean an increasing incidence of injuries but also a gradual devaluing of important matches and especially overseas tours. A fortnight before the 2003 World Cup final, the distinguished Australian lawyer and rugby historian Justice Thomas Hickie summed up the eight years of professional rugby union by quoting Dickens: 'it was the best of times, it was the worst of times'. It was a sentiment shared by many.[5]

And yet. Although rugby union had become a business and its playing had altered dramatically, its values, attitudes and social role had changed remarkably little. As we have seen, the lessons drawn from England's international success by the mainstream British press, and especially after the 2003 World Cup victory, were about the importance of class and character. Time and again, the sentiments articulated were a direct echo of those that could be found in *Tom Brown's Schooldays* almost 150 years ago. 'No other sport requires so much decision-making, leadership and coolness under pressure as rugby. No wonder, perhaps, that since the Boer War more than 200 rugby internationals have been decorated for bravery in battle', explained an article in *Journal of the Royal Air Force College*. 'Manliness, it seems to me, is what rugby is all about it. . . . Rugby players are real men, proper fighting machines, unashamed homages to testosterone', wrote Tiffany Dark the day after England's world cup triumph. Will Greenwood, one of the victors of 2003, even resurrected the analogy between rugby and the Stock Exchange: 'there is a good deal of similarity between an international rugby match and a trading session in the City in the days before it became fully computerised: the pressure in both is enormous, you have to make quick and critical decisions on the hoof, you have to keep a cool head and you need to be bullish and brave.'[6] To rugby's supporters, such comments reflected the timelessness of its appeal. To the less charitable, they indicated how little British society had changed over the past century.

This stability at the core of the game was most strongly reflected in its social composition. In 2003 a Leicester University report on Premiership rugby crowds found that 61 per cent of spectators came from the upper middle and middle classes, with just 17 per cent describing themselves as working class. This compared with soccer's Premier League, in which 44 per cent described themselves as upper middle or middle class and 44 per cent as manual workers. The percentages for the British population as a whole were 27 per cent and 45 per cent respectively.[7] This would seem to indicate that the increase in crowd figures was a result of rugby union deepening its appeal to its historic constituency rather than broadening it to new sectors of society. This can also be seen in the composition of the England side that played in the 2007 World Cup final against South Africa. Of the twenty-two man squad selected for the final, fifteen players had been to fee-paying schools. The England elite squad selected in July 2008 confirmed this trend, with twenty-three of those players for whom we have educational details attending private schools and five at grammar schools, with a lone Phil Vickery representing the comprehensive schools. By way of comparison, around 7 per cent of school-age children went to private schools in 2008.[8] This would suggest that the gradual reduction in the number of privately educated players in the England team, which had taken place over the last quarter of the twentieth century, may now be reversing, a tendency which would reflect the increase in the number of children going to private schools since the late 1980s.[9]

But, despite official claims that the game was attempting to broaden its appeal, these findings should not be surprising. Rugby football came into existence as a way of transmitting the values and mores of the English middle classes through play. Its origins at Rugby School and the articulation of its belief system in *Tom Brown's Schooldays*, and by its numerous other proselytisers, meant that the sport consciously saw itself as a representative of middle-class principles. The struggle for control of the game in the 1890s consolidated its sense of mission and reinforced its moral self-confidence. And this meant that it could occupy a unique place in middle-class recreational culture. Unlike other popular sports, rugby's values were seen as constant and unchanging, impervious to the changing fashions of society and the unwelcome intrusions of the working classes. The defeat of the northern clubs, the experience of the First World War, the conquest of the public and grammar schools, even the defiant support for South Africa, all indicated rugby union's position within traditional middle-class culture. Even cricket did not carry the same moral certainties or cachet of exclusivity.

In this, rugby union demonstrates that sport is a form of 'deep politics' in which social traditions and attitudes are expressed through recreational practices. All sports that have mass appeal reflect the preferences and pre-judices of those sections of society that nurture them. Sport provides meaning to a way of life, by seemingly demonstrating the uniqueness and virtue of that style of living. And because it exists outside of, and often in opposition to, formal politics, the values of the sport are perceived as being self-evident, non-controversial and based on common sense.[10] In sport, opinions about issues of class, race and gender can be expressed in ways that would be unacceptable in normal political discourse. And at its most basic, team sport is a way of enhancing a sense of social unity, not least by offering an opponent or an 'other', because of its essentially binary division into 'us' versus 'them'.

As a national middle-class culture came into being in England in the interwar years, rugby union was one of the conduits through which this new culture emerged. It played a similar role during the expansion of secondary and higher educational opportunities in the 1950s and 1960s, providing the social networks and value systems that enabled young men to enter the ranks of the professional classes. And in the 1980s and 1990s it was one of the expressions of the reinvigorated self-confidence of the middle classes.

It is this constancy that explains the relative ease with which rugby union abandoned amateurism in 1995, in contrast to the civil war that it waged to defend it in 1895. Unlike the late nineteenth century, the essential nature of the sport was not under threat. The debate on professionalism was precisely that, a discussion about the role of commercialism in the future of rugby, rather than a coded dispute about the extent of working-class influence in the sport. There were no fears that the game would become dominated by those of a different social class. All sides in the debate, with the exception of one or two parvenu soccer or boxing interlopers such as Sir John Hall or Frank Warren, were most definitely 'us'.

Even if its exterior principles had changed, rugby union's inner social meaning had endured.

It was still the game of Tom Brown.

Appendix 1

SCHOOLS ATTENDED BY ENGLAND INTERNATIONALS 1871–1995

	Private	Grammar	State	Unknown	Total
1991–95	12	1	8	1	22
1986–90	10	4	5	12	31
1981–85	14	14	9	11	48
1976–80	11	9	5	2	27
1971–75	18	20	6	2	46
1966–70	22	18	6	8	54
1961–65	24	12	5	1	42
1956–60	22	9	1	1	33
1951–55	26	10	2	10	48
1946–50	35	9	3	9	56
1936–40	19	6	2	2	29
1931–35	35	2	0	18	55
1926–30	41	1	2	19	63
1920–25	39	5	2	13	59
1911–14	14	3	3	6	26
1906–10	52	12	4	20	88
1901–05	38	4	2	21	65
1896–1900	36	3	1	32	72
1891–95	29	3	0	27	59
1886–90	23	1	0	21	45
1881–85	29	4	0	13	46
1876–80	37	4	0	11	52
1871–75	69	1	0	7	77
Total	655	155	66	267	1143

Source: U.A. Titley and Ross McWhirter, *Centenary History of the Rugby Football Union*, London, 1970; Raymond Maule, *The Complete Who's Who of England Rugby Union Internationals*, Derby, 1992; *The Save & Prosper Rugby Union Who's Who*, London, 1992–96; *Playfair Rugby Union Annual 1996–97*, London, 1996.

Appendix 2

OCCUPATIONAL BACKGROUNDS OF ENGLAND INTERNATIONALS 1871–1995

	1871–90	1891–1914	1920–39	1946–70	1971–95	Total
Accountant	1	2	3	2	3	11
Actuary				1		1
Aircraft Engineer			2			2
Architect		2	1			3
Army Officer	12	15	16	4	1	48
Artist/Artist's Model		1		1		2
Author	1					1
Banker	3		5	3	5	16
Blacksmith		2				2
Boilermaker		2				2
Boot/Shoemaker		1	1			2
Bricklayer			1			1
Builder		1			3	4
Bus Driver			1			1
Businessman	2		1			3
Business 'Overseas'	2					2
Butcher			1	1		2
Car Mechanic				1		1
Car Salesman		1	1			2
Carpenter		2	1	1		4
Chartered Surveyor			2		7	9
Chief Shipwright			1			1
Civil Engineer	2	2	1	5		10
Civil Servant	4	3	2	3		12
Civil Servant (Imperial)	8	3	5			16
Clergyman	7	8	2	2		19
Coal Exporter		1				1
Coal Merchant		1				1
Colliery Manager		4	1			5
Colliery Owner	1					1
Commercial Chandler			1			1
Company Director/Partner	11	10	24	26	10	81
Computer Consultant					1	1

Cotton Broker	3	1	1			5
Decorator		1				1
Dentist				2	1	3
Dockyard Inspector		1				1
Dock/Shipyard Worker		3	5	1		9
Doctor	17	28	11	10	2	68
Draper			1			1
Draughtsman		3		3		6
Electrical Engineer		1				1
Electrician					2	2
Engineer				3	2	5
Estate/Land Agent	1	2		1	1	5
Factory Manager			2	4	2	8
Factory Worker	1	1				2
Farmer	2	9	9	12	3	35
Financial Consultant					3	3
Fisherman		1				1
Fitter				3		3
Fruit Merchant				3		3
Gardener		1				1
Golf Club Sec	1					1
Haulier			2			2
Heating Engineer			1			1
Hop Merchant	1					1
Hotelier			1			1
Independent Means	2					2
Insurance Broker	1	3	5	3	7	19
Iron Moulder		1				1
Journalist			1		1	2
Labourer		5				5
Landowner	1					1
Lathe Operator				1		1
Leather Dealer	1					1
Management Consultant				3		3
Manager			1	11	1	13
Manufacturer	7					7
Marine Engineer		3				3
Merchant	3	1				4
Miner		3	1			4
Mining Engineer		4		2		6
Naval Officer	1	16	12	3		32
Oil Exec	1					1
Patent Agent	1					1
PE Lecturer				2		2
Pensions Supervisor					1	1
Plater				1		1
Police Inspector				1	1	2
Policeman		2	2	2	7	13
Printing Director			1			1
Public Works Contractor		1				1
Publishing Exec					1	1
Publican	9	12		1		22

	1871–90	1891–1914	1920–39	1946–70	1971–95	Total
RAF Officer		2	3	6	1	12
RAF PT Instructor					1	1
RAF Technician				1	1	2
Railway Clerk	1	1				2
Railway Manager			1			1
Rent Collector					1	1
Research Scientist					1	1
Sailor – Rating			2			2
Sales		3	3	22	12	40
School Master	15	27	19	53	31	145
Sheet Metal Worker				1		1
Ship Broker		1	2			3
Ship Owner	4	2				6
Shipping Manager		1				1
Shoeshop Owner		1				1
Shopworker		1	1			2
Soldier – Ranks		1			1	2
Solicitor	36	21	9	9	4	79
Solicitor's Clerk			1			1
Sports Outfitter					1	1
Steel Agent				1		1
Stockbroker	7	9	8	1	5	30
Stonemason		2				2
Storeman	1					1
Student				1		1
Tailor		1				1
Tea Planter (India)	1	1				2
Timber Merchant	1	3				4
Tool Maker				1	1	2
Town Clerk	1					1
Town Planner					1	1
University Lecturer		3		1		4
Valuer			1			1
Vet				1		1
Wool Merchant	1	2	1			4
Undertaker					1	1
Travel Agent					2	2
RUPA CEO					1	1
Professional Player					1	1

Source: U.A. Titley and Ross McWhirter, *Centenary History of the Rugby Football Union*, London, 1970; Raymond Maule, *The Complete Who's Who of England Rugby Union Internationals*, Derby, 1992; *The Save & Prosper Rugby Union Who's Who*, London, 1992–96; *Playfair Rugby Union Annual 1996–97*, London, 1996.

Appendix 3

CLUBS AFFILIATED TO THE RUGBY FOOTBALL UNION, 1919–20 TO 1989–90

	1919–20	1929–30	1939–40	1949–50	1959–60	1969–70	1979–80	1989–90
Services	33	111	140	106	248	225	322	309
Oxbridge	38	39	34	43	44	45	45	47
Other Universities	1	10	12	26	31	47	48	41
Other Colleges	21	31	30	19	44	73	91	112
Private/Grammar	27	133	141	137/ 55	331	368/ 25[1]	383/ 169[1]	490/ 135[1]
State Schools	–	1	4	6	31	256[1]	1063[1]	1704[1]
Old Boys	19	71	113	135	192	222	211	202
Medical	10	13	13	10	16	19	17	22
Professions	15	37	46	23	27	31	35	39
Locality-based	133	294	341	351	493	603	759	879
Works/Factory	–	19	43	90	141	151	165	169
Other Adult Clubs	–	5	29	23	44	50	38	41
Non-English Clubs	10	15	19	17	30	23	48	81
Total	307	779	965	1041	1672	2138	3394	4271

Notes

[1] Includes schools in membership of the English Schools' Rugby Union.

Source: *RFU Handbooks* 1919–20 to 1989–90.

Appendix 4

LOCATION OF CLUBS AFFILIATED TO THE RFU, 1919–20 TO 1989–90, BY PERCENTAGE

	1919–20	1929–30	1939–40	1949–50	1959–60	1969–70	1979–80	1989–90
London & South East	58	54	56	48	46	40	42	40
South West	10	8	9	13	15	20	15	15
Midlands	8	13	16	17	17	18	19	23
Cumbria/Lcs/Yks	16	20	16	18	19	17	15	18
North East	7	4	3	4	3	5	8	5

Note: due to rounding, totals may not add up to 100 per cent.

Source: *RFU Handbooks* 1919–20 to 1989–90.

NOTES

1 THE SCHOOLBOY'S GAME

1 Thomas Hughes, *Tom Brown's Schooldays*, OUP edition, Oxford, 1989 (hereafter *TBS*), pp. 103–13.

2 *The Origin of Rugby Football: Report (with appendices) of the sub-committee of the Old Rugbeian Society*, Rugby, 1897. I am extraordinarily grateful to Jed Smith and the late Rex King, two former curators of the Museum of Rugby at Twickenham, for allowing me access to this and many more documents, minutes and reports in the Museum's library.

3 As Paul M. Puccio has pointed out, a handful of stories about schoolboy life had been published previously but were largely ignored, possibly because they were written by women. In Dorothy Kilner's 1804 story the principal character even had the name Tom Brown. Paul M. Puccio, 'At the heart of *Tom Brown's Schooldays*: Thomas Arnold and Christian friendship', *Modern Language Studies*, vol. 25, no. 4, Autumn 1995, p. 58.

4 *The Times*, 9 October 1857.

5 Geoffrey Best, *Mid-Victorian Britain 1851–75*, London, 1979, p. 105. K.T. Hoppen, *The Mid-Victorian Generation*, Oxford, 2000, pp. 40–5.

6 *TBS*, p. 1.

7 See the discussion of the cultural impact of the war in Michael Paris, *Warrior Nation: Images of War in British Popular Culture 1850–2000*, London, 2002.

8 On the social composition of Rugby schoolboys and Arnold's aversion to aristocratic boys, see T.W. Bamford, 'Public schools and social class, 1801–51', *The British Journal of Sociology*, vol. 12, no. 3, September 1961, pp. 224–35.

9 *Report of the Commissioners on the Revenues and Management of Certain Colleges and Schools*, British Parliamentary Papers. Public Schools and Colleges, Volume XX, Education, General 9, 1864 (hereafter *Clarendon*), pp. 246–7.

10 Quoted in Lytton Strachey, *Eminent Victorians*, Folio Society edition, London, 1986, p. 171.

11 For a fuller discussion, see W.E. Winn, '*Tom Brown's Schooldays* and the development of Muscular Christianity', *Church History*, vol. 29, no. 1, March 1960, pp. 64–73.

12 A.P. Stanley, *The Life and Correspondence of Thomas Arnold, D.D., Late Head-master of Rugby School, and Regius Professor of Modern History in the University of Oxford*, London, 1845, vol. 2, p. 290.

13 F.D.M., 'Thoughts on ourselves, our position and our prospects', *The Rugby Miscellany*, no. 7, February 1846, pp. 226–8. See also John Chandos, *Boys Together: English Public Schools 1800–1964*, London, 1984 for discussion of this issue.

14 Arnold quoted in Strachey, *Eminent Victorians*, p. 185. Hughes quoted in W.T. Winn '*Tom Brown's Schooldays*. . .', p. 70. *The New Rugbeian*, vol. 3, no. 2, November 1860, p. 81.

15 *TBS*, p. 355.

16 E.C. Mack, *Public Schools and British Opinion 1780–1860*, London, 1938, pp. 336–8, argues that athleticism was a 'perversion of Arnold's thought'. For more on the Muscular Christians and the empire, see J. A. Mangan, *The Games Ethic and Imperialism*, London, 1986.

17 *The Times*, 9 October 1857.

18 Quoted in Sydney Selfe, *Chapters from the History of Rugby School*, Rugby, 1910, p. 157.

19 *TBS*, pp. 178 and 195.

20 *TBS*, pp. 301 and 166. For Hughes' fighting tendencies, see E.C. Mack and W.H.G. Armytage, *Thomas Hughes*, London, 1952, pp. 55 and 79.

21 Quoted in Strachey, *Eminent Victorians*, p. 179.

22 *TBS*, p. 52. John Hughes quoted in Mack and Armytage, *Thomas Hughes*, p. 10.

23 *TBS*, pp. 82–3 and 90.

24 *TBS*, p. 313. Bamford, 'Public schools and social class', p. 230.

25 *Clarendon*, p. 235. Fees are detailed at pp. 259–60. The highest average wages were around 35 shillings a week, earned by skilled workers such as instrument makers or engine drivers. See Best, *Mid-Victorian Britain 1851–75*, p. 115.

26 For deference, Walter Bagehot, *The English Constitution*, CUP edition, Cambridge, 2001, p. 32. For dullness and the importance of stupidity, see Bagehot's 'Letters on the French Coup d'Etat of 1851', *Literary Studies, Volume One*, London, 1911, p. 275.

27 *TBS*, p. 73.

28 *TBS*, pp. 91, 123 and 313. Isabel Quigley, *The Heirs of Tom Brown: The English Public School Story*, London, 1982, p. 52.

29 *TBS*, p. 369. One of the more memorable lines in Sydney Gilliat's screenplay is Basil Radford's rebuke to a telephone operator: 'I'm enquiring about the Test Match in Manchester. Cricket, sir, cricket!! What! You don't know! You can't be in England and not know the Test score!'

30 *The Times*, 9 October 1857.

31 This point is made strongly in Bruce Haley, *The Healthy Body and Victorian Culture*, Harvard, 1978. J.A. Mangan's *Athleticism in the Victorian and Edwardian Public School*, London, 1981 is also a useful discussion about the cult of athleticism.

32 H.H. Almond, 'Athletics and education', *Macmillan's Magazine*, 43, November 1880–April 1881, pp. 285, 283 and 292.

33 *Clarendon*, pp. 40–2, 233 and 298. Punishment of non-playing Rugby pupils is in 'Recollections of Rugby 1863', *Routledge's Every Boy's Annual*, London, no date, *c*.1863, p. 205.

34 *Clarendon*, p. 266.

35 On cricket, see Anthony Bateman '"More mighty than the bat, the pen. . ." Culture, hegemony and the literaturisation of cricket', *Sport in History*, vol. 23, no. 1, Summer 2003, pp. 27–44.

36 *TBS*, p. 111.

37 *The Times*, 9 October 1857.

38 As Tyerman's history of Harrow makes clear, public schools were always fundamentally profit-making enterprises. Christopher Tyerman, *A History of Harrow School*, Oxford, 2000.

39 For Wellington and other schools, adoption of Rugby School rules, see Rev. Frank Marshall and L.R. Tosswill (eds), *Football: The Rugby Union Game*, 2nd edition, London, 1925, p. 33. On the earliest clubs see Adrian Harvey, 'The oldest rugby football club in the world', *Sport in History*, vol. 26, no. 1, April 2006, pp. 150–2.

40 'Stonehenge', *Manual of British Rural Sports*, 3rd edition, London, 1857, p. xiii.

41 H.H. Almond, 'Athletics and education', p. 283.

42 For the Volunteer movement in general, see Hugh Cunningham, *The Volunteers*, London, 1975. For demands that the Volunteers take up sporting activities see the *Leeds Mercury*, 7 April 1864.

43 *The Times*, 5–10 October 1863.

44 The rules agreed at this meeting are published in *Bell's Life in London*, 28 November 1863. For a comprehensive account and analysis of the voting patterns at the FA's foundation meetings, see Adrian Harvey, *Football: The First Hundred Years*, Abingdon, 2005, pp. 143–9.

45 *Bell's Life in London*, 2 January 1859.

46 See the transcript of the discussion in *Bell's Life in London*, 5 December 1863.

47 *Bell's Life in London*, 2 January 1864.

48 *Bell's Life in London*, 7 January 1871. Harvey, *Football: The First Hundred Years*, pp. 161 and 176. C.W. Alcock (ed.), *John Lilywhite's Football Annual*, London, 1868.

49 For the background to the Cambridge rules, see Graham Curry, 'The Cambridge connection', *The Sports Historian*, 2002.

50 *Bell's Life in Victoria and Sporting Chronicle*, (Melbourne) 7 January 1860, quoted in G.M. Hibbins, 'The Cambridge connection: the English origins of Australian Rules Football', in J.A. Mangan (ed.), *The Cultural Bond: Sport, Empire and Society*, London, 1993, p. 109.

51 Gregory de Moore, *Tom Wills: His Spectacular Rise and Tragic Fall*, Sydney, 2008. Geoffrey Blainey, *A Game of Our Own*, Melbourne, 1990.

52 Burridge Spies, 'The imperial heritage', in Albert Grundlingh, Andre Odendaal and Burridge Spies (eds), *Beyond the Tryline: Rugby and South African Society*, Johannesburg, 1995, p. 67.

53 Richard Hodge, 'American college football', *Outing*, vol. 11, no. 6, 1887, p. 486. Bruce Kidd, 'The legacy of Tom Brown in Canada', *International Journal of the History of Sport*, vol. 23, no. 5, August 2006, pp. 701–13.

54 Clifford Putney, *Muscular Christianity. Manhood and Sports in Protestant America, 1880–1920*, Harvard, 2002, p. 20. Robin Lester, *Stagg's University: The Rise, Decline, and Fall of Big-Time Football at Chicago*, Illinois, 1999, p. 12.

55 Quoted in John A. Lucas, 'Victorian Muscular Christianity, prologue to the Olympic Games philosophy', *Olympic Review*, no. 99, January–February 1976, p. 50.

56 See Eugen Weber, 'Gymnastics and sports in Fin-de-Siècle France: opium of the classes?', *American Historical Review*, vol. 76, no. 1, February 1971, pp. 70–98. Philip Dine, *French Rugby Football: A Cultural History*, Oxford, 2001, ch. 1.

57 For details of the London clubs' stance on hacking see *Bell's Life in London*, 7 January 1871.

58 *The Times*, 23 November 1870.

59 *The Times*, 30 November 1870. See also letters in the 26 and 28 November editions. For a broader discussion on medical opposition to the various codes of football, see Roberta J. Park, '"Mended or ended?" Football injuries and the British and American medical press 1870–1910', *The International Journal of the History of Sport*, vol. 18, no. 2, June 2001.

60 *Bell's Life in London*, 8 December 1870. The letter is reprinted in full in Keith Booth, *The Father of Modern Sport: The Life and Times of Charles W. Alcock*, Manchester, 2002, pp. 114–15.

61 *Bell's Life in London*, 24 December 1870.

62 Rugby Football Union minutes, 26 January 1871. A report of the first meeting is in *Bell's Life in London*, 28 January 1871

63 The first set of laws are reproduced in full in O.L. Owen, *The History of the Rugby Football Union*, London, 1955, pp. 59–72.

64 *Bell's Life in London*, 25 March and 1 April 1871.

65 C.W. Alcock, *Football Annual*, London, 1875, pp. 48–9.

2 THE AMATEUR GAME

1 *Leeds Mercury*, 6 January 1894. I am grateful to Huw Richards here for his comments on Anglo-Welsh rugby.

2 *Liverpool Mercury*, 8 January 1894.

3 C.W. Alcock, *Football Annual*, London, 1880, pp. 73–5 and *Football Annual*, London, 1890, pp. 151–8. *Bell's Life in London*, 29 May 1880.

4 *Halifax Guardian*, 1 November 1873 and *Yorkshire Evening Post*, 9 February 1901.

5 *Bell's Life in London*, 31 May 1879.

6 The full story of the emergence of rugby in the north and the 1895 split can be found in Tony Collins, *Rugby's Great Split*, London, 1998.

7 C.W. Alcock, *Football Annual*, London, 1880, pp. 73–5. Graham Williams, *Glory Days, The History of English Rugby Union Cup Finals*, Leeds, 1998.

8 *The Times*, 12 November 1880.

9 Quoted in A.C.M. Croome (ed.), *Fifty Years of Sport at Oxford, Cambridge and the Great Public Schools*, London, 1922, p. 42.

10 *Yorkshire Post*, 25 January 1886.

11 *Chums*, 25 September 1895. *Pastime*, 28 September 1887.

12 *The Yorkshireman Football Number*, March 1891.

13 A Londoner, 'Metropolitan Football' in Marshall, *Football*, p. 329.

14 RFU AGM minutes, 20 September 1893.

15 *Leeds Mercury*, 21 September 1893.

16 *Baily's Magazine of Sports and Pastimes*, 1 November 1893, p. 319.

17 Quoted in the *Leeds Times*, 24 January 1863. I am very grateful to Dr Rob Light for bringing this to my attention.

18 For a discussion of these concepts, see Richard Holt, 'The amateur body and the middle-class man: work, health and style in Victorian Britain', *Sport in History*, vol. 26, no. 3, December 2006.

19 E.H.D. Sewell, 'Rugby football and the colonial tours', *Fortnightly Review*, vol. 82, 1907, p. 427. Letters of Arthur Shrewsbury to Alfred Shaw, 14 March and 22 June 1888, in the Arthur Shrewsbury archive at Trent Bridge Cricket Ground, Nottingham. *Yorkshire Owl*, 18 November 1895. *The Yorkshireman*, 2 May 1888. Pritchett quoted in Frances Stoner Saunders, *Who Paid the Piper?*

London, 1999, p. 332. *Yorkshire Post*, 11 March, 4 October and 13 December 1893.

20 *The Sportsman*, 1 October 1890. *Athletic News*, 17 October 1898.

21 *Yorkshire Evening Post*, 15 January 1900. Huw Richards, *A Game for Hooligans*, London, 2006, p. 63.

22 *Yorkshire Evening Post*, 15 December 1900, and 9 and 22 February 1901.

23 Rev. F. Marshall and L.R. Tosswill (eds), *Football: The Rugby Union Game*, 2nd edition, London, 1925, p. 25. *Yorkshire Evening Post*, 1 and 8 December 1900. *Bell's Life in London*, 1 April 1871.

24 *Yorkshire Evening Post*, 12 January and 22 February 1901.

25 *The Yorkshireman*, 7 November 1885. C.B. Grundy quoted in John Lowerson, *Sport and the English Middle Classes*, Manchester, 1993, p. 84.

26 *Clarendon*, p. 223.

27 Quoted in Howard Marshall, *Oxford v Cambridge, The Story of the University Rugby Match*, London, 1951, p. 119.

28 For the survival of the cult of effortlessness in public schools, see Colin Thubron interviewed in the *Guardian*, 9 September 2006. Simon Gunn also notes the importance of control of the body for the provincial middle classes in the mid-nineteenth century in his 'Class identity and the urban', *Urban History*, vol. 31, no. 1, May 2004, p. 39.

29 See Eric Hobsbawm, *Industry and Empire*, Harmondsworth, 1999, p. 142.

30 Similar stereotyping of body and class occurred in Wales, where the 'Rhondda forward' became synonymous with the manual labourer. See Richards, *A Game for Hooligans*, p. 84.

31 Jennifer Macrory, *Running with the Ball*, London, 1991, pp. 24–5.

32 Peter Lovesey, *The Official Centenary History of the Amateur Athletic Association*, Oxford, 1979, pp. 22–4.

33 *Clarendon*, p. 3.

34 Philip Mason, *The English Gentleman. The Rise and Fall of an Ideal*, London, 1992, p. 9. Philip Trevor, *Rugby Union Football*, London, 1922, p. 22.

35 For the Stoddart affair see Collins, *Rugby's Great Split*, pp. 57–8. George Berney, 'Progress of the R.F.U. from the season 1892–3 to the present time', in Marshall and Tosswill (eds), *Football: The Rugby Union Game*, p. 65. Gedge recounted his tale in *Yorkshire Post*, 6 December 1900.

36 Toni Morrison, *Beloved*, London, 1987, p. 190.

37 RFU AGM minutes, 19 September 1895.

38 *Yorkshire Post*, 21 January 1901, *Athletic News*, 17 October 1898, *Yorkshire Post*, 14 April 1902.

39 *Yorkshire Post*, 20 September 1895.

40 *Yorkshire Post*, 29 September 1897.

41 Occupational statistics taken from U.A. Titley and Ross McWhirter, *Centenary History of the Rugby Football Union*, London, 1970, Raymond Maule, *The Complete Who's Who of England Rugby Union Internationals*, Derby, 1992 and *Yorkshire Post, passim*.

42 Source: RFU *Handbooks*, London, 1895, 1905 and 1910. In contrast the NU numbered 220 clubs in membership in 1905, although by 1910 this had declined to 149; see NRFU *Official Guides* for 1904–05 and 1909–10.

43 For example see letter of S.A. Austin of Belgrave RFC 26 August 1908 to Midland Counties RFU saying that Belgrave Premier Works RFC have induced eight Belgrave players to join them by offering jobs as shoe-making machine operatives (Leicestershire County Archives, DE3097/32).

44 RFU AGM minutes, 28 May 1909.

45 For more on the history of rugby in Coventry see Adrian Smith 'An oval ball and a broken city: Coventry, its people, and its rugby team', *The International Journal of the History of Sport*, vol. 11, no. 3, December 1994, and 'Sport, counterfactual history and rugby's twin codes', *International Journal of the History of Sport*, vol. 21, no. 1, January 2004.

46 For more on the Coventry NU club, see *Yorkshire Post*, 28 September, 7 and 13 October and 1, 3 and 13 December 1909. Graham Williams 'Midlands manoeuvres: a history of Northern Unionism in Coventry', *Code 13*, no. 2, December 1986.

47 The International Rugby Football Board changed its name to the International Rugby Board in 1997. For the sake of simplicity I refer to it throughout the book as the International Board or the IB, the name it was commonly known as throughout the game for most of its existence.

48 For more on the Gould affair, see David Smith and Gareth Williams, *Fields of Praise*, Cardiff, 1980, pp. 92–9 and pp. 108–12. Full details of the RFU and IB deliberations can be found in the *Yorkshire Post*, 12 January, 7 February and 3 March 1898.

49 *Yorkshire Post*, 17 December 1904 and 16 March 1903. *Athletic News*, 28 March 1898.

50 *Yorkshire Post*, 6 February 1909.

51 *Yorkshire Post*, 3 February 1909.

52 *The Field*, 12 January 1884.

53 *Bell's Life in London*, 29 April 1876. RFU committee minutes, 22 January 1878. Rowland Hill, 'The Past Season', in C.W. Alcock, *Football Annual*, London, 1883, p. 17.

54 *The Field*, 12 January 1884.

55 An Old Player, 'The Rugby Union Game in 1888–89', in C.W. Alcock, *Football Annual*, London, 1889, p. 71.

56 *Yorkshire Post*, 19 November 1897 and 18 December 1898.

57 *Yorkshire Post*, 8 February and 1 September 1902.

58 *Yorkshire Post*, 30 June and 26 September 1904, 9 January 1905 and 31 March 1906.

59 *Yorkshire Post*, 15 March 1906.

60 For West Hartlepool's financial troubles, see the *Yorkshire Post*, 14 June 1902.

61 Derek Robinson, *The Combination*, Bristol, 1986.

62 *Yorkshire Post*, 21 September 1900. On Plymouth see T. McLeod, 'Plymouth Argyle', in Clive Leatherdale (ed.), *The Book of Football*, Essex, 1997 reprinted edition, p. 163.

63 RFU AGM minutes, 21 September 1900 and 30 September 1904. Even in 1913 Leicester were approached by the president of Devon Rugby Union to support county's push for the introduction of a league. Leicester turned down the approach, see letter of 9 May 1913 in Leicester FC minute book in Leicestershire County Archives (23D56/1/6).

64 B. Fletcher Robinson, *Rugby Football*, London, 1896, p. 55. *Rugger*, 26 September 1931.

65 FA Council minutes, 12 March 1906.

66 W.J. Morgan and Geoffrey Nicholson, *Report On Rugby* London, 1961, p. 120.

3 THE WAR GAME

1 For more on the relationship between sport and war see Derek Birley, 'Sportsmen and the deadly game', *British Journal of Sports History*, vol. 3, no. 3, 1986, pp. 288–310. Colin Veitch, 'Play up! play up! and win the war! Football, the nation and the First World War', *Journal of Contemporary History*, vol. 20, 1985, pp. 363–77. Other issues relating to war and sport, although sport is sadly ignored in both works, can be found in Paul Fussell, *The Great War and Modern Memory*, London, 1975. Jay Winter, *Sites of Memory, Sites of Mourning: The Great War in European Cultural History*, Cambridge, 1998.

2 *TBS*, p. 104.

3 Robinson, *Rugby Football*, p. 50. H.H. Almond in Rev. Frank Marshall (ed.), *Football: The Rugby Union Game*, London, 1892, p. 55.

4 Walpole story reprinted in Howard Marshall (ed.), *Rugger Stories*, London, 1932, p. 241. Dulwich school song in Geoffrey Best, 'Militarism and the Victorian public school', in M. J. Bradley and B. Simon (eds), *The Victorian Public School*, London, 1975, p. 142.

5 David Cannadine, 'War and death, grief and mourning in modern Britain', in J. Whaley (ed.), *Mirrors of Mortality: Studies in the Social History of Death*, London, 1981, p. 195. See also Peter Parker, *The Old Lie: The Great War and the Public School Ethos*, London, 1987 and J.A. Mangan, *Athleticism in the Victorian and Edwardian Public School*, Cambridge, 1981 and his *The Games Ethic and Imperialism*, London, 1986.

6 Austin in James Morris, *Pax Britannica: The Climax of an Empire*, Folio Society edition, London, 1992, pp. 75–6.

7 H.A. Vachell, *The Hill*, London, 1905, p. 236.

8 FA Council minutes, 12 March 1906.

9 *Yorkshire Post*, 23 October 1906.

10 Indeed, the England team did not defeat a touring national side until 1936 and subsequently managed just two more such victories before the RFU's Centenary in 1971.

11 *The Times*, 10 October 1905. See also John Nauright, 'Colonial manhood and imperial race virility: British responses to post-Boer War colonial rugby tours', in John Nauright and Timothy Chandler (eds), *Making Men: Rugby and Masculine Identity*, London, 1996.

12 Quoted in Edward Bagnall Poulton, *The Life of Ronald Poulton*, London, 1919, p. 145.

13 *The Times*, 4 March 1919.

14 This and the preceding verse of the poem were printed alone on the last page of the *Yorkshire Rugby Football Union Commemoration Book 1914–1919 & Official Handbook 1919–1920*, Leeds, 1920, p. 557.

15 *Athletic News*, 24 August 1914.

16 Letter of 28 August 1914, reprinted in Poulton, *The Life of Ronald Poulton*, p. 308.

17 *The Times*, 9 September 1914.

18 *Athletic News*, 10 August 1914. *The Times*, 21 September 1914.

19 *Athletic News*, 14 September 1914.

20 *Athletic News*, 21 September 1914.

21 *The Alleynian*, March 1915.

22 *Athletic News*, 24 August 1914.

23 *Athletic News*, 31 August 1914.

24 *Yorkshire Post*, 1 September 1914.

25 *Athletic News*, 24 August 1914.

26 Marriott's circular is in the *Yorkshire Rugby Football Union Commemoration Book*, p. 266.

27 *The Times*, 4 September 1914.

28 Peter Simkins, *Kitchener's Army*, Manchester, 1988, pp. 79–103.

29 YRU statement of 9 September 1919 in the *Yorkshire Rugby Football Union Commemoration Book*, p. 267. Letter in *Athletic News*, 28 September 1914.

30 *Athletic News*, 27 November 1916. David Hands, *Leicester F. C. 1880–1980*, Leicester, 1981, p. 33.

31 *Athletic News*, 26 October 1914. Captain Guy Paget, *History of the Raising of the 7th (Service) Battalion, Northamptonshire Regiment*, Aldershot, 1915. H.B. King, *7th (S) Battalion Northamptonshire Regiment 1914–1919*, Aldershot, 1919. S.J. Edwards, *Sportsman and Solider*, privately published by the author, 1998.

32 *Athletic News*, 14 December 1914.

33 *Yorkshire Post*, 1 September 1914.

34 *Yorkshire Post*, 15 September 1914.

35 Ruth Elwyn Harris, *Billie: the Nevill letters 1914–1916*, London, 1991, p. 19. Laurie Milner, *Leeds Pals*, London, 1991, pp. 58–9. *Yorkshire Post*, 1 October 1914.

36 *The Times*, 30 October 1914. *Yorkshire Post*, 14 November 1914. *Athletic News*, 9 November 1914.

37 *The Times*, 14 December 1914. *Yorkshire Post*, 14 December 1914.

38 *Athletic News*, 22 November 1915.

39 *Athletic News*, 11 January and 1 February 1915.

40 *Athletic News*, 18 January and 18 October 1915. Edmund McCabe, 'Rugby and the great war', *Stand To!*, vol. 52, 1998, pp. 41–4. Lyn Macdonald, *Somme*, London, 1983, p. 319. Poulton, *The Life of Ronald Poulton* p. 311. Robert Graves, *Goodbye to All That*, revised edition, London, 1960, p. 149.

41 *The Times*, 4 March 1919.

42 Douglas Clark MS diary, Imperial War Museum, 90/21/1. *Athletic News*, 23 December 1918 and 22 February 1915.

43 J.G. Fuller, 'Popular culture and troop morale in the British and Dominion Forces 1914–1918', D.Phil. thesis, Cambridge, 1988, p. 127.

44 Paul Jones, *War Letters of a Public School Boy*, London, 1918, p. 157.

45 Denis Winter, *Death's Men: Soldiers of the Great War*, London, 1978, p. 155.

46 John Maclaren, *The History of Army Rugby*, Aldershot, 1986, p. 83. For more on the kicking of footballs into No-Man's Land, see Fussell, *The Great War*, pp. 27–8.

47 *Yorkshire Post*, 10 February 1917. *The Times*, 12 and 15 February 1917.

48 A.J. Trollope, secretary of the London Society, in *The Times*, 30 November 1918. *Athletic News*, 3 December 1918. *Yorkshire Post*, 10 February 1919.

49 *Athletic News*, 27 December 1915.

50 *Athletic News*, 16 April 1917.

51 *The Times*, 5 October 1916.

52 *Sheffield Star Sports Special*, 16 October 1915.

53 RFU committee minutes, 14 January 1919.

54 RFU committee minutes, ibid.

55 *The Times*, 15 April 1919.

56 RFU committee minutes, 26 May 1919.

57 *The Times*, 30 December 1918.

58 Letter of Jellicoe reprinted in E.H.D. Sewell, *The Log of a Sportsman*, London, 1923, p. 164.
59 Quoted in *Athletic News*, 18 January 1915.
60 Quoted in Harris, *Billie*, p. 203.
61 *The Times*, 21 April 1919.
62 *Athletic News*, 21 December 1914.
63 Anne Pallant, *A Sporting Century*, Plymouth, 1997, p. 144.
64 Quoted in Modris Eksteins, *Rites of Spring: The Great War and the Birth of the Modern Age*, London, 1989, p. 124. *The Wipers Times: A Facsimile Reprint of the Trench Magazines*, London, 1918, and Fuller, 'Popular culture . . . ', *passim*.
65 Harris, *Billie*, p. 7.
66 Quoted in *Yorkshire Rugby Football Union Commemoration Book*, p. 20. For the widespread use of sporting metaphors by troops see Fuller, 'Popular culture . . . ', p. 202.
67 Jones, *War Letters*, p. 198.
68 *Athletic News*, 7 September 1914.
69 *The Times*, 26 February 1919.
70 J.M. Winter, *The Great War and the British People*, London, 1986, pp. 71–93. England players' war records compiled from U.A. Titley and A.R. McWhirter, *Centenary History of the RFU*, London, 1970 and R. Maule, *The Complete Who's Who of England Rugby Union Internationals*, Derby, 1992. I am indebted to Dr Gwyn Prescott for his valuable insights on this section.
71 *Athletic News*, 10 and 17 March 1919. The Football League lost forty-four players; Simon Inglis, *League Football and the Men Who Made It*, London, 1988, p. 100.
72 J. M. Winter, 'Upper class casualties', *London Review of Books*, 5 March 1987.
73 *The Times*, 30 December 1918.
74 See *Athletic News*, 8 May 1916.
75 *Yorkshire Rugby Football Union Commemoration Book*, p. 272.
76 George Mosse, *Fallen Soldiers. Reshaping the Memory of the World Wars*, Oxford, 1990, especially ch. 5.
77 E.H.D. Sewell, *The Rugby Football Internationals' Roll of Honour*, London, 1919, p. 1. *Yorkshire Rugby Football Union Commemoration Book*, pp. 278, 279 and 276.
78 Winter, *Sites of Memory*, p. 204.
79 Cannadine, *War and Death*, p. 197. *Boy's Own Paper*, November 1919, p. 42.
80 Sewell, *Roll of Honour*, p. 3. Rowland Hill speech quoted in McCabe, *Rugby and the Great War*, p. 44.
81 Jeffrey Richards, 'Popular imperialism and the image of the army in juvenile literature', in J.M. MacKenzie (ed.), *Popular Imperialism and the Military 1850–1950*, Manchester, 1992.
82 *Spectator*, 22 May 1915.
83 F.C. Hawkins and E. Seymour-Bell, *Fifty Years with the Clifton R.F.C. 1872–1922*, Bristol, 1922, p. 92.
84 Martin Pugh, *The Tories and the People 1880–1935*, Oxford, 1985, p. 175.
85 For more on cricket and the war see Jack Williams, *Cricket and England: A Cultural and Social History of the Inter-war Years*, London, 1999, pp. 6–7.
86 Fussell, *The Great War*, pp. 109–10. *The Times*, 3 March 1919.
87 *The Times*, 26 February 1919.
88 *The Times*, 4 March 1919.

89 Eton's adoption of rugby is described in the magazine *Rugby Football*, 16 February 1924.
90 *The Times*, 6 February 1919.
91 *The Times*, 11 and 13 December 1926.
92 C.G., 'The Dawn' reprinted in *Rugby Football Weekly*, 4 October 1924, p. 953.
93 Headmasters' Conference, *Bulletin*, no. 4, 1925, p. 28.
94 Headmasters' Conference see *Report of the 53rd Meeting of the Headmasters' Conference*, 1925, pp. 33–4. *Athletic News*, 27 February and 15 March 1926. *The Times*, 26 June 1926.
95 Figures from RFU *Handbooks* for 1919–20 and 1929–30.
96 *Evening News*, 12 November 1939. H.N., *War-Time Sport, A Structural Analysis*, 14 January 1940. Sport 1937–1947 Box 1, 'Sport in War-Time' Mass-Observation archives, University of Sussex. W.F. Matthews, *Report* (tour diary), 12 September 1939 (Australian Rugby Union archives, Sydney). I am grateful to Judy MacArthur for her assistance in the ARU archives.
97 *Evening Standard*, 17 November 1939.
98 O.L. Owen, *The History of the Rugby Football Union*, London, 1955, p. 205.
99 For more on the challenges faced by amateur sports in the 1940s see Norman Baker's 'The amateur ideal in a society of equality: change and continuity in post-Second World War British sport, 1945–48', *International Journal of the History of Sport*, vol, 12, no. 1, April 1995, pp. 99–126, and 'A more even playing field. Sport during and after the War', in Nick Hayes and Jeff Hill (eds), *Millions Like Us*, Liverpool, 1999, pp. 125–55. For more on the contrasting fortunes of rugby league during wartime, see Tony Collins, *Rugby League in Twentieth Century Britain*, London, 2006.
100 *The Times*, 21 February 2000. *Daily Telegraph*, 7 November 2001.
101 *Daily Telegraph*, 7 November 2001.

4 THE MAN'S GAME

1 W.W. Wakefield and H.P. Marshall, *Rugger*, London, 1927, pp. 61, 29 and 56.
2 Wakefield and Marshall, *Rugger*, p. 61. *The Times*, 5 January 1925. W. Wooller and D. Owen (eds), *Fifty Years of the All Blacks*, London, 1954, p. 87.
3 George Nepia, *I, George Nepia*, 2nd edition, London, 2002, ch. 17. The fullest account of the incident, albeit written with an All Black bias, can be found in chapter 5 of Terry McLean's *Great Days in New Zealand Rugby*, Wellington, 1959. Edwards was later censured by the RFU for 'undue roughness', *The Times*, 15 February 1925.
4 Quoted in Terry Mclean, *Great Days in NZ Rugby*, Wellington, 1959, p. 53.
5 Wakefield and Marshall, *Rugger*, p. 105.
6 Alec Waugh, 'A damn fine show', in *The Loom of Youth*, London, 1917, pp. 216–17.
7 H.H. Almond, 'Football as a Moral Agent', *Nineteenth Century*, vol. 34, 1893. Morgan and Nicholson, *Report on Rugby*, p. 133. Richard Beard, *Muddied Oafs*, London, 2003, p. 205.
8 *TBS*, p. 98.
9 Sydney Selfe, *Chapters from the History of Rugby School*, Rugby, 1910, p. 139.
10 Anon, 'Reminiscences', *The New Rugbeian*, vol. 3, no. 2, November 1860, p. 80.
11 Selfe, *Chapters from the History of Rugby School*, p. 157. Arthur Budd in A. Budd, C.B. Fry, T.A. Cook and B.F. Robinson, *Football*, London, 1897, p. 50.

12 Liam O'Flaherty, 'The Wing Three-Quarter', *The Tent and Other Stories*, London, 1926, pp. 64–5.

13 R.H. Cattell, 'Half-Back Play', *The Book of Football*, London, 1906 (Desert Island Books edition, Essex, 1997), p. 262. Robert M. Rayner, *A Manual of Rugby Football for Public Schools*, London, 1925, p. 15.

14 *The New Rugbeian*, vol. 3, no. 8, November 1861, pp. 296 and 313.

15 Quoted in Jennifer Macrory, *Running with the Ball*, London, 1991, pp. 175–6. *Wakefield Express*, 23 November 1872. For more on British opposition to French 'effeminacy' see Robert and Isabelle Tombs, *That Sweet Enemy: Britain and France, the History of a Love-hate Relationship*, London, 2006.

16 *The Devon Barbarians Magazine*, 1931, Plymouth, p. 12, in Leicester FC archives (Leicestershire County Archives DE3320/42).

17 E.B. Osborn, 'The game', in H.B.T. Wakelam (ed.), *The Game Goes On*, London, 1936, p. 14. The reference to Davenant is to the poet William Davenant's description of football in London in 1634.

18 A.D. Stoop, 'The young idea' in H.B.T. Wakelam (ed.), *The Game Goes On*, p. 56. Philip Howard in *The Times' Six Nations Rugby Handbook 2006*, p. 21.

19 Morgan and Nicholson, *Report on Rugby*, pp. 135–6.

20 Howard Marshall, 'What rugger means to me', in Wakelam (ed.), *The Game Goes On*, p. 73.

21 Quoted in 'An Englishman's audit of Rhodes Scholars', *Harper's*, May 1964, p. 100.

22 *Daily Mirror*, 9 January 1961. *Daily Telegraph*, 17 June 1962. Chris Laidlaw, *Mud in My Eye*, London, 1973, p. 135. Ray French, *My Kind of Rugby*, London, 1979, p. 23.

23 International Rugby Football Board, minutes, 30 March 1964 and 13–14 March 1969. *The Times*, 28 October 1966. John Reason and Carwyn James, *The World of Rugby*, London, 1979, p. 224. Bob Holmes and Chris Thau (eds), *My Greatest Game*, Edinburgh, 1994, p. 97. *The Times*, 2 June 1975.

24 RFU committee minutes, 11 November 1966 and Laws sub-committee, 4 May 1967. Statistics from RFU Laws sub-committee, 8 September 1976 and 5 September 1978.

25 RFU executive committee minutes, 6 and 7 July and 11 December 1978. HMC letter in RFU committee minutes, 24 November 1978. *The Times*, 24 October, 1980.

26 RFU Annual Reports, 1980–1 and 1984–5. *The Times*, 16 September 1985.

27 Anthony Sampson, *Who Runs this Place? The Anatomy of Britain in the 21st Century*, London, 2004, p. 349.

28 *The Yorkshireman*, 18 December 1889. *Rugby Football*, 1 December 1923.

29 John Tosh, *A Man's Place: Masculinity and the Middle-Class Home in Victorian England*, Yale, 1999, especially ch. 7. *Hansard*, vol. CLXXXVII, 6 May 1867–17 June 1867, pp. 817–29.

30 This is discussed in some detail in Linda Dowling's *Hellenism and Homosexuality in Victorian Oxford*, Cornell, 1996.

31 H.H. Almond, 'Athletics and education', *Macmillan's Magazine*, vol. 43, November 1880–April 1881, p. 292.

32 *TBS*, pp. 223 and 218.

33 *TBS*, pp. 233–4. For a broader discussion of these issues, see Paul M. Puccio 'At the heart of *Tom Brown's Schooldays*: Thomas Arnold and Christian friendship', *Modern Language Studies*, vol. 25, no. 4, Autumn 1995, pp. 57–74.

34 Quoted in Noel Annan, 'The cult of homosexuality in England 1850–1950', *Biography*, vol. 13, no. 3, Summer 1980, p. 190. See also Jeffrey Weeks, *Sex,*

Politics and Society, 2nd edition, London, 1989, pp. 49–51 and Roy Porter and Lesley Hall, *The Facts of Life*, Yale, 1995, pp. 141–4.

35 For a thorough discussion on the public schools and the fear of homosexuality, see John Chandos, *Boys Together: English Public Schools 1800–1864*, London, 1984, pp. 284–319.

36 Quoted in W.E. Winn, '*Tom Brown's Schooldays* and the development of Muscular Christianity', *Church History*, vol. 29, no. 1, March 1960, p. 72. For more on the anti-intellectualism of the cult of athleticism, see J.A. Mangan, *Athleticism in the Victorian and Edwardian Public School*, Cambridge, 1981.

37 On latent homosexuality and sport see, for example, Guy Hocquenghem, *Homosexual Desire*, 2nd edition, Duke, 1993, and Michael Messner and Donald Sabo (eds), *Sport, Men and the Gender Order*, Champaign, 1990. It is interesting to note that of the thirty-eight clubs affiliated to the International Gay Rugby Association and Board in February 2008, only fourteen are from the 'traditional' rugby union-playing nations where the game is prized as a marker of masculinity.

38 George Melly obituary, *Independent*, 6 July 2007. *The Times Literary Supplement*, 26 November 1999.

39 See, for example, Michael Green, *Why Was He Born So Beautiful and Other Rugby Songs*, London, 1967, Harry Morgan (ed.), *More Rugby Songs*, London, 1968, and countless depressing others. Long-playing records of the songs were also produced.

40 Watcyn Thomas, *Rugby-Playing Man*, London, 1977, p. 82.

41 *Guardian*, 28 February 2006. For more on initiation rituals see Eric Dunning, 'Sport as a male preserve: notes on the social sources of masculine identity and its transformations', in N. Elias and E. Dunning (eds), *Quest for Excitement: Sport and Leisure in the Civilising Process*, Oxford, 1986, pp. 267–83 and K. Sheard and E. Dunning, 'The Rugby Football Club as a type of male preserve', *International Review of Sport Sociology*, vol. 5, no. 3, 1973, pp. 5–24. For a perspective on rugby union songs in the USA see Steven P. Schacht, 'Misogyny on and off the pitch: the gendered world of male rugby players', *Gender & Society*, vol. 10, no. 5, 1996, pp. 550–65, and Kenneth Muir and Trina Seitz, 'Machismo, misogyny, and homophobia in a male athletic subculture: a participant-observation study of deviant rituals in collegiate rugby', *Deviant Behavior*, vol. 25, no. 4, July–August 2004, pp. 303–27.

42 *Rugger*, 15 January 1947.

43 *The Sunday Times*, 23 November 1969.

44 *Isis* quoted in Peter Howard, *Life and Letters*, London, 1969, p. 33. J.E. Greenwood, *A Cap For Boots*, London, 1977, pp. 104 and 120.

45 Greenwood, *A Cap For Boots*, p. 94.

46 A.W.N. Bond and M.O.H. Doughty, *The House: A History of the Bank of England Sports Club 1908–83*, London, 1984, p. 38. For the Pigalle see Thomas, *Rugby-Playing Man*, p. 37 and Godfrey Smith (ed.), *Take the Ball and Run: A Rugby Anthology*, London, 1991, p. 11.

47 Quoted in Robert Huntley, *Saracens: 125 Years of Rugby*, London, 2001, p. 42.

48 Thomas, *Rugby-Playing Man*, p. 66. For a discussion on sport and drinking cultures, see Tony Collins and Wray Vamplew, *Mud, Sweat and Beers: A Cultural History of Sport and Alcohol*, Oxford, 2002, pp. 74–7.

49 A.E. Freethy to J. Milburn, 26 December 1938, reprinted in *Touchlines*, December 2003. Gadney at RFU AGM minutes, 14 June and 12 July 1963.

50 Philip Warner, *The Harlequins: 125 Years of Rugby Football*, Derby, 1991, p. 188.
51 Quoted in Humphrey Carpenter, *The Brideshead Generation: Evelyn Waugh and His Friends*, London, 1989, p. 74.
52 Undated letter from Vassall to G.H. Harnett (Museum of Rugby library). Rowe Harding quoted in Clem Thomas, *The History of the British Lions*, Edinburgh, 1996, p. 70. Bleddyn Williams speaking at the 1905 All Blacks Centenary conference at Twickenham Stadium, London, 11 September 2005. RFU Executive minutes, 7 October 1965. 'Wreckers' in Laidlaw, *Mud in My Eye*, pp. 63–4 and Thomas, *British Lions*, p. 143. Gadney in RFU AGM minutes, 12 July 1963. RFU AGM, *Report of the Overseas Liaison Committee*, p. 4.
53 *Rugger*, 24 October and 30 January 1931. Marshall 'What rugger means to me', in Wakelam (ed.), *The Game Goes On*, p. 75.
54 *Daily Mirror*, 9 January 1961. RFU Ground sub-committee minutes, 2 January 1964, 30 April 1965, 1 and 13 January 1966, 26 April 1968 and 12 September 1975. Minutes of joint meeting of Coaching sub-committee and Coaching Advisory Panel, 13/14 May 1977.
55 Frank Keating, 'Where is the Twickenham of yesteryear?', *Guardian*, 30 October 1991.
56 *Yorkshire Post*, 15 February 1904, 24 April 1905 and 8 October 1906. *Rugby Football*, 9 February 1924 and 1 December 1923.
57 *Pendleton Reporter* 28 November 1891.
58 A Cardiff Ladies team played a Newport Ladies side in aid of war charities in 1917. During the General Strike of 1926, women played rugby league in West Yorkshire. See Arron Jones, 'A short history of women's rugby', *Touchlines*, October 2003.
59 *Rugger*, 6 February 1932.
60 Philip Trevor, *Rugby Union Football*, London, 1923, p. 4.
61 Frank Morris, *The First 100: History of the London Scottish FC*, London, 1977, p. 39. K.T. Shaw, *Huddersfield R.U.F.C. The First 75 Years*, Huddersfield, 1985, p. 168, although women were allowed into AGMs in 1936.
62 RFU AGM minutes, 28 June 1957.
63 *Bell's Life in London*, 20 January 1872.
64 *Rugby Football & Cricket*, 2 December 1911.
65 Collins, *Rugby's Great Split*, pp. 43–5 and 202.
66 Trevor, *Rugby Union Football*, p. 4. *Rugby Football*, 1 December 1923.
67 *Rugger*, 10 October 1931.
68 Sister Anne, 'Through a woman's eyes', in Wakelam (ed.), *The Game Goes On*, p. 137.
69 J.E. Morpurgo 'Rugger – the manly sport for wives', *The Tatler*, 3 October 1956.
70 Peter Bills, *Passion in Exile, 100 Years of London Irish RFC*, Edinburgh, 1998, p. 109. A.W.N. Bond and M.O.H. Doughty, *The House: A History of the Bank of England Sports Club 1908–83*, London, 1984, pp. 216–17.
71 *Daily Telegraph*, 1 October 1998.
72 I am grateful for much of this information to Laura Stedman, the former collections manager at the Museum of Rugby, Twickenham.
73 RFU Executive minutes, 5 December 1977, 13 January 1978 and 9 February and 5 July 1984.
74 Anonymous player quoted on exhibition panel six at the Museum of Twickenham exhibition *Women's Rugby – A Work in Progress*, 14 March–17 September 2006.

75 Alison Carle and John Nauright, 'Crossing the line: women playing rugby union', in T. Chandler and J. Nauright (eds), *Making the Rugby World: Race, Gender, Commerce*, London, 1999, pp. 128–48. P.D. Howe, 'Women's rugby and the nexus between embodiment, professionalism and sexuality', *Football Studies*, vol. 4, no. 2, October 2001, pp. 77–92. For women's rugby in the USA, see Megan Taylor Shockley, 'Southern women in the scrums', *Journal of Sport History*, vol. 33, no. 2, Summer 2006, pp. 127–55.

76 See, for example, Matthew Campbell, *The Sunday Times*, 9 September 2007, Zoe Brennan, *The Mail on Sunday*, 13 October 2007 and Tony Parsons, *Daily Mirror*, 22 October 2007.

5 THE CLASS GAME

1 *The Magazine of Wellingborough Grammar School*, no. 30, Summer Term 1947, p. 9.

2 *The Times*, 18 and 20 January 1947. John Griffiths, *The Book of English International Rugby, 1871–1982*, London, 1982, pp. 231–5.

3 Sources: Raymond Maule, *The Complete Who's Who of England Rugby Union Internationals*, Derby, 1992. U.A. Titley and R. McWhirter, *Centenary History of the Rugby Football Union*, London, 1970.

4 Frank Ludlam in the *Yorkshire Telegraph and Star*, 12 January 1932.

5 By way of contrast, it is worth noting that just five of 617 British international rugby league players in the same period were privately educated.

6 The universities that provided more than two players to the England side were Birmingham (three), Edinburgh (six), Leeds (four), Manchester (six) and Nottingham (four).

7 Lawrence James, *The Middle Class*, London, 2006, p. 508.

8 Dilwyn Porter, 'Amateur football in England, 1948–63', in Adrian Smith and Dil Porter (eds), *Amateurs and Professionals in Post-War British Sport*, London, 2000, p. 23. Department of Education and Science, *Report of the Committee on Football*, London, 1968, p. 15.

9 RFU *Handbooks*, 1959–60, *passim*. I am grateful to Cathy France for her assistance with these statistics.

10 For a discussion of these themes, see McKibbin, *Classes and Cultures*, p. 46.

11 J.F. Crellin, 'The more things change, the more they stay the same: an analysis of how Saracens and Leicester Football Clubs have managed the transition from amateur sporting clubs to professional sports businesses', unpublished MA thesis, De Montfort University, 1999, p. 36. *Rugby Football*, 17 November 1923. *The Sunday Times*, 23 November 1969.

12 Richard Gordon, *Doctor in the House*, London, 1952, pp. 16–17.

13 Christopher Brooke, *A History of the University of Cambridge, vol. 4, 1870–1990*, Cambridge, 1993, p. 517. *Chums*, 20 June 1914, quoted in Peter Parker, *The Old Lie: The Great War and the Public School Ethos*, London, 1987, p. 132. Quoted in John M. Quail, 'From personal patronage to public school privilege', in Alan Kidd and David Nicholls, *The Making of the British Middle Class?*, Stroud, 1998, p. 181. James Bethell, 'City in a scrum to catch a better class of bruiser', *Independent on Sunday*, 29 May 1995.

14 The first instance of the freemasonry analogy I have located is in the 1 December 1928 issue of *Rugby Football Weekly*, which claimed that 'the game ... is a wonderful freemasonry'. White quoted in John Webb, *Freemasonry and Sport*, Surrey, 1995, p. 32.

15 Peter Clark, *British Clubs and Societies 1580–1800: The Origins of an*

Associational World, Oxford, 2000, p. 444. John Lowerson makes a similar point about sport and clubs in 'Sport and British middle-class culture', *International Journal of the History of Sport*, vol. 21, no. 1, January 2004, p. 38.

16 Margaret Stacey, *Tradition and Change: A Study of Banbury*, Oxford, 1960 and Margaret Stacey, Eric Batstone, Colin Bell and Anne Murcott, *Power, Resistance and Change. A Second Study of Banbury*, London, 1975. C.W. Alcock (ed.), *Football Annual*, London, 1871, p. 46.

17 The definitive word on the foundation of Guy's can be found in Adrian Harvey, 'The oldest rugby football club in the world?', *Sport in History*, vol. 26, no. 1, April 2006, pp. 150–2. The orthodox case is made in T.L.T. Lewis, 'A history of Guy's R.F.C.', *Guy's Hospital Gazette*, 26 October 1968.

18 *Rugby Football & Cricket*, 14 October 1911. *Rugby Football Weekly*, 1 December 1928. Bond and Doughty, *The House: A History of the Bank of England Sports Club 1908–83*, p. 30.

19 For more on old boy societies, see J.R. Honey, *Tom Brown's Universe. The Development of the Victorian Public School*, London, 1977, p. 153.

20 Quoted in *Old Alleynian RFC, 1898–1948*, London, 1948, p. 56 (no author).

21 *A History of the Old Merchant Taylors' RFC*, London, 1982, p. 5 (no author). *Old Alleynian RFC*, p. 145.

22 Old Alleynian RFC committee minutes, 7 January 1920 quoted in *Old Alleynian RFC*, p. 151.

23 *Old Alleynian RFC*, p. 8. *Blackheath Rugby Annual 1938–39*, London, 1938, p. 74.

24 Ian Hubbard, *Old Whitgiftian RFC 1901–51*, London, 1951, p. 12. M.J.P. Fawcett, *A History of Old Cranleighan RFC*, Thames Ditton, 1994. *Old Alleynian RFC*, p. 28.

25 J. Woodward, *Cheltenham RFC 1889–1989*, Cheltenham, 1989, p. 21. Derek Robinson, *The Combination*, Bristol, 1986.

26 Quoted in Simon Gunn and Rachel Bell, *Middle Classes: Their Rise and Sprawl*, London, 2002, p. 83.

27 *Leicester Evening News*, 16 June 1904. H.V. Brodie, *The Midland Rugby Football Annual 1938–39*, London, 1938. On Coventry, see Adrian Smith, 'An oval ball and a broken city: Coventry, its people and its rugby team', *International Journal of the History of Sport*, vol. 9, no. 3, 1994, pp. 506–15 and his 'Sport, counterfactual history, and rugby's twin codes', *International Journal of the History of Sport*, vol. 21, no. 1, 2004, pp. 97–108.

28 *Rugby Football*, 19 January 1924. *One Hundred Years of Cinderford Rugby*, 1986, pp. 130–9 (no author, no place of publication).

29 Leicester FC minutes, 15 September 1893 (Leicester Record Office, 23D56/1/3). *Rugby Football*, 15 September 1923.

30 Leicester FC minutes 14 May 1914 and 11 March 1918 (Leicester Record Office, 23D56/1/6). David Hands, *Leicester Football Club 1880–1980*, Leicester, 1981, p. 63. *Leicester Mercury*, 24 August 1931.

31 Quoted in Hands, *Leicester Football Club 1880–1980*, pp. 73 and 53.

32 S. Hopkins, *Leicestershire Rugby Union 1887–1987*, Leicester, 1986, pp. 46–8.

33 RFU Finance and Emergency committee minutes, 5 December 1949.

34 *Rugger*, 14 November 1931.

35 *Rugger*, 14 January 1947. The Australian dual code international Ken Thornett noted that the system was still in operation during his time with Rosslyn Park in the early 1960s. Ken Thornett with Tom Easton, *Tackling Rugby*, Melbourne, 1956, p. 21.

36 *Blackheath Rugby Annual 1938–39*, London, 1938, p. 60. Sadly we have no record of how many workman or chauffeur tickets were sold.

37 *Rugby Football*, 15 September 1923. English Schools Rugby Union committee minutes, 12 July 1930. RFU schools committee minutes, 31 October 1952.

38 Tom Salmon, *The First Hundred Years: The History of Rugby Football in Cornwall*, Illogan, 1983, p. 6. Allen Buckley, *Bert Solomon: A Rugby Phenomenon*, Truro, 2007, p. 41. In 2004 D.M. Thomas' play based on Solomon's life, *Hellfire Corner*, was staged in Truro. I am grateful to Dr Ian Clarke for this information.

39 Jim Steel to John Wilson, 3 January 1935, Rugby Football League Archives, Leeds.

40 Ray French, *My Kind of Rugby*, London, 1979, p. 14. John Bentley with Neil Squires, *John Bentley: My Story*, London, 1999, p. 26.

41 RFU Finance and Emergency committee minutes, 28 May 1926, 30 June 1932 and 23 June 1933. The Lancashire Rugby Union began a similar scheme for its clubs in 1925 with the proceeds of its county matches.

42 V.A.S. Beanland (ed.), *Merseyside Rugby Union Handbook 1927–28*, Liverpool, 1927, p. 2.

43 The full story of union's relationship with league can be found in Collins, *Rugby League in Twentieth Century Britain*, ch. 9.

44 See for example the poster dated October 1924 held at the RFU's Museum of Rugby, Twickenham.

45 IB minutes, 14 March 1958.

46 Harding to Ward, 30 January 1956, PRO FO 371/122750.

47 RFU committee minutes, 28 May 1920, 28 September 1928, 26 April and 18 January 1935.

48 RFU Finance and Emergency committee, 29 September and 7 November 1933. RFU committee minutes, 1 December 1933 and 14 September 1934. Mark Hoskins and Dave Fox, *Bristol Football Club (RFU) 1888–1945*, Stroud, 2000, p. 91.

49 RFU committee minutes, 18 January 1935.

50 Baxter to Sir E. Henry Palmer, 15 February 1936 and reply of 21 February. Copy of RFU sub-committee 'Subject of Enquiry': all at PRO ED 12/527. RFU committee minutes, 14 February, 20 March and 18 March 1936.

51 RFU Executive committee, 9 February 1962. Northern Counties sub-committee, 23 November 1956.

52 Anne Pallant, *A Sporting Century 1863–1963*, Callington, Cornwall, 1997, p. 111. Bev Risman in *Open Rugby*, January 1986.

53 RFU Executive minutes, 12 June and 11 September 1970.

54 RFU committee minutes, 5 December 1949, 2 January and 25 June 1948 and 6 October 1950. RFU Executive committee, 26 September 1968 and 11 April 1980.

55 *Guardian*, 16 February 1993.

56 Norman Davies, *The Isles: A History*, London, 1999, p. 798.

57 C.F.G. Masterman, *The Condition of England*, London, 1909, p. 59.

58 Minutes of meeting to discuss the rugby union's attitude to amateur rugby league in the north of England, 2 December 1983.

59 RFU Coaching sub-committee minutes, 2 September 1983. A.G.B. Old, *Report on Rugby League*, 2 December 1983.

60 Trevor, *Rugby Union Football*, p. 27.

61 *Guardian*, 24 September 1900.

62 Morgan and Nicholson, *Report On Rugby*, p. 133.

63 Beard, *Muddied Oafs. The Last Days of Rugger*, p. 151.
64 Matthew Arnold, *Culture and Anarchy*, Oxford World's Classic edition, 2006, p. 76. Arnold took the phrase from the line 'young barbarians all at play' in the fourth canto of Byron's *Childe Harold's Pilgrimage*.
65 *Yorkshire Post*, 8, 12 and 29 December 1894.
66 Morgan and Nicholson, *Report On Rugby*, p. 133. Laidlaw, *Mud in Your Eye*, p. 6. One exception to this Conservative trend is former Bedford and England wing Derek Wyatt, who became Labour MP for Sittingbourne and Sheppey in 1997. I am grateful to Huw Richards for numerous stimulating conversations on this and many other related subjects.
67 Marshall, 'What rugger means to me', in Wakelam (ed.), *The Game Goes On*, p. 74. Wakefield and Marshall, *Rugger*, p. 106. Thomas, *Rugby-Playing Man*, p. 24.
68 David Duckham, *Dai for England*, London, 1980, p. 67.
69 Christopher Farman, *The General Strike*, London, 1972, p. 178. H.B.T. Wakelam, *Half-Time*, London, 1938, p. 180. *Daily Worker*, 12 September 1930. *Old Alleynian RFC 1898–1948*, London, 1948, p. 165.
70 Peter Howard, *Life and Letters*, London, 1969, pp. 37–8 and 51–61.
71 Labour Party report on the strength of fascism in Yorkshire, quoted in Keith Laybourn, *Britain on the Breadline*, Stroud, 1990, p. 184.
72 *Action*, 24 September 1936.
73 Richard Aldington, *Death of a Hero*, London, 1929, pp. 285–6.
74 Laidlaw, *Mud in Your Eye*, p. 26.
75 Greenwood, *A Cap For Boots*, p. 101.
76 *Daily Telegraph*, 30 November 2003. *Spectator*, 5 April 2003.
77 The full episode is described in Chapter 3 of Warwick Deeping, *Sorrell and Son*, London, 1925.
78 Tom Jeffrey and Keith McClelland, 'A world fit to live in: the *Daily Mail* and the middle classes 1918–39', in James Curran, Anthony Smith and Pauline Wingate (eds), *Impacts and Influences: Essays on Media Power in the Twentieth Century*, London, 1987, p. 42.
70 Stephen G. Jones, *Sport, Politics and the Working Class*, Manchester, 1991, p. 63. McKibbin, *Classes and Cultures*, p. 89. RFU *Handbooks*, 1919–20 and 1939–40.
80 McKibbin, *Classes and Cultures*, p. 46. W.D. Rubenstein, 'Britain's elites in the interwar period' and Richard Trainor, 'Neither metropolitan nor provincial: the interwar middle class', in Kidd and Nicholls (eds), *The Making of the British Middle Class?*, pp. 196–8 and 204–8.
81 Chester Report, p. 18.

6 THE PLAYER'S GAME

1 *The Times*, 22 January 1962.
2 *The Times*, 9 February 1963.
3 *Daily Telegraph*, 12 March 2008.
4 Mackie was effectively expelled from Rugby when Dr Arnold asked him not return after a Christmas holiday following an 'incident' in which Arnold believed Mackie had let him down. Selfe, *Chapters from the History of Rugby School*, p. 61. One could speculate that, were it not for his expulsion, Mackie may have occupied William Webb Ellis' position in the mythology of rugby.
5 W.D. Arnold ('A Rugbeian'), *The First Day of the Sixth Match*, Rugby, 1851,

p. 19. The most detailed account of the Rugby School game can be found in Macrory, *Running with the Ball*.

6 *Football Rules*, Rugby, 1845, p. 13. These can now be found in Jed Smith, *The Original Rules of Rugby*, Oxford, 2007.

7 *The Country Gentleman*, 24 August 1895, p. 1,070. The same point is made in the unsigned 'Football at the public schools', in *Beeton's Brave Tales*, no. 101, p. 1,021, undated but probably 1863.

8 For a comparison of the rules of the various schools, see C.W. Alcock (ed.), *Football Annual*, London, 1868, pp. 74–5. For shinning see *Bell's Life in London*, 2 and 16 January 1859.

9 Marshall (ed.), *Football: The Rugby Union Game*, pp. 77–8. W.H.H. Hutchinson in *Yorkshire Evening Post*, 1 December, 1900. Hull FC in *Yorkshire Evening Post*, 20 February 1904. Rev. Frank Marshall and L.R. Tosswill (eds), *Football The Rugby Union Game*, 2nd edition, London, 1925 p. 21.

10 A.G. Guillemard, 'The Rugby Union game with hints to players', in Thomas P. Power (ed.), *The Footballer*, Melbourne, 1877, p. 11.

11 Charles Gurdon, 'Football: some hints on the game', *The Union Jack: Every Boy's Paper*, 9 September 1883, p. 228.

12 W. MacLagan and G.L. Jeffrey, 'The different epochs of the Rugby game', in W.A. Morgan (ed.), *The 'House' on Sport*, London, 1898, p. 151. The similarity of this tactic to American football's 'flying wedge' once again shows the linkages between the two sports. For 'two and two' see *Bell's Life in London*, 17 April 1875.

13 The first International between England and Scotland in 1871 saw the sides line up with three full-backs, one three-quarter, three half-backs and thirteen forwards.

14 *Bell's Life in London*, 16 October 1875.

15 *Bell's Life in London*, 12 August 1871.

16 Marshall (ed.), *Football: The Rugby Union Game*, p. 120.

17 At the RFU's general meeting on 31 March 1880, J. Hockey and G.A. Rimmington of Gypsies FC unsuccessfully proposed that heeling out of the scrum should be made illegal.

18 For discussion on the revolutionary effect of the reduction in the size of teams see *Boy's Own Paper*, 13 April 1892, p. 479 and *The Dart*, 9 November 1888.

19 For Marsden and the Newsome brothers, see *Yorkshire Post*, 16 February 1880. For Cheltenham, see Carwyn James and John Reason, *The World of Rugby*, London, 1979, p. 39.

20 For Thornes, see *Yorkshire Evening Post*, 21 and 28 November 1903.

21 For the Welsh evolution of the four three-quarter system, see Gareth Willliams and David Smith, *Fields of Praise*, Cardiff, 1980, p. 61.

22 To complicate matters, the International Board, which the RFU had initially refused to join, awarded a goal from a try four points and an unconverted try two points until 1891.

23 *The Yorkshireman*, 4 April 1893.

24 Admiral Sir Percy Royds, *The History of the Laws of Rugby Football*, Twickenham, 1948, p. 31.

25 *Yorkshire Post*, 9 October 1892.

26 Aubrey Spurling in Morgan (ed.) *The 'House' on Sport*, p. 164. Budd, Fry, Cook and Robinson, *Football*, p. 40. *Guardian*, 18 September 1896.

27 *Rugby Football Weekly*, 12 January 1929. Wakefield foreword to W. Wooller and D. Owen, *Fifty Years of the All Blacks*, London, 1955, pp. 6–7. Wakefield

and Marshall, *Rugger*, p. 288. H.B.T. Wakelam (ed.), *The Game Goes On*, London, 1936, (2nd edition, London, 1954) p. 203. *Rugby Football Weekly*, between 20 October 1923 and 26 January 1924.

28 *Daily Telegraph* (Sydney), 8 July 1923. Col. G.F.C. Campbell, 'Foreword' to *NZ Rugby Annual 1920*, Wellington, 1920, p. 7. *The Referee* (Sydney) 11 May 1921. *Athletic News*, 5 February 1919.

29 RFU committee minutes, 17 October 1919.

30 New South Wales Rugby Union, *Annual Reports*, 1921 and 1931.

31 For the definitive account of the evolution of New Zealand's wing-forward tactics, see Greg Ryan, *The Contest for Rugby Supremacy*, Canterbury, NZ, 2005, ch. 6. Baxter in *Athletic News*, 1 February 1926.

32 Royds, *The History of the Laws of Rugby Football*, pp. 92–103.

33 *Rugby News* (Sydney), 21 May 1932. *Daily Telegraph* (Sydney), 8 July 1932. The dispensations were allowed again in 1936, see RFU committee minutes, 20 March 1936.

34 *Evening Post* (Wellington, NZ), 8 February 1910. I am grateful to Sean Fagan for bringing this article to my attention.

35 J.H. Rogers, 'The rugby game', in Clive Leatherdale (ed.), *The Book of Football*, London, 1906 (1997 edition), p. 190. For Old Leysians, see *Old Alleynian RFC 1898–1948*, London, 1948, p. 64. David Hands, *Leicester FC 1880–1980*, Leicester, 1981, p. 36. *Rugby News* (Sydney), 18 July 1925. *Rugby Football*, 26 January 1924. For Stoop and Harlequins, see *The Sportsman*, 21 October 1907 and James Martens, 'They stooped to conquer: Rugby Union Football 1895–1914', *Journal of Sport History*, vol. 20, no. 1, Spring 1993.

36 Wakefield and Marshall, *Rugger*, p. 41.

37 Wakefield and Marshall, *Rugger*, p. 106. Hands, *Leicester FC 1880–1980*, p. 45; Leicester finally switched back to eight forwards in 1928.

38 *Athletic News*, 1 February 1926. *Edinburgh Review*, January 1928, p. 105. RFU committee minutes, 19 August 1932.

39 Howard Marshall, *Oxford v Cambridge*, London, 1951, pp. 159 and 226.

40 'Lente' in *Rugby Football*, 15 December 1923. Marshall, 'What rugger means to me', in Wakelam (ed.), *The Game Goes On*, p. 73. *Old Alleynian RFC 1898–1948*, London, 1948, p. 147.

41 *Rugby Football*, 24 November 1923 and 5 January 1924. W.D. Gibbon, *First Steps to Rugby Football*, London, 1922, p. 119.

42 *Bell's Life in London*, 29 April 1876.

43 Alec Waugh, 'The young man's game', in *On Doing What One Likes*, reprinted in Howard Marshall (ed.) *Rugger Stories*, London, 1932, p. 43. E.B. Osborn, 'The game', in Wakelam (ed.), *The Game Goes On*, p. 13. Marshall, *Oxford v Cambridge*, p. 8.

44 Trevor, *Rugby Union Football*, p. 25. J.M. Kilburn, *In Search of Rugby Football*, London, 1938, p. 47.

45 *Boy's Own Paper*, February 1920, p. 238. Marshall, *Oxford v Cambridge*, p. 140. Cambridge's 'Jenny' Greenwood had kept the ball in the back row of the scrum until Oxford went off-side. Greenwood, *A Cap For Boots*, p. 110.

46 Waugh, *On Doing What One Likes*, p. 46.

47 James Dundas Hamilton quoted in Gunn and Bell, *Middle Classes: Their Rise and Sprawl*, p. 211.

48 Royds, *The History of the Laws of Rugby Football*, p. 113.

49 Marshall, *Oxford v Cambridge*, p. 10. Wooller quoted in Norman Barrett (ed.), *The Daily Telegraph Chronicle of Rugby*, London, 1996, p. 84.

50 RFU AGM minutes, 3 July 1953. IB minutes, 21 March 1954 (the Australians

had been granted a dispensation in 1951 to penalise direct kicking into touch outside of the kicker's twenty-five yard line). G.V. Wynne-Jones, *Sports Commentary*, London, 1951, p. 170. W. Wooller and D. Owen, *Fifty Years of the All Blacks*, London, 1955, pp. 6–7. *The Times*, 4 February 1958.

51 Denis Lalanne, *The Great Fight of the French Fifteen*, Wellington, NZ, 1960, p. 200.
52 IB minutes, 21 March 1959 and 15 March 1963. *The Times*, 18 March 1963.
53 RFU AGM minutes, 8 July 1966. RFU Laws committee, 4 May 1967.
54 RFU Laws committee minutes, 5 July 1972.
55 *Independent*, 17 April 1992.
56 IRB, *Changes in the Playing of International Rugby Over a Twenty Year Period*, September, 2005, p. 4.

7 THE IMPERIAL GAME

1 *The Times*, 3 March 1884. The RFU statement on the matter is printed in *The Times*, 16 April 1885. Much of the research for this chapter was facilitated by the award of a Research Fellowship to me in 2004 by the Australian Council of State Libraries.
2 *The Times*, 7 May 1888, 30 December 1889 and 29 April 1890.
3 Headmasters' Conference, *Bulletin*, no. 1, 1927, p. 5. H.H. Simson, 'Statement to Member Clubs, 15 May 1928', in A. Thorburn, *The SRU Official History*, Edinburgh, 1928, p. 204.
4 See Greg Ryan, *The Contest for Rugby Supremacy: Accounting for the 1905 All Blacks*, Christchurch, 2005.
5 *Yorkshire Post*, 13 January 1909.
6 *Yorkshire Post*, 20 February 1909. Marriott letter reprinted in *Yorkshire Post*, 19 January 1909, RFU and IB decisions in *Yorkshire Post*, 1 and 20 February 1909.
7 On the Lions name see *The Times*, 18 August 1950 and 22 September 1951.
8 RFU Executive minutes, 17 May and 18 July 1974. For the 1954 controversy over the national anthem of Ireland see Sean Diffley, *The Men in Green*, London, 1973, p. 49.
9 The descriptions of each nation are taken from the media research of Jason Tuck in his fascinating 'Rugby Union and national identity in the British Isles since 1945', unpublished PhD thesis, Loughbrough University, 1999.
10 Donald Swann, *The Songs of Michael Flanders and Donald Swann*, London, 1997, p. 80.
11 *Rugby Football*, 8 September 1923.
12 H.V. Morton, *In Search of England*, London, 1927, p. 202. For more on Morton's ideas on Englishness see Michael Bartholomew, *In Search of H.V. Morton*, London, 2004.
13 John Reason and Carwyn James, *The World of Rugby*, London, 1979, p. 31. Peter Wilby 'Who let him in?', *Observer Sports Monthly*, 2 April 2006.
14 Alun Howkins, 'The discovery of rural England', in Rob Colls and Philip Dodd (eds) *Englishness: Politics and Culture*, London, 1986, p. 62. See also Jeremy Paxman, *The English*, London, 1998, pp. 142–4.
15 Kenneth Pelmear, *Rugby in the Duchy*, Redruth, 1959. Tom Salmon, *The First Hundred Years: The History of Rugby Football in Cornwall*, Illogan, 1983.
16 Andy Seward, 'Cornish rugby and cultural identity', *The Sports Historian*, vol. 18, no. 2, November 1998, pp. 78–94.
17 I am grateful to Andy Seward for this information.
18 *Athletic News*, 1 December 1913.

19 IB minutes, 19 March 1921.
20 Godfrey Elton, 'An Englishman's audit of Rhodes Scholars', *Harper's*, May 1964, p. 102. Philip Zeigler, *Legacy: Cecil Rhodes, the Rhodes Trust and Rhodes Scholarships*, Yale, 2008. Greenwood, *A Cap For Boots*, p. 100. D.J. Wenden, 'Sport', in Brian Harrison (ed.) *The History of the University of Oxford, volume 8, The Twentieth Century*, Oxford, 1994, p. 536.
21 *Rugby Football & Cricket*, 4 November, 1911.
22 *Country Life*, 16 and 23 December 1949.
23 *Rugger*, 18 December 1946. G.V. Wynne-Jones, *Sports Commentary*, London, 1951, p. 167.
24 RFU Committee minutes, 10 December 1935.
25 J.C. Davis, *Official Souvenir – English Team of Rugby Football Players*, Sydney, 1904, p. 3. I am grateful to Mary Bushby for her help and knowledge of Australian rugby history for this chapter.
26 G.R. Hill quoted in *Rugby Football: A Weekly Record of the Game*, 17 November 1923, p. 273.
27 On the link between cricket and anti-Afrikaner provocations in the 1890s, see Dean Allen, 'Logan's Golden Age: cricket, politics and empire in South Africa 1888–1910', unpublished PhD thesis, University of Brighton, 2008, pp. 156–9 and 187–9.
28 Mullineux's views are reported in great detail in the *Australian Field*, 26 August 1899.
29 *Brisbane Courier*, 29 June 1899.
30 H.M. Moran, *Viewless Winds. Being the Recollections and Digressions of an Australian Surgeon*, London, 1939, p. 46.
31 *Sydney Morning Herald*, 7 July 1904.
32 The definitive account of the tour and its aftermath is Ryan, *The Contest for Rugby Supremacy: Accounting for the 1905 All Blacks*. I owe a debt of gratitude to Greg Ryan for sharing his insights and stimulating ideas on the history of New Zealand rugby.
33 Hamish Stuart in the *Otago Witness*, 3 January, 1909, quoted in Greg Ryan, 'A lack of esprit du corps: the 1908 Wallaby tour of Britain', *Sporting Traditions*, vol. 17, no. 1, November 2000, p. 45.
34 McMahon in *Referee*, 31 March 1909.
35 Swann, *The Songs of Michael Flanders and Donald Swann*, p. 82.
36 *Guardian*, 17 December 1906.
37 F. Neville Piggott, *The Springboks History of the Tour 1906–07*, Cape Town, 1907, p. 105.
38 Richards, *A Game for Hooligans*, p. 95.
39 See Sean Fagan, *The Rugby Rebellion*, Sydney, 2005, pp. 155–6.
40 See, for example, Geoff Vincent, 'Practical imperialism: the Anglo-Welsh rugby tour of New Zealand, 1908', *International Journal of the History of Sport*, vol. 15, no. 1, 1998, and Geoff Vincent and Toby Harfield, 'Repression and reform: responses within New Zealand rugby to the arrival of the "Northern game", 1907–8', *New Zealand Journal of History*, vol. 31, no. 2, October 1997.
41 *The Referee*, 11 May and 12 October 1921.
42 Quoted in *The Referee*, 12 September 1917. I am grateful to Sean Fagan for bringing this to my attention.
43 *The Referee*, 4 May 1921. Biographical details from Bruce Montgomerie, *Those Who Played*, Sydney, 2004, p. 119.
44 RFU committee minutes, 17 October 1919. NSWRU management committee minutes, 29 March 1920. NSWRU *Annual Report 1920*, p. 3.

45 IB minutes, 19 March and 23 July 1920. See also NSWRU *Annual Report*, 1921, p. 3.
46 John Hughes, 'Stands rugger yet', *The Referee*, 5 January 1921.
47 IB minutes, 30 November 1923, 14 March and 11 October 1924. *The Times*, 13 December 1924.
48 NSWRU, *Rugby Annual 1927*, Sydney, 1927, p. 21.
49 H.H. Simson, 'Statement to member clubs, 15 May 1928', in A. Thorburn, *The SRU Official History*, Edinburgh, 1928, p. 203.
50 S.F Coopper to A.E. Neilson, 2 January 1931 (RFU Archives, Twickenham). The idea of removing the dispensation had been raised as early as 1929, see IB minutes, 15 March 1929.
51 IB minutes, 29 July 1931. NSWRU *Annual Report*, 1931. The RFU agreed to restore the 'dispensation' on kicking directly into touch to counter rugby league's appeal, see RFU committee minutes, 20 March 1936. The IB eventually brought in the 'dispensation' for the entire game in 1968.
52 A.E. Neilson to S.F Coopper, 6 May 1932
53 'Editorial', *Rugby News*, 12 May 1928, p. 4.
54 F.D. Prentice 'Australasia 1930', in Wakelam (ed.), *The Game Goes On*, p. 154.
55 E.H.D. Sewell, 'The state of the game', *Fortnightly Review*, vol. 89, 1911, pp. 933–48. Northern Union General Council minutes, 12 November 1912. *Rugby Football*, 17 October 1923.
56 For the RFU statement on France see *The Times*, 4 and 10 March 1931. *Rugger*, 19 September and 10 October 1931. For a comprehensive account of this period see Philip Dine, *French Rugby Football; A Cultural History*, Oxford, 2001, ch. 4.
57 RFU Finance and Emergency committee minutes, 11 December 1933. RFU committee minutes, 20 December 1935. S.F. Coopper to J.V. Waite of the USA Rugby Union, 26 February 1936.
58 Hylton Cleaver, *Before I Forget*, London, 1961, p. 94.
59 On Bergougnan see *Daily Mail*, 31 December 1947, *Yorkshire Evening Post*, 7 January 1948 and Gaston Roux, *Arbitration on the Conflict Between the FFR and the FFJXIII*, 10 July 1947 (copy of English translation in RFL Archives, Leeds). On Dauger, see letter from Maurice Blain to Bill Fallowfield, 15 December 1947 (RFL Archives) and IB minutes, 20 March 1953.
60 Harry Thrift (IB secretary) to M. Laurent (FFR secretary), IB minutes, 20 March 1951, IB minutes, 14 March 1952, 20 March 1953 and 20 March 1964. *Daily Telegraph* (London), 6 April and 11 May 1952. Some documents are reprinted in John Reason and Carwyn James, *The World of Rugby*, London, 1979, pp. 95–9.
61 See IB minutes, 21 March 1959, 15 March 1963 and 6 January 1964.
62 IB minutes, 15 March 1963. *The Referee*, 7 October 1937.
63 IB minutes, 17/18 March 1961.
64 For the campaign against apartheid sport, see Douglas Booth, *The Race Game: Sport and Politics in South Africa*, London, 1998, David Black and John Nauright, *Rugby and the South African Nation*, London, 1998. For the impact of the anti-apartheid struggle on Australian rugby, see Thomas Hickie's comprehensive *A Sense of Union*, Sydney, 1998, chs 12 and 13.
65 The full unedifying story of d'Oliveira's treatment is recounted in Peter Oborne, *Basil D'Oliveira: Cricket and Controversy*, London, 2005.
66 RFU Ground sub-committee meeting minutes, 25 September 1969.
67 *Guardian*, 31 October 1969.

68 *Guardian*, 17, 19 and 25 November 1969 and 15 November 1999 for Keating's recollections
69 Peter Hain, *Don't Play With Apartheid*, London, 1971, pp. 148–59. Laidlaw, *Mud in Your Eye*, p. 1.
70 *Guardian*, 27 November, 1969. *The Sunday Times*, 26 November 1969. Nigel Starmer-Smith, in Bob Holmes and Chris Thau (eds), *My Greatest Game*, Edinburgh, 1994, p. 164.
71 *Guardian*, 27 November and 3 December 1969. England fly-half Stuart Barnes later refused to tour South Africa with England in 1984.
72 *The Sunday Times*, 23 November 1969.
73 Rene Cutforth, 'Politics on the pitch', on *Radio Four Reports*, 4 November 1969, transcript at File R47/771/1 Rugby Football, BBC Archives (Caversham). RFU Executive committee minutes, 8 December 1969. Paul Dobson, *Doc: The Life of Danie Craven*, Cape Town, 1994, p. 169.
74 Air Commodore G.C. Lamb, CBE AFC RAF 'The future of South Africa as an apartheid state', Royal College of Defence Studies, 1971, p. 96, copy in the RFU library at Twickenham.
75 John Reason, 'The brink of destruction', *Rugby News*, December 1985.
76 Keating in the *Guardian*, 16 November 1992. Cleary in the *Observer*, 29 November. Botha in the *Daily Telegraph*, 16 November 1992.

8 THE MONEY GAME

1 *Observer*, 21 January 1991.
2 *The Sunday Times*, 21 January 1991. *Independent*, 22 January 1991.
3 CCPR, *Sport and the Community. The Report of the Wolfenden Committee on Sport*, London, 1960, p. 67. Barrett is quoted in Richard Holt and Tony Mason, *Sport in Britain 1945–2000*, London, 2001, p. 47.
4 Martin Polley, 'Amateurism and professionalism in post-war British athletics', in Adrian Smith and Dil Porter (eds), *Amateurs and Professionals in Post-War British Sport*, London, 2000, pp. 88–91. Dil Porter, 'Amateur football in England 1948–63: the Pegasus phenomenon', *Contemporary British History*, vol. 14, no. 2, Summer 2000, pp. 1–30.
5 G.V. Wynne-Jones, *Sports Commentary*, London, 1951, p. 169.
6 RFU AGM, 1951. IB minutes, 27 February 1948 and 15–17 March 1957.
7 *Isis*, 1 May 1968.
8 D.J. Wenden, 'Sport', in Harrison (ed.), *The History of the University of Oxford, volume 8, The Twentieth Century*, pp. 533–5. Laidlaw, *Mud in Your Eye*, p. 161. *Guardian*, 11 December 1996.
9 RFU AGM, 11 July 1975.
10 RFU Executive minutes, 5 May 1968, 17 January, 14 May and 6 June 1969.
11 *The Sunday Times*, 23 November 1969. Laidlaw, *Mud in Your Eye*, p. 153.
12 IB minutes, 19 March 1965 and 13–14 March 1969.
13 RFU Executive minutes, 17 January 1969.
14 RFU Executive minutes, 19 March 1971 and 7 February 1972. RFU Financial Assistance sub-committee minutes, 13 July and 29 December 1972.
15 The story of the cup can be found in Graham Williams, *Glory Days, The History of English Rugby Union Cup Finals*, Leeds, 1998.
16 *The Times*, 4 October 1975 and 13 September 1976. RFU Major Clubs sub-committee, 22 September 1978. Wharton presidential speech at 1977 RFU AGM.
17 *The Times*, 1 November 1975.

18 H.B.T. Wakelam, 'Telling the world', in Wakelam (ed.), *The Game Goes On*, pp. 115–24, and Wakelam, *Half-Time*, p. 187.

19 RFU AGM minutes, 23 June 1950. RFU Finance and Emergency committee minutes, 13 December 1951. Minutes, meeting with BBC, 28 July 1954.

20 Minutes of Home Unions' meeting with the BBC, 15 March 1958. Executive minutes, 8 December 1969. *Observer*, 5 February 1989.

21 RFU Coaching sub-committee, 18 January 1964. RFU Executive, 1 November 1968. Dickie Jeeps at RFU AGM, 1976. The Welsh defeat in South Africa in 1964 led to the same process in Wales.

22 Quoted in Christopher Booker, *The Neophiliacs*, London, 1970, p. 28.

23 Gunn and Bell, *Middle Classes: Their Rise and Sprawl*, p. 211. Harold Perkin, *The Rise of Professional Society: England Since 1880*, London, 2002 edition, p. 270.

24 Derek Wyatt, *Rugby Disunion*, London, 1995, p. 19.

25 IB minutes, 11/12 March 1976. *Rugby World*, September 1965.

26 *The Times*, 19 June 1973.

27 Richards, *A Game for Hooligans*, p. 197.

28 Dave Hammond, *The Club: Life and Times of Blackheath F.C.*, London, 1999, p. 167. RFU Executive minutes, 9 February 1979.

29 RFU Forward Planning sub-committee, 3 May 1979.

30 RFU AGM, 10 July 1970.

31 Burton in *The Times*, 3 September 1982. Welsh players appear to have been the main beneficiaries of Adidas', and other manufacturers, money.

32 RFU Executive minutes, 2 September 1983.

33 First Report of the Committee on Standards in Public Life, Cm 2850 I, London, 1995, p. 16. James Dundas Hamilton quoted in Gunn and Bell, *Middle Classes: Their Rise and Sprawl*, p. 195. For the Stock Exchange, see David Kynaston, *The City of London, Volume IV: A Club No More, 1945–2000*, London, 2002.

34 See, for example, Steve Bale, 'How professional have amateurs become?', *Independent*, 15 December 1993.

35 D.D. Serfontein, *Circular to Clubs in Membership*, 6 May 1993. For an overview of this period, see Peter Williams, 'Battle lines on three fronts: the RFU and the lost war against professionalism', *International Journal of the History of Sport*, vol. 19, no. 4, December 2002, pp. 114–36.

36 *The Official Rugby Union Club Directory 1990–91*, London, 1990, p. 6.

37 *The Times*, 17 and 18 January 1978. IB minutes, 21/22 March 1979.

38 RFU Executive minutes, 1 November 1968. IB minutes, 13–14 March 1969.

39 *The Times*, 28 May 1983 and *Sydney Morning Herald*, 16 October 2003.

40 For an analysis of the IB's attitude to the World Cup, see Derek Wyatt, *Rugby Disunion: The Story of Three World Cups*, London, 1995, pp. 30–1.

41 For France, see Louis Bonnery, *Le Rugby à XIII*, Limoux, 1996, pp. 251–2. For Italy, 'Italy's pro circus', *Rugby World & Post*, September 1993. For Japan, Siggy Konno, letter to Max Mannix, 2 August, 1994 (copy in David Hinchliffe Archive, Rugby Football League, Leeds). Haden in the *Independent on Sunday*, 7 October 1990.

42 Welsh Rugby Union, *Report of Inquiry into the Involvement of Welsh Players in the Centenary Celebration of the SARB*, August 1989, sections C.1 and C.2.c (document in David Hinchliffe Archive, Leeds).

43 RFU AGM, 8 July 1994.

44 O.L. Owen, 'Introduction', in Kenneth Pelmear (ed.), *Rugby Football: An Anthology*, London, 1958, p. 10. IB minutes, 15 March 1963 and 6 January 1964.

45 RFU committee minutes, 18 October 1985. 1985 RFU AGM minutes. *1986–87 Annual Report and Financial Statement*, p. 1.
46 *Independent*, 13 October 1990.
47 *The Times*, 21 January 1991. *Guardian*, 4 May 1995.
48 *Independent*, 14 April 1995 and 9 July 1994.
49 David Hare, *Plenty*, London, 1978, p. 79.
50 Phil Dine, *French Rugby Football*, 2001, p. 177.
51 See, for example, *Independent*, 4 July 1992.
52 Phil Kearns speaking on the Australian Broadcasting Corporation DVD, *Stealing Rugby*, Sydney, 2006.
53 Stuart Barnes, *The Year of Living Dangerously*, London, 1995, p. 153. Peter Fitzsimons, *The Rugby War*, Sydney, 1996, p. 312.
54 Fitzsimons, pp. 15–20. *Daily Telegraph*, 24 June 1995.
55 For the full story of the WRC see Fitzsimons and especially the DVD, *Stealing Rugby*. Ieuan Evans and Peter Jackson, *Bread of Heaven*, Edinburgh, 1995, p. 202.
56 *Independent*, 14 April 1995.
57 Franz Kafka, *The Trial*, London, Penguin edition, 2000, p. 172.
58 Welsh Rugby Union, *Report of Inquiry into the Involvement of Welsh Players in the Centenary Celebrations of the South African Rugby Board: Conclusions and Recommendations*, August 1989, Cardiff, 1991, pp. 3–5.
59 Bernard Lapasset, F.C.H. McLeod, Rob Fisher and Vernon Pugh, *Report of the IRB Amateurism Working Party*, February 1995, pp. 3–4 (Museum of Rugby, Twickenham). Bizarrely, throughout the report the split with league is continually referred to as having happened in 1893, rather than 1895. T.A. Kemp speaking at the 1971 RFU AGM.
60 Lawrence James, *The Middle Class: A History*, London, 2006, p. 5.

9 THE WHOLE NEW BALL GAME?

1 For the Byzantine intricacies of the debates during this period, see Peter Williams, 'Cycle of conflict: a decade of strife in English professional rugby', *International Journal of the History of Sport*, vol. 25, no. 1, 2008, pp. 65–81, Adrian Smith, 'The impact of professionalism on Rugby Union 1995–99', in Adrian Smith and Dil Porter (eds), *Amateurs and Professionals in Post-War British Sport*, London, 2000, pp. 146–89, Ian Malin, *Mud, Blood and Money*, Edinburgh, 1997, and Donald McRae, *Winter Colours: Changing Seasons in World Rugby*, Edinburgh, 1998.
2 Quoted in Dominic Hobson, *The National Wealth*, London, 1999, p. 893.
3 By way of comparison, the aggregate attendance for all twelve Guinness Premiership clubs in 2007–08 was still less than that of Manchester United in the same season. Clubs in soccer's Championship averaged crowds of 17,023 and those in the third tier, Division One, 7,991. Rugby League's Super League averaged 10,246 for its 2007 season.
4 IRB, *Changes in the Playing of International Rugby Over a Twenty Year Period*, September, 2005, p. 6.
5 *Guardian*, 22 November 2004. For injuries see Gwyn Jones, 'Playing a dangerous game,' *Observer Sports Monthly*, October 2005, pp. 40–5. Thomas V. Hickie, 'The amateur ideal in the era of professional rugby', in Mary Bushby and Thomas V. Hickie, *Rugby History: The Remaking of the Class Game*, Melbourne, 2007, p. 17.
6 Pat Carter, 'Who needs officer qualities?', *Journal of the Royal Air Force*

College, LXXIII, March 2002, p. 14. I am grateful to Dr Eliza Reidi for bringing this to my attention. *The Sunday Times*, 23 November 2003 and 3 October 2004.

7 Report of the Sir Norman Chester Centre at the University of Leicester into Premiership Rugby supporters, press release dated 13 May 2003 at www. scrum.com/news/news.asp?newsid=18338 (accessed 27 August 2008).

8 *Daily Telegraph*, 22 July 2008.

9 James, *The Middle Class: A History*, p. 515.

10 For the importance of ideas about common sense and 'conventional wisdom' for middle-class conservatism see Ross McKibbin, 'Class and conventional wisdom', in his *The Ideologies of Class*, Oxford, 1991, pp. 259–94, and David Jarvis, 'British conservatism and class politics in the 1920s', *English Historical Review*, vol. 111, no. 440, February 1996, pp. 59–84.

BIBLIOGRAPHY

Archive sources

Australian Rugby Union Archives, Sydney, New South Wales Rugby Union, minute books and tour reports 1919–1939.

Batley Rugby Union Football Club, West Yorkshire Archive Service, Wakefield, minutes 1919–1939.

BBC Written Archives, Caversham, File R47/771/1 Rugby Football.

David Hinchliffe Archive, Rugby Football League, Leeds, documents relating to the Sports (Discrimination) Bill, 1989–1995.

Douglas Clark Papers, Imperial War Museum, London, manuscript diary.

English Schools Rugby Union, Museum of Rugby, London, committee minutes.

Headmasters' Conference, Leicester, minute books and bulletins, 1918–1939.

International Rugby Football Board, Museum of Rugby, London, committee minute books, 1886–1995.

Leicester Football Club, Leicestershire County Archives, minute books and press cuttings, 1892–1930.

Mass-Observation Archive, University of Sussex, Brighton, Sport 1937–1947 Box 1, 'Sport in War-Time'.

Rugby Football League, Leeds, committee minute books, 1899–1985.

Rugby Football Union, Museum of Rugby, London, committee minute books, correspondence and reports, 1871–1995.

The National Archives, Kew, PRO ED 12/527 and PRO FO 371/122750.

Government and official reports

Central Council for Physical Recreation, *Sport and the Community. The Report of the Wolfenden Committee on Sport*, London, 1960.

Department of Education and Science, *Report of the Committee on Football*, London, 1968.

First Report of the Committee on Standards in Public Life, Cm 2850 I, London, 1995.

Hansard Report of the Commissioners of the Schools Inquiry, 1867–8. Education General 17, 1868.

Report of the Commissioners on the Revenues and Management of Certain Colleges and Schools, British Parliamentary Papers. Public Schools and Colleges, volume XX, Education, General 9, 1864.

Newspapers and periodicals

Action
Athletic News
Australian Field
Baily's Magazine of Sports and Pastimes
Bell's Life in London
Bell's Life in Victoria and Sporting Chronicle (Melbourne)
Boy's Own Paper
Brisbane Courier
Chums
Country Life
Daily Mail
Daily Mirror
Daily Telegraph
Daily Telegraph (Sydney)
Daily Worker
Evening News
Evening Post (Wellington, NZ)
Evening Standard
Financial Times
Guardian
Halifax Guardian
Independent
Independent on Sunday
Isis
Leeds Mercury
Leeds Times
Leicester Evening News
Leicester Mercury
Liverpool Mercury
Mail on Sunday
Observer Sports Monthly
Open Rugby
Pastime
Pendleton Reporter
Rugby Football
Rugby Football & Cricket
Rugby Football Weekly
Rugby Football: a weekly record of the game
Rugby News (Sydney)
Rugby World & Post
Rugger

Sheffield Star
Spectator
Sport in Industry
Sporting Chronicle
Sportsman
Sydney Morning Herald
Tatler
The Country Gentleman
The Dart
The Devon Barbarians Magazine
The Field
The Magazine of Wellingborough Grammar School
The New Rugbeian
The Referee (Sydney)
The Sunday Times
The Times
The Times Literary Supplement
The Yorkshireman
Touchlines
Wakefield Express
Western Mail
Yorkshire Evening Post
Yorkshire Owl
Yorkshire Post
Yorkshire Telegraph and Star

Annuals, directories and yearbooks

Alcock, C.W. (ed.), *John Lilywhite's Football Annual*, London, 1868.
Beanland, V.A.S. (ed.), *Merseyside Rugby Union Handbook 1927–28*, Liverpool, 1927.
Blackheath Rugby Annual 1938–39, London, 1938.
Brodie, H.V., *The Midland Rugby Football Annual 1938–39*, London, 1938.
New Zealand Rugby Annual 1920, Wellington, 1920.
Northern Rugby Football Union, *Official Guide*, Leeds.
Rugby Football Union, *Handbooks*, London.
The Official Rugby Union Club Directory 1990–91, London, 1990.
The Times' Six Nations Rugby Handbook 2006.

Books

A History of the Old Merchant Taylors' RFC, London, 1982 (no author).
Adonis, Andrew and Pollard, Stephen, *A Class Act: The Myth of Britain's Classless Society*, Harmondsworth, 1998.
Aldington, Richard, *Death of a Hero*, London, 1929.

Arnold, John, Spearritt, Peter and Walker, David (eds), *Out of Empire. The British Dominion of Australia*, Port Melbourne, 1993.

Arnold, Matthew, *Culture and Anarchy*, Oxford World's Classic edition, 2006.

Arnold, W.D., *The First Day of the Sixth Match*, Rugby, 1851.

Auty, T.W., *Centenary History of Headingley Football Club*, Leeds, 1978.

Bagehot, Walter, *Literary Studies, volume One*, London, 1911.

Bagehot, Walter, *The English Constitution*, CUP edition, Cambridge, 2001.

Bagnall Poulton, Edward, *The Life of Ronald Poulton*, London, 1919.

Bailey, P., *Leisure and Class in Victorian England*, 2nd edition, London, 1987.

Balaam, L., *Manchester Football Club 1860–1985*, Manchester, 1985.

Bale, J., *Sport and Place*, London, 1982.

Barak, M., *A Century of Rugby At Sale*, Sale, 1962.

Barnes, Stuart, *The Year of Living Dangerously*, London, 1995.

Bartholomew, Michael, *In Search of H.V. Morton*, London, 2004.

Beard, Richard, *Muddied Oafs. The Last Days of Rugger*, London, 2003.

Bentley, John, with Squires, Neil, *John Bentley: My Story*, London, 1999.

Best, Geoffrey, *Mid-Victorian Britain 1851–75*, London, 1979.

Bills, Peter, *Passion in Exile, 100 Years of London Irish RFC*, Edinburgh, 1998.

Birley, D., *Sport and the Making of Britain*, Manchester, 1993.

Birley, D., *Land of Sport and Glory: Sport and British Society 1887–1910*, Manchester, 1995.

Black, David and Nauright, John, *Rugby and the South African Nation*, London, 1998.

Blainey, Geoffrey, *A Game of Our Own*, Melbourne, 1990.

Bond, A.W.N. and Doughty, M.O.H., *The House: A History of the Bank of England Sports Club 1908–83*, London, 1984.

Bonnery, Louis, *Le Rugby à XIII*, Limoux, 1996.

Booker, Christopher, *The Neophiliacs*, London, 1970.

Booth, Alan, *The British Economy in the Twentieth Century*, London, 2001.

Booth, Douglas, *The Race Game: Sport and Politics in South Africa*, London, 1998.

Booth, Keith, *The Father of Modern Sport: The Life and Times of Charles W. Alcock*, Manchester, 2002.

Bourke, Joanna, *Dismembering the Male: Men's Bodies, Britain and the Great War*, London, 1996.

Bradley, M.J. and Simon, B. (eds), *The Victorian Public School*, London, 1975.

Branson, Noreen, *Britain in the Nineteen Twenties*, London, 1975.

Branson, Noreen and Heinemann, Margot, *Britain in the Nineteen Thirties*, London, 1971.

Briggs, A., *Victorian People*, London, 1965.

Briggs, Asa, *The History of Broadcasting in the UK. volume Four: Sound and Vision*, revised edition, Oxford, 1995.

Brooke, Christopher, *A History of the University of Cambridge, vol. 4, 1870–1990*, Cambridge, 1993.

Brown, Judith M. and Lewis, W.R. (eds), *The Oxford History of the British Empire, vol. 4: The Twentieth Century*, Oxford, 1999.

Buckley, Allen, *Bert Solomon: A Rugby Phenomenon*, Truro, 2007.

Budd, A., Fry, C.B., Cook, T.A. and Robinson, B.F., *Football*, London, 1897.

Bushby, Mary and Hickie, Thomas V. (eds), *Rugby History: The Remaking of the Class Game*, Melbourne, 2007.

Calder, Angus, *The People's War: Britain 1939–1945*, London, 1969.

Cannadine, David, *Class in Britain*, Yale, 1998.

Carpenter, Humphrey, *The Brideshead Generation: Evelyn Waugh and His Friends*, London, 1989.

Chandler, T. and Nauright, J. (eds), *Making Men: Rugby and Masculine Identity*, London, 1996.

Chandler, T. and Nauright, J. (eds), *Making the Rugby World: Race, Gender, Commerce*, London, 1999.

Chandos, John, *Boys Together: English Public Schools 1800–1964*, London, 1984.

Clark, Peter, *British Clubs and Societies 1580–1800: The Origins of an Associational World*, Oxford, 2000.

Cleaver, Hylton, *Before I Forget*, London, 1961.

Collini, Stefan, *English Pasts*, Oxford, 1999,

Collins, Tony, *Rugby's Great Split*, London, 1998.

Collins, Tony, *Rugby League in Twentieth Century Britain*, London, 2006.

Collins, Tony and Vamplew, Wray, *Mud, Sweat and Beers: A Cultural History of Sport and Alcohol*, Oxford, 2002.

Colls, Robert, *Identities of England*, Oxford, 2002.

Colls, R. and Dodd, P. (eds), *Englishness, Politics and Culture 1880–1920*, London, 1986.

Crick, Bernard, *George Orwell, A Life*, Harmondsworth, 1980.

Croome, A.C.M. (ed.), *Fifty Years of Sport at Oxford, Cambridge and the Great Public Schools*, London, 1922.

Croxford, W.B., *Rugby Union in Lancashire and Cheshire*, Liverpool, 1950.

Cunningham, Hugh, *Leisure in the Industrial Revolution*, London, 1980.

Cunningham, Hugh, *The Volunteer Force*, London, 1975.

Dalglish, J.R.A., *Red, Black & Blue, The First 125 Years of Liverpool Football Club*, Swinton, 1983.

Davie, Michael, *Anglo-Australian Attitudes*, London, 2000.

Davies, Norman, *The Isles: A History*, London, 1999.

Davis, J.C., *Official Souvenir – English Team of Rugby Football Players*, Sydney, 1904.

De Groot, Gerald, *Blighty: British Society in the Era of the Great War*, London, 1996.

De Moore, Gregory, *Tom Wills: His Spectacular Rise and Tragic Fall*, Sydney, 2008.

Deeping, Warwick, *Sorrell and Son*, London, 1925.

Diffley, Sean, *The Men in Green*, London, 1973.

Dine, Philip, *French Rugby Football: A Cultural History*, Oxford, 2001.

Dobbs, B., *Edwardians At Play*, London, 1973.

Dobson, Paul, *Doc: The Life of Danie Craven*, Cape Town, 1994.

Dowling, Linda, *Hellenism and Homosexuality in Victorian Oxford*, Cornell, 1996.

Duckham, David, *Dai for England*, London, 1980.

Dunn, Andrew, *Australia and the Empire*, Sydney, 1984.

Dunning, E. and Sheard, K., *Barbarians, Gentlemen & Players*, New York, 1979.

Dyos, H.J. and Wolff, M. (eds), *The Victorian City: Images and Realities*, London, 1973.

Edwards, S.J., *Sportsman and Solider* (privately published by the author), 1998.

Eksteins, Modris, *Rites of Spring: The Great War and the Birth of the Modern Age*, London, 1989.

Ensor, R.C.K., *England 1970–1914*, London, 1936.

Evans, Ieuan and Jackson, Peter, *Bread of Heaven*, Edinburgh, 1995.

Fagan, Sean, *The Rugby Rebellion*, Sydney, 2005.

Farman, Christopher, *The General Strike*, London, 1972.

Fawcett, M.J.P., *A History of Old Cranleighan RFC*, Thames Ditton, 1994.

Fishwick, Nicholas, *English Football and Society 1910–50*, Manchester, 1989.

Fitzsimons, Peter, *The Rugby War*, Sydney, 1996.

French, Ray, *My Kind of Rugby*, London, 1979.

Fussell, Paul, *The Great War and Modern Memory*, London, 1975.

Gibbon, W.D., *First Steps to Rugby Football*, London, 1922.

Gill, E., *Skipton R.U.F.C. Centenary*, Skipton, 1974.

Golby, J. (ed.), *Culture and Society in Britain 1850–1890*, London, 1986.

Golby, J.M. and Purdue, A.W, *The Civilisation of the Crowd*, London, 1984.

Gordon, Richard, *Doctor in the House*, London, 1952.

Graves, Robert, *Goodbye To All That*, London, 1960.

Green, Michael, *Why Was He Born So Beautiful and Other Rugby Songs*, London, 1967.

Greenland, W.J., *The History of the Amateur Football Alliance*, London, 1965.

Greenwood, J.E., *A Cap For Boots*, London, 1977.

Griffiths, John, *The Book of English International Rugby, 1871–1982*, London, 1982.

Grundlingh, Albert, Odendaal, Andre and Spies, Burridge (eds), *Beyond the Tryline: Rugby and South African Society*, Johannesburg, 1995.

Gunn, Simon, *The Public Culture of the Victorian Middle Class*, Manchester, 2000.

Gunn, Simon and Bell, Rachel, *Middle Classes: Their Rise and Sprawl*, London, 2002.

Haight, G. (ed.), *A Victorian Reader*, New York, 1972.

Hain, Peter, *Don't Play With Apartheid*, London, 1971.

Haley, Bruce, *The Healthy Body and Victorian Culture*, Harvard, 1978.

Hammond, Dave, *The Club: Life and Times of Blackheath F.C.*, London, 1999.

Hands, David, *Leicester F.C. 1880–1980*, Leicester, 1981.

Hare, David, *Plenty*, London, 1978.

Hargreaves, Jennifer (ed.), *Sport, Culture and Ideology*, London, 1982.

Hargreaves, John, *Sport Power and Culture: A Social and Historical Analysis of Popular Sports in Britain*, Cambridge, 1986.

Harris, Ruth Elwyn, *Billie: The Nevill Letters 1914–1916*, London, 1991.

Harrison, J.F.C., *Late Victorian Britain 1875–1901*, London, 1990.

Harvey, Adrian, *Football: The First Hundred Years*, Abingdon, 2005.

Hawkins, F.C. and Seymour-Bell, E., *Fifty Years with the Clifton R.F.C. 1872–1922*, Bristol, 1922.

Hayes, N. and Hill, J. (eds), *Millions Like Us*, Liverpool, 1999.

Hickie, Thomas V., *A Sense of Union*, Sydney, 1998.

Hill, Jeff, *Sport, Leisure and Culture in Twentieth Century Britain*, London, 2003.

Hill, Jeff and Williams, Jack (eds), *Sport and Identity in the North of England*, Keele, 1996.

History of the Lancashire Football Association, Blackburn, 1928.

Hobsbawm, Eric, *Industry and Empire*, Harmondsworth, 1999.

Hobson, Dominic, *The National Wealth*, London, 1999.

Hocquenghem, Guy, *Homosexual Desire*, North Carolina, 1993.

Holmes, Bob and Thau, Chris (eds), *My Greatest Game*, Edinburgh, 1994.

Holt, Richard and Mason, Tony, *Sport in Britain 1945–2000*, London, 2001.

Holt, Richard, *Sport and the British*, Oxford, 1989.

Honey, J.R., *Tom Brown's Universe. The Development of the Victorian Public School*, London, 1977.

Hope-Simpson, J.B., *Rugby Since Arnold*, London, 1967.

Hopkins, S., *Leicestershire Rugby Union 1887–1987*, Leicester, 1986.

Hoppen, K.T., *The Mid-Victorian Generation*, Oxford, 2000.

Hoskins, Mark and Fox, Dave, *Bristol Football Club (RFU) 1888–1945*, Stroud, 2000.

Houghton, W.E., *The Victorian Frame of Mind*, London, 1957.

Howard, Peter, *Life and Letters*, London, 1969.

Hubbard, Ian, *Old Whitgiftian RFC 1901–51*, London, 1951.

Hughes, Thomas, *Tom Brown's Schooldays*, OUP edition, Oxford, 1989.

Huntley, Robert, *Saracens: 125 Years of Rugby*, London, 2001.

Hynes, S., *The Edwardian Turn of Mind*, Princeton, 1968.

Inglis, Simon, *League Football and the Men Who Made It*, London, 1988.

James, Lawrence, *The Middle Class: A History*, London, 2006.

Jones, Paul, *War Letters of a Public School Boy*, London, 1918.

Jones, Stephen G., *Sport, Politics and the Working Class*, Manchester, 1991.

Jones, Stephen, *Midnight Rugby*, London, 2001.

Kafka, Franz, *The Trial*, Penguin edition, London, 2000.

Kidd, A. and Nicholls, D. (eds), *The Making of the British Middle Class?* Stroud, 1998.

Kilburn, J.M., *In Search of Rugby Football*, London, 1938.

King, H.B. *7th (S) Battalion Northamptonshire Regiment 1914–1919*, Aldershot, 1919.

Kynaston, David, *The City of London, volume IV: A Club No More, 1945–2000*, London, 2002.

Laidlaw, Chris, *Mud in My Eye*, London, 1973.

Lalanne, Denis, *The Great Fight of the French Fifteen*, Wellington, NZ, 1960.

Laybourn, Keith, *Britain on the Breadline*, Stroud, 1990.

Leatherdale, Clive (ed.), *The Book of Football*, facsimile edition, Essex, 1997.

Lester, Robin, *Stagg's University: The Rise, Decline, and Fall of Big-Time Football at Chicago*, Illinois, 1999.

Lovesey, Peter, *The Official Centenary History of the Amateur Athletic Association*, Oxford, 1979.

Lowerson, John, *Sport and the English Middle Classes*, Manchester, 1993.

Lowerson, J. and Myerscough, J., *Time to Spare in Victorian England*, Sussex, 1977.

Macdonald, Lyn, *Somme*, London, 1983.

Mack, E.C., *Public Schools and British Opinion 1780–1860*, London, 1938.

Mack, E.C. and Armytage, W.H.G., *Thomas Hughes*, London, 1952.

MacKenzie, J.M. (ed.), *Popular Imperialism and the Military 1850–1950*, Manchester, 1992.

Maclaren, John, *The History of Army Rugby*, Aldershot, 1986.

Macrory, Jennifer, *Running with the Ball*, London, 1991.

Malin, Ian, *Mud, Blood and Money*, Edinburgh, 1997.

Mangan, J.A., *Athleticism in the Victorian and Edwardian Public School*, London, 1981.

Mangan, J.A., *The Games Ethic and Imperialism*, London, 1986.

Mangan, J.A. (ed.), *The Cultural Bond: Sport, Empire and Society*, London, 1993.

Marsden, A., *Preston Grasshoppers' Centenary Brochure*, Preston, 1969.

Marshall, Rev. F. (ed.), *Football: The Rugby Union Game*, London, 1892.

Marshall, Rev. F. and Tosswill, L.R. (eds), *Football: The Rugby Union Game*, 2nd edition, London, 1925.

Marshall, Howard (ed.), *Rugger Stories*, London, 1932.

Marshall, Howard, *Oxford v Cambridge, The Story of the University Rugby match*, London, 1951.

Marwick, Arthur, *British Society Since 1945*, Harmondsworth, 1982.

Mason, Philip, *The English Gentleman. The Rise and Fall of an Ideal*, London, 1992.

Mason, Tony (ed.), *Sport in Britain, A Social History*, Cambridge, 1985.

Masterman, C.F.G., *The Condition of England*, London, 1909.

Maule, Raymond, *The Complete Who's Who of England Rugby Union Internationals*, Derby, 1992.

McIntosh, P.C., *Physical Education in England since 1800*, London, 1968.

McKibbin, Ross, *Classes and Cultures. England: 1918–1950*, Oxford, 1998.

McKibbin, Ross, *The Ideologies of Class*, Oxford, 1991.

McLean, Terry, *Great Days in New Zealand Rugby*, Wellington, 1959.

McRae, Donald, *Winter Colours: Changing Seasons in World Rugby*, Edinburgh, 1998.

Meller, H., *Leisure and the Changing City, 1870–1914*, London, 1976.

Messner, Michael and Sabo, Donald (eds), *Sport, Men and the Gender Order*, Champaign, 1990.

Milner, Laurie, *Leeds Pals*, London, 1991.

Montgomerie, Bruce, *Those Who Played*, Sydney, 2004.

Moran, H.M., *Viewless Winds. Being the Recollections and Digressions of an Australian Surgeon*, London, 1939.

Morgan, Harry (ed.), *More Rugby Songs*, London, 1968.

Morgan, Kenneth O., *Wales 1880–1980*, Oxford, 1981.

Morgan, W.A. (ed.), *The 'House' on Sport*, London, 1898.

Morgan, W.J. and Nicholson, Geoffrey, *Report On Rugby*, London, 1961.

Morris, Frank, *The First 100: History of the London Scottish FC*, London, 1977.

Morris, James, *Pax Britannica: The Climax of an Empire*, Folio edition, London, 1992.

Morris, R.J. and Rodger, R. (eds), *The Victorian City, A Reader in British Urban History*, Essex, 1993.

Morrison, Toni, *Beloved*, London, 1987.

Morton, H.V., *In Search of England*, London, 1927.

Mosse, George, *Fallen Soldiers. Reshaping the Memory of the World Wars*, Oxford, 1990.

Moynihan, John, *The Soccer Syndrome*, London, 1968.

Nelson, Donald M., *Anatomy of Game*, Delaware, 1994.

Nepia, George, *I, George Nepia*, 2nd edition, London, 2002.

Neville Piggott, F., *The Springboks History of the Tour 1906–07*, Cape Town, 1907.

O'Flaherty, Liam, *The Tent and Other Stories*, London, 1926.

Oborne, Peter, *Basil D'Oliveira: Cricket and Controversy*, London, 2005.

Old Alleynian RFC, 1898–1948, London, 1948 (no author).

Old Rugbeian Society, *The Origin of Rugby Football: Report (with appendices) of the Sub-Committee of the Old Rugbeian Society*, Rugby, 1897.

One Hundred Years of Cinderford Rugby (no author, no place of publication), 1986.

Owen, O.L., *The History of the Rugby Football Union*, London, 1955.

Paget, Captain Guy, *History of the Raising of the 7th (Service) Battalion, Northamptonshire Regiment*, Aldershot, 1915.

Pallant, Anne, *A Sporting Century*, Plymouth, 1997.

Paris, Michael, *Warrior Nation: Images of War in British Popular Culture 1850–2000*, London, 2002.

Parker, Peter, *The Old Lie: The Great War and the Public School Ethos*, London, 1987.

Paxman, Jeremy, *The English*, London, 1998.

Pearson, G., *Hooligan: A History of Respectable Fears*, London, 1983.

Pelmear, Kenneth (ed.), *Rugby Football: An Anthology*, London, 1958.

Pelmear, Kenneth, *Rugby in the Duchy*, Redruth, 1959.

Perkin, Harold, *The Rise of Professional Society: England Since 1880*, London, 2002.

Polley, Martin, *Moving The Goalposts: A History of Sport and Society Since 1945*, London, 1998.

Porter, Roy and Hall, Lesley, *The Facts of Life*, Yale, 1995.

Pugh, Martin, *The Tories and the People 1880–1935*, Oxford, 1985.

Putney, Clifford, *Muscular Christianity. Manhood and Sports in Protestant America, 1880–1920*, Harvard, 2002.

Quigley, Isabel, *The Heirs of Tom Brown: The English Public School Story*, London, 1982.

Rayner, Robert M., *A Manual of Rugby Football for Public Schools*, London, 1925.

Read, D., *The Age of Urban Democracy*, London, 1979.

Reason, John and James, Carwyn, *The World of Rugby*, London, 1979.

Richards, Huw, *A Game for Hooligans*, London, 2006.

Robbins, Keith, *The British Isles, 1901–1951*, Oxford, 2002.

Robinson, Bertram F., *Rugby Football*, London, 1896

Robinson, Derek, *The Combination*, Bristol, 1986.

Routh, G., *Occupation and Pay in Great Britain 1906–79*, London, 1980.

Royds, Sir Percy, *The History of the Laws of Rugby Football*, Twickenham, 1948.

Rubinstein, W.D., *Capitalism, Culture and Decline in Britain 1750–1990*, London, 1993.

Rugby School, *Football Rules*, Rugby, 1845 (no author).

Ryan, Greg, *Forerunners of the All Blacks*, Canterbury, NZ, 1993.

Ryan, Greg, *The Contest for Rugby Supremacy*, Canterbury, NZ, 2005.
Ryan, Greg (ed.), *Tackling Rugby Myths*, Otago, NZ, 2006.
Said, Edward, *Culture and Imperialism*, London, 1993.
Salmon, Tom, *The First Hundred Years: The History of Rugby Football in Cornwall*, Illogan, 1983.
Sampson, Anthony, *Who Runs this Place? The Anatomy of Britain in the 21st Century*, London, 2004.
Samuel, Raphael, *Island Stories: Unravelling Britain*, London, 1998.
Sandiford, K., *Cricket and the Victorians*, Aldershot, 1994.
Searle, G.R., *A New England? Peace and War 1886–1918*, Oxford, 2004.
Selfe, Sydney, *Chapters from the History of Rugby School*, Rugby, 1910.
Sewell, E.H.D., *The Rugby Football Internationals' Roll of Honour*, London, 1919.
Sewell, E.H.D., *The Log of a Sportsman*, London, 1923.
Shaw, K.T., *Huddersfield R.U.F.C. The First 75 Years*, Huddersfield, 1985.
Simkins, Peter, *Kitchener's Army*, Manchester, 1988.
Smith, Adrian and Porter, Dilwyn (eds), *Amateurs and Professionals in Post-War British Sport*, London, 2000.
Smith, David and Williams, Gareth, *Fields of Praise*, Cardiff, 1980.
Smith, Godfrey (ed.), *Take the Ball and Run: A Rugby Anthology*, London, 1991.
Smith, Jed, *The Little Book of English Rugby*, London, 2007.
Smith, Jed, *The Original Rules of Rugby*, Oxford, 2007.
Stacey, Margaret, Batstone, Eric, Bell, Colin and Murcott, Anne, *Power, Resistance and Change. A Second Study of Banbury*, London, 1975.
Stacey, Margaret, *Tradition and Change: A Study of Banbury*, Oxford, 1960.
Stanley, A.P., *The Life and Correspondence of Thomas Arnold, D.D., Late Headmaster of Rugby School, and Regius Professor of Modern History in the University of Oxford*, London, 1845.
Stevenson, John and Cook, Chris, *Britain in the Depression: Society and Politics 1929–39*, 2nd edition, London, 1994.
Stevenson, John, *British Society 1914–45*, Harmondsworth, 1984.
'Stonehenge', *Manual of British Rural Sports*, 3rd edition, London, 1857.
Stonor Saunders, Frances, *Who Paid the Piper?* London, 1999.
Strachey, Lytton, *Eminent Victorians*, Folio Society edition, London, 1986.
Swann, Donald, *The Songs of Michael Flanders and Donald Swann*, London, 1997.
Taylor, A.J.P., *Essays in English History*, Harmondsworth, 1976.
Thomas, Clem, *The History of the British Lions*, Edinburgh, 1996.
Thomas, Watcyn, *Rugby-Playing Man*, London, 1977.
Thompson, F.M.L. (ed.), *The Cambridge Social History of Britain 1750–1950*, Cambridge, 1990.
Thompson, P., *The Edwardians*, London, 1975.
Thorburn, A., *The SRU Official History*, Edinburgh, 1928.
Thornett, Ken, with Easton, Tom, *Tackling Rugby*, Melbourne, 1965.
Thornton, A.P., *The Habit of Authority*, London, 1966.
Titley, U.A. and McWhirter, Ross, *Centenary History of the Rugby Football Union*, London, 1970.
Tombs, Robert and Isobel, *That Sweet Enemy: Britain and France, the History of a Love-hate Relationship*, London, 2005.

Tosh, John, *A Man's Place: Masculinity and the Middle-Class Home in Victorian England*, Yale, 1999.

Trevor, Philip, *Rugby Union Football*, London, 1923.

Tyerman, Christopher, *A History of Harrow School*, Oxford, 2000.

Vachell, H.A., *The Hill*, London, 1905.

Vamplew, W., *Pay Up and Play the Game*, Cambridge, 1988.

Wakefield, W.W. and Marshall, H.P., *Rugger*, London, 1927.

Wakelam, H.B.T. (ed.), *The Game Goes On*, London, 1936.

Wakelam, H.B.T., *Half-Time*, London, 1938.

Waller, P.J., *Town, City and Nation: England 1850–1914*, Oxford, 1983.

Walton, John and Walvin, James (eds), *Leisure in Britain 1780–1930*, Manchester, 1983.

Walvin, James, *The Peoples' Game. The History of Football Revisited*, Edinburgh, 1994.

Ward, Stuart (ed.), *British Culture and the End of Empire*, Manchester, 2001.

Ward, Stuart, *Australia and the British Embrace*, Melbourne, 2001.

Warner, Philip, *The Harlequins: 125 Years of Rugby Football*, Derby, 1991.

Waugh, Alec, *The Loom of Youth*, London, 1917.

Waugh, Alec, *On Doing What One Likes*, London, 1932.

Webb, John, *Freemasonry and Sport*, Surrey, 1995.

Weeks, Jeffrey, *Sex, Politics and Society*, 2nd edition, London, 1989.

Weight Richard, *Patriots. National Identity in Britain, 1940–2000*, London, 2002.

Williams, Graham, *The Code War*, Harefield, 1994.

Williams, Graham, *Glory Days, the History of English Rugby Union Cup Finals*, Leeds, 1998.

Williams, Jack, *Cricket and England: A Cultural and Social History of the Inter-War Years*, London, 1999.

Winter, Denis, *Death's Men: Soldiers of the Great War*, London, 1978.

Winter, J.M., *The Great War and the British People*, London, 1986.

Winter, Jay, *Sites of Memory, Sites of Mourning: the Great War in European Cultural History*, Cambridge, 1998.

Wipers Times: A Facsimile Reprint of the Trench Magazines, London, 1918.

Woodward, J., *Cheltenham RFC 1889–1989*, Cheltenham, 1989.

Wooller, W. and Owen, D. (eds), *Fifty Years of the All Blacks*, London, 1954.

Wyatt, Derek, *Rugby Disunion*, London, 1995.

Wynne-Jones, G.V., *Sports Commentary*, London, 1951.

Zeigler, Philip, *Legacy: Cecil Rhodes, the Rhodes Trust and Rhodes Scholarships*, Yale, 2008.

Articles and chapters in books

Almond, H.H., 'Athletics and education', *Macmillan's Magazine*, vol. 43, November 1880–April 1881.

Almond, H.H., 'Football as a moral agent', *Nineteenth Century*, vol. 34, 1893.

An Old Player, 'The Rugby Union game in 1888–89', in Alcock, C.W. (ed.), *Football Annual*, London, 1889.

Annan, Noel, 'The cult of homosexuality in England 1850–1950', *Biography*, vol. 13, no. 3, Summer 1980.

Anon, 'Recollections of Rugby 1863', *Routledge's Every Boy's Annual*, London, c. 1863.

Arscott, C. and Wolff, J., 'Cultivated capital', *History Today*, vol. 37, 1987.

Baker, Norman, 'A more even playing field. Sport during and after the War', in Hayes, N. and Hill, J. (eds), *Millions Like Us*, Liverpool, 1999.

Baker, Norman, 'The amateur ideal in a society of equality: change and continuity in post-Second World War British sport, 1945–48', *International Journal of the History of Sport*, vol. 12, no. 1, April 1995.

Baker, W.J., 'William Webb Ellis and the origins of Rugby Football: the life and death of a Victorian myth', *Albion*, vol. 13, 1981.

Bamford, T.W., 'Public schools and social class, 1801–51', *The British Journal of Sociology*, vol. 12, no. 3, September 1961.

Barlow, S., 'The diffusion of "Rugby" Football in the industrialised context of Rochdale, 1868–90', *International Journal of the History of Sport*, vol. 10, no. 1, April 1993.

Bateman, Anthony, '"More mighty than the bat, the pen. . ." Culture, hegemony and the literaturisation of cricket', *Sport in History*, vol. 23, no. 1, Summer 2003.

Best, Geoffrey, 'Militarism and the Victorian public school', in Bradley, M. J. and Simon, B. (eds), *The Victorian Public School*, London, 1975.

Birley, Derek, 'Sportsmen and the deadly game', *British Journal of Sports History*, vol. 3, 1986.

Cannadine, David, 'War and death, grief and mourning in modern Britain', in Whaley, J. (ed.), *Mirrors of Mortality: Studies in the Social History of Death*, London, 1981.

Carle, Alison and Nauright, John, 'Crossing the line: women playing rugby union', in Chandler, T. and Nauright, J. (eds), *Making the Rugby World: Race, Gender, Commerce*, London, 1999.

Carter, Pat, 'Who needs officer qualities?' *Journal of the Royal Air Force College*, LXXIII, March 2002.

Coleman, D.C., 'Gentlemen and players', *Economic History Review*, vol. 26, no. 1, 1973.

Collins, Tony, 'History, theory and the "civilising process"', *Sport in History*, vol. 25, no. 2, August 2005.

Collins, Tony, 'The first Rugby Union World Cup? The 1919 inter-services tournament', in Bushby, Mary and Hickie, Thomas V. (eds), *Rugby History: The Remaking of the Class Game*, Melbourne, 2007.

Curry, Graham, 'The Cambridge Connection', *The Sports Historian*, 2002.

Curry, G., Dunning, E. and Sheard, K., 'Sociological versus empiricist history: some comments on Tony Collins's "History, Theory and the 'Civilizing Process'"', *Sport in History*, vol. 26, no. 1, April 2006.

Dunning, Eric, 'Sport as a male preserve: notes on the social sources of masculine identity and its transformations', in Elias, N. and Dunning E., *Quest for Excitement: Sport and Leisure in the Civilising Process*, Oxford, 1986, pp. 267–83.

Elton, Godfrey, 'An Englishman's audit of Rhodes Scholars', *Harper's*, May 1964, p. 102.

F.D.M., 'Thoughts on ourselves, our position and our prospects', *The Rugby Miscellany*, no. 7, February 1846, pp. 226–8.

'Football at the public schools', *Beeton's Brave Tales*, issue 101 (no author), *c.* 1863.

Guillemard, Arthur, 'The Rugby Union game with hints to players', in Power, Thomas P. (ed.), *The Footballer*, Melbourne, 1877.

Gunn, Simon, 'Class identity and the urban', *Urban History*, vol. 31, no. 1, May 2004, p. 39.

Gurdon, Charles, 'Football: some hints on the game', *The Union Jack: Every Boy's Paper* (undated).

Halladay, E., 'Of pride and prejudice: the amateur question in English nineteenth century rowing', *The International Journal of the History of Sport*, vol. 4, no. 1, May 1987.

Harrison, B., 'Religion and recreation in nineteenth century England', *Past and Present*, no. 38, December 1967.

Harvey, Adrian 'The oldest Rugby Football Club in the world?', *Sport in History*, vol. 26, no. 1, April 2006, pp. 150–2.

Hibbins, G.M., 'The Cambridge connection: the English origins of Australian Rules Football', in Mangan, J.A. (ed.), *The Cultural Bond: Sport, Empire and Society*, London, 1993.

Hickie, Thomas V., 'The amateur ideal in the era of professional rugby', in Bushby, Mary and Hickie, Thomas V. (eds), *Rugby History: The Remaking of the Class Game*, Melbourne, 2007.

Hill, Rowland, 'The past season', in Alcock, C.W. (ed.), *Football Annual*, London, 1883.

Hodge, Richard, 'American college football', *Outing*, vol. 11, no. 6, 1887.

Holt, Richard, 'The amateur body and the middle-class man: work, health and style in Victorian Britain', *Sport in History*, vol. 26, no. 3, December 2006.

Howe, P.D., 'Women's rugby and the nexus between embodiment, professionalism and sexuality', *Football Studies*, vol. 4, no. 2, October 2001, pp. 77–92.

Howkins, Alun, 'The discovery of rural England', in Colls, R. and Dodd, P. (eds), *Englishness: Politics and Culture*, London, 1986.

Jarvis, David, 'British conservatism and class politics in the 1920s', *English Historical Review*, vol. 111, no. 440, February 1996 pp. 59–84.

Jeffrey, Tom and McClelland, Keith, 'A world fit to live in: the *Daily Mail* and the middle classes 1918–39', in Curran, J., Smith, A. and Wingate, P. (eds), *Impacts and Influences: Essays on Media Power in the Twentieth Century*, London, 1987, p. 42.

Jones, Aaron, 'A short history of women's rugby', *Touchlines*, October 2003.

Kidd, Bruce, 'The legacy of Tom Brown in Canada', *International Journal of the History of Sport*, vol. 23, no. 5, August 2006.

Kirby, H.T., 'Some notes on the Bloxam Family of Rugby', *Essays in Honour of Philip B Chatwin*, Oxford, 1962.

Lewis, T.L.T., 'A history of Guy's R.F.C.,' *Guy's Hospital Gazette*, 26 October 1968.

Lowerson, John, 'Sport and British middle-class culture', *International Journal of the History of Sport*, vol. 21, no. 1, January 2004.

Lucas, John A., 'Victorian Muscular Christianity, prologue to the Olympic Games philosophy', *Olympic Review*, no. 99, January–February 1976, p. 50.

MacLagan, W. and Jeffrey, G.L., 'The different epochs of the Rugby game', in Morgan, W.A. (ed.), The 'House' on Sport, London, 1898.

Martens, James, 'They stooped to conquer: Rugby Union Football 1895–1914', Journal of Sport History, vol. 20, no. 1, Spring 1993.

McCabe, Edmund, 'Rugby and the Great War', Stand To!, vol. 52, 1998, pp. 41–4.

Morris, R.J., 'Middle class culture 1700–1914', in Fraser, Derek (ed.), A History of Modern Leeds, Manchester, 1980.

Mount, Ferdinand, 'Double-barrelled dolts', London Review of Books, vol. 28, no. 16, July 2006, p. 6.

Muir, Kenneth and Seitz, Trina, 'Machismo, misogyny, and homophobia in a male athletic subculture: a participant-observation study of deviant rituals in collegiate rugby', Deviant Behavior, vol. 25, no. 4, July–August 2004 , pp. 303–27.

Nauright, J., 'Sport, manhood and Empire', International Journal of the History of Sport, vol. 8, no. 2, September 1991.

Nauright, John, 'Colonial manhood and imperial race virility: British responses to post-Boer War colonial rugby tours', in Chandler, T. and Nauright, J. (eds), Making Men: Rugby and Masculine Identity, London, 1996.

Park, Roberta J., '"Mended or Ended?" Football injuries and the British and American medical press 1870–1910', The International Journal of the History of Sport, vol. 18, no. 2, June 2001.

Polley, Martin, 'Amateurism and professionalism in Post-War British athletics', in Smith, Adrian and Porter, Dilwyn (eds), Amateurs and Professionals in Post-War British Sport, London, 2000.

Porter, Dilwyn, 'Amateur football in England 1948–63: the Pegasus phenomenon', Contemporary British History, vol. 14, no. 2, Summer 2000, pp. 1–30.

Puccio, Paul M., 'At the heart of Tom Brown's Schooldays: Thomas Arnold and Christian Friendship', Modern Language Studies, vol. 25, no. 4, Autumn 1995, p. 58.

Quail, John M., 'From personal patronage to public school privilege', in Kidd, Alan and Nicholls, David, The Making of the British Middle Class?, Stroud, 1998.

Reid, D.A., 'Folk-football, the aristocracy and cultural change: a critique of Dunning and Sheard', International Journal of the History of Sport, vol. 5, no. 2, September 1988.

Rhind, N., 'Blackheath Football Club 1862–1870', Transactions of the Greenwich and Lewisham Antiquarian Society, vol. 10, no. 1, 1985.

Richards, Jeffrey, 'Popular imperialism and the image of the army in juvenile literature', in MacKenzie, J.M. (ed.), Popular Imperialism and the Military 1850–1950, Manchester, 1992.

Rubenstein, W.D., 'Britain's elites in the interwar period', in Kidd, A. and Nicholls, D. (eds), The Making of the British Middle Class?, Stroud, 1998.

Russell, D., '"Sporadic and curious": the emergence of rugby and soccer zones in Yorkshire and Lancashire c. 1860–1914', International Journal of the History of Sport, vol. 5, no. 2, September 1988.

Ryan, Greg, 'A lack of esprit du corps: the 1908 Wallaby tour of Britain', Sporting Traditions, vol. 17, no. 1, November 2000.

Schacht, Steven P., 'Misogyny on and off the pitch: the gendered world of male rugby players', Gender & Society, vol. 10, no. 5, 1996, pp. 550–65.

Seward, Andy, 'Cornish rugby and cultural identity', *The Sports Historian*, vol. 18, no. 2, November 1998, pp. 78–94.

Sewell, E.H.D., 'Rugby football and the colonial tours', *Fortnightly Review*, vol. 82, 1907, p. 427.

Sewell, E.H.D., 'The state of the game', *Fortnightly Review*, vol. 89, 1911.

Sheard, K. and Dunning, E., 'The Rugby Football Club as a type of male preserve', *International Review of Sport Sociology*, vol. 5, no. 3, 1973, pp. 5–24.

Shockley, Megan Taylor, 'Southern women in the scrums' *Journal of Sport History*, vol. 33, no. 2, Summer 2006, pp. 127–55.

Smith, Adrian, 'An oval ball and a broken city: Coventry, its people, and its rugby team', *The International Journal of the History of Sport*, vol. 11, no. 3, December 1994.

Smith, Adrian, 'The impact of Professionalism on Rugby Union 1995–99', in Adrian Smith and Dil Porter (eds), *Amateurs and Professionals in Post-War British Sport*, London, 2000, pp. 146–89.

Smith, Adrian, 'Sport, counterfactual history and rugby's twin codes', *International Journal of the History of Sport*, vol. 21, no. 1, January 2004.

Spies, Burridge, 'The imperial heritage', in Grundlingh, Albert, Odendaal, Andre and Spies, Burridge (eds), *Beyond the Tryline: Rugby and South African Society*, Johannesburg, 1995.

Trainor, Richard, 'Neither metropolitan nor provincial: the interwar middle class', in Kidd, A. and Nicholls, D. (eds), *The Making of the British Midde Class?*, Stroud, 1998.

Veitch, Colin, 'Play up! play up! and win the war! Football, the nation and the First World War', *Journal of Contemporary History*, vol. 20, 1985, pp. 363–77.

Vincent, Geoff and Harfield, Toby, 'Repression and reform: responses within New Zealand rugby to the arrival of the "Northern game", 1907–8', *New Zealand Journal of History*, vol. 31, no. 2, October 1997.

Vincent, Geoff, 'Practical imperialism: the Anglo-Welsh Rugby tour of New Zealand, 1908', *International Journal of the History of Sport*, vol. 15, no. 1, 1998.

Waites, B.A., 'The effect of the First World War on class and status in England, 1910–20', *Journal of Contemporary History*, vol. 11, no. 1, January 1976.

Weber, Eugen, 'Gymnastics and sports in fin-de-siècle France: opium of the classes?' *American Historical Review*, vol. 76, no. 1, February 1971, pp. 70–98.

Wenden, D.J., 'Sport', in Brian Harrison (ed.), *The History of the University of Oxford, volume 8, The Twentieth Century*, Oxford, 1994.

Williams, Graham, 'Midlands manoeuvres: a history of northern unionism in Coventry', *Code 13*, no. 2, December 1986.

Williams, Peter, 'Battle lines on three fronts: the RFU and the lost war against professionalism', *International Journal of the History of Sport*, vol. 19, no. 4, December 2002, pp. 114–36.

Williams, Peter, 'Cycle of conflict: a decade of strife in English professional rugby', *International Journal of the History of Sport*, vol. 25, no. 1, 2008, pp. 65–81.

Winn, W.E., '*Tom Brown's Schooldays* and the development of Muscular Christianity', *Church History*, vol. 29, no. 1, March 1960.

Theses

Allen, Dean, 'Logan's Golden Age: cricket, politics and empire in South Africa 1888–1910', PhD thesis, University of Brighton, 2008.

Blackledge, P., 'William Cail, amateurism and the Rugby Football Union', MA thesis, University of Northumbria, 1994.

Crellin, J.F., '"The more things change, the more they stay the same": an analysis of how Saracens and Leicester Football Clubs have managed the transition from amateur sporting clubs to professional sports businesses', MA thesis, De Montfort University, 1999.

Fuller, J.G., 'Popular culture and troop morale in the British and Dominion Forces 1914–1918', D.Phil. thesis, Cambridge, 1988.

Lamb, Air Commodore G.C., 'The future of South Africa as an apartheid state', Royal College of Defence Studies, 1971.

Lewis, R.W, 'The development of professional football in Lancashire, 1870–1914', PhD thesis, University of Lancaster, 1993.

Martens, J.W., 'Rugby Union Football and English society 1871–1914', PhD thesis, University of Manitoba, 1988.

Tuck, Jason 'Rugby Union and national identity in the British Isles since 1945', PhD thesis, Loughbrough University, 1999.

Audio-visual sources

Australian Broadcasting Corporation, *Stealing Rugby*, DVD, Sydney, 2006.

Rugby World, *The Official History of English Rugby*, DVD, London, 2003.

INDEX

Routledge Sport

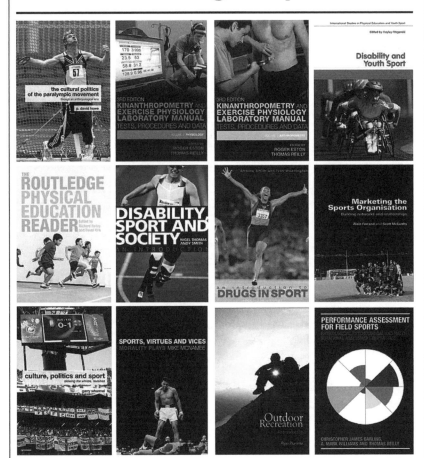

Routledge
Taylor & Francis Group

www.routledge.com/sport